CENTER FOR JAPANESE STUDIES

BIBLIOGRAPHICAL SERIES

NUMBER 4

JAPANESE HISTORY:

A GUIDE TO JAPANESE REFERENCE

AND RESEARCH MATERIALS

JAPANESE HISTORY:
A GUIDE TO JAPANESE REFERENCE AND RESEARCH MATERIALS

_____John W. Hall

GREENWOOD PRESS, PUBLISHERS
WESTPORT, CONNECTICUT

The Library of Congress has catalogued this publication as follows:

Library of Congress Cataloging in Publication Data

Hall, John Whitney, 1916–
    Japanese history.

    Reprint of the ed. published by University of
Michigan Press, Ann Arbor, which was issued as no. 4
of Bibliographical series, University of Michigan,
Center for Japanese Studies.
    1. Japan—History—Bibliography. I. Title.
II. Series: Michigan. University. Center for
Japanese Studies. Bibliographical series, no. 4.
[Z3306.H27 1973]   016.952   73-3013
ISBN 0-8371-6830-9

First Greenwood Reprinting 1973

Library of Congress Catalogue Card Number 73-3013

ISBN 0-8371-6830-9

Printed in the United States of America

EDITOR'S FOREWORD ON THE BIBLIOGRAPHICAL SERIES

The Bibliographical Series of the Center for Japanese Studies has for its main purpose the listing and evaluating of the major Japanese works pertaining to the humanities and social sciences, particularly as they deal with Japan and the areas immediately adjacent to Japan. It is assumed that Western materials pertaining to Japan are adequately covered in the bibliographies of Pagés, von Wenckstern, Nachod, Praesent-Haenisch, Pritchard, Gaskill, etc., and that Western specialists in the several fields will know how to get at the Western materials in their respective fields.

The bibliographies in the present series are intended to serve as an introduction to the native research materials in the several disciplines and hence as an aid to research for teachers and students. In each case an attempt has been made to describe or to evaluate each work that is listed, or at least to justify the inclusion of each item. The authors have also attempted to indicate the American libraries at which each item may be found. Scholars and librarians will perhaps find that the several bibliographies in this series will serve as useful guides to buying programs which they may wish to initiate.

The bibliographies are selective. Each item listed is believed to be of some value or interest to the scholarly user. In those cases in which it has been impossible to examine a book or article of known value, it still is included. A book or article is thus included if it is written by a competent scholar, if it is included in a bibliography which is itself competently compiled, if it appears to treat its subject matter in detail and with an approach to completeness, if it is frequently quoted, if it is well reviewed, or if it is referred to as being authoritative. Wherever possible, notes as to why an item seems to be of value have been given.

The scope of each bibliography is defined by the compiler or compilers in their introductions, but in general each of the bibliographies lists (a) important source materials, and (b) secondary sources dating from a fixed date in the recent past, as, for instance, the Meiji Restoration, 1900, 1910, etc.

Although the materials in most cases deal with the Japanese islands, each compiler has set the limits of the geographical area which his materials cover. In certain cases expansion into areas that are outside Japan appears to be justified by the fact that Japanese research has been the dominant research for these areas. Hence one or more of the bibliographies will cover Japanese materials on Formosa, Korea, Manchuria, and the Mandated Islands.

The format is uniform within each volume. In general the name of each author or compiler is given both in romanization and characters. The surnames are given first and the given names next, as the practice is in Japan. The names of corporate authors, such as government offices, are given in romanization and characters; they are then translated. The title of each book or article is given in romanization and characters; it is then translated. The place of publication and the name of the publisher are given in romanization alone, but a separate listing within each bibliography gathers together the names of the publishers, with the characters used in writing their names.

1. Long $\bar{a}$, $\bar{o}$, and $\bar{u}$ are indicated by macrons over the vowels.
2. Only the first letters of initial words and proper nouns are capitalized.
3. In the bibliographical data, the compilers have given both the edition and the printing of the work cited. Significant textual variations sometimes occur between different printings of the same edition of a given work.
4. When dealing with an item composed of one volume, complete pagination is given for that volume, including all separately paged sections. If any title is in more than one volume, only the total number of volumes is given, without paging.
5. In the event that the item cited happens to be part of a series or collection, the compilers have given in brackets introduced by an equals sign the title, characters, and translated title of that series or collection and the number of the volume concerned.
6. The location of each item in American libraries is shown by means of the symbols used in the Union List of Serials. The symbols for the major libraries concerned are as follows:

    CCC - Claremont Colleges
    CSt - Stanford General Library
    Cst-H - Hoover War Library
    CtY - Yale
    CU - University of California
    DLC - Library of Congress
    ICU - Chicago
    IEN - Northwestern
    MH - Harvard
    MiU - Michigan
    NN - New York Public Library
    NNC - Columbia
    WaU - University of Washington

7. Works such as encyclopedias, dictionaries, yearbooks, series, and collections are cited by title; the name of the editor or compiler, in romanization and characters, is usually given after the title.
8. In the case of articles found in journals, quotation marks surround the Japanese title, characters, and translated title.
9. Abbreviations are explained in lists, if necessary.

10. If any volume of a journal is continuously paged, number and month may be omitted. If it has both continuous volume pagination and separate pagination for each issue, only the volume, year, and the continuous volume pagination may be given. If more than one volume appears in any single year, and each is separately and continuously paged, the procedure has been to give the volume, inclusive months of the issues in the volume, year, and continuous volume pagination.

11. In the case of a single article comprising a chapter or a section of a book which is a compilation of articles by a number of authors, this fact is shown by inserting the word "in" between the title of the article and compilation in which it is found. Following the "in," a complete citation of the book in question is given.

12. All descriptions, evaluations, criticisms, and comments pertaining to a volume or article follow the citations in separate, indented paragraphs. These may include brief biographies of the authors or compilers, but only one biography per author or compiler is given in each bibliography. Cross-references from one citation to another are used to call attention to comments, biographies, etc.

13. A list of the standard professional journals is given whenever found to be convenient.

The following remarks may interest the growing number of scholars who are concerned with the problem of publishing materials in the lesser known fields, in which the number of copies to be distributed is necessarily small and in which special problems, such as the one here faced of giving names and titles in characters, must be met. An electric typewriter was first used to type the materials in romanization. The characters were then written in, in spaces left for the purpose. The over-all dimensions of the typed area was 10 by 14 and 1/2 inches. This was reduced to the present size in photographing the pages. The photographs thus taken were then made the basis for reproduction by offset process. Except in the case of the introductory material, no attempt was made to justify the right-hand margins.

Joseph K. Yamagiwa

Note on John W. Hall's Japanese History: a Guide to Japanese Reference and Research Materials

Users of the present work will find that Professor Hall is a historian who takes a wide-angle view of his subject. He has thus listed the principal bibliographies, reference works, anthologies, periodicals, and survey histories for such fields as geography, government, law, economics, education, religion, literature, art, and science. Students in all these areas, as well as historians proper, will—it is hoped—welcome this volume.

Since the inception of this bibliographical series, Far Eastern libraries in the United States have made substantial additions to their Japanese collections. Because of the rapidity with which these materials are still being acquired, it is no longer possible to indicate for each of the items listed in any bibliography the libraries which own it. The present series will therefore discontinue the practice of indicating these libraries.

J. K. Y.

AUTHOR'S INTRODUCTION

A glance through the shelves of the major Japanese collections in the United States will reveal a great preponderance of works in the historical field. The student of Japanese history, first approaching these collections, is likely to find himself overwhelmed by the vast resources in reference works, source materials, and scholarly studies of all varieties which confront him. Since World War II, with the rapid expansion of Japanese library facilities in this country, and the increased use of Japanese materials by American scholars, the need for a bibliographical guide to Japanese publications in the field of history has become acute. It was with this need in mind that the present work was undertaken.

In view of the scope and complexity of the subject, it has not been feasible to compile a single-volume guide which would cover all aspects of Japanese history to the satisfaction of the specialist. It was determined, therefore, for the purposes of the bibliographical series being published by the Center for Japanese Studies at the University of Michigan, to divide the field of history into several parts. The present volume, which is the first to appear, comprises a general introduction covering reference aids, published sources, scholarly journals, and a selected offering of survey literature of recent origin. This introductory volume will not attempt to discuss primary sources, pre-modern historical writings, or periodical articles. Such detailed coverage will be left to later volumes which will confine themselves to smaller segments of Japanese history.

In preparing this work for the non-specialist the greatest problems which the writer has confronted have been those of selection and balance: selection which would make this work a guide of manageable size rather than a mere book-list; balance which would afford an impartial coverage of the many subjects embraced within the historical field. The writer realizes acutely the difficulties of achieving either of these goals. He is aware that a compilation of this nature cannot avoid numerous errors both of fact and judgment. The specialist in each field will discover much to disagree with either in the choice of entries or in the prefaces and annotations. Unfortunately, a bibliography is at best a perishable commodity. As the work is being labored over new publications make many of the entries obsolete. A further balance is enforced upon the compiler, a balance between bibliographical perfection and currency or utility. In this introductory volume the emphasis has been placed upon utility. For its inadequacies the writer asks the indulgence of the reader and sincerely solicits his suggestions and comments. Since it is proposed eventually to revise the several bibliographies published separately in the Bibliographical Series of the Center for Japanese Studies and to combine them into a coordinated whole, any suggestions which the reader may care to offer will be doubly welcome.

In compiling this work the writer has attempted constantly to keep in mind the needs of the general non-specialist in the field of Japanese history. In selecting entries he has above all sought to avoid works of a technical or restricted nature. Since other bibliographies in this series will cover the contemporary period, emphasis has been placed upon reference works and historical surveys covering the pre-1868 phase of Japanese history, with only a minimum coverage devoted to the more recent period. Generally, works dealing with only a limited period of history have also been eliminated. However, in fields in which adequate survey literature is non-existent, outstanding works of limited scope have been included. Finally, works of recent appearance have been given general priority over those of earlier origin. This is not only because such recent works appear to offer more to the contemporary scholar but because more adequate guides to the earlier materials are available.

While thus limiting the amount of detail contained within the individual sections of this volume, the author has attempted to interpret the scope of the field of history broadly so as to embrace as wide a variety of subjects as possible within both the social sciences and humanities. Such an approach to history, it was felt, was especially necessary when dealing with a people as alien to us as the Japanese. Where political, social, economic, cultural, and religious traditions differ markedly from our own, the historian must inquire more widely into the entire fabric of the past if he is to understand the factors of causation or bring his subject to life. It is hoped also that this more inclusive approach to the many facets of Japanese historiography will better serve to impress the reader with the breadth and variety of the work of Japanese historians.

Organization of materials has naturally presented a major problem. In arranging the following works, the writer decided against the adoption of some rigid scheme approved either by Japanese or Western bibliographers, but permitted the categories to take shape as entries were collected. This has resulted in a somewhat unorthodox grouping of subjects but one which, it is believed, will be more useful to the active research worker.

While the process of selection and organization is in itself a form of evaluation, the writer has sought to go farther by providing, through introductory comments and individual annotations, information for the guidance of the research worker. The task of annotation has been made especially difficult in two ways. First of all, the writer can claim to have specialized knowledge of only a few of the many sub-fields included in this work. Secondly, it has been physically impossible even to glance through all of the material listed. Thus, although the writer has attempted whenever possible to base his bibliographic data and annotations on direct observation, he has had to rely to a considerable extent on standard bibliographic materials or guides to historical literature, and on the advice of native experts. This procedure has made unavoidable the inclusion of a certain percentage of unannotated or even incomplete entries (since Japanese bibliographies seldom provide complete bibliographical information). It has furthermore greatly magnified the possibility of error both in bibliographic data and in the evaluations. The writer is especially aware of the difficulty of securing impartial judgment on works of the postwar period. With the Japanese academic world split rather sharply into conflicting schools of interpretation, many of the most recent guides to historical literature have revealed deep-seated biases.

A GUIDE TO JAPANESE REFERENCE AND RESEARCH MATERIALS

A final difficulty of a more technical nature involves two problems of romanization. One of these is the question of how to split or combine the long compound words employed by the Japanese, and in particular what to do with terminal elements such as shi (history), kō (treatise), or ron (essay). The general practice adopted below has been to split long compounds into as small segments as possible but to assimilate dangling elements without the use of hyphens (thus bunkashi, not bunka shi or bunka-shi). A more frustrating problem has been the lack of consistency in the romanizations employed by Japanese publishers when they themselves provide romanized titles. In most instances of this kind the publishers' romanization has been ignored for the sake of consistency. In a few cases, however, chiefly in the section on periodicals, where customary romanizations have become established, such spellings have been retained and enclosed in parentheses. (Thus "Zinbun" and "Nippon-Rekishi," not Jimbun and Nihon rekishi).

The research on which this work is based was conducted over the course of several years. During the spring of 1951, the writer, with the aid of graduate students of the Center for Japanese Studies, made use of the Japanese collection at the University of Michigan together with standard Japanese historical bibliographies to lay a foundation for the project. In the summer of the same year a research grant from the Center of Japanese Studies and a travel grant from the Horace H. Rackham School of Graduate Studies enabled the writer to visit the major Japanese collections in this country, principally those at Harvard University, Columbia University, the Library of Congress, the University of California at Berkeley, Stanford University, and the Hoover Institute and Library on War, Revolution and Peace. Further work was done on the bibliography during the course of the writer's residence in Japan from February of 1952 to January, 1953.

During this rather lengthy and diverse process of compilation, the writer has incurred an indebtedness to numerous individuals. For helpful suggestions and kind assistance in facilitating library search, the writer is grateful to Mr. Robert T. Paine, Jr. and Mr. K. Tomita of the Museum of Fine Arts, Boston, Professor Serge Elisséeff and Dr. Kai-ming Chiu of the Harvard-Yenching Institute, Mr. Edwin Beal of the Library of Congress, Professor Donald H. Shively of the University of California, Berkeley, and Dr. Nobutake Ike of the Hoover Library. While the writer was in Japan, Messrs. Kanai Madoka and Sugiyama Hiroshi of the Tokyo University Historiographical Institute painstakingly went over the manuscript and cards and made valuable suggestions and recommendations. Professor Kaji Shinzō of Tokyo University also gave freely of his time to help in facilitating this bibliographic project.

On the University of Michigan campus the writer wishes to acknowledge the inspiration received from the first volume in the present Bibliographic Series, the work by Professor Robert E. Ward. For their efforts in reading the completed manuscript and offering valuable criticisms the writer wishes to thank Professor Sumio Taniguchi and Mr. Raymond Nunn. Finally a debt of gratitude goes to the editor of this series, Professor Joseph K. Yamagiwa, for his critical editorial suggestions and his careful review of the manuscript, and to the director of the Center for Japanese Studies, Professor Robert B. Hall, for his support and constant encouragement of the project.

J. W. H.

Ann Arbor, July, 1953

TABLE OF CONTENTS

A GUIDE TO JAPANESE REFERENCE AND RESEARCH MATERIALS

I. BIBLIOGRAPHIES

The historian is fortunate in having at his disposal a large number of bibliographical reference works covering the entire range of Japanese history. His chief problem is that of selecting from these an adequate number of aids which will offer easy and reasonably complete access to the sources in which he is interested. Naturally the number of works he consults will depend upon the degree of completeness which he desires. But a certain minimum number will be imperative if he is to achieve more than superficial coverage of his field.

Since working bibliographies generally grow as research progresses, the historian will wish to begin by selecting secondary works in his field which contain useful bibliographical notes or appendices. If his topic is sufficiently broad, he may find one of the recent "introductions" to Japanese history, such as Tōyama Shigeki's Nihonshi kenkyū nyūmon (Introduction to the study of Japanese history) (Entry 683) the place to start. This work discusses the significant literature on the major aspects of Japanese history. With the third edition it also appends an excellent introductory list of books and articles chosen for the historian whose special interest is in the social sciences.

Many of the standard histories of Japan listed in Part V, Chapter 2 of this guide contain bibliographical references. Of these, the earlier works tend to cite primary sources while those written since the middle thirties more often refer to secondary materials. In the first group Kuroita Katsumi's Kokushi no kenkyū (The study of Japanese history) (Entry 25) and the seven-volume Sōgō Nihonshi taikei (Synthetic survey of Japanese history) (Entry 748) are outstanding. Of the more recent prewar works Heibonsha's Nihonshi (History of Japan) (Entry 739), Mikasa Shobō's Nihon rekishi sensho (Complete series on Japanese history) (Entry 737), and Chijin Shokan's Taikan Nihon bunkashi zensho (Survey of Japanese cultural history series) (Entry 749) are most consistent and generous in their bibliographical citations. A postwar series, still in the process of publication, has the advantage of containing the results of most recent Japanese historical scholarship. This multivolume work entitled Nihon rekishi kōza (Japanese history series) (Entry 734) is issued by Kawade Shobō. Individual articles vary, but in general they are consistent in their citation of selected readings.

For more limited subjects a starting point will be found in the specialized monographs listed in Part V, Chapters 3 through 12 of this book. Specific recommendations will be found in the introductory passages to these chapters. It will also be noted that the entries in certain of the historical dictionaries conclude with bibliographical recommendations. While these are never exhaustive, they indicate the best-known sources for any given subject and therefore constitute a convenient starting point for further research. The new Heibonsha's Sekai rekishi jiten (Encyclopedia of world history) (Entry 232) when complete will constitute the best such source. The articles on Japanese historical subjects in this work are written by the most active postwar historians and contain up-to-date bibliographical citations.

After acquainting himself with the above survey literature, the scholar will be ready to begin in earnest the augmentation of his bibliography through reference to the standard bibliographical guides listed in the next three chapters. Here his task will divide itself rather sharply into two distinct phases. His most immediate problem will be to gain access to the latest and most authoritative products of contemporary Japanese scholarship. But having done this, and wishing to pursue his subject farther, he will find it necessary to turn to the primary sources themselves. No single bibliographical guide will answer both of these needs. Instead, the scholar will find that each phase of his bibliographical task involves a number of separate problems, the first of which is that of acquiring familiarity with bibliographies of bibliographies.

1. BIBLIOGRAPHIES OF BIBLIOGRAPHIES

Works devoted exclusively to the listing of Japanese bibliographies are not numerous. Furthermore those which exist are, for the most part, incomplete or obsolete. For information on bibliographies published prior to 1933, the historian will find two works of special value. Amano Keitarō's Hompō shoshi no shoshi (A bibliography of Japanese bibliographies) (Entry 1) is a standard classified but unannotated list of bibliographical literature published from ancient times to 1932. It is especially complete in its coverage of bibliographies published since the Restoration. To this should be added the essay by the French Japanologist, Émile Gaspardone, entitled "Les bibliographies japonaises" (Entry 2), written in 1933. This essay classifies and evaluates the major catalogues and bibliographies of pre-Restoration history, geography, religion, literature, etc.

For bibliographical literature published after 1933 the historian's problem is more complicated. Nearly all of the standard types of bibliography listed in the succeeding Sections a through d contain lists of book catalogues, and bibliographies. The specialist, depending upon the nature of his research problem, will need to consult some or all of these more general publications. Guides to their use are suggested in the introductory paragraphs which follow.

1. Amano Keitarō 天野敬太郎, Hompō shoshi no shoshi 本邦書誌の書誌 (A bibliography of Japanese bibliographies), Tōkyō, Ōsaka, Mamiya Shoten, 1933, 370 pp.

The single most important work in this field, now considerably out-dated. It covers all bibliographical literature from ancient times through 1932. Part one is devoted to pre-Restoration bibliographies and book lists, part two to materials published after 1868. The second part is extensively classified. Late entries are added as a supplement and not integrated with the main body of the work. Bibliographic entries are for the most part unannotated and are frequently incomplete. Subject and author indexes are provided.

2. Gaspardone, Émile, "Les bibliographies japonaises," <u>Bulletin de la Maison Franco-Japonaise</u>, v. 4, 1933, pp. 29-116.

   A bibliographical essay especially important for its coverage of materials on pre-Restoration history, religion and literature. The essay is divided into nine sections: 1) general indexes, 2) periodical publications, 3) biography, 4) history, 5) geography, 6) economics and law, 7) language and linguistics, 8) religion, and 9) literature. More specialized fields such as mathematics, astronomy, and calligraphy are treated in an appendix. Because the author has attempted to present his bibliographical information in a smooth literary style, his citations are often left incomplete.

3. Hoshino Kō 星 野 恒, Shigaku sōsetsu 史 学 叢 説 (Collected historical essays), Tōkyō, Fuzambō, 富 山 房, 1909, 2v. 776+774 pp.

   v. 1, pp. 559-775 contains an important essay on annotated bibliographies of pre-Restoration works.

2. GENERAL BIBLIOGRAPHIES

For access to contemporary historical literature the historian will find three general annotated bibliographies of indispensable service. The most extended in its coverage of fields is the work by Hatano and Yayoshi entitled <u>Kenkyū chōsa sankō bunken sōran</u> (General survey of reference works for study and research) (Entry 8). This work covers the entire range of Japanese scholarship although its citations are limited largely to standard reference works and basic texts. More specifically historical in scope is Kurita Motoji's <u>Sōgō kokushi kenkyū</u> (General guide for research in Japanese history) (Entry 24). Most entries in this work are annotated, and the various sections are provided with extensive introductory paragraphs full of bibliographical recommendations. Of outstanding importance, especially for the historian with the social science point of view, is the bibliographical series edited by Honjō Eijirō, <u>Nihon keizaishi bunken</u> (Bibliography of Japanese economic history) and its two successor volumes (Entries 10, 11, and 12). These bibliographies interpret economic history in its broadest sense and include nearly all subjects exclusive of literature and fine arts. Their value is immeasurably increased by the inclusion of references to a large number of periodical articles in addition to books. Entries which cite books are annotated.

While the above works will suffice for most purposes, they none the less have severe limitations. All three are selective and tend to be arbitrary in their choice of bibliographical entries, while the first two mentioned works are by now severely dated. These volumes must be supplemented, therefore, in two ways, first for the sake of completeness and second for the purpose of acquiring more up-to-date bibliographical information. For the first of these two tasks the historian should refer to the more complete Ministry of Home Affairs and National Diet Library catalogues, the catalogues and accession lists of major libraries, and to those bibliographies devoted specifically to the listing of periodical articles. These steps are outlined in Sections <u>b</u> through <u>e</u> of this chapter.

For continuing up-to-date coverage, the historian will find at his disposal several annual bibliographical publications. Most useful are the yearly bibliographical summaries of historical literature compiled by the major scholarly organizations in Japan. The first of these is the series begun in 1916 by Kyoto Imperial University and published in <u>Shirin</u>. This series was later taken up by the Yoyogikai, then by the Tsukuba Kenkyūbu, and is now published in modified form by the Tokyo University Shigakkai (Institution of Historical Science). It is included annually in <u>Shigaku zasshi</u> (Journal of historical science) as "Sen kyūhyaku[　]nen no rekishi gakkai (Historical studies in Japan, 19[　])." (Entries 37, 52, 50, and 39). The Shigakkai brought out in 1952 a combined bibliographical survey for the years 1946-50 entitled <u>Shigaku bunken mokuroku 1946-50</u> (Bibliography of historical studies, 1946-50) (Entry 41). Since the work covers both Chinese and Western history as well as Japanese history, its listings of materials on the latter subject are limited. Nevertheless it provides one of the best surveys of historical literature in postwar Japan. It lists both books and articles and contains an author index. A second annual series has been edited by the Rekishigaku Kenkyūkai (commonly called Rekken). Begun in 1930 as the <u>Rekishigaku nempō</u> (Annual report of historical studies) (Entry 35), it has continued in recent years as <u>Rekishigaku no seika to kadai</u> (Historical studies; accomplishments and problems) (Entry 36). Number 1 of the postwar series covered the years 1944-49 in analytical summaries only. Number 2 published in 1951 covers the year 1950 and contains not only articles analyzing the year's historical accomplishments but includes also a selected list of books and articles classified by historical periods. To these annuals should be added the chief publishers' yearbooks discussed in Section <u>d</u> of this chapter, the periodic indices to periodical literature discussed in Section <u>e</u>, and the review and current bibliography sections of the chief journals listed in Part IV.

Access to primary material and works written before the advent of modern historical scholarship in Japan is a somewhat more difficult task. Here again a double problem presents itself. First comes the work of accumulating references to primary and pre-modern sources, next the need to acquire information concerning the nature and location of these sources. To aid in the first step there exist a number of classified but unannotated catalogues and indices. Of first importance is the chronological index to primary sources prepared by the Tokyo University Historiographical Institute as part of its monumental project of compiling the <u>Dai Nihon shiryō</u> (Historical materials of Japan). It is entitled <u>Shiryō sōran</u> (Main points of the Historical materials of Japan) (Entry 48) and is arranged chronologically by historical incident. Under each incident are listed the major historical sources which relate to it. Naturally many of the sources so listed are extremely obscure and will be generally available only when the <u>Dai Nihon shiryō</u> is complete. Furthermore the <u>Shiryō soran</u> is considerably dated and often inaccurate. A further limitation is its coverage which terminates with the year 1583.

Of more general use, therefore, are two less pretentious indices. The first of these is Mozume Takami's <u>Gunsho sakuin</u> (Bibliographical index) (Entry 27), which classifies minutely under individual subjects over ten thousand pre-modern sources. The second, Ban Nobutomo and Koizumi Yasujiro's <u>Nihon shiseki nempyō</u> (Chronological table of Japanese historical materials) (Entry 18), indicates in tabular form the standard sources covering any given year from ancient times to 1868. The encyclopedic <u>Koji ruien</u> (Encyclopedia of ancient matters) (Entry 207) may also be used to gain access to primary sources, as may also Tsuji Zennosuke's <u>Dai Nihon nempyō</u> (Japanese chronological table) (Entry 346). In the latter work each citation of an historical fact is followed by a code word which indicates the source from which it was taken.

For entrance into less formalized historical materials, the various indices to series and miscellanies discussed in Section f of this chapter will be found indispensable. The historian will also want to know of the excellent classified list of historical sources included in Endō and others' Shiseki kaidai (Annotated bibliography of history) (Entry 5). This list (pp. 231-250) arranges chronologically and topically the major sources used by modern Japanese historians. Finally, for maximum completeness the scholar may have to consult the catalogues of some of the major libraries in Japan. These works are difficult to use, however, because of their lack of adequate classification.

Since few of the above bibliographical materials supply more than the bare titles of books and manuscripts, the historian is still faced with the problem of acquiring information on the contents and location of the works to which he has been referred. At this point he must bring into play still another set of reference materials, the kaidai or annotated bibliographies of pre-modern materials. Two general kaidai of great value are listed below. The first of these is Samura Hachiro's Zōtei kokusho kaidai (Annotated bibliography of Japanese books, revised and enlarged) (Entry 38). This work lists and briefly annotates some twenty-seven thousand Japanese works in all fields written before 1868, and indicates the location of modern printed editions when such exist. The other is Endō and others' Shiseki kaidai (Annotated bibliography of history) (Entry 5), a work of smaller and more strictly historical scope. Annotated bibliographies limited to single fields have been listed later in the chapters dealing with specialized bibliographies.

Neither of the above works indicates the location of unpublished materials. This final problem has no easy solution. Since Japan has no centralized national archives, manuscripts are scattered among many private and institutional collections, few of which are adequately catalogued. The previously mentioned Nihon shiseki nempyō by Ban Nobutomo and Koizumi Yasujiro is, to the author's knowledge, the only work which indicates the location of manuscript sources. For manuscripts not listed in this work, the only recourse seems to be to consult individually the catalogues of the major Japanese libraries or archival collections, both public and private.

The following list of general bibliographies is highly selective and includes for the most part only works in book form completely devoted to the subject of historical bibliography. Naturally a good deal of excellent bibliographical material lies hidden in the appendices of books on history and in the various historical journals. Such sources have not been systematically listed in the following section. However, the author has attempted to indicate in his annotations of the major journals and secondary works on Japanese history the existence of review sections and bibliographical appendices. It should also be pointed out that the following list makes no attempt to cover with any degree of completeness bibliographies dealing exclusively with government publications. Since the Meiji period, the various branches of the Japanese government have published such a quantity of material that orientation in this field of publication is an entire subject in itself. For most purposes, however, the historian should find the government publications series published by the Cabinet Printing Office (Entries 29 and 30) and the National Diet Library (Entry 20) sufficiently complete. It should also be noted that the general catalogues published by the National Diet Library (Entries 58 and 59) and the yearbook issued by the Shuppan Nyūsusha (Entry 89) list government publications.

a. General

4. Chiyoda Ken 千代田謙, Matsumoto Hikojirō 松本彦次郎, and Matsui Hitoshi 松井等, Shigaku meicho kaidai 史学名著解題 (Annotated bibliography of famous books on history), Tōkyō, Kyōritsusha, 1931, 357 pp.

This work, volume 15 of the Gendai shigaku taikei (Outline of contemporary historiography), is composed of three bibliographical essays on Western, Japanese, and Chinese historiography. Matsumoto Hikojirō's section on Japan comprises nearly half the volume and is devoted to critical commentaries on the chief historical works written in Japan from ancient times through the Tokugawa period.

5. Endō Motoo 遠藤元男, Suzuki Satoshi 鈴木俊, Hara Taneyuki 原種行, and Tanaka Masayoshi 田中正義, Kokushi Tōyōshi Seiyōshi shiseki kaidai 国史東洋史曲洋史籍解題 (An annotated bibliography of Japanese, Oriental and Occidental history), Tōkyō, Heibonsha, 1936, 250+281+139+8+93+82 pp.

This work is volume 25 of the Sekai rekishi taikei (Outline of world history) series. Together with Samura's Kokusho kaidai (Entry 38) it is the most important of the annotated bibliographies of pre-modern historical sources. The book is arranged in three parts: Japan, Orient, and Occident. Two hundred and fifty pages plus eighty-two pages of index are devoted to Japan. Entries are arranged by title. Each work is extensively annotated giving date of authorship, résumé of contents, full table of contents if the work is a collection, and location of modern printed editions. The index is very exhaustive since it includes not only the major citations but titles contained in serial publications. Pages 231-250 comprise a classified list of historical reference works, providing a convenient introduction to the major pre-modern sources in the field of history.

6. Gaimushō Bunshoka Toshogakari 外務有文書課図書係 (Ministry of Foreign Affairs, Archives, Chief Archivist), Hompō shokanchō kaisha kyōkai dantai kankō kakushu sōsho shiryō oyobi panfuretto mokuroku 本邦諸官庁,会社,協会,団体,刊行各種叢書史料及パンフレット目録. (A catalogue of various series, research materials and pamphlets published by various Japanese governmental offices, firms, associations and organizations), Tōkyō, Gaimushō Bunshoka Toshogakari, 1930-31, 3 v.

7. Gaimushō Jōhōbu Shōgaika Bunkahan 外務省情報部渉外課文化班 (Ministry on Foreign Affairs, Intelligence Bureau, Liaison Division, Cultural Section), A bibliography of representative writings of Japanese culture and science, Tōkyō, Gaimushō, 1947, 122-11 pp.

An unannotated list compiled by Japanese specialists at the request of the Washington Documents Center. It lists about twenty basic books in each of fifty fields including history and related fields. Selections are arbitrary and tend to include older works. Bibliographical citations are often incomplete.

8. Hatano Ken'ichi 波多野賢一 and Yayoshi Mitsunaga 彌吉光長, <u>Kenkyū chōsa sankō bunken sōran</u> 研究調査参考文献総覧 (General survey of reference works for study and research), Tōkyō, Asahi Shobō, 1934, 877 pp.

    The most valuable of the general annotated bibliographies, it covers reference works and standard texts in all fields published from ancient times to 1932. Arrangement is by decimal system. Within each field a section is devoted to history. There is a section on foreign bibliographies and an appendix on the types and uses of reference works. A detailed index of Japanese titles covers pages 741-865. This book relies rather heavily on Amano Keitaro's <u>Hompō shoshi no shoshi</u> (Entry 1) and thus perpetuates errors contained in that work. Annotations tend to be at a minimum and approximately one-fifth of the citations are unannotated. Bibliographical entries are frequently incomplete.

9. Hibiya Toshokan 日比谷図書館 (Hibiya Library), <u>Hōbun sankōsho mokuroku</u> 邦文参考書目録 (A catalogue of Japanese reference works), Tōkyō, Hibiya Toshokan, 1927, 36 pp.; rev. and enl. ed., Tōkyō, Isseidō, 1929, 40 pp.; 2nd rev. and enl. ed., Tōkyō, Isseidō, 1931, 47 pp.

    A list of essential dictionaries, bibliographies, indexes, histories, biographical dictionaries, yearbooks, etc.

10. Honjō Eijiro 本庄栄治郎, <u>Kaihan Nihon keizaishi bunken</u> 改版日本経済史文献 (Revised bibliography of Japanese economic history), Tōkyō, Nihon Hyōronsha, 1933, 10+703+195 pp.

    This volume combines and brings up to date two previous bibliographies published in 1924 and 1926. Much more than just a bibliography of economic history, it covers the history of all social science fields in comprehensive fashion. Though it touches on intellectual and religious history, it is weak in these fields and neglects altogether literature and the arts. Annotations are largely written to explain the value of the entries to the economic historian. Volumes two and three of this series (see following entries), bring the entire coverage up to 1950. The Honjō bibliographies have a number of unique features which make them indispensable to the historian: 1) they include both books and articles; 2) the sections on historical materials break down the contents of the major collections and briefly annotate each item; 3) they include separate lists of local histories; and 4) they include separate bibliographies of Western works on Japanese social and economic history. The indices are full and contain references to both book titles and to the contents of the major collections. Articles are not indexed.

11. Honjō Eijiro 本庄栄治郎, <u>Nihon keizaishi shin'bunken</u> 日本経済史新文献 (New bibliography of Japanese economic history), Tōkyō, Nihon Hyōronsha, 1942, 12+709 pp.

    This volume brings the excellent bibliographical coverage of the social sciences, begun in the previous entry, up to 1941. Largely based on the yearly <u>Keizaishi nenkan</u> (Yearbook of economic history) (Entry 28) published in <u>Keizaishi kenkyū</u>, it contains as a special feature a checklist of major journals and serial publications.

12. Honjō Eijiro 本庄榮治郎, Yoshikawa <u>Hidezo</u> 吉川秀造, and Matsuyoshi Sadao 松好貞夫, <u>Nihon keizaishi daisan bunken</u> 日本経済史第三文献 (Bibliography of Japanese economic history, number three), Tōkyō, Nihon Hyōronshinsha, 1953, 12+600 pp.

    This work continues the coverage of books and articles begun in the previous volumes from January 1941 through December 1950. A new feature of this volume is the annotation of some of the articles cited.

13. Ishin Shiryō Hensan Jimukyoku 維新史料編纂事務局 (Office for the Compilation of Historical Materials Concerning the Restoration), <u>Ishin shiryō kōyō</u> 維新史料綱要 (Summary index of historical materials on the Restoration), Tōkyō, Ishin Shiryō Hensan Jimukyoku, 1937-.

    The compilation office is now incorporated into the Shiryō Hensansho or the Historiographical Institute of Tokyo University. This series constitutes a simplified guide to materials found in the great collection of documents on the Restoration, the <u>Dai Nihon Ishin shiryō</u> (Entry 379). Like the <u>Shiryō sōran</u> (Entry 48) it provides a chronology of events with documents listed for each incident. By 1939, ten volumes had been published covering the period 1853-69.

14. Jimbun Kagaku Iinkai 人文科学委員会 (Committee on Humanistic Science), "Bunken mokuroku 文献目録 (Bibliography)," in <u>Zinbun</u>, March 1947-May 1951, 9 numbers, 8 v.

    Zinbun, published irregularly by a committee of the Ministry of Education, devoted from a quarter to a half of each issue to a selected, classified bibliography of Japanese books and articles in the fields of literature, history, philosophy, law, and economics. Entries were submitted by the Tokyo University Philosophy Department, the Waseda University Literary Department, the Tokyo Geographical Research Institute and the Institute for Ethnological Research. The last two numbers constitute a single-volume special issue. The series covers the years 1946-1949, a period which is inadequately treated in other standard references. The bibliographical feature was dropped when the Committee on Humanistic Science became a private organization in 1951.

15. Kamba Takeo 神波武夫, <u>Kihonteki sankō tosho mokuroku</u> 基本的参考図書目録 (Catalogue of basic reference books). Osaka, Mamiya Shoten, 1929, 42 pp.

    A list of basic reference works for use by Japanese libraries. Books are entered under the following categories: 1) general (including bibliographies, dictionaries, yearbooks, newspapers, encyclopedias, etc.); 2) spiritual sciences; 3) historical sciences; 4) social sciences; 5) natural sciences; 6) engineering; 7) industry; 8) fine arts; 9) language; and 10) literature.

16. Kawai Eijirō 河合榮治郎 and Kimura Takeyasu 木村健康, ed., <u>Kyōyō bunken kaisetsu</u> 敎養文献解説 (An annotated bibliography of educational materials). Tōkyō, Shakai Shisō Kenkyūsho Shuppambu, enlarged ed. 1950, 2 v.
    A collection of introductory bibliographical essays in a large variety of fields with emphasis on the social sciences. Most of the essays are written to introduce to Japanese scholars the basic Western literature in such fields as philosophy, sociology, economics, etc. The historian, however, will find useful sections on Shinto, Japanese Buddhism, and Japanese Christianity in volume 1; volume 2 contains two excellent articles, one by Takasaka Masaaki on Japanese historiography, the other by Fujiki Kunihiko on Japanese history. Bibliographical citations are incomplete but the authors include valuable evaluative comments.

17. Kōbe Kōtō Shōgyōgakkō Shōgyō Kenkyujo 神戸高等商業学校商業研究所 (Commercial Research Institute of the Kobe Higher Commercial School), <u>Keizai hōritsu bunken mokuroku</u> 經濟法律文献目録 (Catalogue of economic and legal literature), Tōkyō and Ōsaka, Hōbunkan, 1927 and 1932, 2 v.
    For the student of recent history this thorough though unannotated bibliography will be of utmost value. Its coverage includes books, pamphlets, and articles appearing in a large number of journals and newspapers from 1916 to 1930. Entries are classified according to 36 major categories including contemporary Japanese economics, social conditions, politics, administration, law, foreign relations, etc. Each volume contains a detailed subject index. Volume 2, which covers the period 1926-30, does not list newspaper articles.

18. Koizumi Yasujirō 小泉安次郎, <u>Nihon shiseki nempyō</u> 日本史籍年表 (Chronological table of Japanese historical materials), Tōkyō, Yoshikawa Kōbunkan, 1911, 6+38+383+5+5+268+8 pp.
    An amplified and completed version of a work begun by Ban Nobutomo, the late Tokugawa scholar. This work consists of two tables. Table 1, chiefly the work of Ban, covers the years 888-1602; table 2 covers 1603-1868. Each table is divided into yearly sections. Each section presents a list of sources which contain references to events of that year. Generally between 20 and 50 works are listed. These works are divided into three categories. In table 1 the categories are: 1) archival material recommended by Ban Nobutomo, 2) amplification of 1), 3) diaries and biographical materials. In table 2 these categories are: 1) documents relating to the Imperial court, 2) materials on the Shogunal government, 3) miscellaneous. Pertinent chapters of works are identified; the location of manuscript copies is indicated by a code character. On the first occurrence of each work, significant bibliographical data is recorded. This constitutes one of the most important tools for gaining information on primary Japanese historical sources and for obtaining information on the location of manuscript copies of such sources.

19. <u>Kokumin keizai zasshi</u> 国民經济雑誌, (Journal of national economics), Kōbe, Hōbunkan, June 1906-. Monthly.
    This journal is edited by the Institute of Commercial Studies, Kōbe Commercial University. Each number from 1909 includes a classified bibliographical section entitled <u>(Naikoku) bunken mokuroku</u> (Bibliography of Japanese publications) which lists books and articles in all social science fields. Useful primarily for its coverage of contemporary problems, it is of limited value to the historian.

20. Kokuritsu Kokkai Toshokan 国立国会図書館, <u>Kancho kankōbutsu sōgōmokuroku</u> 官斤刊行物總合目録 (General catalogue of government publications), Tōkyō, Kokuritsu Kokkai Toshokan, 1952, 650 pp.
    A comprehensive catalogue of government publications from September 1945 to December 1950. Entries are classified by subject. There is an index by government agency.

21. Kokusai Bunka Shinkōkai 国際文化振興会 (Society for International Cultural Relations), <u>Bibliographical register of important books written in Japanese on Japan and the Far East published during the year ...</u> (1932-), Tōkyō, Kokusai Bunka Shinkōkai, 1937-.
    Prewar numbers were published annually. Postwar publication was resumed in 1951 in modified form. This bibliography attempts to cover all major fields of Japanese scholarship in a highly selective fashion. Each volume lists publications appearing during a given year (volume 1 covers 1932 and volume 8, 1938). The appearance of new journals is noted. Bibliographical entries are in Japanese and English. One special use which this series has is that it gives romanized readings of the names of contemporary Japanese authors. Unfortunately the lag between coverage and publication diminishes the value of this series.

22. Kokusho Kankōkai 国書刊行会 (Society for the publication of national literature), <u>Gunsho biko</u> 群書備考 (Notes on books), Tōkyō, Kokusho Kankōkai, 1916, 4+48+540 pp.
    An annotated bibliography compiled in 1827 by Murai Yōrei. It was subsequently revised by Itō Chikara and Saitō Matsutarō. Loosely arranged and difficult to use, it nevertheless contains a great deal of information on pre-modern sources hard to obtain elsewhere. The usefulness of the modern edition is enhanced by the addition of a title index.

23. Konakamura Kiyonori 小中村清矩, <u>Kokushigaku no shiori</u> 国史学の栞 (A guide to Japanese historiography), Tōkyō, Yoshikawa Hanshichi, 1895, 11+2+136+2+1 pp.
    An early but still useful guide to the chief materials necessary for the study of pre-Restoration Japanese history.

24. Kurita Motoji 栗田元次, <u>Sōgō kokushi kenkyū</u> 綜合国史研究 (General guide for research in Japanese history), Tokyo, Dobun Shoin, 1935, 3 v.
    This work along with Kuroita Katsumi's <u>Kokushi no kenkyū</u> (Entry 25) is one of the most indispensable historiographical guides. Its historiographical importance derives from the excellent introductory essays which Kurita has prefaced to the various bibliographical sections of his work. It ranks with Hatano and Yayoshi's <u>Kenkyū chōsa sankō bunken sōran</u> (Entry 8), and Honjo's bibliographies of economic history

(Entries 10 to 12) as one of the best of the selective annotated bibliographies. Its special focus is upon historical reference works, collections of historical sources, and upon secondary works in a broad variety of historical fields. The entries are descriptively annotated but little critical comment is added. Except for the fact that the work is now considerably out-of-date, it forms an excellent starting point for the student of Japanese history. The index contains references not only to the chief bibliographical entries but to titles mentioned in the historiographical prefaces and to the titles included in the large serial collections of historical materials.

25. Kuroita Katsumi 黒板勝美 , Kokushi no kenkyū 国史の研究 (Study of Japanese history), Tōkyō, Iwanami Shoten, rev. ed., 1931-36, 4 v.
Undoubtedly the most famous of modern Japanese histories, this work has a large number of bibliographical uses. Volume 1, entitled Sōsetsu (General introduction), contains a number of bibliographical chapters; the most useful are: 1) a discussion of historical geography, and 2) of genealogies; 3) an historiographical essay which concludes with 4) a chronological listing of important Japanese works on Japanese history published from 1868 to 1930; 5) a similar list of Western language works published from 1364 to 1930; 6) bibliographical essays and recommended books and articles on the major period and subject divisions of Japanese history. The remaining three volumes constitute a standard political history of Japan. The author's documentation affords a valuable source of information on pre-Restoration bibliography. It is important to note that the materials used by Kuroita became the standard sources for the Tokyo Imperial University school of Japanese historiography.

26. Masamune Atsuo 正宗敦夫 , Nihon koten zenshū, shomokushū 日本古典全集書目集 (Complete collection of Japanese classics; book catalogues), Tōkyō, Kokusho Kankōkai, 1931-2, 3 v.
A collection of four important pre-Restoration book and manuscript catalogues, useful to the specialist who fails to find Samura's Kokusho kaidai (Entry 38) complete enough. A supplementary volume appeared in 1937.

27. Mozume Takami 物集高見 , Gunsho sakuin 群書索引 (Bibliographical index), Tōkyō, Kōbunko Kankōkai, 1916-7, 3 v.
A monumental classified index to pre-Restoration literature which became the basis of the encyclopedic Kōbunko (Entry 206). The work is arranged in syllabic order by subject. Under each subject are listed those sources which in whole or in part deal with it. Citations are more numerous than in either the Kōbunko or the Koji ruien (Entry 207). For the student of pre-modern Japanese history this work is of primary importance.

28. Nihon Keizaishi Kenkyūjo 日本経済史研究所 (Institute for the study of Japanese economic history), Nihon keizaishi nenkan 日本経済史年鑑 (Yearbook of economic history), yearly special issue of Keizaishi kenkyū, Tōkyō, Nihon Hyōronsha, 1932-44.
An annual survey of Japanese works on Japanese, Oriental, and Occidental economic history. Part 1 contains critical reviews of the previous year's scholarship in a large variety of fields. Except for the 1934 issue, part 2 consists of a classified annotated bibliography of books and articles in economic history. Part 3 is a classified index of the contents of Keizaishi kenkyū during the previous year. Although the bibliographical data of this series is consolidated in Honjō's Nihon keizaishi shin'bunken (Entry 11), and Nihon keizaishi daisan bunken (Entry 12), the review notes of part 1 continue to be of importance.

29. Naikaku Insatsukyoku 内閣印刷局 (Cabinet Printing Office), Kanchō kankō tosho mokuroku 官庁刊行図書目録 (Catalogue of government publications), Tōkyō, Naikaku Insatsukyoku, 1927-37. Quarterly.
A quarterly catalogue of all books, serial publications, pamphlets, etc., published by government offices. Each issue is divided into two parts. Part 1 lists publications according to government agency, part 2 according to classified subject. Entries in part 2 are sometimes annotated. Lack of a cumulative index to this series makes its use extremely inconvenient. After 1937 this quarterly was succeeded by the monthly Kanchō kankō tosho geppo (see following entry).

30. Naikaku Insatsukyoku 内閣印刷局 (Cabinet Printing Office), Kanchō kankō tosho geppō 官庁刊行図書月報 (Monthly catalogue of governmental publications), Tōkyō, Naikaku Insatsukyoku, January 1938-43. Monthly.
A continuation of the quarterly Kanchō kankō tosho mokuroku (See previous entry).

31. Nihon Toshokan Kyōkai 日本図書館協会 (Japanese Library Association), Nihon Toshokan Kyōkai sentei shinkan tosho mokuroku 日本図書館協会選定新刊図書目録 (Japanese Library Association's catalogue of selected new publications), Tōkyō, Nihon Toshokan Kyōkai, 1914—. Monthly.
The emphasis in selection is on reference works. Publication of this catalogue was taken over in 1924 by the Toshokan zasshi (Entry 643) in which it appears as an appendix. Since the war it has appeared separately under the title Sentei tosho sōmokuroku (General Catalogue of selected works).

32. Nishimura Kanefumi 西村兼文 , Zoku gunsho ichiran 続群書一覧 (A bibliographical survey, continued), revised by Irita Seizō 入田整三 Tōkyō, Nichiyō Shobō, 1926, 2+3+1002+58 pp.
Completed in 1892, this work corrects and supplements Ozaki Masayoshi's Gunsho ichiran (Entry 34).

33. Ōmori Kingorō 大森金五郎, Shiseki kaisetsu 史籍解説 (Annotated bibliography of historical materials), Tōkyō, Sanseidō, 1937, 4+240+13 pp.

A useful reference work for the student of pre-Restoration Japan. Part 1 consists of descriptive annotations of important reference works and modern collections of historical materials. Part 2 contains full annotations of major pre-modern historical sources arranged in chronological order. Parts 3 and 4 deal with books on ancient court procedure and antiquarian practices. Annotations are unusually clear and full. There is an index.

34. Ozaki Masayoshi 尾崎雅喜, Gunsho ichiran 群書一覧 (A bibliographical survey), modern edition revised and supplemented, and index by Irita Seizō 入田整三, Tōkyō, Nichiyō Shobō, 1931, 4+8+29+29+1090+370 pp.

This work, originally completed in 1801, is an old style annotated bibliography listing some 2000 books and manuscripts. Entries are arranged in irregular fashion under broad subject headings. Much of the material contained in this and its companion work, Nishimura Kanebumi's Zoku gunsho ichiran (Entry 32), has been incorporated into Samura Hachirō's Kokusho kaidai (Entry 38).

35. Rekishigaku Kenkyūkai 歴史学研究会, "Rekishigaku nempō 歴史学年報 (Annual report of historical studies)," Rekishigaku kenkyū, v. 1, 1933-44.

This annual special number of Rekishigaku kenkyū (Entry 568) parallels in its coverage the series begun by Shirin (See entry 37). The series was interrupted during World War II and resumed in 1950 with a second series under the title Rekishigaku no seika to kadai (See following entry). Each of the prewar volumes surveys a year's activity in the fields of Japanese, Oriental and Occidental history. Early issues contain both review essays and classified bibliographies of books and articles on the whole range of historical studies. Later issues become increasingly interpretive and hence contain less bibliographical information. As a whole, however, this series affords one of the best coverages on historical books and articles for the period 1936-43.

36. Rekishigaku Kenkyūkai 歴史学研究会, Rekishigaku no seika to kadai 歴史学の成果と課題 (Historical studies: accomplishments and problems), Tōkyō, Iwanami Shoten, 1950—.

An annual supplement to Rekishigaku kenkyū (Entry 568). The first issue after the war covered the years 1944-49 and thus filled in the interval from the termination of the prewar "Rekishigaku nempō" series (See previous entry). Volume 2 covers the year 1950. Volume 1 contains interpretive essays on the activity of Japanese historians in the fields of Japanese, Oriental, and Occidental studies. Volume 2 revives the feature of a selected, classified bibliography of books and articles. Users should be aware of the historical bias of the postwar Rekishigaku Kenkyūkai.

37. "Sakunen no shigaku 昨年の史学 (Historiography during the previous year)," Shirin, v. 1-14 (1916-29).

This annual feature of Shirin (Entry 580) gives excellent coverage of historical literature for the years 1915-28. Later issues of this series include separate bibliographical sections on archeology and geography as well as history. Each issue contains a critical survey of historical literature in each of the major historical fields with copious references to the most significant books and articles published during the previous year. This survey was carried on by the Yoyogikai after Shirin dropped it in 1930.

38. Samura Hachiro 佐村八郎, Zōtei kokusho kaidai 増訂国書解題 (Annotated bibliography of Japanese books, revised and enlarged), revised by Samura Toshio 佐村敏郎, Tōkyō, Rokugōkan, 1926, 2 v.

This monumental annotated bibliography of books and manuscripts of pre-Restoration Japan was first published in 1900 and affords the most complete and satisfactory coverage of earlier Japanese historical literature. The body of the work consists of an annotated bibliography of some twenty-seven thousand works listed by title in syllabic order. Annotations contain date of authorship, description of content, information on printed editions, and a note on the author. Volume 2 contains the following useful appendices:

1) An author index which includes pennames.
2) A classified index of works cited in the bibliography. Classification is based on the "traditional" system and hence difficult to use.
3) A title index by strokes, a most useful feature especially when the reading of a title is obscure.
4) A list of major serial publications plus a detailed breakdown of their contents.

Indexes 1, 2, and 3 are not complete. Index 4 was prepared by Hamano Tomosaburō (See entry 107).

39. "Sen kyūhyaku [ ] nen no rekishi gakkai 19 [ ]年の歴史学会 (Historical studies in Japan, 19 [ ]," in Shigaku zasshi, v. 58 (1949), no. 1—.

This annual special issue of Shigaku zasshi (Entry 578) continues in somewhat abridged form the yearly summary of historical activities in Japan compiled by the Tsukuba Kenkyūbu (Entry 50) up to the beginning of World War II. Each issue contains interpretive articles on publications in the fields of Japanese, Oriental, and Western history produced during the previous year in Japan. The section on Japan is divided into the following sections: 1) general, 2) ancient, 3) feudal, 4) Meiji restoration, and 5) recent history. There is no separate bibliographical list or index.

40. Shakai Keizaishi Gakkai 社会経済史学会, "Shakai keizai shigaku no hattatsu 社会経済史学の発達 (Social and economic history of Japan, its recent development)," Shakai keizaishigaku, v. 10 (1941) nos. 9-10.

This is a special number of Shakai keizaishigaku (Entry 612) edited by Ono Takeo. It contains articles by individual specialists on the development of Japanese scholarship in such fields as: agriculture, industry, commerce, thought, society, administration, law, and customs. Though the quantity of bibliographical information varies greatly from article to article, this work constitutes a valuable introductory guide to the general field of history as a social science. It has been widely used by contemporary Japanese historians.

41. Shigakkai 史学会, Shigaku bunken mokuroku 1946-50 史学文献目録 1946-50 (Bibliography of historical studies, 1946-50) Tōkyō, Yamakawa Shuppansha, 1951, 2+7+204 pp.

This work represents one of the most valuable efforts in the field of historical bibliography to come out of postwar Japan. It is a selected and classified list of books and articles by Japanese scholars in the fields of Japanese, Oriental, and Occidental history. Some nine thousand items are listed of which 4800 deal with Japan. Over four hundred journals are represented. An especially valuable feature of this work is its index by author.

42. Shiryō Hensangakari 史料編纂掛, (Department of Historiography), Shiryō hensangakari biyō tosho mokuroku 史料編纂掛備用図書目録 (Catalogue of books in the Department of Historiography), Tōkyō, Shiryō Hensangakari, 1905, 1498 pp.

Since its founding in 1888, the present Tokyo University Historiographical Institute, Shiryō Hensansho, has acquired, through purchase or by hand-written facsimile copy, a vast collection of basic historical materials. These have been used in the preparation of the various documentary series issued by the institute. They have also formed the basis of the research of many of Japan's leading historians. Unfortunately, this catalogue is now seriously dated. But until a more up-to-date catalogue is issued, this one will remain valuable as a list of important documentary materials.

43. Shiryō Hensangakari 史料編纂掛 (Department of Historiography), Shiryō hensangakari biyō shashin gazō zugarui mokuroku 史料編纂掛備用寫眞畫像図畫類目録 (Catalogue of photographs, portraits, and drawings in the Department of Historiography), Tōkyō, Shiryō Hensangakari, 1905, 36+28+182+24 pp.

A companion volume to the previous entry.

44. Takahashi Ryūzō 高橋隆三, Shiseki kaidai 史籍解題 (An annotated bibliography of historical sources), in Dai Nihonshi koza 大日本史講座 (Series on Japanese history), Tōkyō, Yūzankaku, 1938, v. 18, 173+8 pp.

Largely a descriptive bibliography of historically important diaries. Titles are arranged chronologically and are accompanied by notes on contents and authors. Unfortunately, no information is given on how to locate copies. For its limited field, however, the work supplements the more general kaidai.

45. Takagi Shintarō 高木眞太郎, Kokushi shincho kaidai 国史新著解題 (An annotated bibliography of newly published works in Japanese history), Tōkyō, Shunjūsha, 1943-44, 2 v.

This work, started as an annual undertaking, was apparently interrupted by World War II. Each volume begins with a review article on historical activity during the previous year. Following this the author gives lengthy reviews of approximately five major works published in each of several fields of history: political, economic, intellectual, religious, etc. Volume 1 provides, in addition, a selected checklist of important works published during 1942 in each of the above fields. Volume 2 does the same for 1943 and also lists articles. A very valuable work for the years it covers.

46. Takaichi Yoshio 高市慶雄, Meiji bunken mokuroku 明治文献目録 (Catalogue of Meiji literature), Tōkyō, Nihon Hyōronsha, 1932, 316 pp.

Useful primarily for students of Meiji history, this work consists of a classified catalogue of works published from 1868 to 1890. Entries are listed both under subject and by author's name.

47. Tanaka Kei 田中敬 and Mori Miyahiko 毛利宮彦, Naigai sankō tosho no chishiki 内外参考図書の知識 (Guide to Japanese and foreign reference works), Tōkyō, Toshokan Jigyō Kenkyūkai, 1929, 325 pp.

The first 216 pages of this work are devoted to an annotated bibliography of Japanese reference works. Useful but less comprehensive than Hatano and Yayoshi's Kenkyū chōsa sankō bunken sōran (Entry 8).

48. Tōkyō Teikoku Daigaku Bungakubu Shiryō Hensansho 東京帝国大学文学部史料編纂所 (Tōkyō Imperial University, Faculty of Letters, Historiographical Institute), Shiryō sōran 史料綜覧 (Main points of the historical materials of Japan), Tōkyō, Chōyōkai 1923+.

By 1938, ten volumes of this important index had been completed. Work on the index has paralleled the preparation of the great archival collection by the Tokyo University. Eventually the index will cover the years 888 to 1868. This work is arranged chronologically, recording the important events under each date. For each event an exhaustive list of primary sources is listed, many of which will be generally available only when the Dai Nihon shiryō (Entry 382) is complete. Volume 10 brings the coverage down to 1572.

49. Tokushi Yūshō 秃氏裕祥, Shomoku shūran 書目集覧 (A collection of book catalogues), Kyōto, Tōrin Shobō, 1928-31, 2 v.

A facsimile reproduction of five important book dealer's catalogues of the seventeenth and eighteenth centuries. Of use only for the most exacting bibliographical research of pre-nineteenth century literature.

50. Tsukuba Kenkyūbu 筑波研究部, Shōwa[　　　]nen no kokushi gakkai 昭和[　　]年の国史学界 (Historical studies in Japan during the year [　　]), Tōkyō, Tsukuba Kenkyūbu, 1937-43. Annual.

A continuation of the yearly survey of historical literature in Japan begun in Shirin (Entry 37) and subsequently taken over by the Yoyogikai (Entry 52). The volumes edited by the Tsukuba Kenkyūbu unfortunately omit the analytical essays which made the previous surveys so valuable. The 1943 issue was edited jointly by Tsukuba Fujimaro and Sakamoto Tarō. The Shigaku zasshi has continued this series in somewhat modified form (See entry 39).

51. Wada Hidematsu 和 田 英 松, Honchō shojaku mokuroku kōshō 本 朝 書 籍 目 録 考 證 (A study of Honcho shojaku mokuroku), Tōkyō, Meiji Shoin, 1936, 28+29+664 pp.
    The Honchō shojaku mokuroku (Catalogue of Japanese literature) is a work dated variously from the 13th to 15th century containing valuable bibliographical information for the student of early Japanese history. Professor Wada has added annotations in the light of modern scholarship and discusses the present status of the works listed, whether they are still in existence, and if so where. A title index has been added.

52. Yoyogikai 代 々 木 会, Shōwa [   ] nen no kokushi gakkai 昭 和 [   ] 年 ノ 国 史 学 界 (National history during the year [   ]), Tōkyō, Yoyogikai, 1930-36. Annual.
    An annual review of Japanese historical literature continuing the series begun by Shirin (See entry 37). In addition to providing the usual critical surveys of the major historical fields the Yoyogikai began the practice of including a separate list of books and articles classified under 17 categories. In 1937 the series was taken up by the Tsukuba Kenkyūbu (Entry 50).

b. Ministry of Home Affairs and National Diet Library Catalogues

    Prior to World War II, the Japanese government customarily issued lists of titles submitted to the Ministry of Home Affairs for copyright and censorship purposes. These lists provide a nearly exhaustive coverage of all commercially published books, especially for the period after 1924. Before that date the coverage was somewhat spotty.
    Following World War II the book collecting function of the Home Ministry was partially taken over by the National Diet Library. As yet, however, the bibliographical lists published by this library are not as complete as those of the prewar Home Ministry. This is due to the fact that the National Diet Library lacks legal powers to require all new publications to be deposited with it.
    While the above category of bibliographical materials is important for the completeness of its coverage, the scholar will find it somewhat difficult to use because of the lack of cumulative volumes prior to 1948. Thereafter the Zen—Nihon Shuppambutsu sōmokuroku (General catalogue of works published in Japan) (Entry 59) affords one of the most complete and accessible repositories of current bibliography available. The entries which follow have been chronologically listed since in a sense they constitute a single series.

53. Naimushō Toshokyoku 内 務 省 図 書 局 (Ministry of Home Affairs, Bureau of Books), Hanken shomoku 版 権 書 目 (Catalogue of copyrights), Tōkyō, Naimushō Toshokyoku, 27 nos. in 6 v., 1876-83 and 1921-23.
    This is the first of the Home Ministry's catalogues of books deposited for copyright purposes. The series is of interest chiefly for the historian of the early Meiji period. Titles contained in this series are cumulated in the Naimushō Toshokyoku's Toshokyoku shomoku (1883, 2 v.) and the Dai ni Toshoka shomoku (1886, 3 v.). The present series was succeeded by the monthly bulletin described in the following entry.

54. Naimushō Toshokyoku 内 務 省 図 書 局 (Ministry of Home Affairs, Bureau of Books), Shuppan shomoku geppō 出 版 書 目 月 報 (Monthly bulletin of publications), Tōkyō, Naimushō Toshokyoku, 114 nos., 1878-87.
    A continuation of the Home Ministry's listings of books deposited with it. Most of the entries in this series were accumulated in the Toshokyoku shomoku and Dai ni Toshoka shomoku (see previous entry). This series was succeeded after a break by the Naimushō nōhon geppō series (Following entry).

55. Naimushō nōhon geppō 内 務 省 納 本 月 報 (Monthly list of books deposited with the Ministry of Home Affairs), Tōkyō, Tosho Kenkyūkai, v. 1-3, 1926-29. Monthly.
    Privately compiled under authorization of the Home Ministry this series continues a practice begun in 1912 and carried on by a number of publishing houses. Because of the complex nature of this series, its previous bibliographical history is condensed under this entry. Originating in 1912 in the Dokusho no tomo 読 書 ノ 友 (Readers' world); the Bukkuman ブ ッ ク マ ン (Bookman), Tōkyō, Yomiuri, v. 1-2, 1924-25; the Yomuhito 讀 む 人 (The reader), Tōkyō, Yomiuri, v. 3, nos. 1-6, 1926; the Bukkuman, v. 3, nos. 7-9, 1926; the Bukku rebyū ブ ッ ク レ ビ ュ ー (Book review), Tōkyō, Tosho Kenkyūkai, v. 1-2, 1926-28; and again the Bukkuman, Tosho Kenkyūkai, v. 2, no. 11-v. 3, no. 5, 1928-29. Bibliographic information is compiled from daily mimeographed releases of the Home Ministry. Contents are divided into 22 subject categories. After October 1930 this series was published under different auspices (see below).

56. Naimushō nōhon geppō 内 務 省 納 本 月 報 (Monthly list of books deposited with the Ministry of Home Affairs), Tōkyō, Ōsakayagō Shoten, v. 1, no. 1-v. 7, no. 5, October 1930-March 1937. Monthly.
    A monthly classified version of the daily Naimushō nōhon nippō (Daily list of books deposited with the Ministry of Home Affairs). It continues the series described in the previous entry. Actual compilation was performed as before by the Tosho Kenkyūkai.

57. Nōhon geppō 納 本 月 報 (Monthly report of books deposited), Tōkyō, Kokuritsu Kokkai Toshokan, Sept. 1948-July 1949. Monthly.
    This series may be said to have revived the work of the Home Ministry and the Tosho Kenkyūkai which had been interrupted by World War II. It is a classified list of commercially printed books and journals deposited with the National Diet Library. Classification is by Dewey Decimal System. A quarterly publication, Nōhon kihō, was begun concurrently but dropped almost immediately. The Nōhon geppō was superseded by the Kokunai shuppambutsu mokuroku (Following entry).

58. Kokunai shuppambutsu mokuroku 国 内 出 版 物 目 録 (Japanese national bibliography), Tōkyō, Kokuritsu Kokkai Toshokan, Aug.-Sept. 1949—. Monthly.
    A monthly classified list of copyrighted publications. It continues in more comprehensive fashion the series begun in the Nōhon geppō (Previous entry). Each issue has two major divisions: a classified list of government publications, and a classified list of commercially published books. Some issues also list phonograph records. An alphabetical title index is generally provided.

59. Zen-Nihon shuppambutsu sōmokuroku 全日本出版物總目錄 (General catalogue of works published in Japan), Tōkyō, Kokuritsu Kokkai Toshokan, 1951–. Yearly.
   A cumulative summary of the monthly index of government and copyrighted publications issued in Nōhon geppō (Entry 57) and the Kokunai shuppambutsu mokuroku (Entry 58). Volume 1 covers the period April 1948-March 1949. The work is divided into three major sections: 1) government publications, 2) commercially published books and journals, and 3) children's literature. Later volumes list periodicals and such miscellaneous items as works in braille, movies, film strips, and slides.

c. Library Catalogues and Accession Lists

   The historian will find the catalogues and accession lists of Japan's major libraries of importance in two ways: first as a source of bibliographical information on pre-modern historical materials, especially on the availability of manuscript copies and rare items, and secondly for the coverage they afford of recently published literature. For the latter purpose, other more convenient guides exist, though few are as complete.
   Most Japanese libraries issue two series of catalogues, one with titles arranged in syllabic order (the kanabetsu or shomei series) the other by classification under broad categories (the bunrui or kemmei series). The latter is more convenient, but categories are often too general for easy use.
   The value of individual library catalogues naturally varies greatly with the institution. A discussion of the history of library collections and their present status is reserved to Part III, Chapter 1 below. Here it need only be pointed out that for coverage of pre-Restoration materials the catalogues of the Imperial Household Library (Kunaishō Toshokan), the Cabinet Library (Naikaku Bunko), the Imperial Library (Teikoku Toshokan, now the Ueno Library), the Seikadō Library, the Sonkeikaku Library, and the Tōkyō and Kyōto [Imperial] University Libraries are the most complete. For books of recent publication, the catalogues of the prewar Imperial Library and the postwar National Diet Library are most complete, since copies of nearly all commercially printed books are customarily deposited in these two libraries.
   In the following list, catalogues of only the most important libraries have been entered. Entries are classified by publishing library and thereafter chronologically.

60. Kokuritsu Kokkai Toshokan 国立国会図書館 (National Diet Library), Shūsho tsūhō 收書通報 (Current acquisitions), Tōkyō, Kokuritsu Kokkai Toshokan, Nov. 1948–.
   The National Diet Library, modeled after the United States Library of Congress, has taken over the government's centralizing activities formerly carried on by the Home Ministry and the Cabinet Library. Most major public libraries of the Tokyo area are now incorporated as branches of this library. The even numbered issues of this series list Japanese books while the odd numbered ones list Western books. Classification is by the Dewey Decimal System.

61. Kunaishō Zushoryō 宮内省図書寮 (Imperial Household Ministry, Librarian), Teishitsu wakan tosho mokuroku 帝室和漢図書目録 (Catalogue of Japanese and Chinese books held by the Imperial Household Library), Tōkyō, Kunaishō, 1916 and 1926, expanded ed., 2 v.
   Volume 1 is a classified list of the library's holdings to the end of 1915. Volume 2 is a classified accession list for 1916-24. Books are listed under 23 general categories encompassing the humanities, social and natural sciences.

62. Kyōto Teikoku Daigaku Fuzoku Toshokan 東京帝国大学附属図書館 (Kyoto Imperial University Library), Wakansho bunrui mokuroku 和漢書分類目録 (Classified catalogue of Japanese and Chinese books), Kyōto, Kyōto Teikoku Daigaku Fuzoku Toshokan, 1938+.
   When complete this catalogue will be one of the most important of its type. Five volumes have appeared to date, each volume being devoted to a major field of learning. Volume 1 on general reference works is of use to the historian; the others are on the natural sciences.

63. Naikaku Kirokukyoku 内閣記録局 (Cabinet Archives Office), Naikaku Bunko tosho mukuroku. Washomon kanabun 内閣文庫図書目録 和書門假名分 (Catalogue of the Cabinet Library. Kana index to Japanese works), Tōkyō, Naikaku Kirokukyoku, 1889-90, 3 v.
   A catalogue of works held by the Cabinet Library up to the time of publication. Entries are in syllabic order but are given rough subject grouping under each syllabic section. Valuable for reference to rare historical materials and public documents. Accessions are listed in the following entry.

64. Naikaku Shokikanshitsu Kirokuka 内閣書記官室記録課 (Cabinet, Secretariat, Archives Section), Naikaku Bunko washo kanabetsu tsuika mokuroku. Dai ni hen 内閣文庫和書假名別追加目錄 第二編 (A supplementary kana catalogue of Japanese books held by the Cabinet Library. Volume 2), Tōkyō, Naikaku Shokikanshitsu Kirokuka, 1902, 492 pp.
   An accessions list bringing the coverage of the catalogue listed in the previous entry up to 1901.

65. Naikaku Kirokukyoku 内閣記録局 (Cabinet, Archives Office), Naikaku bunko tosho mokuroku. Washomon ruibetsu 内閣文庫図書目録 和書門類別 (Catalogue of the Cabinet Library. Classified index to Japanese works), Tōkyō, Naikaku Kirokukyoku, 1889-90, 3 v.
   A classified catalogue with entries arranged under broad categories. Within each category titles are listed in syllabic order. Far more convenient to use than the unclassified list noted above, it is continued by the work listed in the following entry.

66. Naikaku Shokikanshitsu Kirokuka 内閣書記官室記録課 (Cabinet, Secretariat, Archives Section), Naikaku bunko washo ruibetsu tsuika mokuroku. Dai ippen 内閣文庫和書類別追加目録第一編 (Supplementary classified catalogue of Japanese books held by the Cabinet Library. Volume 1), Tōkyō, Naikaku Shokikanshitsu Kirokuka, 1900, 157 pp.
>   A sequel to the catalogue listed above. It continues the coverage down to 1900.

67. Ōsaka Furitsu Toshokan 大阪府立図書館 Osaka Furitsu Toshokan zōka wakan tosho mukuroku 大阪府立図書館増加和漢図書目録 (Classified accession list of Japanese and Chinese books held by the Osaka City Library), Ōsaka, Ōsaka Furitsu Toshokan, 1908-.
>   Volumes of this series have appeared at nearly yearly intervals. Volume 31 published in 1942 covers accessions from April, 1940 to March, 1941. Classification is detailed and modern in conception. Consequently this series affords one of the most convenient coverages of recent literature to be found among the library publications.

68. Seikadō Bunko 静嘉堂文庫 (Seikadō Library), Seikadō Bunko kokusho bunrui mokuroku 静嘉堂文庫国書分類目録 (Classified catalogue of Japanese books in the Seikadō Library), Tōkyō, Seikadō Bunko, 1929, 16+1201+227 pp.
>   This library, established by the Iwasaki family, is famous for its possession of a large number of rare historical materials and manuscripts. Items are classified under broad general headings. A title index is provided at the end of the volume. A supplementary volume was published in 1939. A parallel catalogue of Chinese books also exists.

69. Shōkōkan Bunko 彰考館文庫 (Shōkōkan Library), Shōkōkan tosho mokuroku 彰考館図書目録 (Catalogue of books in the Shōkōkan), Tōkyō, Shōkōkan Bunko, 1918, 1240 pp.
>   A classified catalogue of Chinese and Japanese holdings. This collection is of special interest to the historian since the Shōkōkan was the library of the Mito branch of the Tokugawa house and was established for the compilation of the famous Dai Nihonshi (History of Japan).

70. Sonkeikaku Bunko 尊經閣文庫 (Sonkeikaku Library), Sonkeikaku Bunko kokusho bunrui mokuroku 尊經閣文庫国書分類目録 (A classified catalogue of Japanese works in the Sonkeikaku library), Tōkyō, Ishiguro Bunkichi, 1939, 11+795+176 pp.
>   Founded as the library of the Maeda family, this collection is noteworthy for its inclusion of valuable historical manuscripts. This list covers works of national interest. A separate catalogue of works relating to the Kaga domain is planned. There is a title index.

71. Tōkyō Toshokan 東京図書館 (Tokyo Library), Tōkyō Toshokan wakansho kana mokuroku 東京図書館和漢書假名目録 (Kana catalogue of Japanese and Chinese books in the Tokyo Library), Tōkyō, Tōkyō Toshokan, 1886, 428 pp.
>   Before 1894 the Teikoku Toshokan was called the Tōkyō Toshokan 東京図書館. After World War II it became the Ueno Toshokan 上野図書館 and was incorporated under the National Diet Library as one of its branches. Its holdings have been listed in various catalogues under several titles. See following entries. The present work is the basic list of holdings of the original Tokyo Library. This catalogue and its supplements are superseded by the later series published during the period (1894-1947) when the library was named the Teikoku Toshokan.

72. Tōkyō Toshokan 東京図書館 (Tokyo Library), Wakan bunrui mokuroku 和漢分類目録 (Classified catalogue of Japanese and Chinese books), Tōkyō, Tōkyō Toshokan, 1885, 2 v.
>   This is the classified catalogue of the library's basic holdings up to the time of publication. It was supplemented by the three volumes listed in the following entry. This catalogue and its numerous supplements are superseded by the Teikoku Toshokan's revised catalogue published in the period 1900-07 (Entry 77).

73. Tōkyō Toshokan 東京図書館 (Tokyo Library), Tōkyō Toshokan zōkasho mokuroku, dai [   ] hen, Wakansho no bu 東京図書館増加書目録第 [ ] 編, 和漢書の部 (Catalogue of accessions to the Tokyo Library, Supplement [   ], Japanese and Chinese books), Tōkyō, Tōkyō Toshokan, 1889, 1892 and 1894, 3 v. (Supplements 1-3).
>   This series supplements the library's basic classified catalogue noted above and brings coverage down through 1893. The series is continued under different title as noted in the next entry.

74. Teikoku Toshokan 帝国図書館 (Imperial Library), Teikoku Toshokan zōkasho mokuroku, dai [   ] hen, wakansho no bu 帝国図書館増加書目録第 [   ]編, 和漢書の部 (Catalogue of accessions to the Imperial Library, Supplement [   ], Japanese and Chinese books), Tōkyō, Teikoku Toshokan, 1897, 1899 and 1901, 3 v. (Supplements 4-6).
>   After 1894 the Tōkyō Toshokan became the Teikoku Toshokan. Supplements to the 1885 catalogue were renamed accordingly. Serial numbering remained continuous. This series completes the coverage through 1899. Thereafter accessions were listed in the library's Teikoku Toshokan wakansho kemmei mokuroku (Entry 76).

75. Teikoku Toshokan 帝国図書館 (Imperial Library), <u>Teikoku Toshokan wakan tosho shomei mokuroku</u> 帝国図書館和漢図書書名目録 (Title catalogue of Japanese and Chinese books in the Imperial Library), Tōkyō, Teikoku Toshokan, 1899-1944, 1 basic catalogue plus 10 supplements.

> The Tōkyō Toshokan became the Teikoku Toshokan in 1894. This catalogue lists the holdings of the library as of the end of 1893, while supplements bring its coverage up to 1935. This series thus supersedes the one begun in 1886 by the old Tōkyō Toshokan. The classified series which parallels this catalogue is much more convenient to use (See entries 77 and 78).

76. Teikoku Toshokan 帝国図書館 (Imperial Library), <u>Teikoku Toshokan wakansho kemmei mokuroku (Zōkasho mokuroku, dai shichi hen)</u> 帝国図書館和漢書件名目録（増加書目録，第七編）(Classified catalogue of Japanese and Chinese books in the Imperial Library [Catalogue of accessions, Supplement 7]), Tōkyō, Teikoku Toshokan, 1905, 794+196+35 pp.

> This classified catalogue, also published as volume 1 of a new series, and its continuation published in 1909, cover accessions since 1899. It supplements the 1900-07 catalogue up through 1907. Thereafter accessions were listed in the <u>Teikoku Toshokampō</u> noted below.

77. Teikoku Toshokan 帝国図書館 (Imperial Library), <u>Teikoku Toshokan wakan tosho bunrui mokuroku</u> 帝国図書館和漢図書分類目録 (Classified catalogue of Japanese and Chinese books in the Imperial Library), Tōkyō, Teikoku Toshokan, 1900-07, 9 v.

> This complete classified catalogue of the library's holdings up through 1899 supersedes the previously listed 1885 catalogue and its supplements. The fields covered by the nine volumes are as follows: 1) Religion, Philosophy, Education; 2) Literature; 3) History, Biography; 4) Local History; 5) Law, Economics, Sociology; 6-8) Natural Sciences; 9) General Reference Works and Series Publications. Each volume is classified under elaborate subject headings and has a separate title index. Subsequent accessions are covered by the following entry.

78. <u>Teikoku Toshokampō</u> 帝国図書館報 (Bulletin of the Imperial Library), Tōkyō, Teikoku Toshokan, May, <u>1908-March, 1944.</u>

> A classified bulletin of accessions to the Imperial Library published as a quarterly to 1929, then bimonthly, and after 1931 as a monthly. This series affords an unusually complete coverage of books published in Japan since 1908. Unfortunately, there is no cumulative listing.

79. Tenri Toshokan 天理図書館 (Tenri Library), <u>Tenri Toshokan tosho bunrui mokuroku</u> 天理図書館図書分類目録 (Classified catalogue of books in the Tenri Library), Tambaichi, Tenri Toshokan, 1932-35, 6 v.

> A collection of considerable importance, especially for its coverage of religious history. Each volume is devoted to a single broad field of learning as follows: 1) General Reference Works, 2) Spiritual Sciences, 3) Historical Sciences, 4) Social Sciences, 5) Natural Sciences, Technology, Productive Arts, and 6) Literature.

80. Tōkyō Teikoku Daigaku Fuzoku Toshokan 東京帝国大学附属図書館 (Tokyo Imperial University Library), <u>....Wakansho bunrui mokuroku ....</u> 和漢書分類目録 (Classified catalogue of Japanese and Chinese books in the collection of the Tōkyō Imperial University Library), Tōkyō, Tōkyō Teikoku Daigaku, 1893-1923. Irregular.

> The first volume of this series is a classified catalogue of the old Tokyo Imperial University holdings as of 1888. Subsequent volumes bring the coverage up to the time of the destruction of the library in the earthquake of 1923. Twenty-one major classifications and numerous sub-categories are used, and a romanized title index provided. A title catalogue paralleled this classified series. It is, however, much less convenient to use. Since this collection is no longer in existence, these catalogues are useful only as a bibliographical reference.

81. Tōkyō Teikoku Daigaku Fuzoku Toshokan 東京[帝国]大学附属図書館 (Tōkyō [Imperial] University Library, <u>Tōkyō [Teikoku] Daigaku wakan tosho mokuroku</u> 東京[帝国]大学和漢図書目録 (Catalogue of Japanese and Chinese books in the Tokyo [Imperial] University Library), Tōkyō, editor, 1938-.

> The Tokyo [Imperial] University Library was rapidly rebuilt after 1923, though it still lacks the rare historical materials of the older collection. In 1935 it began to compile a new catalogue of holdings up to that year. Up to the present only a few volumes have appeared. The following is the publication plan. Those entries with publication dates have already appeared in print.
>
> Hon mokuroku 本目録 (Main catalogue 1924-35)
> The main catalogue will be composed of the following ten volumes:
> Dai ippen 第一編 (1st fascicle): Sōki 總記 (General) and
>   Zassai 雑載 (Miscellaneous................. 1949
> Dai ni-hen: Tetsugaku 哲学 (Philosophy), Shūkyō 宗教 (Religion) and
>   Kyōiku 教育 (Education)............
> Dai sampen: Gogaku 語学 (Languages), Bungaku 文学 (Literature) and
>   Geijutsu 藝術 (Fine Arts)...........
> Dai shi-hen: Rekishi 歴史 (History) and Chiri 地理 (Geography)..........
> Dai go-hen: Hōritsu 法律 (Law) and Seiji 政治 (Politics)............. 1943
> Dai roppen: Keizai 經済 (Economics) and Shakai 社会 (Sociology)........
> Dai shichi-hen: Rigaku 理学 (Science)............
> Dai hachi-hen: Kōgaku 工学 (Engineering), Heiji 兵事 (Military and Navy Sciences)
>   and Sangyō 産業 (Industries)..........
> Dai kyū-hen: Igaku 医学 (Medicine) and Yakugaku 藥学 (Pharmacy).......
> Dai jippen: Nōgyō 農業 (Agriculture)..........

The main catalogue will be supplemented by yearly listings. The following have appeared to date.
Zōka dai-ichi 増加第一 (1st supplement):
      Nov. 1935-Oct. 1936. 1938
Zōka dai-ni: Nov. 1936-Oct. 1937 1939
Zōka dai-san: Nov. 1937-Dec. 1938 1940
Zōka dai-shi: Jan.-Dec. 1939 1941
Zōka dai-go: Jan.-Dec. 1940 1942
Zōka dai-roku: Jan.-Dec. 1941 1945

82. Tōyō Bunko 東洋文庫 (Oriental Library), Iwasaki Bunko wakansho mokuroku 岩崎文庫和漢書目録 (Catalogue of Japanese and Chinese books in the Iwasaki Library), Tōkyō, Tōyō Bunko, 1934, 1102 pp.
    The Iwasaki collection is of special importance for its holdings of rare manuscripts and old printed works. This collection is now held in the Tōyō Bunko.

d. Publishers' and Bookdealers' Yearbooks and Catalogues

Various yearbooks of publications (Shuppan nenkan) afford an excellent and convenient means of keeping abreast of historical materials published in Japan since the early 1920s. Yearbooks have been issued by the major publishing associations in Japan and contain, in addition to classified lists of a year's publications, valuable information on publishers, authors, libraries, cultural organizations and the like. It should be borne in mind that such yearbooks are not all-inclusive, since they list only the works printed or handled by member firms. However, since the large majority of Japanese publishers belong to a number of associations, the chief yearbooks cover nearly all new commercially printed works for the year.
    Of the prewar publishers' yearbooks, the Tokyōdō series (Entries 91, 85, and 86) which began in 1930 and the Tōkyō Shosekishō Kumiai series (Entry 92) begun in 1929 are most complete and should be used in parallel to supplement each other. The former series continued under varying auspices until 1948. The only currently available yearbook is the Shuppan nenkan (Entry 89) issued by the Shuppan Nyūsusha. This series began publication in 1951. Hence books published during the years 1948 and 1949 are not covered by publishers' annuals.
    Of the publishers' catalogues, the Tōkyō Shosekishō Kumiai's Toshoso mokuroku (General catalogue of books) (Entry 93), issued at irregular intervals since 1893, is of major importance. Each issue represents a cumulation of titles currently handled by the association's member firms.
    It should be mentioned that the major publishers' associations are in the habit of issuing periodic catalogues, generally at monthly, or even more frequent, intervals. Since the yearly volumes are based on these catalogues and cumulate information from them in more convenient form, the prewar monthly and weekly compilations have been omitted from the following list. However, the scholar who wishes to keep informed of new publications as they appear will do well to subscribe to one of three weekly series: the Shuppan Nyūsusha's Shuppan nyūsu (Publication news) (Entry 90), the Shuppan Kyōkai's Nihon dokusho shimbun (Japan readers' weekly) (Entry 88), or the Tosho shimbun (Publication weekly) (Entry 95). All three contain news and reviews of current literature. Of them the Tosho shimbun takes a somewhat more liberal editorial stand. The general user will probably find the Shuppan nyūsu most accessible.
    Although bookdealers' catalogues (Kosho mokuroku) are of primary interest to those who wish to purchase books, they are of considerable use to the research worker in that they often list rare primary and secondary sources and give a great deal of forgotten information concerning them. Certain large book dealers compile price lists of books on hand. These are issued irregularly and are often poorly mimeographed, but they are usually classified. The following is a list of the major book dealers, all of them in Tokyo, which publish catalogues of value to the historian. No attempt has been made to itemize individual catalogues.

Bunkyūdō   Keiō Shobō
Gannandō Shoten   Komiyama Shoten
Ganshōdō   Meijidō Shoten
Isseidō Shoten

    A second-hand book catalogue published in 1950 by the Isseidō Shoten entitled Isseidō kihon tosho mokuroku (Isseidō's catalogue of basic books) (Entry 83) is of special value as a practical guide to basic materials in all publication fields. Since this work was issued as a handbook for bookdealers, the work does not reflect the actual availability of the books it lists. Finally, the historian should find the well-known bookdealers' monthly, Nihon kosho tsūshin (Entry 87), of use for the information it contains on the current state of the used book market and on the movement of private library collections.

83. Isseidō Shoten 一誠堂書店, Isseidō kihon tosho mokuroku 一誠堂基本図書目録 (Isseidō's catalogue of basic books), Tōkyō, Isseidō Shoten, 1950, 96 pp.
    A convenient check list of basic materials in all fields of Japanese publication. Compiled by a major dealer in second-hand books. Although each item is given a price, this catalogue is not intended as an actual price list of second-hand books but as a guide to book dealers.

84. Kokusai Shichōsha 国際思潮社, Shuppan nenkan 出版年鑑 (Yearbook of publications), Tōkyō, Kokusai Shichōsha, 1927-28.
    A short-lived standard publisher's yearbook succeeded by the Tōkyō Shosekishō Kumiai's Shuppan nenkan (Entry 92).

85. Nihon Shuppan Bunka Kyōkai 日本出版文化協会 (Japan Publishing Culture Association), Shoseki nenkan 書籍年鑑 (Yearbook of publications), Tōkyō, Kyōdō Shuppansha, 1942.
    This yearbook covering the year 1941 is a successor to the Tokyōdō's Shuppan nenkan series (Entry 91). It in turn was succeeded by the following entry.

86. Nihon Shuppan Kyōdō Kabushiki Kaisha 日本出版協同株式会社 (Japan Publishing Association), Nihon shuppan nenkan 日本出版年鑑 (Yearbook of Japanese publications), Tōkyō, Nihon Shuppan Kyōdō K. K., 1943-48.

   This successor to the Tōkyōdō's Shuppan nenkan (Entry 91) is important for its coverage of the war and immediate postwar years. The 1943 issue covers 1942, the 1947 issue, 1943-45, and the 1948 issue, 1946-47. The over-all size of this series is considerably smaller than that of the prewar Tōkyōdō series, owing in part to the wartime decline in publications. Each postwar volume is divided into two or more parts, each part covering a year. Within the individual parts the make-up of the work is similar to that of other yearbooks. Section 1 surveys briefly the significant activities in each of the major publishing fields. Section 2 relates to the publishing industry itself. Section 3 is a classified but unannotated list of outstanding works for the period covered by the yearbook. Section 4 is a classified list of magazines and journals. Section 5 is a list of publishing houses and their addresses.

87. Nihon kosho tsūshin 日本古書通信 (Japan bookdealers' monthly), Tōkyō, Nihon Kosho Tsūshinsha, 1935-. Monthly.

   A useful monthly journal in standard use by all second-hand bookdealers in Japan. Each issue contains a few short essays on items of bibliographic interest and a number of lists of books and prices submitted by major book dealers. A feature of several issues during 1952 has been a list of basic works in all fields of publication, "Kihon tosho mokuroku."

88. Nihon dokusho shimbun 日本讀書新聞 (Japan readers' weekly), Tōkyō, Nihon Shuppan Kyōkai, 1933-. Weekly.

   A publishers' weekly containing review articles and a list of new publications of the week. This weekly and the Tosho shimbun perform a similar function to the New York Times' "Sunday Book Review Section" in this country.

89. Shuppan Nyūsusha 出版ニュース社 , Shuppan nenkan 出版年鑑 (Yearbook of publications), Tōkyō, Shuppan Nyūsusha, 1951-.

   One of the most comprehensive yearbooks, and the only one currently available. It devotes over 1000 pages to a single issue. Each number covers publications during the year immediately preceding its issue. Arrangement and coverage are similar to those of the Tōkyōdō yearbook (Entry 91). This series, however, does not continue the helpful practice of including brief annotations for each bibliographic entry. On the other hand it adds several important new sections: a classified catalogue of government publications, lists of libraries and cultural organizations, and a list of authors, giving pertinent data such as age, address, birthplace, university, specialty, and present occupation. The 1952 edition contains four valuable indexes to 1) titles, 2) authors, 3) subject content of the yearbook, and 4) advertisements. The 1953 edition has dropped the listing of government publications.

90. Shuppan nyūsu 出版ニュース (Publication news), Tōkyō, Shuppan Nyūsusha, 1949-, 3 times a month.

   Features notes and reviews on new and future publications. Early issues were somewhat unreliable in their coverage of the publication field. From 1953 each issue has carried a list of new publications classified under the NDC system. Coverage is one month behind the date of each issue.

91. Tōkyōdō 東京堂 , Shuppan nenkan 出版年鑑 (Yearbook of publications), Tōkyō, Tōkyōdō, 1930-41.

   The best of the pre-World War II yearbooks. Each volume covers the year immediately preceding its issue. Though it lists only works handled by member firms, these include a large proportion of all new books published in Japan. Government publications are not included. Each volume is divided into seven parts. Part 1 covers in survey fashion news of the publishing world and of various fields of publication, lists of banned and outstanding books, and a section on bibliographical materials. Part 2 is devoted to publishing statistics. Part 3 gives a classified bibliographical coverage of the year's publications. All important bibliographical data are included together with a one-sentence description of the contents of each entry. Part 4 is a classified list of magazines and journals published during the year. Bibliographical data are supplemented with a brief note on the general interest or emphasis of each journal. Parts 5-7 concern publishing houses. For succeeding volumes in this series see entries 85 and 86.

92. Tōkyō Shosekishō Kumiai 東京書籍商組合 (Tōkyō Bookdealers' Association), Shuppan nenkan 出版年鑑 (Yearbook of publications), Tōkyō, Tōkyō Shosekishō Kumiai Jimusho, 1929-. Annual.

   A standard publishers' yearbook discontinued since World War II. Although somewhat less useful than the Tōkyōdō's publication by the same name (Previous entry), it should be used in parallel to supplement the latter series. Each issue contains the usual sections on publishing news and statistics and devotes the majority of its pages to a classified, but unannotated, list of the year's publications.

93. Tōkyō Shosekishō Kumiai 東京書籍商組合 (Tokyo Bookdealers' Association), Tosho sōmokuroku 図書總目録 (General catalogue of books), Tōkyō, Tōkyō Shosekishō Kumiai Jimusho, 1893, 1898, 1906, 1911, 1918, 1923, 1929, 1933 and 1940.

   The most important of the general publishers' catalogues. Each issue is a list of books currently handled by the association's member organizations. The listings, therefore, are not cumulative nor restricted to works published since the previous catalogue. Most issues are divided into three sections: a title catalogue, a publisher's catalogue, and a classified catalogue. The 1933 edition added an author's catalogue. Bibliographical information is complete but no annotations are given.

94. Tosho kenkyūkai 図書研究会, Sōgō shuppan nenkan 綜合出版年鑑 (General yearbook of publications), Tōkyō, Tosho Kenkyūkai, 1928—. Annual.
A yearbook, now discontinued, with a make-up somewhat different from others listed in this section. It attempts to cover all new commercially published books which appeared in Japan during the year preceding its issue. Bibliographical sections are classified, but entries are listed by month, hence most inconvenient to use. For 1928-29 the series was issued under the title Shinkansho sōmokuroku 新刊書總目録; for 1930-31 under the title Shuppan nenkan (sōgō). The present title was adopted in 1932.

95. Tosho shimbun 図書新聞 (Publication weekly), Tōkyō, Tosho Shimbunsha, 1949—. Weekly.
A weekly newspaper of publications, less useful than the Nihon dokusho shimbun (Entry 88) because of its lack of any systematic listing of new books.

e. Guides to Periodical Literature

Unfortunately, there is no single all-inclusive, cumulative bibliographical guide to Japanese periodical literature comparable to the Readers' Guide to Periodical Literature in this country. Nonetheless, the field of history is more fortunate than others in this respect, since a number of selective guides to historical literature are available.
Periodical guides are of two general types: those which offer information on the journals themselves, and those which analyze the contents of journals. Information of the first variety is best found in the various publishers' annuals (shuppan nenkan) discussed in the previous section. The Tōkyōdō yearbook, for instance, contains a classified listing of journals, giving publication history and information on the editorial slant of each item. Similar coverage is given newspapers by the Shimbun sōran (General survey of newspapers) (Entry 99) and the Nihon shimbun nenkan (Japan newspaper yearbook) (Entry 100). More recently the National Diet Library has published annual surveys of periodical publications as special issues of its monthly catalogue of copyrighted works (Entry 98).
The above compilations are of little use, however, for journals and newspapers published before the early 1920s. For earlier coverage the catalogue of periodical and newspaper holdings of the Teikoku Toshokan (Imperial Library) (Entry 103) and Seki Hironao's Tōkyō Teikoku Daigaku Hōgakubu Meiji shimbun zasshi bunko shozō mokuroku (Catalogue of Meiji newspapers and magazines in the library of the Faculty of Law of Tokyo Imperial University) (Entry 102) should be consulted. Despite the existence of these catalogues and yearbooks, the problem of ascertaining accurate publication histories of Japanese periodicals is most difficult. Many prewar journals are now defunct, and most journals had to abandon publication for a number of years during the war.
Guides to periodical and newspaper articles are available in many forms. Certain of the general bibliographies noted previously contain selected references to articles. Honjō Eijirō's three volumes on economic history (Entries 10, 11, and 12) and the series included in the journal Zinbun (Entry 14) contain references to periodical articles, as do the selected historical bibliography covering the years 1946-50 put out by the Shigakkai (Entry 41) and the annual issued by the Rekishigaku Kenkyūkai (Entry 36). To these general works should be added three selective guides which deal exclusively with periodical materials. Indispensable to the historian is the Ōtsuka Shigakkai's Sōgō kokushi rombun yōmoku (Combined catalogue of selected articles on Japanese history) (Entry 101) which covers historical journals published between 1868 and 1938. For articles chosen on the basis of more contemporary interest the historian will find Amano Keitarō's two-volume Hōsei keizai shakai rombun sōran (A guide to articles on law, politics, economics and sociology) (Entry 96) and the Kōbe Kōtō Shōgyōgakkō Shōgyō Kenkyūjo's Keizai hōritsu bunken mokuroku (Catalogue of economic and legal literature) (Entry 147) of value. Since World War II the Kokuritsu Kokkai Toshokan (National Diet Library) has issued a monthly classified index to the content of all periodicals received by the library. This series, entitled Zasshi kiji sakuin, (Entry 97), is published in two series, one devoted to natural sciences and the other to the humanistic sciences. Though cumbersome to use, this series affords by far the most complete coverage of postwar periodical articles. For an easily accessible check list of articles in the field of history there exists the list of recent articles at the back of each issue of Shigaku zasshi (Entry 578). Beginning with 1951 this list was expanded from an accessions list to a more complete record of recently published articles.
One of the most rewarding methods of acquiring references to historical articles is through the general indexes of the major historical journals, especially since the great proportion of important research is published in only a handful of scholarly periodicals. The following table indicates the location of indexes which will be of most use to the historian.

Journal	Index	Volumes Covered
Keizaishi kenkyū	v. 19. 2 (1938)	v. 1 - 100
Kokka gakkai zasshi	v. 42. 10 (1928)	v. 1 - 499
Rekishi chiri	Nihon Rekishichiri Gakkai (1933)	v. 1 - 60
Shakai keizaishigaku	v. 11. 2 (1941)	v. 1 - 10
Shigaku	Mita Shigakkai (1937)	v. 1 - 15
Shigaku zasshi	Fuzambō (1940)	v. 1 - 50
	Yamakawa Shuppansha (1953)	v. 1 - 60
Shigaku kenkyū	v. 10. 3 (1939)	v. 1 - 10
Rekishi to chiri	(1935)	v. 1 - 53
Shikai	v. 38 (1896)	v. 1 - 38
Shirin	Shigaku Kenkyūkai (1935)	v. 1 - 20

The only regular subject index for a newspaper is that prefaced to the monthly reduced-size editions of the Tōkyō Asahi (Entry 104).

96. Amano Keitarō 天野敬太郎, Hōsei keizai shakai rombun sōran 法政經濟社会論文總覽 (A guide to articles on law, politics, economics, and sociology), Tōkyō, Tōkō Shoin, 1927 and 1928, 2 v.
　　Volume 1 covers 96 journals of a strictly economic or legal nature down to 1926. Few articles deal with pre-modern Japan. Volume 2 brings the coverage of these journals up to the end of 1927 and adds complete coverage up to this date of 18 journals not previously listed. Among these new additions are the major historical journals. Volume 2, therefore, is of considerable use to the historian. Articles are listed by title and elaborately classified under detailed subject headings. Volume 2 contains an author index for both volumes. Unfortunately, the work as a whole is extremely selective in its inclusion of entries.

97. Kokuritsu Kokkai Toshokan 国立国会図書館 (National Diet Library), Zasshi kiji sakuin 雑誌記事索引 (Japanese periodicals index), Tōkyō, Kokuritsu Kokkai Toshokan, 1949—.
　　A monthly classified index to periodical articles appearing in journals received at the library. Two series are now issued concurrently, one dealing with the natural sciences, the other with the humanities and social sciences. Each issue covers a month approximately half a year prior to the time of issue. The first month covered is September, 1948. Entries are classified by subject; a list of journals is included at the end of each issue. This series undoubtedly affords the best coverage of post-World War II Japanese journals of all types.

98. Kokunai shuppambutsu mokuroku, Teiki kankōbutsu 国内出版物目録. 定期刊行物 (Japanese national bibliography—Periodicals and newspapers published in 1950), Tōkyō, Kokuritsu Kokkai Toshokan, 1951—.
　　A special issue of the National Diet Library's series Kokunai shuppambutsu mokuroku (Entry 58). This volume provides a comprehensive listing of periodical publications appearing during 1950. Government publications are listed under agency, general periodicals are classified by subject, newspapers are listed alphabetically. Each entry provides information on frequency of publication, current volume and issue number, publishing institution, and price. The years 1948 and 1949 are covered in similar fashion by special issues of the NDL's Nohon geppō (Entry 57).

99. Nihon Dempō Tsūshinsha 日本電報通信社 (Japan Telegraphic News Agency), Shimbun sōran 新聞總覽 (General survey of newspapers), Tōkyō, Nihon Dempō Tsūshinsha, 1907—. Annual.
　　An annual survey of Japanese newspapers. Metropolitan and local newspapers are arranged by place of publication. Each entry includes information on history, ownership, management, circulation, etc.

100. Nihon shimbun nenkan 日本新聞年鑑 (Japan newspaper yearbook), Tōkyō, Shimbun Kenkyūjo, 1922—; Nihon Shimbun Kyōkai, 1947—.
　　The 1947 edition of this annual includes a survey of the previous fifteen years of newspaper activity. Detailed coverage is given to current newspapers, their personnel and policies. Non-member publications and specialized papers are also listed.

101. Ōtsuka Shigakkai Kōshi Bukai 大塚史学会高師部会 (Otsuka Historical Society, Higher Normal School Branch), Sōgō kokushi rombun yōmoku 綜合国史論文要目 (Combined catalogue of selected articles on Japanese history), Tōkyō, Tōkō Shoin, 1939, 627 pp.
　　This work combines and supersedes two previous bibliographies issued by the same compilers in 1931 and 1934. The single most important selected catalogue of articles on Japanese history, it covers 169 scholarly journals and collections from 1868 to 1938. Entries are classified and listed by author under a wide variety of subjects.

102. Seki Hironao 瀬木博尚, ed., Tōkyō Teikoku Daigaku Hōgakubu Meiji shimbun zasshi bunko shozō mokuroku 東京帝国大学法学部明治新聞雑誌文庫所蔵目録 (Catalogue of Meiji newspapers and magazines in the library of the Faculty of Law of Tokyo Imperial University), Tōkyō, by the editor, 1930-41, 3 v.
　　This series affords the best coverage of newspapers and magazines published during the Meiji (1868-1912) period. It gives complete bibliographic data on a great variety of papers and periodicals first published during these years, and in addition lists books and articles relating to this class of publication. Of unusual interest is the list of special numbers of newspapers and magazines. This series is generally listed under its decorative title Tōtenkō 東天紅.

103. Teikoku Toshokan 帝国図書館, Teikoku Toshokan zasshi shimbun mokuroku 帝国図書館雑誌新聞目録 (Catalogue of journals and newspapers in the Imperial Library), Tōkyō, Teikoku Toshokan, 1937, 157 pp.
　　A list of holdings as of the end of 1935. It constitutes a valuable reference for the history of publication of periodicals and newspapers of the earlier period.

104. Tōkyō Asahi Shimbun shukusatsuban 東京朝日新聞縮刷版 (Reduced-size edition of the Tōkyō Asahi Newspaper), Tōkyō, Tōkyō Asahi Shimbunsha, 1920—. Monthly.
　　A bound and reduced-size edition of the Tōkyō Asahi. This edition provides one of the only regular subject indexes of newspaper articles in Japan. Though limited to articles appearing in only the one paper, news coverage is excellent. Each bound edition contains an elaborate subject index of the volume's contents.

105. Zasshi nenkan 雑誌年鑑 (Yearbook of periodicals), Tōkyō, Nihon Dokusho Shimbunsha, 1939-41. Kyōdo Shuppansha, 1942.
　　A standard yearbook, it includes a classified list of periodicals published during the preceding year, brief notes on publication policy and pertinent bibliographic data.

f. Guides to Series, Collections and Miscellanies

The historian will find a large body of historical literature, both primary and secondary, published in the form of series (sōsho), collections (zenshū), lectures (kōza), or miscellanies (zuihitsu). Many of the more general bibliographies considered up to now do not include references to this type of literature, or do so in only superficial fashion. The historian will thus require the use of a number of specialized guides for access to these collections.

Guides to collectanea are of two types: those which describe and classify the collections themselves, and those which list the contents of the individual collections. Of the former type Kawashima Gonzaburō's Sōsho zenshū shomoku (Catalogue of series and collections) (Entry 109) is of greatest use. This work classifies nearly all multiple-volume works published between 1868 and 1936. It is supplemented and brought up to 1945 by a similar work published by Kawashima and Yagi Toshio (Entry 110).

Indexes to the contents of collectanea are found in a large number of widely scattered places. Naturally many of the collections themselves contain detailed indexes. Some of them are, in addition, annotated. The major series and collections of interest to the historian are also analyzed in some of the general bibliographies such as Kurita Motoji's Sōgō kokushi kenkyū (Entry 24), Honjō Eijirō's bibliographies of economic history (Entries 10 to 12), Endo Motoo and others' Shiseki kaidai (Entry 5), and Samura Hachirō's Kokusho kaidai (Entry 38). Giving more specialized and complete coverage, however, is Hirose Bin's Nihon sōsho sakuin (Index of Japanese series) (Entry 108) and Ōta Tamesaburō's Nihon zuihitsu sakuin (Index to Japanese miscellanies) (Entries 111 and 112). These two works go beyond the mere listing of individual components of collections, for they provide elaborate indexes to the subject contents of these components. Both works are especially complete in their coverage of pre-Restoration materials.

106. Achikku Myūzeamu アチック・ミューゼアム, Sōsho saishū Nihon koten shomoku sakuin 叢書採輯日本古典書目索引 (Index of Japanese classics contained in series), Tōkyō, Achikku Myūzeamu, 1938, 6+205+33 pp.
A special issue of the bibliographical series of the Attic Museum, it provides an index to the contents of 86 pre-modern series (sōsho). The works are primarily of literary and historical interest. Appendices contain an author index and a list of readings for obscure titles.

107. Hamano Tomosaburō 濱野知三郎, Nihon sōsho mokuroku 日本叢書目錄 (A catalogue of Japanese series), Tōkyō, Rikugōkan, 1927, 256 pp.
This work is also contained in an appendix to v. 2 of the 1926 revised edition of Samura Hachirō's Kokusho kaidai (Entry 38). It covers series published from the beginning of the Tokugawa period (1600) to 1912. Series are listed by title. Complete bibliographical data are provided together with a breakdown of the contents of each collection.

108. Hirose Bin 廣瀬敏, Nihon sōsho sakuin 日本叢書索引 (Index of Japanese series), Tōkyō, Musashino Shoin, 1939, 2+3+13+65+4+9+573+96 pp.
An important reference guide to the contents and subject matter of collectanea. It covers series published in Japan up through 1930. Series are largely of literary and historical interest, having been written before 1878. The following features of the work will be of use: 1) a catalogue of series and collections arranged by title with information on whether works exist in printed form or in manuscript; 2) bibliographical data on the collections listed in section 1 together with a detailed title breakdown of the contents of each; 3) an index of manuscript series; 4) a detailed classified index to the subject contents of the various printed series; under each subject are listed individual works (component parts of series) which contain references to the subject; unfortunately volume and page references are omitted; 6) a content analysis of unpublished manuscript series.

109. Kawashima Gonsaburō 川島五三郎, Sōsho zenshū shomoku 叢書全集書目 (Catalogue of series and collections), Tōkyō, Tōkyō Koshosekishō Kumiai, 1931-36, 5 v.
This work provides the most complete title index to series and collections published between 1868 and 1936. Series are listed under a broad system of classification. For each series the compiler gives pertinent bibliographical data and lists the component parts. Volumes 1-2 cover general series and collections, volume 3 those relating to government, law, social affairs and economics, volume 4 those in the field of history and geography, and volume 5 religion, philosophy, and education. For a successor to this work see, Kawashima and Yagi, Zōtei zenshū sōsho kakaku sōran (Following entry).

110. Kawashima Gonsaburo 川島五三郎 and Yagi Toshio 八木敏夫, Zōtei zenshū sōsho kakaku sōran 增訂全集叢書價格總覽 (Enlarged and revised price list for collections and series), Tōkyō, Nihon Kosho Tsūshinsha, 1947, 18+236 pp.
Less detailed but more up to date than Kawashima's Sōsho zenshū shomoku (See previous entry), it claims to cover all series and collections printed from 1868 through 1945. The work lists sōsho and zenshū in syllabic order with pertinent bibliographic data and list prices. Ten major collections are further analyzed and given a complete content listing. These include collections of special importance to the historian such as the Dai Nihon shiryō and Dai Nihon komonjo. A 1950 edition of this work brings the coverage up to 1949 and adds a special section on post-World War II series publications.

111. Ōta Tamesaburō 太田為三郎, Nihon zuihitsu sakuin 日本隨筆索引 (Index to Japanese miscellanies), Tōkyō, Iwanami Shoten, revised ed. 1925, 2+4+803+19 pp.
An elaborate content index of 250 well-known miscellanies (zuihitsu), most of them written before the Restoration. The works tend to be literary but there are many of historical value. This book arranges under subject headings references to pertinent chapters of miscellanies. It is unfortunate that contents of miscellanies are not analyzed beyond individual chapter headings. But aside from this defect, since zuihitsu make up the contents of a large number of series and collections, this work affords a convenient content index to many of the best-known series. A supplement was published in 1932 (See next entry).

112. Ōta Tamesaburō 太 田 爲 三 郎 , Zoku Nihon zuihitsu sakuin 續 日 本 隨 筆 索 引 (Index to Japanese miscellanies continued), Tōkyō, Iwanami Shoten, 1932, 6+13+895 pp.
> A supplement tò Ōta's previous index (See above), this work covers 178 miscellanies omitted from the earlier work. Emphasis is on works written during the Tokugawa period (1600-1868).

113. Tarumi Nobuhide 垂 水 延 秀 , Nihon sōsho nempyō tsuki bunrui oyobi shomei sakuin 日 本 叢 書 年 表 附 分 類 及 書 名 索 引 (Chronology of Japanese collections, with subject and title indexes), Ōsaka, Mamiya Shoten, 1930, 205 pp.
> An extremely useful reference work for Japanese collectanea. Part 1 lists all non-manuscript collections by year of publication from 1213-1930 and includes bibliographical data. Part 2 lists manuscript collections and indicates their library locations. Part 3 is a subject index of titles, and Part 4 a syllabic index of titles.

3. SPECIALIZED BIBLIOGRAPHIES

While the general and historical bibliographies noted in Section 2 above are sufficient for most purposes of historical research, the scholar may find that the intricacies of his subject require the use of more specialized bibliographic guides. His need in this respect will be first to obtain more detailed information on the pre-modern sources in a given field, and second to acquire additional specialized references to monographs and articles of a more recent date. Guides to aid in the first task are plentiful and easily accessible. Indexes to current literature in specialized fields, however, are more difficult to come by, since such lists are usually buried in the various technical journals. The location of specialized bibliographical material prior to 1932 is well covered in Amano Keitarō's Hompō shoshi no shoshi (A bibliography of Japanese bibliographies) (Entry 1) and in Hatano and Yayoshi's Kenkyū chōsa sankō bunken sōran (General survey of reference works for study and research) (Entry 8). After that date there is no adequate guide to such literature. Each specialist will be obliged to acquire leads to specialized bibliographies through the review sections of the journals in his field or through the various publishers and scholarly yearbooks.

The following brief list of only the most obviously important specialized bibliographies has been prepared without pretense to completeness. Annotations have been kept to a minimum, since in most cases the titles alone are sufficient indication of content.

a. Historiography

Japanese historians have devoted a great deal of attention to the problems of historiography and the philosophy of history. Most of their writings in this field show the direct impact of Western interpretations of history, chiefly of the Southwest German, the materialist, or the recent American schools. The following bibliographies, therefore, refer in large number to Japanese translations of Western works on historical technique and interpretation. Perhaps the most accessible introduction to Japanese historiographical literature is through Kawai Eijirō's Gakusei to rekishi (The student and history) (Entry 670), published as part of the Gakusei sōsho (Student series).

114. Kōsaka Masaaki 高 坂 正 顯 , "Rekishigaku 歴 史 学 (Historiography)" and "Rekishi tetsugaku 歴史哲学 (Philosophy of history)," in Kawai and Kimura, Kyōyō bunken kaisetsu, Tōkyō, 1950 (Entry 16), pp. 63-71, 72-82.
> Two excellent annotated and interpretive bibliographical articles on historiography by a modern expert on the philosophy of history. Emphasis is on the impact of Western historiography on Japanese thinking.

115. "Shigakushi kankei bunken mokuroku 史 学 史 関 係 文 献 目 録 (Bibliography of works on historiography)," Shigaku kenkyū, v. 11 (March, 1940), no. 3-4, pp. 435-483.
> An unannotated list of works, both Japanese and Western, on historiography and historical theory. Classification is by period.

116. Matsumoto Yoshio 松 本 芳 夫 and Ariga Haruo 有 賀 春 雄 , "Shigaku riron bunken mokuroku 史 学 理 論 文 献 目 録 (Catalogue of literature on the theory of history)" Shigaku, v. 11 (Feb., 1933), no. 4, pp. 621-78.
> An unannotated chronological listing of Japanese language works on historiography, many of which deal with interpretations of Western historical theories. Covers from 1868 to 1933.

b. Guides to Biographical Literature

Because of the general adequacy of Japanese biographical dictionaries, the historian is left with only two possible problems in this aspect of his research. He may wish to acquire additional facts or details on the lives of those individuals in whom he is especially interested, or he may wish to locate material on the lives of individuals who do not warrant inclusion in even the largest dictionaries.

A number of the biographical dictionaries provide citations to the sources from which their facts are selected. Investigation of these leads will often turn up a great deal of additional information. The general indexes and guides to series and miscellanies mentioned in 2e above also provide references to the location of biographical materials. For a more specialized and exhaustive coverage, however, the historian will find the works published by the Hibiya Library, notably Hatano Ken'ichi's Denki shiryō sakuin (An index of biographical materials) (Entry 117), most useful in augmenting his knowledge of major historical figures.

The acquisition of information on the lives of little-known persons is naturally a more difficult task. For pre-nineteenth century biographies of lesser historical figures the scholar will need to consult the indexes to such major sources of biographical information as the Rikkokushi (Six national histories), the Dai Nihonshi (History of Japan), the Dai Nihon yashi (Unofficial history of Japan), and the Kansei chōshū shokafu (The Kansei collated genealogies) listed below. These works cover the field of Japanese biography up to approximately the beginning of the nineteenth century. Beyond this date the task of the historian becomes immensely complicated, for he will find almost nothing in the way of consolidated bibliographical references. This subject will be left to later bibliographies in the Michigan series.

117. Hatano Ken'ichi 波 多 野 賢 一 , Denki shiryo sakuin 傳 記 資 料 索 引 (An index of biographical materials), Tōkyō, Hibiya Toshokan, 1928-29, 2 v.
    An important index to biographies, articles, portraits, and other types of biographical material, both modern and pre-modern. An appendix in v. 2 lists selected bibliographical references.

118. Hibiya Toshokan 日 比 谷 図 書 館 (Hibiya Library), Denki shiryo sakuin 傳 記 資 料 索 引 (Index of biographical sources), Tōkyō, Hibiya Toshokan, 1928-35, irregularly published in parts.

119. Heki Shōichi 日 置 昌 一 , Nihon rekishi jimmei jiten 日 本 歴 史 人 名 辞 典 (A dictionary of Japanese historical figures), Tōkyō, Kaizōsha, 1938, 991 pp.
    The introduction to this work contains a list of biographical sources used for the compilation of the dictionary. Though a bare list of titles, it constitutes one of the most complete listings of such materials to be found. Titles are grouped by period.

120. "Kansei chōshū shokafu sōsakuin 寛 政 重 修 諸 家 譜 總 索 引 (Index to the Kansei chōshū shokafu)," in Tokyo Teikoku Daigaku Shiryo Hensansho, Tokushi biyo, Tōkyō, Naigai Shoseki K.K., rev. ed. 1942, pp. 1259-1445.
    An index to the most comprehensive bibliographical source for the first half of the Tokugawa period. The difficulty of using the original work has given rise to this index. Names are classified under court and provincial titles. References are to chapters in the Kansei chōshū shokafu.

121. Dai Nihon Yūbenkai 大 日 本 雄 辯 会 , Dai Nihonshi kiden jimmei sakuin 大 日 本 史 記 傳 人 名 索 引 (A biographical index to the annals and biographies sections of the Dai Nihonshi), Tōkyō, Dai Nihon Yūbenkai Kōdansha, 1929.
    This work makes up volume 17 of the 1929 edition of the Dai Nihonshi. It offers an index to the biographies contained in one of the most important sources for the period prior to 1392.

122. Mori Senzō 森 銑 三 , "Kinsei jimbutsu shiryō sōran 近 世 人 物 資 料 總 覧 (A survey of biographical materials for the modern period)," Denki, v. 3 (1936).
    A detailed index to biographical material for the Tokugawa period (1600-1868). Names are entered in syllabic order with all known biographical sources listed under each name. The work appears to have been only partially completed.

123. Saeki Ariyoshi 佐 伯 有 義 , Rikkokushi sakuin 六 国 史 索 引 (Index to the Rikkokushi), in Rikkokushi 六 国 史 (Six national histories), Tōkyō, Asahi Shimbusha, 1931, v. 10.
    The six official histories of the Nara and early Heian period cover the history of Japan down to 887. Together they form one of the best sources of biographical information for the eighth and ninth centuries.

124. Yamada An'ei 山 田 安 榮 , "Yashi honden sakuin 野 史 本 傳 索 引 (Index to biographies in Yashi)," in Iida Tadahiko, Yashi, Tōkyō, Yoshikawa Kōbunkan, rev. ed. 1909, v. 1, 41 pp.
    This index to the Dai Nihon yashi provides easy access to biographies in one of the chief sources for the period from 1392 to 1817.

c. Local History, Local Government, and Historical Geography

    Two types of research organization in Japan have been active in preparing specialized guides to material on local history and geography. The first of these are the prefectural or city libraries and historical societies, which in the course of collecting local documents or compiling local histories have issued catalogues of materials at hand. Such materials for the most part cover the pre-Restoration or, at the latest, the pre-twentieth century field of local history and administration. It is interesting to note that these materials are being used increasingly by contemporary Japanese historians. For the non-Japanese, however, the raw materials of local history are most difficult to handle. He will consequently be more concerned with the modern printed editions of local histories and gazetteers published by prefectural or city historical organizations. A comprehensive catalogue of these printed works, which appeared from 1868 to 1950, is fortunately available in Honjō Eijirō's bibliographies of economic history (Entry 125). A journal of recent origin, the Chihoshi kenkyū (Local history) (Entry 588), published by the nationally organized Chihoshi Kenkyū Kyōgikai (Committee for the Study of Local History), is full of recent bibliographical information on local historical studies in Japan.
    The second type of research organization is primarily concerned with the problems of modern local administration or of urban growth. Of these the most active has been the Tōkyō Shisei Chōsakai (Tokyo Municipal Research Society) whose publications provide an excellent guide to recent material on modern local development. It should also be borne in mind that all levels of local government in Japan issue quantities of publications ranging from statistics to local histories. The historian will find no systematic guide to this type of literature.

125. Honjō Eijirō 本 庄 榮 治 郎 , "Chiho shishi bunken 地 方 史 誌 文 献 (A bibliography of local gazetteers)," in Kaihan Nihon keizaishi bunken, Tōkyō, 1932, Appendix, pp. 1-85; continued in Nihon keizaishi shin bunken, Tōkyō, 1942, pp. 615-664, and in Nihon keizaishi daisan bunken, Tōkyō, 1953, pp. 563-570.
    The most convenient and complete catalogue of printed works on local history. The three lists cover many hundreds of provincial and city histories and gazetteers compiled and published during the years 1868-1951. Such works are especially important for the study of the Tokugawa period (1600-1868). Many of the works are themselves indexes to local historical materials. Entries are arranged by locality and are unannotated.

126. Jimbun Chiri Gakkai 人文地理学会 (Society for the Study of Human Geography), "Toshi kenkyū shiryo 都市研究資料 (Municipal research materials)" in Toshi chiri kenkyū 都市地理研究 (Studies of urban geography), Tōkyō, 1929, pp. 253-55.
A   Useful for the post-Restoration period of urban development.

127. Kawaguchi Takeo 川口丈夫 , "Toshi chiri kenkyū bunken 都市地理研究文献 (Literature for research in urban geography)," in Toshi chiri kenkyū 都市地理研究 (Studies of urban geography), Tōkyō, 1929, pp. 237-52.
A   Compiled for the Society for the Study of Human Geography (Jimbun Chiri Gakkai).   Emphasis is on recent urban development.

128. "Ken-gun-shi-chō-sonshi mokuroku 縣郡市町村史目録 (Catalogue of prefectural, district, city, town and village histories)," Chihōshi kenkyū 地方史研究 (The study of local history), v. 4, pp. 6-7.
A   A brief list of local histories published since 1945 or in the process of compilation.

129. Kokubu Gōji 国分剛二 , "Kyōdo shishi mokuroku kō 郷土史誌目録稿 (Draft catalogue of local histories and gazetteers)," Shigaku 史学 , 8 (1929) 4. 607-654.
A   A listing by provinces of books and manuscripts held in the library of Keiō University.

130. "Kyōdoshi kenkyū sankō bunken ryakumoku 郷土史研究参考文献略目 (An abridged list of reference works for the study of local history)," Rekishi kyōiku, special number for 1930 entitled "Kyōdoshi wa ika ni kenkyū subeki ka 郷土史は如何に研究すべきか (How should local history be studied?)."

131. Nagasaki Kenritsu Nagasaki Toshokan 長崎縣立長崎図書館 (Nagasaki Prefectural Library), Kyōdo shiryō mokuroku 郷土誌料目録 (Catalogue of local materials), Nagasaki, Nagasaki Kenritsu Toshokan, 1923-36, 2 v.
A   A bibliography of local records and historical materials of special interest to the student of early relations between Japan and the West.

132. Naimushō Chirikyoku 内務省地理局 (Ministry of the Interior, Geographic Section), Chishi mokuroku 地誌目録 (Catalogue of local gazetteers), Tōkyō, Ookayama Shoten, 1935, 202 pp.
A   A comprehensive catalogue of materials for the study of local historical geography.

133. Kuroita Katsumi 黒板勝美 , Kōtei kokushi no kenkyū, Sōsetsu 更訂国史の研究總説 (Revised study of Japanese history, General introduction), Tōkyō, Iwanami Shoten, 1931, pp. 89-112, "Rekishi chiri 歴史地理 (Historical geography)."
A   A helpful introductory article on the problems of historical geography is followed by a selective list of old local gazetteers, fudoki, travel diaries, Tokugawa maps, and meisho zue.

134. Sako Keizō 佐古慶三 , Shisei kankei shiryō kaidai 市政関係資料解題 (Annotated bibliography of materials on municipal administration), Osaka, Naniwa Sōsho Kankōkai, 1926, 6 pp.

135. Takagi Toshita 髙木利太 , Kazō Nihon chishi mokuroku 家藏日本地誌目録 (A catalogue of Japanese geographical gazetteers in the author's collection), Osaka, by the author, 1927-30, 2 v.
A   A valuable study of local histories and gazetteers.   Volume 1 contains a brief survey of the compilation of local histories in Japan.   The body of the work constitutes a briefly annotated bibliography of nearly 2000 local gazetteers.   A large number of the entries are manuscripts or old printed copies.

136. Tōkyō Shisei Chōsakai 東京市政調査会 (Tokyo Municipal Research Society), Hōbun tosho mokuroku 邦文図書目録 (A catalogue of Japanese books), Tōkyō, Tōkyō Shisei Chōsakai, 1927, 381 pp.
A   A useful bibliography for the study of recent municipal administration and public administration.

137. Wada Mankichi 和田萬吉 , Kohan chishi kaidai 古版地誌解題 (An annotated bibliography of old printed editions of geographical gazetteers), Tōkyō, Wada Tsunashirō, 1916, 2+2+5+332 pp.
A   Descriptions of over eighty gazetteers printed during the Tokugawa period (1600-1868).   Entries are listed by locality.

d. Government, Politics, and Law

The following section includes only a very selective and partial listing of the many specialized bibliographies which exist for the numerous fields of government and politics.   A fuller list will be found in the guide to political science materials published in this series by Robert Ward.   For the historian such subjects are generally well enough covered by the more comprehensive general bibliographies of economics, law, and social affairs noted in Section e of this chapter.   Of special interest to the historian in the following list is the work by Ikebe Yoshikata entitled Nihon hōseishi shomoku kaidai (Annotated bibliography of the history of Japanese legal institutions) (Entry 139), a work which analyzes pre-Restoration laws and presents an excellent working bibliography of works on legal history.   Also the historian will find in the two works listed elsewhere by Ishii Ryōsuke excellent selected bibliographic lists.   The first, Nihon hōseishi gaisetsu (Introduction to the history of Japanese jurisprudence) (Entry 880), contains references to primary works on various problems of the pre-Meiji period. The second, Nihon hōseishiyō (Essentials of Japanese legal history) (Entry 881), contains a classified list of secondary works in all field of Japanese legal history.

138. Hosokawa Kameichi 細川亀市 , "Hōseishi seijishi ni kansuru jūyō bunken 法政史政治史に関する 重要文献 (Significant literature on legal and political history)," Shomotsu tembō, v. 7, July, 1937.
The compiler is an expert on medieval law and Tokugawa economic history.

139. Ikebe Yoshikata 池辺義象 , Nihon hōseishi shomoku kaidai 日本法政史書目解題 (Annotated bibliography of the history of Japanese legal institutions), Tōkyō, Daitōkaku, 1918, 1 v. ed., 815 pp.
A most valuable reference work for the legal historian, it covers the entire field of pre-Restoration Japanese law. Part 1 comprises what might be termed an annotated source book of ancient legal materials. Beginning with Shōtoku Taishi's 17 Articles, the work covers all major collections of laws quoting extensively their main passages. Parts 2 and 3 provide annotated lists of general and specialized works, ancient and modern, on Japanese laws and legal history. Both books and articles are included.

140. Imanaka Tsugumaro 今中次麿 , Seiji shisōshi 政治思想史 (History of political thought), Tōkyō, Iwanami, 1927, v. 1, pp. 871-80, "Seiji shishōshi sankō shomoku 政治思想史参考書目 (Bibliography of reference works on the history of political thought)."

141. Konakamura Kiyonori 小中村清矩 , "Hōritsushi kōkyū shomoku 法律史考究書目 (A bibliography for the study of legal history)," in Kokugakuin 国学院 , Hōsei ronsan 法政論纂 (Essays on law and government), Tōkyō, Nihon Tosho K.K., 1903, 1 v.
An important interpretive article on the bibliography of legal history by one of the pioneer modern legal historians.

142. Paul F. Langer and A. Rodger Swearingen, Japanese Communism, an Annotated Bibliography of Works in the Japanese Language with a Chronology, 1921-52, New York, I.P.R., 1953, 12+95 pp.
An important work for the study of Japanese communism. The work is divided into 5 parts dealing with: 1) Marxist theory and interpretation of Japanese society, 2) history of Japanese communism, 3) party organization, 4) strategy, and 5) foreign relations. A list of authors and their writings and a subject index are provided.

143. Ōhara Shakai Mondai Kenkyūsho 大原社会問題研究所 , Nihon shakaishugi bunken 日本社会主義文献 (Bibliography of Japanese socialism), Tōkyō, Dōjinsha shoten, 1929.
A chronological unannotated list.

e. Economic and Social History

The specialized interests of the social and economic historian in Japan have been closely related to those of the general historian. The following list of bibliographies repeats to a large extent, therefore, works which were noted above under general bibliographies. One new category of aids has been added. This includes the catalogues of pre-modern materials which form the basis of contemporary research on pre-Restoration economics and social organization. Particularly useful in this respect is Takimoto Seiichi's Nihon keizai tenzekikō (A survey of early works on Japanese economics) (Entry 161) which is an annotated bibliography of the most important works collected in his Nihon keizai taiten (Compendium of Japanese economics) (Entry 460). Ono Takeo's "Nōmin shiryō kaisetsu (An annotated bibliography of historical materials on the peasantry)" (Entry 153) is useful for its coverage of materials published in the Kinsei jikata keizai shiryō (Materials relating to early modern local economy) (Entry 457) and the Nihon nōmin shiryō shūsei (Collected materials on the history of the Japanese peasantry) (Entry 462).
Since many of the following bibliographies are extremely voluminous, it may be worth while to point out a number of more limited and selective guides to works in the field of economic and social history. The student may find, for instance, that for introductory purposes the classified and briefly annotated lists in Horie Yasuzo's Nihon keizaishi (Economic history of Japan) (Entry 967), Miyamoto Mataji's Nihon shōgyōshi (History of commerce in Japan) (Entry 1089), and Honjō Eijirō's Nihon keizaishi sōran (Collected essays on Japanese economic history) (Entry 966) are of more immediate value to him than the cumbersome but exhaustive works listed below.

144. "Fūzokushi ni kansuru zasshi yōmoku 風俗史に関する雑誌要目 (An index to periodical articles dealing with the history of customs)," Fūzoku kenkyū, v. 105 (1929)—.
An annual feature of this journal.

145. Honjō Eijirō 本庄栄治郎 , Kaihan Nihon keizaishi bunken 改版日本経済史文献 (Bibliography of Japanese economic history, revised), Tōkyō, Nihon Hyoronsha, 1933, 897 pp.
This work previously annotated under general bibliographies (Entry 10), is of greatest use to the social and economic historian. Its coverage of books and articles on such specialized subjects as village and city, population, mining, forestry, fishing, agriculture, taxation, commerce, trade, industry, finance, currency, banking, social classes, and social problems is especially complete. This volume covers material published in Japan from 1868 to 1931. Supplements bring the coverage up to 1951. (See entries 11 and 12). A special feature is its annotation of the various component parts of the great economic collections such as the Nihon keizai taiten (Entry 460).

146. "Keizaishi nenkan 経済史年鑑 (Yearbook of economic history)," Keizaishi kenkyū, v. 48 (1932)-44.
This series, previously annotated under Entry 28, began in 1932. Unfortunately, the journal was discontinued during World War II. Volume 1 covers Japanese works on Japanese, Oriental, and Occidental economic history from 1868 to 1931. The succeeding volumes cover a single year span. With volume 3 a review section which summarized and evaluated in essay fashion the main developments within various economic fields was added. The bibliographic contents of this series were cumulated in Honjō's bibliographical series (Entries 10 to 12).

147. Kōbe Kōtō Shōgyō Gakkō Shōgyō Kenkyūjo 神戸高等商業学校商業研究所 (Commercial Research Institute of the Kobe Higher Commercial School), Keizai hōritsu bunken mokuroku 經済法律文献目錄 (Catalogue of economic and legal literature), Tōkyō and Ōsaka, Hōbunkan, 1927 and 1932, 2 v.
    See entry 77 for a complete annotation. This work should be used in combination with Honjō's volumes on economic history (Entries 10 to 12) since it gives primary coverage to recent economic developments.

148. Kokushō Iwao 黒正巖 and Kikuta Tarō 菊田太郎, Keizai chirigaku bunken sōran 經済地理学文献總覽 (General survey of literature on economic geography), Tōkyō, Sōbunkaku, 1937, 478+ 320 pp.
    A specialized classified but unannotated bibliography of general economic geography. It is divided into two parts. Part 1 lists Japanese and Chinese materials; part 2 lists Western works. Classifications are precise and coverage is extended to Japanese works on non-Japanese economy. This work should be used to supplement Honjō's bibliographies of economic history (Entries 10 to 12).

149. Matsumoto Jun'ichirō 松本淳一郎, Nihon shakaigaku 日本社会学 (Japanese sociology), Tōkyō, Jichōsha, 1937, 162 pp.
    A history and bibliographical survey of sociology as a discipline in Japan. The bibliographical information is excellent for the understanding of the theory, methodology, and development of Japanese sociology.

150. "Nihon keizai koten sōran 日本經済古典綜覽 (A general survey of Japanese economic classics)," in Bunken sakuin 文献索引 (Bibliographical indices), Tōkyō, Achikku Myūzeamu, 1936.
    This index is contained in the first volume of the Attic Museum's bibliographical series. The work is an annotated index to the contents of the major compendiums of pre-Restoration economic writings, among them the Nihon keizai taiten, the Tsūzoku keizai bunko, and the Kinsei jikata keizai shiryō (Entries 460, 468, and 457). Each work is annotated. Notes are also provided on the authors.

151. Nihon zaisei keizai shiryō sakuin 日本財政經済史料索引 (Index to the Nihon zaisei keizai shiryo), Tōkyō, Zaisei Keizai Gakkai, 1925.
    This is the index to one of the important repositories of materials on Japanese economic history (See entry 465).

152. Nōmukyoku, Dai Nihon nōshi, Tōkyō, Hōbunkan, 1891, 274 pp., "Nōji sankosho kaidai 農事参考書解題 (Annotated bibliography of agricultural reference works)."
    This work is published as an appendix to the Dai Nihon nōshi (Entry 1053). It is an annotated bibliography of some 870 works relating to agricultural matters written from 729 to 1865. Entries are classified under various sub-heads such as land-tax, fisheries, stock farming, silk-worm culture, crafts, etc.

153. Ono Takeo 小野武夫, "Nōmin shiryō kaisetsu 農民史料解說 (Annotated bibliography of historical materials on the peasantry)," in Nihon shihonshugi hattatsushi kōza. Tōkyō, Iwanami Shoten, 1933.
    Professor Ono was a specialist on Tokugawa agrarian history. This is an annotated catalogue of works compiled by the Nōshōmusho (Ministry of Agriculture and Commerce) and published in such collections as the Nihon Keizai taiten, the Kinsei jikata keizai shiryō, and the Nihon nomin shiryō shūsei (Entries 460, 457, and 462).

154. Ōsaka Shiritsu Daigaku, Keizai Kenkyūsho 大阪市立大学經済研究所 (Osaka City University, Institute of Economic Studies), Keizaigaku shōjiten 經済学小辞典 (Concise dictionary of economics), Tōkyō, Iwanami Shoten, 1951, 1288 pp.
    The most recent and useful of the general dictionaries of economics, the bibliographical citations at the end of each item provide a useful introduction to the basic literature in many economic fields.

155. Ōsaka Shōka Daigaku Keizai Kenkyūsho 大阪商科大学經済研究所 (Economics Research Institute of the Ōsaka Commercial College), Keizaigaku bunken taikan 經済学文献大鑑 (A catalogue of literature on economics), Ōsaka, Ōsaka Shōka Daigaku Keizai Kenkyūsho, 1934-39, 4 v.
    While the emphasis of this work is primarily recent and specifically economic, the economic historian may find it of use. Volume 1 deals with finance, volumes 2 and 3 currency and banking, and volume 4 commerce. Works in Western languages are included.

156. Osaka Shōka Daigaku, Keizai Kenkyūsho 大阪商科大学經済研究所 (Osaka Commercial University Institute of Economic Research), Shakai kagaku bunken kaisetsu 社会科学文献解說 (The social sciences: bibliography and notes), Various publishers, 1947—. Twice a year.
    A survey of books and articles in the social sciences appearing in Japan from the beginning of 1947. Each volume contains a classified bibliography and carries lengthy reviews of a few of the most significant works. Emphasis is exclusively contemporary. There is little of historical interest.

157. Rekishigaku Kenkyūkai 歴史学研究会, Nihon shakai no shiteki kyūmei 日本社会の史的究明 (The historical investigation of Japanese society), Tōkyō, Iwanami Shoten, 1949, 340 pp.
    An appendix (pp. 291-340) to this work provides an excellent, though somewhat biased, critical review of Japanese works on social history. It is prepared by Matsushima Eiichi and Nagahara Keiji.

158. "Saikin no keizaishigakkai 最近の經済史学界 (Recent developments in the field of economic history)," Keizaishi kenkyū, no. 26 (1931)-.
    A regular feature of each issue of Keizaishi kenkyū (Entry 606) until the termination of the journal during the war. This section contained bibliographical notes and reviews in somewhat more detail than the yearly Keizaishi nenkan (Entry 146).

159. Shakai Keizaishi Gakkai 社会經済史学会, "Shakai keizaishigaku no hattatsu 社会經済史学 の発達 (Social and economic history of Japan, its recent development)," Shakai keizaishigaku, v. 10 (1941), nos. 9+10.
　　　See entry 40 for a full annotation.

160. "Shakai keizaishigaku bunken mokuroku 社会經済史学文献目録 (A catalogue of works on social and economic history)," Shakai keizaishigaku, v. 2, no. 4 (1932)— v. 7, no. 1 (1937).
　　　An irregular feature of the journal Shakai keizaishigaku (Entry 612). Issues were alternately devoted to Japanese and Western language sources. Entries are classified and include books and journals. This series provides excellent and detailed coverage of the period 1932-36.

161. Takimoto Seiichi 瀧本誠一, Nihon keizai tenzekiko 日本經済典籍考 (A survey of early works on Japanese economics), Tōkyō, Nihon Hyōronsha, 1928, 454 pp.
　　　This work is an annotated bibliography of a large number of pre-Restoration works of economic significance. Most works are to be found in the great economic compendium, the Nihon keizai taiten (Entry 460), edited by Takimoto. Annotations provide bibliographic data, descriptions of contents and notes on authors.

162. Tōkyō Shōka Daigaku, Hitotsubashi Shimbunbu (Tokyo University of Commerce, Hitsubashi Newspaper Department), Keizaigaku kenkyū no shiori 經済学研究の栞 (A guide to the study of economics), Tōkyō, Shunjusha, 1950, 4 v.
　　　A guide to problems, methodology, and bibliography in the field of economics both Eastern and Western. Volume 1 deals with theory, volume 2 with economic policies, volume 3 with economic history of the West, and volume 4 with the economic history of Japan and China. Contributions on Japanese economic history are made by Matsumoto Shimpachiro and Shinobu Seizaburo. Their recommendations thus favor the Marxist school.

163. Uchida Ginzō 内田銀蔵, Nihon keizaishi no kenkyū, Tōkyō, Dōbunkan, 1929, 2 v., "Nihon keizaishi kenkyū sankōsho 日本經済史研究参考書 (Reference works for the study of Japanese economic history)."
　　　A bibliographical essay of special importance to the study of pre-Meiji economics by a pioneer economic historian. First published in Kokumin keizai zasshi (v. 7, 3 - 11, 6) but most accessible in the above collection of Uchida's essays.

164. Yoshida Hideo 吉田英雄, Nihon shakai keizai hennenshi 日本社会經済編年史 (Annals of Japanese social economics), Tōkyō, Kaizōsha, 1928, 641 pp.
　　　This work, though primarily a chronological history, is useful as a general bibliographical guide to economic facts. The work covers Japanese economic development from ancient times to 1925. Each fact is given one or more bibliographical references. A list of all works so cited is contained at the end of the book.

f. Education

　　　The history of education in Japan has an extensive literature which cannot fully be covered here. The following bibliography, however, should prove sufficient for most needs of the general historian. Compiled in postwar Japan with American bibliographic aid, it is comprehensive and well classified.

165. Kokuritsu Kyōiku Kenkyūsho 国立教育研究所 (National Research Institute of Education), Kyōiku bunken sōgo mokuroku 教育文献總合目録 (Union list of educational books located in Japan), Tōkyō, Kokuritsu Kyōiku Kenkyūsho, 1950, 9+380 pp.
　　　A comprehensive, classified catalogue of works on education published in Japan from 1868 to 1949. There is an extensive section on the history of education.

g. Religion

1) Shinto

　　　Pre-modern literature on Shinto is vast and largely inaccessible except to the specialist. The following catalogues attest to the volume of such material but shed little light on the nature of the works listed, since none is annotated to any appreciable degree. Bibliographies of modern scholarship on Shinto are extremely rare.

166. Inoue Tetsujirō 井上哲次郎 and Saiki Yūgi 佐伯有義, Shinto bunrui sōmokuroku 神道分類總目録 (A classified bibliography of Shinto), Tōkyō, Shun'yōdō, 1937, 1 v.
　　　A classified and partially annotated catalogue of pre-modern works in the field of Shinto.

167. Jingū Shichō 神宮司庁 (Office of Shrine Affairs), Jingū bunko tosho mokuroku 神宮文庫図書目録 (Catalogue of the Ise Shrine Library), Kyōto, Jingū Shichō, 1922, 2+14+682+217 pp.
　　　A classified catalogue of the Ise Shrine Library holdings as of 1921. Many of the books are of a general nature but a large percentage deal with Shinto.

168. Shinten sakuin 神典索引 (An index to Shinto scriptures) Yokohama, Ōkura Seishinbunka Kenkyūsho 大倉精神文化研究所, 1937, 396 pp.
　　　A subject index to the major Shinto classics. Subjects include names of deities and place names. Entries are listed syllabically; kana readings are given for most names. Thus this work provides an excellent method of arriving at the readings of many difficult names of Shinto deities.

169. Katō Genchi 加藤玄智 , Shintō shoseki mokuroku 神道書籍目録 (A bibliography of Shinto), Tōkyō Dōbunkan, 2nd ed. 1943, 17+646+2 pp..
> The most complete and thoroughly useful of the Shinto catalogues. It covers works on Shinto written be-before 1868 only. Entries are classified and arranged chronologically within each category. Each title is followed by its romanization and complete bibliographical information. Location of manuscripts in various libraries is indicated. Author and title indexes in syllabic order are provided.

2) Buddhism

The field of Buddhist studies is one of the most complex which faces the student of Japanese history. Undoubtedly much of the field is closed except to the specialist. However, the general historian, especially if his interest is in pre-seventeenth century Japanese history, will find a modicum of knowledge of Buddhist bibliography essential. Hatano and Yayoshi's general bibliography (Entry 8) is unusually complete in its coverage of this field. The following entries have been taken largely from his suggestions. They have been selected to provide a guide to classical Buddhist sources as well as to modern scholarship in the field of the history of Buddhism. Among them Ono Gemmyō's Bussho kaisetsu daijiten (Dictionary of Buddhist books with explanations) (Entry 175) is worthy of special mention. This work is a monumental annotated bibliography of Buddhist works in Sanskrit, Chinese, and Japanese. Since the work is arranged in dictionary fashion by title, it is not of use in acquiring bibliographical references to any particular subject.

170. "Bukkyō gakkai sōran 佛教学界總覧 (Survey of Buddhist scholarship)," in Ryūkoku Daigaku ronsō 龍谷大学論叢 (Ryukoku University review), Kyōto, Ryūkoku Daigaku, 1930+.
> This annual review feature of the journal Ryūkoku Daigaku ronsō (Entry 622) appears first to have been carried by the journal Mujintō 無盡燈 , v. 17-24 (1912-19), and subsequently taken over by Bukkyō kenkyū 佛教研究 , v. 1-8 (1920-27).

171. Bukkyō shoseki mokuroku 佛教書籍目録 (Catalogues of Buddhist books) [vol. 1 and 2 of Dai Nihon Bukkyō zensho 大日本佛教全書 (Complete collection of Japanese Buddhist literature)], Tōkyō, Bussho Kankōkai, 1913-14, 2 v.
> These two volumes contain over 75 lists and catalogues of Japanese writings in the field of Buddhism. Useful only to the specialist, they afford a comprehensive index to pre-modern Buddhist literature in Japan.

172. Butten Kenkyūkai 佛教研究会 (Association for the Study of Buddhist Texts), Bukkyō rombun sōmokuroku 佛教論文總目録 (General catalogue of articles on Buddhism), Tōkyō, Ushio Shobō, 1931, 648 pp.
> A classified unannotated catalogue of over 12,000 articles in the field of Buddhist studies culled from the major Buddhist journals published during the years 1868-1930. A revised edition was published in 1935. Perhaps the most useful bibliography of its kind for the general historian.

173. Ogiwara Unrai 荻原雲来 , Daizōkyō Nanjō mokuroku hosei sakuin 大藏經南條目録補正索引 (English title Japanese alphabetical index of Nanjō's catalogue of the Buddhist Tripitaka), Tōkyō, Maruzen, 1930.
> The most convenient index to the Chinese version of the Buddhist Tripitaka. Based on Nanjō Bun'yū's monumental work published in London in 1883, it supplements and revises the former by making of it an index rather than a mere catalogue. References are to the Japanese Taishō edition of the Tripitaka.

174. Ōmura Seigan 大村西崖 and Nakano Gishō 中野義照 , Nihon Daizōkyō bussho kaidai 日本大藏經佛書解題 (Annotated bibliography of the Japanese Tripitaka), Tōkyō, Zōkyō Shoin, 1922, 2 v.
> This work is a revision of the Nihon Daizōkyō kaidai (Annotated bibliography of the Japanese Tripitaka): vols. 2 and 3 of the Nihon Daizōkyō (Entry 488).

175. Ono Gemmyō 小野玄妙 , Bussho kaisetsu daijiten 佛書解説大辞典 (Dictionary of Buddhist books with explanations), Tōkyō, Daitō Shuppansha, 1932, 12 v.
> A comprehensive annotated bibliography of Buddhist literature. For each entry the following information is provided: name of work in characters, Sanskrit equivalent, number of volumes or chapters, whether still available and if so where, note on author or translator, history or translation, description of contents, history of transmission of ms., history of printed copies, present status of old copies. Volume 12 contains essays on the history of Chinese translations of Buddhist writings and on the history of the Tripitaka.

176. Ryūkoku Daigaku Toshokan 龍谷大学図書館 (Ryūkoku University Library), Bukkyōgaku kankei zasshi rombun bunrui mokuroku 佛教学関係雑誌論文分類目録 (A classified catalogue of periodical articles in the field of Buddhist studies), Kyōto, Ryūkoku Daigaku Shuppambu, 1931, 498 pp.

177. Ryūkoku Daigaku Toshokan 龍谷大学図書館 (Library of Ryūkoku University), Ryūkoku Daigaku wakansho bunrui mokuroku, Bukkyō no bu 龍谷大学和漢書分類目録 佛教之部 (Classified catalogue of Japanese and Chinese books held by Ryūkoku University, section on Buddhism), Kyōto, Ryūkoku Daigaku, 1929, 17+806+100 pp.
> This catalogue of the library of one of the major Buddhist seminaries in Japan is an excellent bibliographical source for Buddhist literature. The 1929 edition lists holdings as of 1928. A supplement published in 1935 covers accessions up through 1934.

178. Shinsho Hanayama, "Orientation in the Study of Japanese Buddhism," in Kokusai Bunka Shinkōkai, A Guide to Japanese Studies, Tōkyō, K.B.S., 1937, pp. 87-135.
> One of the better articles in this book, it is of real value to the historian seeking orientation in Buddhist studies.

179. Shōwa hōbō sōmokuroku 昭和法室總目録 (General index to the Shōwa edition of the Tripitaka), Tokyo, Taishō Issaikyō Kankōkai, 1929, 2 v., Daizo Shuppan K.K., 1 v. (3 v. in all).

    Part of the great Taisho Shinshū edition of the Tripitaka, it contains a collection of indices to not only the Taishō edition but to a large number of previous editions and collections of Buddhist materials.

3) Christianity

    The history of Christianity in Japan has been most widely studied by Westerners.   Unfortunately, perhaps because of the long years of anti-Christian persecution in Japan, native materials from which the history of early Christian activities might be studied are extremely scarce.   While detailed bibliographic guides to Western language sources have been prepared by such men as Murdoch, Nachod, Cordier, Boxer, and Johannes Laures, no comparable studies have been made of native materials.   A search of the writings of such Japanese specialists as Shimmura Izuru, Ebizawa Arimichi, and Okamoto Ryōchi will reveal only a limited amount of new bibliographical information.   The following work is chiefly concerned with religious writings.   It is not by any means a general guide to Japanese sources on Japanese Christianity.

180. Ebizawa Arimichi 海老澤有通, Kirishitan tenzeki sōkō 切支丹典籍叢芳 (Collected essays on books dealing with Christianity), Tokyo, Takubundō, 1943, 261 pp.

    Notes on Christian writings of the "Christian Century" and the early Meiji periods.   Works listed are largely religious in nature and consist of missionary tracts or the works of early converts together with the anti-Christian polemics which paralleled them.

h. Literature

    Because of the specialized nature of the field of Japanese literature, no attempt has been made to cover the subject except in extremely general fashion.   Fortunately, however, a number of excellent guides and reference aids are available for the student of Japanese literary history.   A recent and extremely handy introduction is to be found in volume 8 of the Kawade Shobō's Nihon bungaku kōza (Series on Japanese literature) (Entry 191). This volume, entitled Nihon bungaku kenkyūhō (Methodology for the study of Japanese literature), brings up to date the methodological and bibliographical sections of the older Iwanami Shoten's Nihon bungaku (Iwanami series on Japanese literature) (Entry 190).   An appendix, "Nihon bungaku kenkyū bunken kaidai (An annotated bibliography for the study of Japanese literature)," lists and annotates the major literary collections and modern studies of literary works.   Beyond this work the student will find Fujimura Saku's Nihon bungaku daijiten (Dictionary of Japanese literature) (Entry 331) sufficient for most purposes of identifying literary works.   Moreover, the articles in this dictionary are provided with brief but excellent bibliographic references.

    One work which all students of Japan's early literature will need to know is Ishiyama Tetsurō's Nihon bungaku shoshi (Bibliography of Japanese literature) (Entry 183), which gives the most thorough annotated coverage of Japanese literary works up to the end of the sixteenth century.

    Bibliographies of recent books and articles on literary history are numerous.   The best of these appear to be the two series appearing in the journals Bungaku (Literature) (Entry 189) and Jimbun kenkyū (Studies in the humanities) (Entry 186).

181. Numazawa Tatsuo, Nihon bungakushi hyōran, Tokyo Meiji Shoin, 1934, v. 1, pp. 166-171, "Bungakushirui chosaku nempyō 文学史類著作年表 (A chronological classified list of works on the history of Japanese literature."

    Contained in the first volume of the author's Nihon bungakushi hyōran (Entry 329), this list presents chronologically under broad classifications the major studies of Japanese literary history published in Japan from 1868 to 1932.   Bibliographical references are incomplete, but the work provides a useful check list.

182. Georges Bonneau, Bibliographie de la Littérature Japonaise Contemporaine, Tokyo, Maison Franco-Japonaise, 1938, 102+280 pp.

    A useful annotated guide to contemporary Japanese belles-lettres.   In an introduction the author discusses collections of literature and historical studies of contemporary literature.   The main body of the work is a bibliographical dictionary arranged by author.   There is an index.

183. Ishiyama Tetsurō 石山徹郎, Nihon bungaku shoshi 日本文学書誌 (Bibliography of Japanese Literature), Tokyo, Okura Kōbundō, 1934, 6+24+932 pp.

    The most authoritative annotated bibliography of early Japanese literature, this work covers important works written up to the middle of the sixteenth century.   The book is divided into periods and by genre under each period.   For each entry it gives kana reading of name, a brief description of contents, a note on the author, a detailed history of its transmission, and present status of manuscript or printed copies, a list of commentaries, and a list of reference works and scholarly monographs concerning the work.

184. Kaito Matsuzo 垣内松三 and Mōri Akira 毛利昌, Kokubungaku shomoku shūran 国文学書目集覧 (Comprehensive bibliography of Japanese literature), Tokyo, Meitokudō, 6th printing 1934, 19+434+52+20+10 pp.

    A convenient guide to the study of Japanese literature from an historical point of view.   The work is divided into two parts.   Part 1 is a discussion of methodology with bibliographical references on each of the points discussed.   Part 2 is an annotated bibliography of pre-1868 Japanese literature by genre.   Individual titles are arranged by period and are briefly annotated.   Appendices provide a breakdown of the contents of major literary collections, a list of reference materials, and a title index to part 2.

185. Katsura Koson 桂 湖 村, <u>Kanzeki kaidai</u> 漢 籍 解 題 (An annotated bibliography of Chinese works), Tōkyō, Meiji Shoin, 1922.
    An authoritative bibliography of classical Chinese works, it is of great use in obtaining information on Chinese titles which so often appear in Japanese pre-Restoration literature. Arranged in standard Ssu-k'u chuan-shu categories. An index makes for easy finding of titles. The Chinese section of Endō Motoo's <u>Shiseki kaidai</u> (Entry 5) performs a similar function for the historian interested in Chinese literature.

186. "Kokubun gakkai tembō 国 文 学 界 展 望 (Survey of the field of Japanese literary studies)," <u>Jimbun kenkyū</u> 人 文 研 究 (Studies in the humanities), Ōsaka Shiritsu Daigaku Bungakkai, v. 1 (1950), no. 7—.
    A semi-annual feature of a new journal. Material is gathered by Maeda Masato 前 田 正 人. Each survey covers a period of approximately half a year and includes a classified list of books and articles on Japanese literature. Material is largely of non-historical interest.

187. Kyōto Kokubun Gakkai 京 都 国 文 学 界 (Literary Association, Kyoto), <u>Kokugo kokubun zasshi kenkyū rombun sakuin</u> 国 語 国 文 雑 誌 研 究 論 文 索 引 (An index to periodical articles on the study of Japanese language and literature), Kyōto, Bunken Shoin, 1931, 2+2+8+424 pp.
    The most complete index to native research in the field of Japanese literature, it covers some 300 journals published from 1868 to 1929. Entries are elaborately classified under genre and individual literary works. In addition to literature a number of related subjects such as literary geography and customs are covered. A companion volume was published in 1933 (See next entry).

188. Kyōto Kokubun Gakkai 京 都 国 文 学 会 (Literary Association, Kyoto), <u>Kokugo kokubun kenkyū zasshi sakuin</u> 国 語 国 文 研 究 雑 誌 索 引 (An index to periodicals in the field of Japanese language and literature), Kyōto, Bunken Shoin, 1933.
    A supplement to the bibliography noted above. It includes materials on myths, customs, court practices, etc.

189. "[   ]nen Nihon bungaku kenkyū bunken mokuroku [   ] 年 日 本 文 学 研 究 文 献 目 録 (A classified index to materials for the study of Japanese literature published during [   ])," in <u>Bungaku</u> 文 学 (Literature), Tōkyō, Iwanami Shoten, 1931—.
    An annual feature appearing usually in the March issue, it covers in classified fashion the output of literary studies, including both books and articles, for the previous year. There is a section on history of literature and a useful list of reference works and series.

190. <u>Nihon bungaku shomoku kaisetsu</u> 日 本 文 学 書 目 解 説 (An annotated catalogue of Japanese literature), in <u>Iwanami kōza: Nihon bungaku</u> 岩 波 講 座 日 本 文 学 (Iwanami series on Japanese literature), Tōkyō, Iwanami Shoten, 1931-33, 9 v.
    Nine pamphlets in this series are devoted to bibliographic descriptions of the major works of Japanese literature. Each pamphlet covers a specific historical period. Writers are authorities of the prewar period.

191. Origuchi Shinobu 折 口 信 夫, <u>Nihon bungaku kenkyūhō</u> 日 本 文 学 研 究 法 (Methodology for the study of Japanese literature), in <u>Nihon bungaku kōza</u> 日 本 文 学 講 座 (Series on Japanese literature), v. 8, Tōkyō, Kawade Shobō, 1951, 235 pp.
    The first part of this volume contains five essays on methodology. Pages 101-180 consist of an appendix entitled "Nihon bungaku kenkyū bunken kaidai. (An annotated bibliography for the study of Japanese literature)." The bibliography is divided into six parts: 1) general, 2) early ancient, 3) late ancient, 4) medieval, 5) modern, and 6) recent. Each part is compiled by one or more contemporary specialists. Covers major collections and authoritative aids and studies in the field of Japanese literature. A great deal of attention is given to historical studies and to the lives of writers.

i. <u>Art and Science</u>

    The study of fine arts in Japan is well advanced. Several organizations of national importance have been active in producing reference works in the field. Of these the Bijutsu Kenkyūsho (Institute of Art Research) of Tokyo has contributed most to general bibliographical knowledge with its two series listed below. While it is not the purpose of this work to deal with the natural sciences the following work by Yuasa Mitsutomo has been included because of its coverage of literature in the field of history of Japanese science.

192. Bijutsu Kenkyūsho 美 術 研 究 所 (Institute of Art Research), <u>Nihon bijutsu nenkan</u> 日 本 美 術 年 鑑 (Japan art yearbook), Tōkyō, Bijutsu Kenkyūsho, 1936—.
    Each issue of this series contains a lengthy classified bibliographical section which lists both books and articles. Volume 9, published in 1949, covered the years 1944-46. It was compiled by the Kokuritsu Hakubutsukan (National Museum). Volume 10, published in 1952, covered the years 1947-51. Compilation was again by the Institute of Art Research.

193. Bijutsu Kenkyūsho 美 術 研 究 所 (Institute of Art Research), <u>Tōyō bijutsu bunken mokuroku</u> 東 洋 美 術 文 献 目 録 (Classified bibliography of Far Eastern art), Tōkyō, Zayūhō Kankōkai, 1941—.
    A comprehensive index to Japanese research in the field of Japanese, Chinese, and Korean art, this work cumulates the entries of the Institute's annual Nihon bijutsu nenkan (see above), but lists only articles. Volume 1 covers articles in some 550 periodicals published from 1868 to 1935. Entries are classified and cover architecture and archeology as well as the graphic arts. There is a section on art history. Volume 2, published in 1948, covers the years 1936-45 and is better classified.

194. Yuasa Mitsutomo 湯浅光朝, Kagaku bunkashi nempyō 科学文化史年表 (Chronological tables of science and culture), Tōkyō, Chūō Kōronsha, 1950, 250 pp.
  A work packed with information in tabular form on the development of science and technology throughout the world. Pages 241-246 provide an excellent bibliography of the history of Japanese science.

4. LIBRARY SCIENCE

The subject of this section is of somewhat marginal interest to the research worker in Japanese history. However, in the course of his bibliographic activities the historian is often faced with problems of library usage and cataloguing technique. The following are a few selected works which will answer problems arising out of the peculiarities of library science in Japan.

195. Amano Keitarō 天野敬太郎, Toshokan sōran 図書館總覧 (A library handbook), Kōbe, Bunkyō Shoin, 1951, 10+242 pp.
  This work affords a comprehensive survey of the present state of Japanese libraries and library science. Sections deal with: libraries, their history and present condition; library associations; a bibliographical list of works on libraries and library science; library terms and their usages; and men in the library world.

196. Amano Keitarō 天野敬太郎, "Toshokan yōgo jii no kaidairyaku 図書館用語辞彙の解題略 (Brief annotated bibliography of dictionaries of library terminology)," Toshokan kenkyū, v. 7 (October, 1934), no. 4, pp. 491-500.
  An annotated bibliography of works on library terminology together with a list of standardized translations for a large number of Japanese bibliographical terms.

197. Mamiya Fujio 間宮不二雄, Ō-wa taiyaku toshokan jiten 欧-和対譯図書館辞典 (Dictionary of library terms, European languages to Japanese), Ōsaka, Bunyūdō Shoten, 1925, 118+69+5+4+3+39 pp.

198. Ōta Tamesaburō 太田為三郎, Wakan tosho mokurokuhō 和漢図書目録法 (Cataloguing rules for Japanese and Chinese works), Tōkyō, Geisōkai, 1931.
  A guide to library technique in pre-World War II Japan.

199. Toshokan nenkan 図書館年鑑 (Yearbook of libraries), Urawa (Saitama), Toshokan Shiryōsha, 1951, 263 pp.

200. "Tosho oyobi toshokan kankei rombun ichiran 図書及図書館関係論文一覧 (Survey of articles on books and libraries)," Toshokan zasshi, v. 24 (1930), no. 11—.
  This bibliographical section became a regular feature of each issue after November, 1930.

201. Uemura Chōzaburō 植村長三郎, Shoshigaku jiten 書誌学辞典 (Dictionary of bibliographical science), Kyōto, Kyōiku Tosho K.K., 1942, 602 pp.
  This work could more accurately be entitled a dictionary of library science. It is extremely useful for its explanation of library and bibliographical terms and for its coverage of modern Japanese libraries and their histories. It is arranged by subject in dictionary fashion. There is an index of Western library terms used in the text together with their Japanese equivalents and an index of Japanese terms.

202. Uemura Chōzaburō 植村長三郎, Tosho, toshokan jiten 図書図書館事典 (Dictionary of books and libraries), Tōkyō, Buntokusha, 1951, 599 pp.

II. REFERENCE WORKS

The Western student of Japanese history will find himself particularly dependent upon reference works such as encyclopedias, dictionaries, and chronologies. This is due first of all to the very nature of historical research which embraces a wide variety of subjects drawn from a diversity of fields. But beyond this the need for general references is accentuated by the fact that the Western scholar constantly meets in his work terms and references with which he is unfamiliar. Broad acquaintance with reference works and a knowledge of their proper selection and use is therefore essential for those who wish to carry on research in the field of Japanese history. Fortunately, the Japanese are prolific compilers of such reference materials. Satisfactory aids exist in almost every field to which the historian will need to turn. The following chapter lists a limited number of such works selected to be of most use to the Western student of Japanese history. Items are listed alphabetically by title.

1. ENCYCLOPEDIAS

The compiling of encyclopedias has a long tradition in Japan going back beyond the Restoration. In this the Japanese have followed the lead of the Chinese and their encyclopedic compilations, termed lei-shu 類書. Pre-modern works of this type are now largely superseded, but a number of them are still of use to the historian for antiquarian purposes. Furthermore, references to such works are frequent enough to warrant their inclusion in the following list. A modern encyclopedia compiled in the lei-shu tradition is the Koji ruien (Encyclopedia of ancient matters) (Entry 207). This work is indispensable to the historian since it brings together quotations from a great variety of sources on every conceivable aspect of pre-modern Japan. Of the modern encyclopedias modeled after the Encyclopedia Britannica the Heibonsha Dai hyakka jiten (Great encyclopedia) (Entry 203) is the latest and most comprehensive. Its companion work, Daijiten (Encyclopedia) (Entry 204), covers in dictionary fashion an encyclopedic number of terms and phrases, personal and geographical names, and literary works.

203. <u>Dai hyakka jiten</u> 大百科事典 (Great encyclopedia), Tōkyō, Heibonsha, 1931–, 28 v. + supplements. The most complete of the great modern encyclopedias. The main body of the work is in 28 volumes. Supplementary volumes are periodically added to bring the contents up to date. Supplement 3 was published in 1950. Contents deal primarily with Japanese subjects or those general or foreign subjects of interest to Japanese. All articles are signed. Coverage is best for matters of contemporary interest, hence this work has not superseded for the historian the older <u>Nihon hyakka daijiten</u> (Encyclopedia Japonica) (Entry 209). Since the war an edition of the <u>Dai hyakka jiten</u>, in smaller format, has been in press.

204. Shimonaka Yasaburō 下中彌三郎, <u>Daijiten</u> 大辞典 (Encyclopedia), Tōkyō, Heibonsha, 1934-36, 26 v.
In actuality a dictionary, this work nevertheless is of encyclopedic proportions. It covers not only words and terms but biography, geography, and literary titles and phrases. Equally thorough in its coverage of ancient and modern Japan, it is one of the most indispensable research tools for the historian. The last volume is a <u>kana</u> index. Users are cautioned that quotations of literary phrases have not always been verified and hence are sometimes inaccurate.

205. Kitamura Nobutaka 喜多村信節, <u>Kiyū shōran</u> 嬉遊笑覽 (Survey of interesting and entertaining facts), Tōkyō, Kondō Shuppanbu, ed. 3, 1916, 12+1 v.
An antiquarian encyclopedia of rather limited use to the general historian, it was completed some time before the author's death in 1856. The arrangement is haphazard but an index in the modern edition makes the work usable. The emphasis of the work is on the life, dwellings, costumes, customs, and natural environment of the Japanese of the Tokugawa period (1600-1868). A two-volume edition was published in 1932 by the Rikugōdō.

206. Mozume Takami 物集高見, <u>Kobunko</u> 廣文庫 (Storehouse of literature), Tōkyō, Kobunko Kankōkai, 1916-18, 20 v.
This monumental work by the author of the <u>Gunsho sakuin</u> (Entry 27) in actuality performs for the research worker the task of looking up the references listed in the earlier index. The work is arranged in dictionary fashion; under each subject, the author has quoted pertinent passages from a large variety of sources. It should be noted that not all of the references listed in Mozume's previous index are quoted here. Thus the earlier work is still of use. The <u>Kobunko</u> is more literary and cultural in its subject content than the <u>Koji ruien</u> (Entry 207). Hence it is of special importance in tracking down early literary allusions and the significance of terms and usages. The lives of a large number of historical persons are also covered in this work.

207. Jingūshichō 神宮司庁, <u>Koji ruien</u> 古事類苑 (Encyclopedia of ancient matters), Tōkyō, Koji Ruien Kankōkai, 1896-1914, 51 v.; revised popular edition 1936, 60 v.
A monumental encyclopedic repository of primary materials covering all phases of pre-modern Japan, this work is modeled on the great Chinese encyclopedias. Each chapter deals with a separate field and is introduced by a concise résumé of the subject. Following the introduction, selected passages from primary sources are quoted in classified order. Attempt is made to bring together first references or primary laws and ordinances concerning a given subject or institution. A comprehensive subject index (v. 60 of the 1936 edition) makes the work convenient to use. Volumes of special significance include those on the calendar, emperors, court ranks and practices, feudal administration, land-tax systems, law, currency, foreign affairs, military affairs, biography, and customs.

208. Yashiro Kōken 屋代弘賢 and others, <u>Kokon yōrankō</u> 古今要覽稿 (Draft encyclopedia of matters old and new), Tōkyō, Kokusho Kankōkai, 1905-07, 6 v.
An antiquarian encyclopedia compiled by shogunal order between 1821 and 1843. It is based on Yamaoka's <u>Ruijū meibutsukō</u> (Entry 210).

209. Saitō Seisuke 齊藤精輔, <u>Nihon hyakka daijiten</u> 日本百科大辞典 (Encyclopedia Japonica), Tōkyō, Sanseido [v. 1-6] and Nihon Hyakka Daijiten Kanseikai [v. 7-10], 1908-19, 10 v.
An early and extremely authoritative encyclopedia modeled on the <u>Encyclopedia Britannica</u>. It emphasizes matters of special interest to Japanese. Not entirely superseded for the historian by the <u>Dai hyakka daijiten</u> (Entry 203).

210. Yamaoka Shummei 山岡浚明, <u>Ruijū meibutsukō</u> 類聚名物考 (Classified notes on names and things), revised by Inoue Raikoku 井上頼圀 and Kondō Heijō 近藤瓶城, Tōkyō, Kondō Kappanjo, 1903-05, 7 v.
An eighteenth century encyclopedia covering a wide variety of practices, customs, and objects common to Japanese life. Each subject item is followed by numerous quotations from related sources. The modern edition is thoroughly revised. Volume 7 is an index.

211. Terajima Ryōan 寺島良安, "<u>Wakan sansai zue</u> 和漢三才圖会 (Illustrations of the three powers from China and Japan)," in <u>Nihon zuihitsu taisei</u> 日本随筆大成 (Collection of Japanese miscellanies), Tōkyō, Yoshikawa Kōbunkan, 1927-28, 2 v.
The Japanese version of the 16th century Ming encyclopedia of the physical world, <u>San-t'sai t'u-hui</u> 三才図会, compiled by Wang Ch'i 王圻. This work was first published in Japan in 1713 and contains numerous illustrations and explanations of astronomical, zoological, botanical, and geographical matters, and details on agricultural technique, arts, and crafts of the seventeenth century and therefore for the late pre-modern period in general. A difficult work to use but often quoted by Japanese scholars.

2. DICTIONARIES AND HANDBOOKS

a. Japanese Language and Character Dictionaries

The historian working with Japanese sources must accept the role of translator, a role which becomes increasingly difficult as he goes back to older or more specialized material. The following dictionaries are undoubtedly familiar to all who have dealt with problems of reading Japanese texts. They have been included, however, because of the necessity of clarifying the special features for which each is valuable. The belief that one "good" dictionary is sufficient for the needs of the historian is hardly valid. Adequate understanding of Japanese texts requires the use of a number of general as well as specialized dictionaries.

In the following annotations, the term "Japanese language dictionary" refers to word dictionaries in which ideographs are subordinated to their kana readings. "Character dictionaries," sometimes referred to as Chinese-Japanese dictionaries, are arranged by order of character with compounds listed under each character. Since the titles of many of the dictionaries are decorative rather than functional, translations have sometimes been omitted.

212. Ōtsuki Fumihiko 大 槻 文 彦 , Daigenkai 大 言 海 , Tōkyō, Fuzambo, 1932-37, 5 v.
This work is based upon one of the great pioneer modern dictionaries of the Japanese language, the same author's Genkai 言 海 published in 1884. Though rather hard to use, the Daigenkai is considered the most authoritative of the large dictionaries. Volume 4 is an index.

213. Ueda Mannen 上 田 万 年 , Daijiten 大 辞 典 , Tōkyō, Keiseisha, 1940, 25+2602+210 pp.
The best-known "character" dictionary, and widely used in this country by virtue of its wartime publication by the Harvard University Press. Most useful for its large number of compounds, the listing of readings of characters when used in proper names, and the convenient feature of numbering the radicals, it is nevertheless deficient in that it does not adequately define the meanings of the various readings of each character.

214. Shimonaka Yasaburō 下 中 彌 三 郎 , Daijiten 大 辞 典 , Tōkyō, Heibonsha, 1934-36, 26 v.
The most exhaustive of the great "Japanese" dictionaries, its encyclopedic character has been described above (Entry 204). As a translation tool this work is of special value for its coverage of quotations and literary allusions. It is also provided with an index. Users are cautioned, however, that quotations are not always accurately extracted.

215. Ueda Mannen 上 田 万 年 and Matsui Kanji 松 井 簡 治 , Dai Nihon kokugo jiten 大 日 本 国 語 辞 典 , Tōkyō, Kinkōdō and Fuzambo, 1915-28, 5 v.
Considered the most inclusive of the Japanese language dictionaries, this work is especially useful for the numerous illustrative quotations which it cites. Its inclusion of many dialect terms is also a special feature. Volume 5 contains kana and character indices.

216. Fujii Otoo 藤 井 乙 男 , Gengo daijiten 諺 語 大 辞 典 (Dictionary of proverbs), Tōkyō, Yūhōdō Shoten, 1926, 1159 + 254 pp.

217. Shimmura Izuru 新 村 出 , Genrin 言 林 , Kyōto, Zenkoku Shobō, 1949, 14+2470+41 pp.
A successor to Jien (Entry 218), but not to be confused with it. This work is in some ways more complete, especially in its coverage of modern terms, but the general level is elementary. It lacks the coverage which Jien gave to historical terms. The print is small and hard to read.

218. Shimmura Izuru 新 村 出 , Jien 辞 苑 , Tōkyō, Hakubunkan, 1935, 8+2285 pp.
One of the best one-volume "Japanese" dictionaries. Semi-encyclopedic in nature, it is similar to the French Petite Larousse. The work has many references to historical terms, persons, practices, and events. An abridged version of this has appeared under the title Gen'en 原 苑 .

219. Haga Yaichi 芳 賀 矢 一 , Kakugen daijiten 格 言 大 辞 典 (Dictionary of proverbs), Tōkyō, Bunshōkaku, 1916, 1045 pp.

220. Kanazawa Shōzaburō 金 澤 庄 三 郎 , Kōjirin 廣 辞 林 , Tōkyō, Sanseidō, 1948, 1936 pp.
An encyclopedic dictionary of the Japanese language similar to the Jien (Entry 218). Compared to the latter this has more words of recent and foreign origin. It is perhaps the most used of its kind among contemporary Japanese scholars.

221. Mombushō 文 部 省 , Kokugo no kakiarawashikata 国 語 の 書 き 表 わ し 方 (How to write Japanese), Tōkyō, Mombushō, 1950, 165 pp.
A handbook of the Japanese written language. It is especially useful for its rules on correct kana spellings of words and its lists of abbreviated characters.

222. Kōjimachi Kōji 麹 町 幸 二 , Modan yōgo jiten モ ダ ン 用 語 辞 典 (Dictionary of modern terms), Tōkyō, Jitsugyō no Nihonsha, 1930.
Useful for its coverage of current words and phrases many of them of foreign origin.

223. Inoue Raikoku 井 上 頼 圀 , Nankun jiten 難 訓 字 典 (Dictionary of difficult readings), Tōkyō, Keiseisha, 1933, 424 pp.
A useful source for the reading of difficult proper names.

224. Hattori Unokichi 服部宇之吉 and Koyanagi Shigita 小柳司氣太, <u>Shōkai kanwa daijiten</u> 詳解 漢和大字典 (Detailed Chinese-Japanese dictionary), Tōkyō, Fuzambō, 1929, 3+8+18+2212 pp.
   A character dictionary, its special merit lies in the fact that it not only gives the readings of characters but defines the meanings of each reading—a feature lacking in Ueda's <u>Daijiten</u> (Entry 213). Its coverage of classical Chinese phrases is also superior.

225. Hōshokai 法書会, <u>Zōho gotai jirui</u> 増補五体字類 (Five styles of writing, revised and enlarged), Tōkyō, Seito Shobō, 1921, 615+35 pp.
   Useful for deciphering hand written manuscripts.

226. Ochiai Naobumi 落合直文 and Haga Yaichi 芳賀矢一, <u>Nihon daijiten kotoba no izumi</u> 日本大 辞典言泉, Tōkyō, Ōkura Shoten, revised and enlarged, 1931-32, 6 v.
   One of the best "Japanese" dictionaries and of invaluable use to the historian dealing with early materials. Its coverage of classical and historical terms is excellent. Definitions are clear and well illustrated. The last volume consists of a character index to the work arranged by stroke. (The radical arrangement is unusual.) This index thus acts as one of the most useful tools for arriving at the pronunciation of difficult phrases and proper names.

227. Tōjō Misao 東條操, <u>Zenkoku hōgen jiten</u> 全国方言辞典 (Dictionary of Japanese dialects), Tōkyō, Tōkyōdō, 1951, 881 pp.

b. Historical Dictionaries and Handbooks

   Japanese historical scholarship has not produced as yet an adequately exhaustive dictionary of Japanese history. Of the prewar works Yashiro Kuniharu's <u>Kokushi daijiten</u> (Dictionary of Japanese history) (Entry 229) is the only completed full-size dictionary. Its approach, however, is outdated and overly formal. The Fuzambō dictionary <u>Kokushi jiten</u> (Dictionary of Japanese history) (Entry 230) is, unfortunately, only half complete, though it provides answers to more of the questions which the historian as a social scientist will ask. Of special use in this respect is the Nihon Keizai Kenkyūjo's <u>Nihon keizaishi jiten</u> (Dictionary of Japanese economic history) (Entry 291) which includes a great deal of information on matters of political and social history as well as the expected coverage of economic affairs.
   Postwar Japan has produced two historical dictionaries of note. Heibonsha's <u>Sekai rekishi jiten</u> (Encyclopedia of world history) (Entry 232) gives an eighteen-volume coverage to Japanese, Oriental and Occidental history. The approach is modern and its contributors represent the best of postwar Japanese scholarship. Unfortunately, the work devotes less than one-third of its space to Japan. Wakamori Tarō's <u>Nihon rekishi jiten</u> (Dictionary of Japanese history) (Entry 231) provides a less specialized dictionary for the beginning student of Japanese history.
   The <u>Tokushi biyō</u> (Handbook of Japanese history) (Entry 233), prepared by the Historiographical Institute of the University of Tokyo, can be of immense use to the historian once he masters its contents. So much miscellaneous information is packed into this work that the scholar will have to be constantly on the alert to make the most use of it. Similar to this work is the <u>Chihōshi kenkyū hikkei</u> (Manual for the study of local history) (Entry 228) which has brought together much information on Japanese local history.

228. Chihōshi kenkyū kyōgikai 地方史研究協議会, <u>Chihōshi kenkyū hikkei</u> 地方史研究必携 (Manual for the study of local history), Tōkyō, Iwanami Shoten, 1952, 316 pp.
   An extremely handy volume which does for local history what <u>Tokushi biyō</u> (Entry 233) does for Japanese history in general. The work is divided according to historical periods. Under each period paragraphs deal with local administrative and economic systems. There are lists of official titles, of peasant uprisings, fluctuations in the price of rice, statistics on tenantry, political parties, national production, education, and almost every conceivable subject which the student of Japanese local history might meet. An appendix is devoted to art forms, the calendar, weights and measures, and a bibliography of published local histories. Coverage is from the origins of the Japanese people to 1951.

229. Yashiro Kuniharu 八代国治, Hayakawa Junzaburō 早川純三郎, and Inobe Shigeo 井野辺茂雄, <u>Daizōtei kokushi daijiten</u> 大増訂国史大辞典 (Further revised and supplemented dictionary of Japanese history), Tōkyō, Yoshikawa Kōbunkan, 1925-26, 6 v.
   Originally compiled in 1903, this work remains the only complete major dictionary of Japanese history. Unfortunately, it is somewhat dated and stilted in its approach. Its coverage of pre-Restoration political, institutional, and biographical history is most complete. Most articles provide references to primary sources. Illustrated by plates, drawings, maps and charts. A one-volume edition was published in 1936.

230. <u>Kokushi jiten</u> 国史辞典 (Dictionary of Japanese history), Tōkyō, Fuzambō, 1940, 4 v.
   Unfortunately, this dictionary remains unfinished. Compiled from a social science approach it features lengthy articles on political, economic, social, and cultural developments in each of the major historical periods. A fair portion of the articles gives skeleton bibliographies. Attractively put out and well illustrated. Volume 4 carries only part way through syllable <u>shi</u>.

231. Wakamori Tarō 和歌森太郎, <u>Nihon rekishi jiten</u> 日本歴史事典 (Dictionary of Japanese history), Tōkyō, Jitsugyō no Nihonsha 実業之日本社, 1952, 521 pp.
   Not to be confused with the small pamphlet with the identical title published in the <u>Atene bunko</u> (Athena library), this work is one of the most complete of the recent dictionaries of Japanese history. Somewhat popular in its approach, its easy style makes it ideal as an introductory reference work for the Western student of Japanese history.

232. <u>Sekai rekishi jiten</u> 世界歴史事典 (Encyclopedia of world history), Tōkyō, Heibonsha 平凡社, 1950–.

Scheduled to run to eighteen volumes, this work represents one of the most ambitious of Japan's postwar encyclopedic efforts. The encyclopedia unfortunately devotes less than one-third of its space to Japanese history. Articles are contributed by the best of Japan's postwar historians and tend to deal with Japanese history in terms of broad problems. Bibliographical citations are given.

233. Tōkyō Teikoku Daigaku Shiryō Hensansho 東京帝国大学史料編纂所 (Tokyo Imperial University, Historiographical Institute), <u>Tokushi biyō</u> 讀史備要 (Handbook of Japanese history), Tōkyō, Naigai Shosekisha, 1933, 2154 pp.

An extremely useful collection of historical data covering all aspects of Japanese history from ancient times to 1932. The following are some of its helpful features: 1) a comparative table of regnal, zodiacal, Japanese, Chinese, Korean, and Western style dates, 2) a chronological listing of important events in Japanese history, 3) tabular histories of Japanese emperors and their courts, of shogun, and of <u>daimyō</u>, 4) tables of holders of chief offices in the Tokugawa government, 5) charts depicting the administrative system of each period in Japanese history, 6) histories of Japanese <u>kuni</u> and <u>gun</u>, 7) tables of Shinto shrines and Buddhist sects, 8) a calendar of festivals and observances during the year, 9) tables of fluctuations in currency and rice values, 10) genealogies and tables of succession to office of heads of religious sects, schools of philosophy, schools of art and of crafts, acting groups, teachers of military arts, 11) indexes to biographical literature on court nobles, military houses, and priests, and 12) a list of death dates of prominent persons.

234. <u>Tōyō rekishi daijiten</u> 東洋歴史大辞典 (Encyclopedia of Oriental history), Tōkyō, Heibonsha, 1937-39, 9 v.

The most comprehensive and authoritative work of its kind in any language, it represents the combined efforts of the faculties of Tokyo and Kyoto Imperial Universities. Coverage is exclusively continental, but Japanese relations with the continent are also included.

c. Antiquarian Dictionaries

Specialized terms referring to ancient court titles and official practices and usages are a never-ending source of difficulty to the historian working in pre-Restoration materials. The historian should know of the existence of a number of modern antiquarian dictionaries which deal specifically with such terms. Works of this nature, but of more encyclopedic proportions, have already been noted in the section on encyclopedias. The <u>Koji ruien</u> (Encyclopedia of ancient matters) (Entry 207) is not surpassed by any except the most specialized modern dictionaries. The most useful of these, Wada Hidematsu's <u>Shūtei kansoku yōkai</u> (Revised dictionary of official titles) (Entry 241), is hardly more than an abridgement of material found in the volumes on titles and ranks (<u>Kan'ibu</u>) of the <u>Koji ruien</u>.

The following dictionaries deal primarily with terms and usages current among the pre-modern aristocracy. Works relating to words and customs of more plebeian origin will be listed below in Section <u>h</u>.

235. Sekine Masanao 関根正直 and Katō Teijirō 加藤貞次郎, <u>Kaitei yūsoku kojitsu jiten</u> 改訂有職故実辞典 (Revised dictionary of ancient practices and usages), Tōkyō, Rimpei Shoten, 1940, 2+864+73 pp.

The standard antiquarian dictionary, its chief emphasis is on early court practices and bureaucratic titles.

236. Kanno Dōmei 簡野道明, <u>Koji seigo daijiten</u> 故事成語大辞典 (A dictionary of archaic Japanese), Tōkyō, Meiji Shoin 明治書院 1908, 4 ffnc.+2+4+1630+165+[1] pp.

A dictionary devoted to the explanation of archaic terms in such fields as astrology, the calendar, court titles, ceremonies, and music. The terms are largely of Chinese origin.

237. Ema Tsutomu 江馬務, <u>Kokubun kojitsu fūzokugo shūshaku: Yōgi fukushoku hen</u> 国文故実風俗語集釈 容儀服飾篇 (Commentary on terms relating to ancient practices and customs in Japanese literature: customs and accessories), Tōkyō, Kyōritsusha, 1935, 6+8+508+12+4 pp.

238. Amemiya Shin'ichirō 雨宮信一郎, <u>Nihon bunkashi jibutsu kigen jiten</u> 日本文化史事物起源辞典 (Dictionary of things cultural and their origins in Japan), Tōkyō, Tōkō Shoin, 1933, 356 pp.

239. Matsuoka Shizuo 松岡静雄, <u>Nihon kogo daijiten</u> 日本古語大辞典 (Dictionary of archaic Japanese), Tōkyō, Tōkō Shoin, 1929, 2 v.

A dictionary dealing with archaic Japanese words found in such early pieces of literature as the <u>Kojiki</u>, <u>Nihon shoki</u>, and <u>Man'yōshū</u>.

240. Ema Tsutomu 江馬務, <u>Shinshū yūsoku kojitsu jiten</u> 新修有職故実辞典 (Newly revised dictionary of ancient practices and usages), Kyōto, Hoshino Shoten, 1930, 329 pp.

A work by the leading expert on ancient customs, clothing, and practices. This book covers Japanese history from the Heian period to modern times but emphasizes the Heian. There are numerous illustrations and photographic recreations of early court scenes in authentic costume. Further enlarged in 1937.

241. Wada Hidematsu 和田英松, <u>Shūtei kansoku yōkai</u> 修訂官職要解 (Revised dictionary of official titles), Tōkyō, Meiji Shoin, 1926, 372 pp.

A useful and authoritative reference work for the explanation of pre-Restoration officialdom and official titles. Divided into periods, under each period the administrative structure, both court and military, is laid out and explanations given of the functions of each office. There is an index and a conversion table between native Japanese official names and T'ang terminology.

242. Kawabata Sanehide 河 鰭 実 英, <u>Yūsoku kojitsu zufu</u> 有 職 故 実 図 譜 (Illustrated manual of ancient practices and usages), Kyōto, Jimbun Shoin, 1941.
> A useful illustrated handbook of ancient practices, it covers such subjects as cloth, clothing, armor, domestic architecture, and utensils. There is no index.

d. <u>Biographical Aids</u>

1. <u>Dictionaries</u>

Biographical aids may be considered under three general headings: biographical dictionaries, Who's Whos, and genealogies. Most useful to the historian is the general biographical dictionary which covers eminent Japanese of all periods. Among such dictionaries Heibonsha's <u>Shinsen daijimmei jiten</u> (Newly selected biographical dictionary) (Entry 253) is outstanding for the fullness of its biographical notes. As an aid to arriving at the identity of historical figures mentioned only by their personal names or by one of their numerous pseudonyms, Haga Yaichi's <u>Nihon jimmei jiten</u> (Biographical dictionary of Japan) (Entry 251) is without peer. For names which do not appear in either of these two works the scholar is referred to the indices to the standard biographical sources such as the <u>Rikkokushi</u> (Six national histories), the <u>Dai Nihonshi</u> (History of Japan), Yashi (Unofficial history of Japan), and the <u>Kansei chōshū shokafu</u> (Kansei collated genealogies) listed in Part 5, Chapter 4 of this work.

243. Dai Nihon Jimmei Jisho Kankōkai 大 日 本 人 名 辞 書 刊 行 会 (Society for the Publication of the Biographical Dictionary of Japan), <u>Shinteiban Dai Nihon jimmei jisho</u> 新 訂 版 大 日 本 人 名 辞 書 (Biographical dictionary of Japan, revised edition), Tōkyō, Naigai Shoseki K.K., 1937, 5 v.
> Originally published in 1885-86 and many times revised, this work covers famous Japanese from earliest times down to the present. Biographical sketches are short but entries are numerous. Volume 5 consists of genealogical tables, lists of swordsmiths and other artisans, and an index.

244. Takamure Itsue 高 群 逸 枝, <u>Dai Nihon josei jimmei jisho</u> 大 日 本 女 性 人 名 辞 書 (A biographical dictionary of Japanese women), Tōkyō, Kōseikaku, rev. ed., 1942, 20+640+5 pp.
> Useful for a limited purpose. There is a classified index by type (empresses, writers, etc.) and a character index. Biographical articles all have bibliographical notes.

245. Ogawa Kandō 小 川 貫 道, <u>Kangakusha denki oyobi chojutsu shūran</u> 漢 学 者 傳 記 及 著 述 集 覧 (A general index to biographies and writings of Kangaku scholars), Tōkyō, Seki Shoin, 1935, 44+781+12 pp.
> For each entry the following information is given: name with <u>kana</u> reading, other literary names, birthplace, age at time of death, school or tradition, a list of chief writings, a biographical reference.

246. Takebayashi Kan'ichi 竹 林 貫 一, <u>Kangakusha denki shūsei</u> 漢 学 者 傳 記 集 成 (Collection of biographies of Kangakusha), Tōkyō, Seki Shoin, 1928, 9+7+9+13+1381+37+16 pp.
> A biographical history of the Confucian movement in Japan, this work covers nearly 400 names. Biographical sketches are made up largely of extracts from Tokugawa biographies. There is an index.

247. Ōkawa Shigeo 大 川 茂 雄 and Minami Shigeki 南 茂 樹, <u>Kokugakusha denki shūsei</u> 国 学 者 傳 記 集 成 (Collection of biographies of Kokugaku scholars), Tōkyō, Dai Nihon Tosho K.K., 1904, 7+2+12+10+1700+30 pp.
> This work covers over six hundred writers of the period 1593-1903 who were active in or in any way associated with the Kokugaku movement. Biographical sketches consist largely of quotations from previous biographies. The work is somewhat hard to use but an index prepared by the Nihon Bungaku Shiryō Kenkyūkai (see next item) is available.

248. Nihon Bungaku Shiryō Kenkyūkai 日 本 文 学 資 料 研 究 会 (Society for the Study of Japanese Literary Materials), <u>Kokugakusha denki shūsei myōgō sōsakuin</u> 国 学 者 傳 記 集 成 名 号 總 索 引 (A comprehensive personal and penname index to the Kokugakusha denki shūsei), Tōkyō, Kokuhon Shuppansha, 1935, 47 pp.
> Prepared because of the lack of completeness in the indices contained in the <u>Kokugakusha denki shūsei</u>. (See previous item.)

249. Washio Junkei 鷲 尾 順 敬, <u>Nihon Bukka jimmei jisho</u> 日 本 佛 家 人 名 辞 書 (A biographical dictionary of Japanese Buddhists), Tōkyō, Kōyūkan, 1911, 1317 pp.
> This is a revised edition of a work originally published in 1903. It covers some 6000 names of priests, nuns, and Buddhist painters and artisans. There are numerous illustrations and charts.

250. Sawada Akira 澤 田 章, <u>Nihon gaka jiten (jimmei hen)</u>, 日 本 畫 家 辞 典 (人 名 編) (A dictionary of Japanese painters, biographical section), Tōkyō, Kigensha, 1927, 700 pp.
> The first pages of this work consist of genealogies and charts of schools. The bibliographical section is arranged in syllabic order by painters' brushnames. Each biographical sketch gives reference to original sources.

251. Haga Yaichi 芳 賀 矢 一, <u>Nihon jimmei jiten</u> 日 本 人 名 辞 典 (Biographical dictionary of Japan), Tōkyō, Ōkura Shoten, 1914, 203+1174 pp.
> Though only a one-volume work, this is nonetheless the most comprehensive of the biographical dictionaries. A special feature of this work is the stroke index to personal names and pseudonyms—most valuable since historical documents often fail to provide the surname. There is also a character index to surnames. Biographical sketches are short but give essential data on dates and official positions.

252. Nihon tōjiki meikō ryakuden 日本陶磁器名工畧傳 (Short biographies of Japanese pottery and porcelain masters), Ōsaka, Yamanaka Shoka, 1934, 45 pp.

253. Shinsen daijimmei jiten 新撰大人名辞典 (Newly selected biographical dictionary), Tōkyō, Heibonsha, 1937-41, 9 v.
    The most satisfactory biographical dictionary because of its size and the lengthy biographies which it provides. It lists fewer names than Haga Yaichi's work (Entry 251). Famous men, both modern and ancient, are included. Many of the sketches contain bibliographical notes. Volume 7 deals with contemporary names. Volume 8 gives selective coverage to foreign names. Volume 9 is an index.

2. Who's Whos

    The above general biographical dictionaries give only a very selective coverage to contemporary Japanese. For the recent period, therefore, the scholar will need to avail himself of one or more of the Who's Whos and professional directories which exist in considerable profusion. Of these, the Nihon shinshiroku (Who's who in Japan) (Entry 263) has the widest coverage, though its biographical information is limited. The Jinji kōshinroku (Information about people) (Entry 261) has a less extensive coverage of names but includes longer biographical sketches. For information on contemporary scholars and writers the historian will find two useful types of publication. The first includes lists of academic personnel and holders of the doctorate. Of these Iseki Kurō's Gakui taikei hakushiroku (Outline of the academic status of persons holding the doctorate) (Entry 257) contains perhaps the most satisfactory biographical and professional information. More specialized lists of scholars are frequently published by the Ministry of Education. The second type of biographical aid includes handbooks of current writers put out by several of the Japanese publishing and copyright associations. Of these the Bunka jimmeiroku (A who's who of persons in cultural activities) (Entry 254) will be found most useful by virtue of its completeness and the fact that kana readings of all names are given.

254. Bunka jimmeiroku 文化人名録 (A who's who of persons in cultural activities), Tōkyō, Nihon Chosakuken Kyōgikai, 1951, 787+201 pp.
    Valuable as a reference work on contemporary scholars, this work covers copyright holders in the fields of art, language, philosophy, economics, law, politics, criticism, history, geography and many other fields. Entries are arranged by discipline and syllabically within each division. Names are written in both characters and kana. Biographical information includes place of birth, present address, education, academic specialties, current position, membership in professional societies, and major publications. Additional sections provide tables of publishers, cultural organizations, publishing houses and the newspapers and journals which they publish. A comprehensive index to the biographical sections is appended. A 1953 edition has appeared.

255. Izeki Kurō 井関九郎, Dai Nihon hakushiroku 大日本博士録 (A list of Japanese holders of the doctorate), Tōkyō, Hattensha, 1922, 6 v.
    A who's who of holders of the doctorate. Each entry gives name, dissertation, other publications, and honors. Volume 1 covers doctors of law and pharmacology. Volume 5 covers doctors of literature which includes most scholars in the humanities and social sciences. The other volumes deal with medicine, natural science, etc. An index is appended.

256. Mombushō Semmon Gakumukyoku 文部省専門学務局 (Ministry of Education, Special Office of School Affairs), Gakuiroku 学位録 (List of doctorates), Tōkyō, Mombusho, 1922—. Annual.
    An annual cumulative list of holders of the doctorate. Classification is by discipline and is chronological within each discipline.

257. Izeki Kurō 井関九郎, Gakui taikei hakushiroku 学位大系博士録 (Outline of the academic status of persons holding the doctorate), Tōkyō, Hattensha, 1939, variously paged.
    A who's who of holders of the doctorate in Japan classified by field. Information is given on date of degree, title of dissertation, whether or not published, present position, and address. There is an index.

258. Jimbun Kagaku Iinkai 人文科学委員会, Gakujutsu Kaigi yūhensha meibo 学術会議雄篇者名簿 (Roster of outstanding writers in the Gakujutsu Kaigi), Tōkyō, Jimbun Kagaku Iinkai,
    A convenient selective list of postwar Japanese scholars in the field of humanities.

259. Nihon Shuppan Kyōdō Kabushiki Kaisha 日本出版協同株式会社 (Japanese Publishing Association, Ltd.), Gendai shuppan bunkajin sōran 現代出版文化人総覧 (Survey of contemporary writers), Tōkyō, Nihon Shuppan Kyōdō K.K., 1947, 408 pp.
    A useful reference to contemporary writers and scholars. Part 1 is an index of authors classified by fields. Part 2 is a list of authors who have published books or articles since August, 1945, giving in some instances kana readings and for all entries pertinent data on the career, education, present position and address, professional societies, and major publications. Part 3 is a list of authors who have died since January, 1943.

260. Kyōdō Shuppansha Hensambu 協同出版社編纂部 Gendai shuppan bunkajin sōran 現代出版文化人総覧 (Comprehensive survey of contemporary writers), Tōkyō, Kyōdō Shuppansha, 1943, 848 pp.
    A valuable source of biographical data on writers and scholars. This work combines the information contained in the Kyōdō Shuppansha's Shoseki Nenkan and Zasshi nenkan (Entries 85 and 105). The following 6 parts comprise the chief features of the work: 1) a list of journals and their editors, 2) a similar list of newspapers, 3) a list of publishers with pertinent data on their publishing activities, 4) a list of chief officers of publishing houses, 5) a list of writers including kana reading of name, pertinent biographical data, and major publications for each entry, and 6) an index of writers classified by fields.

261. Jinji kōshinroku 人 事 興 信 録 (Information about people), Tōkyō, Jinji Koshinjo, 1903—. Tre innial.
An extremely detailed who's who of contemporary Japanese. Number 15 (1948) is in two volumes and covers over 30,000 persons including Japanese residing abroad. Each entry gives information on careers, business interests, family relationships, etc. Arranged by syllabic order. There is an index of initial characters.

262. Shishido Shinzan 宍 戸 新 山, Meiji Taishō Shōwa taikanroku 明 治 大 正 昭 和 大 官 錄 (Roster of high officials of the Meiji, Taishō, and Shōwa eras), Tōkyō, Daitō Shimbunsha, 1931.
A detailed record of the establishment and subsequent changes in the Japanese civil service from 1868 to 1930. It indicates in tabular form names of official posts and their occupants for this period.

263. Nihon shinshiroku 日 本 紳 士 錄 (Who's who in Japan), Tōkyō, Kōjunsha, 1889—. Annual
Covers about 13,000 prominent Japanese and foreigners living in the chief metropolitan centers of Japan. Selection is based on amount of taxes paid. There are separate lists of highest local taxpayers, members of chambers of commerce, etc. An issue came out in 1950.

264. Igarashi Eikichi 五 十 嵐 榮 吉, Taishō jimmei jiten 大 正 人 名 辞 典 (Biographical dictionary of the Taishō era [1912-26]), Tōkyō, Tōyō Shimpōsha, 1914, 38+1868+126 pp.

265. Taishū jinjiroku 大 衆 人 事 錄 (The popular who's who), Tōkyō, Teikoku Himitsu Tanteisha, No. 13 (1940), 5 v.
A biennial who's who of very wide coverage. Entries are listed by area within Japan. In the 1940 edition each volume deals with one major geographical region. There is a separate index for each volume.

3. Genealogies

Genealogical collections are of primary use only in certain specialized instances. But since most works of this nature offer considerably more than bare genealogical tables, they can be used as well for the general information they contain on the histories of families and their various branches. Of the works listed below Ōta Akira's two works entitled Seishi kakei daijiten (Dictionary of surnames and genealogies) and Keizu to keifu (Genealogy) (Entries 271 and 267) are most satisfactory. The first is a dictionary of genealogies with discussions of the origins and development of important surnames. The second is a general discussion of names, their origin, and their study. Besides such general collections it should be realized that Japanese historical literature contains detailed individual genealogies for nearly every historically important family.

266. Ishin Shiryō Hensankai 維 新 史 料 編 纂 会 (Society for the Compilation of Historical Materials Concerning the Restoration), Gendai kazoku fuyō 現 代 華 族 譜 要 (Genealogies of the contemporary nobility), Tōkyō, Nihon Shiseki Kyōkai, 1929, 720+73+31 pp.
A dictionary of genealogies of 957 Japanese noble families existing in 1928. Brief histories of each family are included along with genealogies. Tables listing the new and old peerage and indices of noble families by type of origin (kuge, buke, etc.).

267. Ōta Akira 太 田 亮, Keizu to keifu 系 図 と 系 譜 (Genealogy), Tōkyō, Sōgensha, 1941, 366 pp.
A general discussion of genealogical science in Japan by its foremost authority. Chapters deal with surnames and personal names, their origin and development; genealogies, their transmission and authenticity; and methodology.

268. Heki Shōichi 日 置 昌 一, Nihon keifu sōran 日 本 系 譜 綜 覧 (Collected tables of Japanese genealogies), Tōkyō, Kaizōsha, 1936, 984 pp.
A collection of genealogies classified under the following heads: Imperial family, courtiers, military families, Buddhist sects, chief scholarly schools, art and craft schools. There is a special chart of daimyō and their domains and of the confiscation of fiefs by the Tokugawa.

269. Numata Raisuke 沼 田 賴 輔, Nihon monshogaku 日 本 紋 章 学 (The study of Japanese heraldry), Tōkyō, Meiji Shoin, 1926.
A comprehensive study of the origin, meaning, and development of Japanese family crests by the foremost expert on the subject.

270. Araki Ryōzō 荒 木 良 造, Seimei no kenkyū 姓 名 の 研 究 (Study of names), Kyōto, Asada Bummeidō, 1929, 464 pp.
A study of Japanese surnames and personal names, their origins, and the complex problem of variant readings.

271. Ōta Akira 太 田 亮, Seishi kakei daijiten 姓 氏 家 系 大 辞 典 (Dictionary of surnames and genealogies), Tōkyō, Seishi Kakei Daijiten Kankōkai, 1934-36, 3 v.
The most complete treatment of Japanese families and their genealogies. The origin of families and their major branches is minutely discussed together with such matters as crests and genealogical tables. The same author has published a one-volume work entitled Seishi kakei jisho, Tōkyō, 1910.

272. Yabuki Masae 屋 葺 政 衛, Shūsei gokeifu kō 集 成 御 系 譜 考 (A study of collected Imperial genealogies), Tōkyō, Yabuki Masae, 1916, 4 v.
A detailed genealogical history of the Imperial family and its many branches and family connections. Volume 4 covers contemporary members of the family. The introduction to volume 1 contains an excellent list of genealogical sources.

e. Place Name Dictionaries, Atlases and Maps

The standard place name dictionary for historical use is Yoshida Togo's Dai Nihon chimei jiten (Dictionary of Japanese place names) (Entry 274). Heibonsha's Nihon chimei jiten (Japanese place name dictionary) (Entry 277) is of more recent date but its entries are generalized and contain little historical information. For the reading of current place names there exists Ogawa Takuji's Shi-chō-son-ōaza yomikata meii (Classified list of readings of the names of cities, towns, villages, and hamlets) (Entry 278).

The only adequate historical atlas of Japan is Yoshida and Ashida's Dai Nihon dokushi chizu (Historical atlas of Japan) (Entry 275), a work by now considerably dated. The historian will find, on the other hand, that the detailed contour 25,000:1 and 50,000:1 maps formerly prepared by the General Staff and now by the Geodetic Office of the Ministry of Construction (Kensetsushō, Chiri Chōsasho) (see Entry 273) are of use not alone to the geographer or the field worker. Because of their precise inclusion of detail, these maps indicate the location of a large number of historical remains, a feature which most other maps lack. Finally, it should be pointed out that reproductions of old maps are most likely to be located in the collections of local historical materials, some of which are listed in Part III, Chapter 2b2 and Part V, Chapter 3 of this work.

273. Kensetsushō Chiri Chōsasho 建設省地理調査所 (Ministry of Construction, Geodetic Office), Chikeizu 地形図 (Contour maps), Tōkyō, Chiri Chōsasho, 1949-51.
    Published in several series and constantly being revised, the currently available 25,000:1 series was revised in 1949, while the 50,000:1 series was revised in 1951. These maps are like our Coast and Geodetic Survey maps and provide contours and minute physical details. The 250,000:1 series lacks detail and is of limited value for historical purposes. Key maps are available for each series.

274. Yoshida Tōgo 吉田東伍, Dai Nihon chimei jiten 大日本地名辞典, (Dictionary of Japanese place names), Tōkyō, Fuzambō, 1922-23, rev. ed., 6 v.
    The most famous of the great place name dictionaries and of indispensable use to the historian. Arrangement of places is by geographical locality, but an index makes the work easy to use. This dictionary is especially known for the wealth of historical data given for the various places identified.

275. Yoshida Tōgo 吉田東伍 and Ashida Koreto 芦田伊人, Dai Nihon dokushi·chizu 大日本読史地図 (Historical atlas of Japan), Tōkyō, Fuzambō, 6th rev. ed., 1939, 4+4+27+141 pp.
    The only adequate historical atlas of Japan, its emphasis is primarily pre-Restoration. Sixty-six maps cover old political boundaries, campaign diagrams of major wars, trade routes, important cities, feudal holdings, etc.

276. Sawada Hisao 澤田久雄, Nihon chimei daijiten 日本地名大辞典 (Comprehensive dictionary of Japanese place names), Tōkyō, Nippon Shobō, 1939, 6 v.
    A standard place name dictionary arranged in syllabic order. It is of considerable value to the historian for its listing of minor places of historical interest such as shrines, temples, etc., under each larger locality. Of value also are the extensive quotations from historical sources.

277. Nihon chimei jiten 日本地名辞典 (Japanese place name dictionary), Tōkyō, Heibonsha, 1937, 6 v.
    A standard geographical dictionary for modern Japan and her possessions as of 1937.

278. Ogawa Takuji 小川琢治, Shi-chō-son-ōaza yomikata meii 市町村大字読方名彙 (Classified list of readings of the names of cities, towns, villages, and hamlets), Ōsaka and Tōkyō, Seizōdō, 1925, 403+5+43+2 pp.
    A useful postal guide showing characters and kana readings for contemporary Japanese place names down to the aza 字 level.

279. Fujita Motoharu 藤田元春, Shin Nihon zuchō 新日本図帖 (New atlas of Japan), Tōkyō, Tōkō Shoin, 1934.
    The handiest one-volume modern atlas of Japan. There are 34 colored topographical maps. Detail is excellent and easy to read. A separate kana index to names is provided together with a table of names which are considered difficult to read.

280. Tomimoto Tokijirō 富本時次郎, Teikoku chimei daijiten 帝国地名大辞典 (Great dictionary of place names in the Japanese empire), Tōkyō, Yūkan Seikadō, 1902, 4 v.
    An old but still useful place name dictionary. Its coverage of places of historical interest is especially good.

f. Law, Government, and Politics

The following entries represent but a small selection of reference dictionaries in the field of law, government, and politics. Of the general dictionaries of jurisprudence Iwanami's five-volume Hōritsugaku jiten (Dictionary of jurisprudence) (Entry 283) is most complete. It, however, does not cover the postwar period and hence should be supplemented by Suekawa's recent Hōgaku jiten (Entry 282). For more specialized reference works in this field the scholar is referred to Robert E. Ward's A Guide to Japanese Reference and Research Materials in the Field of Political Science.

281. Kawase Sohoku 河瀬蘇北, Atarashii seiji seido no jibiki 新しい政治制度の字引 (Dictionary of the new political system), Tōkyō, Jitsugyō no Nihonsha, 1924.
    Explains legal, social and political terms used in modern Japanese administrative organization and practice.

282. Suekawa Hiroshi 末川 博, Hōgaku jiten 法学辞典 (Dictionary of jurisprudence), Tōkyō, Nihon Hyōronsha, 1951, 1040 pp.
     The newest and one of the best of the general dictionaries of jurisprudence.

283. Suehiro Izutarō 末弘厳太郎 and Tanaka Kōtarō 田中耕太郎, Horitsugaku jiten 法律学辞典 (Dictionary of jurisprudence), Tōkyō, Iwanami Shoten, 1934-37, 5 v.
     One of the best of the general legal dictionaries, its coverage is primarily modern. It treats all major fields of law, both Japanese and Western.

284. Watanabe Manzō 渡辺万蔵, Hōritsu jisho 法律辞書 (Legal dictionary), Tōkyō, Hōritsu Jisho Kankōkai, 1926 (Supplements in 1928 and 1929).
     An excellent general dictionary of jurisprudence. Much of the work is given over to the explanation of Western legal terms and Japanese terms of foreign origin.

285. Noda Teruo 野田照夫, Hōritsu keizaigo jiten 法律経済語辞典 (Dictionary of legal and economic terms), Tōkyō, Hogaku Shoin, 1942, 190 pp.

286. Kobayashi Eisaburō 小林英三郎 and Uchino Sōji 内野壮兒, Kyōsanshugi jiten 共産主義辞典 (Dictionary of communism), Tōkyō, Nisshin Shoten, 1949, 342 pp.
     A semi-official publication of the Japanese Communist Party, it explains some 1600 Japanese and Western terms on communist social and political theory and gives biographical sketches of leading Japanese party members. A complete index is appended.

g. Economics and Economic History

     Two dictionaries prepared by Osaka University of Commerce and published by Iwanami Shoten dominate the field of general economics. The first, Keizaigaku jiten (Dictionary of economics) (Entry 289), is the more complete, though it devotes most of its space to non-Japanese subjects. The second, Keizaigaku shōjiten (Concise dictionary of economics) (Entry 290), is a product of the latest postwar scholarship and gives considerable coverage to Japanese economic history. For the field of economic history, however, the dictionary issued by the Kyoto University Institute of Japanese Economic History stands alone. This work, entitled Nihon keizaishi jiten (Dictionary of Japanese economic history) (Entry 291), is one of the historian's most useful tools because it deals extensively not only with the economic but the social and political history of Japan.

287. Keizai daijisho 経済大辞書 (Dictionary of economics), Tōkyō, Dōbunkan, 1910-16, 9 v.
     Part of the Dai Nihon hyakka jisho series. It covers the entire field of economics, drawing heavily on Western sources and theory. Sections on Japan are of limited use to the economic historian. A large number of indices make the work easy to use.

288. Minami Nobuyoshi 南信好, Eiwa hōsei keizai shōgyō jiten 英和法政経済商業辞典 (English-Japanese dictionary of legal, political, economic, and commercial terms), Tōkyō, Shun'yōdō, 1929, 558+918 pp.

289. Ōsaka Shōka Daigaku Keizai Kenkyūsho 大阪商科大学経済研究所 (Osaka University of Commerce, Institute for Economic Studies), Keizaigaku jiten 経済学辞典 (Dictionary of economics), Tōkyō, Iwanami Shoten, 1930, 6 v.
     The most complete of the general economic dictionaries, its emphasis is primarily modern and international and hence the coverage of Japan is limited. Articles covering major economic developments devote some space to events taking place in Japan, however. Volume 6 is an index to the set.

290. Ōsaka Shiritsu Daigaku Keizai Kenkyūsho 大阪市立大学経済研究所 (Osaka Municipal University, Institute for Economic Studies), Keizaigaku shōjiten 経済学小辞典 (Concise dictionary of economics), Tōkyō, Iwanami Shoten, 1951, 1264 pp.
     The best one-volume dictionary of economics and a product of the latest postwar scholarship. Emphasis is primarily modern and international. However, the coverage of Japanese economics and economic history is excellent for such a work.

291. Nihon Keizaishi Kenkyūsho 日本経済史研究所 (Institute of Japanese Economic History), Nihon keizaishi jiten 日本経済史辞典 (Dictionary of Japanese economic history), Tōkyō, Nihon Hyōronsha, 1940, 2 v. + separate index.
     The outstanding dictionary of Japanese economic history, compiled under the editorship of Honjō Eijirō. The work covers all aspects of Japanese economic life down into the Meiji period. Lengthy articles are included on major topics. All articles include a note on suggested reading. Coverage of the Tokugawa period is especially complete. Indispensable to the historian with a social science approach.

292. Satō Kanji 佐藤寛次, Nōgyō daijiten 農業大辞典 (Dictionary of agriculture), Tōkyō, Nihon Hyōronsha, 1934, 2 v.
     Largely a working dictionary for the modern Japanese agricultural technician. The emphasis of this work is on agriculture in general and not specifically on agriculture in Japan. It includes, however, a number of useful articles on Japanese terms and problems.

293. Ōno Shirō 大野史郎, Nōgyō jibutsu kigen shūsei 農業事物起源集成 (A compendium of agricultural terms and their origins), Tōkyō, Maruyamasha, 1935, 594 pp.

h. Ethnology, Sociology and Social Science

The fields of folklore studies and abstract sociology are well advanced in Japan. As elsewhere, however, pursuit of the social sciences as "sciences" has been a recent development. Prewar dictionaries in this group of fields tend either to concern themselves with folkloristic details and abstract sociology or to deal with general social problems and theories in the fashion of the Encyclopedia of the Social Sciences. Dictionaries of the latter type give relatively little coverage to Japan and draw heavily on Western sources.

Since the war several excellent dictionaries in the fields of Japanese ethnology and sociology have made their appearance. A general dictionary of excellent scholarly caliber is the Nihon shakai minzoku jiten (Dictionary of Japanese sociology and ethnology) (Entry 299). This work covers a wide variety of subjects in the fields of sociology, politics, economics, custom, art, religion and folklore. Emphasis is strongly historical. Strictly folkloristic and ethnological in coverage is the Minzokugaku jiten (Dictionary of folklore) (Entry 295). Nevertheless, this work is of importance to the historian for its detailed treatment of the history of family and social institutions in Japan. For the field worker, the series of folk vocabularies published by Yanagida Kunio (Entry 294) represent a most valuable tool. These vocabularies are not of much help, however, in reading local historical documents.

294. Yanagida Kunio 柳田国男, Bunrui nōson goi 分類農村語彙 (Classified vocabularies of agricultural villages), Tōkyō, Tōyōdō, 1948, 2 v.
    One of the series of vocabularies by the same author. In addition to these two volumes the series consists of the following 11 works:

    1. Village vocabularies:

        Bunrui sanson goi   分類山村語彙   (mountain villages)
        Bunrui gyoson goi   分類漁村語彙   (fishing villages)

    2. Customs:

        Fukusō shūzoku goi   服装習俗語彙   (clothing)
        Kinki shūzoku goi   禁忌習俗語彙   (taboos)
        Kon'in shūzoku goi   婚姻習俗語彙   (marriage)
        Minjū shūzoku goi   民住習俗語彙   (dwellings)
        San'iku shūzoku goi   産育習俗語彙   (child birth and child raising)
        Saiji shūzoku goi   歳時習俗語彙   (yearly observances)
        Zokusei shūzoku goi   族制習俗語彙   (family system)

295. Minzokugaku Kenkyūsho 民族学研究所 (Institute of Ethnology), Minzokugaku jiten 民族学辞典 (Dictionary of folklore), Tōkyō, Tōkyōdō, 1951, 714 pp.
    Primarily concerned with Japan, this dictionary provides an excellent reference to ethnological terms as applied to Japan. The work covers such matters as customs, festivals, mythology, folklore, house types, social patterns, family organization, and many other similar matters. Articles generally include a note on suggested reading. This work may be thought of as bringing together in convenient form the great mass of data on Japanese life and customs collected by Yanagida Kunio and his school.

296. Nakayama Tarō 中山太郎, Nihon minzokugaku jiten 日本民俗学辞典 (Dictionary of Japanese ethnology), Tōkyō, Shōwa Shobō, 1933, 921 pp.
    An early and now somewhat outdated work coming out of Professor Nakayama's school of folklore studies, now superseded by the publication of the Minzokugaku Kenkyūsho (Entry 295) and the Nihon Minzokugaku Kyōkai (Entry 299).

297. Ono Takeo 小野武夫, Nihon Nōminshi goi 日本農民史語彙 (A glossary of terms related to the history of the Japanese peasantry), Tōkyō, Kaizōsha, 1926, 465+8 pp.
    Arranged in syllabic order. Each entry is followed by quotations from sources which indicate the meaning of the term or the particular use of a given agricultural implement.

298. Keizai Zasshisha 經濟雜誌社, Nihon shakai jii 日本社会辞彙 (Encyclopedia of Japanese society), Tōkyō, Keizai Zasshisha, 1907-08, 3v.
    Edited by Taguchi Ukichi, this work is by now seriously outdated. It remains, however, one of the few works specifically concerned with Japanese social affairs. It is of special interest to the historian for its treatment of pre-Meiji government, law, economics, social patterns, customs, religion, and a variety of other subjects. Volume 3 is an index.

299. Nihon Minzokugaku Kyōkai 日本民族学協会 (Japanese Ethnological Association), Nihon shakai minzoku jiten 日本社会民俗辞典 (Dictionary of Japanese sociology and ethnology), Tōkyō, Seibundō Shinkōsha, 1952—, 3 v.
    Because of its broad coverage of social, political, economic, religious, and folkloristic problems, this dictionary, when complete, will be an indispensable tool for the historian. Contributing scholars represent the best in their respective postwar fields. Articles generally offer notes on suggested reading.

300. Ono Takeo 小野武夫 , Nōson mondai jiten 農村問題辞典 (Dictionary of agricultural village problems), Tōkyō, Hibonkaku, 1934.

301. Shimmei Masamichi 新明正道 , Shakaigaku jiten 社会学辞典 (Dictionary of sociology), Tōkyō, Kawade Shobō, 1944, 850 pp.
One of the best dictionaries of its kind giving broad coverage to the field of sociology. It is especially useful for its biographies and critiques of foremost Japanese sociologists and for the light it sheds on the development of sociology as a discipline in Japan.

302. Miki Kiyoshi 三木清 , Shakai kagaku shinjiten 社会科学新辞典 (New dictionary of the social sciences), Tōkyō, Kawade Shobō, 1941, 457 pp.
Written as a general reference work for the social sciences, this work gives only incidental coverage to Japan. It is nonetheless useful as a guide to the development of social science thinking in prewar Japan.

303. Shakai Shisōsha 社会思想社, Shakai kagaku daijiten 社会科学大辞典 (Dictionary of the social sciences), Tōkyō, Kaizōsha, 1932, rev. ed., 26+1269+131 pp.
An excellent work for its type giving broad coverage to terms related to modern social and political movements, social problems, and social philosophy. Emphasis is universal rather than specifically Japanese. There is a detailed subject index and an index of Western names and phrases.

304. Sugimori Kōjirō 杉森孝次郎, Shakai kagaku jiten 社会科学辞典 (Dictionary of sociology), Tōkyō, Shakai Shisō Kenkyūsho, 1929, 907 pp.
A general reference to terms and expressions relating to social problems, social movements, education, social theory, and the like.

305. Takahata Motoyuki 髙畠素之 , Shakai mondai jiten 社会問題辞典 (Dictionary of social problems), Tōkyō, Shinchōsa, 1925, 755 pp.
A dictionary giving wide coverage to terms and developments relating to modern political, social, and economic movements and problems.

306. Tadokoro Teruaki 田所輝明 , Shakai undō jiten 社会運動辞典 (Dictionary of social movements), Tōkyō, Hakuyōsha, 1928, 487 pp.

i. Philosophy and Religion

1) General

    General dictionaries of philosophy and religion published in Japan deal mostly with Western intellectual systems. The historian specifically interested in Eastern philosophies or religions will therefore have to turn to more specialized works than those listed below. The following works are mentioned, however, as having some limited value to the intellectual historian.

307. Iwanami tetsugaku jiten 岩波哲学辞典 (Iwanami's dictionary of philosophy), Tōkyō, Iwanami Shoten, rev. ed., 1930, 1015+5+5+104+88 pp.
The best of the general dictionaries of philosophy and religion, its coverage is heavily slanted in the direction of Western subjects. There is a romanized index of Japanese subjects, a Western language index, and a Sanskrit index.

308. Miki Kiyoshi 三木清 , Gendai tetsugaku jiten 現代哲学辞典 (Dictionary of contemporary philosophy), Tōkyō, Nihon Hyōronsha, 1936, 535+73 pp.
Treats contemporary philosophical problems in a series of lengthy articles. Each article gives a list of recommended reading.

309. Kido Mantarō 城戸幡太郎, Kyōikugaku jiten 教育学辞典 (A dictionary of education), Tōkyō, Iwanami Shoten, 1939, 5 v.
Affords a very broad coverage of education in Japan, China, and the West. Considerable space is devoted to Japan. Volume 5 contains a number of useful tables which arrange the entries in the first four volumes in subject sequences so as to provide running histories of education and educational institutions. There is a subject and personal name index.

310. Nihon Shūkyō Remmei 日本宗教聯盟, Mombushō, Shūkyō Kenkyūkai 文部省宗教研究会, and Jiji Tsūshinsha 時事通信社, Shūkyō benran 宗教便覧 (Handbook of religion), Tōkyō, Jiji Tsūshinsha, 1948, 496 pp.
An extremely useful handbook of religious matters in contemporary Japan. The work is divided into four parts as follows: 1) histories and general descriptions of the religious sects still active in Japan; these include Shinto, Buddhist, and Christian sects; 2) the current status of the above-mentioned sects, their activities, and associated institutions; 3) the contemporary religious world; religious problems; 4) bibliographies of writings of and about the active religious sects; tables, statistics, and chronologies.

2) Shinto

    The following works should be of help to the historian who confronts Shinto names and problems of doctrine in his research. For Shinto in pre-Meiji Japan the Heibonsha Shintō daijiten (Dictionary of Shinto) (Entry 315) is perhaps most generally useful. For the more modern period Ogura Kenji's Kokutai jingi jiten (Dictionary of national polity and Shinto deities) (Entry 313) is of particular value.

311. Sugimori Kichiji 椙 杜 吉 次 , Dai Nihon jimmei jisho 大 日 本 神 名 辞 書 (A dictionary of the names of Japanese deities), Tōkyō, Ganshōdō, rev. ed., 1926.
    This work provides explanations of the numerous names in the Shinto pantheon. Sources from which information was taken are indicated. The work was compiled by members of the Meiji Jinja Shiryō Hensansho (Meiji Shrine Historiographical Office).

312. Yamakawa Uichi 山 川 鵜 市 , Jingi jiten 神 祇 辞 典 (Dictionary of Shinto), Tōkyō, Heibonsha, 1924, 15+828+2 pp.
    A general dictionary of Shinto covering a wide variety of subjects such as deities, shrines, festivals, etc. There are two indices, one a kana index, the other a character index by number of strokes. This second index is extremely useful since it provides a method of arriving at the kana reading of obscure Shinto names.

313. Ogura Kenji 小 倉 鏗 爾 , Kokutai jingi jiten 国 体 神 祇 辞 典 (A dictionary of national polity and Shinto deities), Tōkyō Kinseisha, 1940, 142+1656 pp.
    A most valuable work which brings together the writings of prominent Tokugawa and contemporary scholars on a wide variety of subjects involving national polity and Shinto. Under each entry extensive passages are quoted from a large number of sources, so as to provide a well-balanced treatment of the subject. There is an index.

314. Fujimoto Kōzaburō 藤 本 弘 三 郎 and others, Nihon shaji taikan 日 本 社 寺 大 観 (Catalogue of Japanese temples and shrines), Kyōto, Hinode Shimbunsha, 1933, 2v.
    Volume 1 is devoted to shrines and contains a useful preface on the general subject. Shrine names are arranged geographically. Entries give a brief note on the history of each shrine and the related institutions. There is a catalogue by shrine rank and a general index. Volume 2 gives the same coverage to Buddhist temples.

315. Shintō daijiten 神 道 大 辞 典 (Dictionary of Shinto), Tōkyō, Heibonsha, 2nd ed., 1937-40, 3 v.
    The best and most modern dictionary of Shinto. It covers all aspects of the subject, deities, shrines, ceremonies, terms, etc.

3) Buddhism

    The field of Buddhist studies is one of the best supplied with reference aids. Undoubtedly the general historian will find Mochizuki's Bukkyō daijiten (Dictionary of Buddhism) (Entry 317) and Ono Gemmyō's Bussho kaisetsu daijiten (Dictionary of Buddhist books with explanations) (Entry 175) sufficient for most purposes. Beyond these two works a host of more specialized aids exists. Every major sect has its own dictionary which may be consulted when the general dictionaries fail to provide the answer to a specific problem. Although somewhat outdated, Rosenberg's Bukkyō kenkyū meijishū (Introduction to the study of Buddhism, vocabulary) (Entry 320) is an aid in locating entries in these more obscure dictionaries. The student of literary history will find Kawakami's Yōbun shōroku Daizōkyō sakuin (Phrase index of the Buddhist Tripitaka) (Entry 325) of special value. This work provides an excellent means of tracing the origins of Buddhist phrases which appear in literary texts.

316. Ryūkoku Daigaku 龍 谷 大 学 (Ryūkoku University), Bukkyō daijii 佛 教 大 辞 彙 (Dictionary of Buddhism), Tōkyō, Fuzambō, rev. ed., 1935-36, 6 v.
    One of the most useful of the Buddhist dictionaries, heavily slanted toward the Shin sect. It covers such general subjects as Buddhist terms and doctrines, history of sects, biographies of priests and nuns, iconography, and ceremonial. There are many excellent illustrations. Unfortunately, there is no index. This work was originally published between 1914 and 1922.

317. Mochizuku Shinkō 望 月 信 亨 , Bukkyō daijiten 佛 教 大 辞 典 (Dictionary of Buddhism), Tōkyō, Bukkyō Daijiten Hakkōsho, 1931-36, 6 v.
    The latest and most scientific of the general Buddhist dictionaries, it is undoubtedly the single most satisfactory work of its kind and largely replaces the earlier Fuzambō dictionary (Entry 316). Articles are clearly written and in most cases list recommended reading. Each entry is followed by its romanization. The work is profusely illustrated. Volume 6 is composed of maps and Sanskrit, Pali, and character indices.

318. Oda Tokunō 織 田 得 能 , Bukkyō daijiten 佛 教 大 辞 典 (Dictionary of Buddhism), Tōkyō, Ōkura Shoten, rev. ed., 1927, 1 v.
    The best one-volume work, it actually has more entries than Mochizuki's dictionary (Entry 317). Explanatory articles are short but clear and in most cases indicate sources. There is an index.

319. Ui Hakuji 宇 井 伯 壽 , Bukkyō jiten 佛 教 辞 典 (Dictionary of Buddhism), Tōkyō, Daitō Shuppansha, 1938, 1874+118 pp.
    A convenient one-volume dictionary with a large number of entries. Definitions are simply written.

320. Rosenberg, O., Bukkyō kenkyū meijishū 佛 教 研 究 名 辞 集 (Introduction to the study of Buddhism, vocabulary), Petrograd, Faculty of Oriental Languages, Imperial University of Petrograd, 1916, 11+527+4+17 pp.
    A useful though somewhat outdated work which provides a combined index to some 150 dictionaries and collections dealing with Buddhism in Japanese and Western languages. It thus provides a means of arriving at definitions of obscure Buddhist terms not found in the general dictionaries. Indices provide useful information on Sanskrit equivalents to Chinese terms, Chinese readings, and Japanese readings.

321. <u>Dai Nihon jiin sōran</u> 大 日 本 寺 院 總 覽 (A dictionary of Buddhist temples in Japan), Tōkyō, Meiji Shuppansha, 1916, 2+722 pp.
Locates and gives the historical background for all Buddhist institutions in Japan.

322. Tomita Gakujun 富 田 敦 純, <u>Himitsu jirin</u> 秘 密 辞 林 (Dictionary of esoteric Buddhism), Tōkyō, Kaji Sekai Shisha, 1911, 1134 pp.
A dictionary of esoteric Buddhism with emphasis on Tendai.

323. Shishiō Bunko Hensambu 獅 子 王 文 庫 編 纂 部, <u>Honge seiten daijirin</u> 本 化 聖 典 大 辞 林 (A comprehensive dictionary of Honge scriptures), Tōkyō, Shishiō Bunko, 1918-23, 4 v.
A specialized dictionary covering the doctrine and organization of the Nichiren sect. The chief editor was Tanaka Chigaku 田 中 智 学.

324. Mikkyō Jiten Hensankai 密 敎 辞 典 編 纂 会 (Esoteric Buddhist Dictionary Compilation Society), <u>Mik-kyō daijiten</u> 密 敎 大 辞 典 (Dictionary of esoteric Buddhism), Kyōto, Mikkyō Jiten Hensankai, 1931-33, 3 v.
Compiled by the faculty of the Tōji seminary, this work covers the special field of esoteric Buddhism with emphasis on Shingon. Entries are in syllabic order and treat such matters as doctrine, sutras, mandala, ceremonies, regulations, and the lives of important priests. Volume 3 consists of indices.

325. Kawakami Kozan 川 上 孤 山, <u>Yobun shōroku Daizōkyō sakuin</u> 要 文 抄 錄 大 藏 經 索 引 (Phrase index of the Buddhist Tripitaka), Tōkyō, Daizōkyō Sakuin Kankōkai, 1927, 4 v.
A monumental phrase index to the Tripitaka and many other Buddhist writings. Phrases are classified under subject categories which are sometimes hard to anticipate. The location of each quotation is given. Thus this work is an excellent tool for determining the origin of phrases appearing in literary texts.

326. Yamada Kōdō 山 田 孝 道, <u>Zenshū jiten</u> 禪 宗 辞 典 (Dictionary of Zen Buddhism), Tōkyō, Kōyūkan, 1915, 1145 pp.
Covers doctrines, terms, expressions, ceremonies, priests, temples, and literature for the field of Zen Buddhism.

j. Literature

The historian will find that for reference works in the field of literature he will need little more than Fujimura Saku's <u>Nihon bungaku daijiten</u> (Dictionary of Japanese literature), now thoroughly enlarged and revised (Entry 331). While this work should be sufficient for all general needs, a number of other more specialized aids may also be found useful. Numazawa Tatsuo's <u>Nihon bungakushi hyōran</u> (Tables for the study of Japanese literary history) (Entry 329), though now somewhat obsolete, can be of great help to the historian because of its convenient arrangement in tabular form of a great deal of information on literary and cultural history. The more recent Hanawa Shobō's <u>Bungaku benran: Nihon-hen</u> (Handbook of literature: Japan) (Entry 327) is also conveniently arranged to provide easy access to much specialized information.

327. <u>Bungaku benran: Nihon-hen</u> 文 学 便 覽 日 本 編 (Handbook of literature: Japan), Tōkyō, Hanawa Shobō, 1949.
A useful handbook crammed with much information. The following sections will be of special interest: 1) history of Japanese literature together with bibliographies of general and specialized studies of Japanese literary history; 2) an annotated bibliography of important literary works; 3) a glossary of terms; 4) a biographical section on important writers; 5) a chronology; and 6) an annotated bibliography of reference works for the study of Japanese literature.

328. Kindai Bungakusha 近 代 文 学 社 (Contemporary Literary Association), <u>Gendai Nihon bungaku jiten</u> 現 代 日 本 文 学 辞 典 (Dictionary of contemporary Japanese literature), Tōkyō, Kawade Shobō, 1949, 568+20 pp.
Covers Japanese literary works and writers from 1868 to 1945. Treatment is somewhat overly selective but several features recommend it as a guide to the contemporary literary scene. Of most use is the practice of providing extensive bibliographical citations after each article. There is a chronology and an author index as well as a title and subject matter index.

329. Numazawa Tatsuo 沼 澤 龍 雄, <u>Nihon bungakushi hyōran</u> 日 本 文 学 史 表 覽 (Tables for the study of Japanese literary history), Tōkyō, Meiji Shoin, 1934, 2v.
This work can be of great use to the historian once he has mastered the complicated arrangement. Volume 1 contains the following sections: 1) chronological tables of Japanese literature arranged in columns by genre, 2) tabular descriptions of customs, arts and crafts, and illustrations of ancient practices and usages, 3) a chronology of Japanese literature by periods, 4) a bibliography of Japanese secondary works on Japanese literature classified by genre, 5) an index to contents of lecture series (kōza) on Japanese literature, 6) a table of Western translations of Japanese literary works, 7) an index to literary series (sōsho) and collections both modern and ancient, 8) an index to works mentioned in volume 1. Volume 2 consists of the following folding charts: 1) an historical chronological table, 2) a chart of major literary schools with diagrammatic explanation of influences between them, 3) a chart of historical periods, and 4, 5) charts of the life span of major writers arranged by literary schools.

330. Shuzui Kenji 守 随 憲 治, Yamagishi Tokuhei 山岸 德平, and Imaizumi Tadayoshi 今 泉 忠 義, Nihon bungaku jiten: koten-hen 日 本 文 学 辞 典, 古 典 編 (Dictionary of Japanese literature: the classics), Tōkyō, Sōmeisha, 1950, 1027 pp.
> Largely an annotated bibliography of Japanese literary works from ancient times to 1868. Arrangement is by syllabic order.

331. Fujimura Saku 藤 村 作, Zōho kaitei Nihon bungaku daijiten 増 補 改 訂 日 本 文 学 大 辞 典 (Dictionary of Japanese literature, enlarged and revised), Tōkyō, Shinchōsha, 1950-52, 8 v.
> The single most important and satisfactory dictionary of Japanese literature giving extensive coverage of all Japanese literature and writers, ancient and modern. Literary works are described and criticized; writers are given full coverage and evaluation. Articles frequently include bibliographical citations. The work was revised after the war and volume 8 of the revised edition contains over a thousand new items. Volume 7 is an index.

k. Fine Arts and Crafts

While the field of fine arts and crafts is rather specialized, the general cultural historian will wish to have at his disposal a minimum number of reference works on this subject. The following selected works will aid in the identification of artists' names, the history of master works and their present location, and the meaning of technical art terms. While a great many more general dictionaries of art have been published by the Japanese, these have been omitted because they deal largely with Western art and their usefulness to the student of Japanese history is limited.

332. Araki Tadashi 荒 木 矩, Dai Nihon shoga meika taikan 大 日 本 書 畫 名 家 大 鑑 (General survey of famous Japanese calligraphers and painters), Tōkyō, Dai Nihon Shoga Meika Taikan Kankōkai, 1934, 4 v.
> Volumes 1 and 2 of this series contain artists' biographies. Names are listed by number of stroke in the first character of the artist's art name. Volume 3 deals with seals and signatures. Volume 4 consists of indices: 1) an index to artists by surname, 2) an index of artists by variant art names, and 3) an index to signatures.

333. Ei-Wa insatsu shoshi hyakka jiten 英 和 印 刷 書 誌 百 科 辞 典 (English-Japanese dictionary of graphic art terms), Tōkyō, Nihon Insatsu Gakkai, 1943, 804 pp.

334. Shimizu Kōkyō 清 水 孝 敬, Kantei hiyaku tōkō tankō jiten 鑑 定 秘 譯 刀 工 鐔 工 辞 典 (A dictionary of swordsmiths and fitting makers together with a discourse on the evaluation of swords), Tōkyō, Taiyōdō, 1928.
> A standard reference work on the history and evaluation of swords and their fittings. The work contains biographies and lists of swordsmiths, articles on the history of swordmaking and on how to judge fine swords, tables of swords, swordsmiths' signatures, etc.

335. Noma Seiroku 野 間 清 六 and Tani Shin'ichi 谷 信 一, Nihon bijutsu jiten 日 本 美 術 辞 典 (Dictionary of Japanese art), Tōkyō, Tōkyōdō, 1952, 726 pp.

336. Nakamura Tatsutarō 中 村 達 太 郎, Nihon kenchiku jii 日 本 建 築 辞 彙 (Dictionary of Japanese architecture), Tōkyō, Maruzen Shuppan K.K., rev. ed., 1931, 1 v.
> A dictionary of technical architectural terms and techniques.

337. Yamato Kai 大 和 会, Nihon kobijutsu annai 日 本 古 美 術 案 内 (A guide to pre-modern Japanese art), Tōkyō, Heigo Shuppansha, 1931, 2 v.
> A useful handbook which provides information on the location of art objects in private and public collections. This work is especially valuable since much of the best of Japanese art is found in private collections or in scattered temples and monasteries.

338. Ikeda Tsunetarō 池 田 常 太 郎, Nihon shoga kottō daijiten 日 本 書 畫 骨 董 大 辞 典 (Dictionary of Japanese calligraphy, painting, and art objects), Tōkyō, Shūhōkaku, rev. and enl. ed., 1926, 2254 pp.
> A useful illustrated guide to artists and art objects, arranged as follows: 1) a character index to biographical references contained in the book; 2) calligraphic masterpieces chronologically arranged and described; biographies of calligraphers, 3) paintings and painters' biographies; 4) craft objects. There is no adequate index.

339. Nakamura Ryūsetsu 中 村 立 節, Sōsho daijiten 草 書 大 辞 典 (Dictionary of sōsho), Tōkyō, Ryūbunkan, 1913, 2 v.
> This dictionary gives facsimile examples of characters written by a large variety of Japanese and Chinese calligraphers. Arrangement is by character.

340. Ono Ken'ichirō 小 野 賢 一 郎, Tōki daijiten 陶 器 大 辞 典 (Dictionary of ceramics), Tōkyō, Fuzambō, 1934-36, 6 v.
> A standard illustrated dictionary of ceramics covering Japan, China, and the West. Volume 6 includes a supplement and indices.

3. CHRONOLOGIES

a. Comparative Lunar and Solar Calendars

   Chronologies (nempyō) are an extremely common form of reference work in Japan, doubtless because of the complexities of Oriental calendrical systems. All chronologies have as their basis a comparison by years of at least three methods of recording dates: 1) the Japanese lunar (kigen) system with year 1 set at 660 B.C., the mythical origin of the Japanese state; 2) the Chinese lunar system using the hexagenary cycles; and 3) the Western solar system. Such comparative tables are useful but must be used with care if the historian is to arrive at accurate date equivalents between Eastern and Western events. While most chronologies offer only a yearly concordance, a few specially constructed tables provide a day-to-day comparison between the solar and lunar calendars. The appearance recently of Tsuchihashi's Japanese chronological tables (Entry 342) supersedes the other works of this type listed below.

341. William Bramsen, "Japanese chronological tables, showing the date, according to the Julian or Gregorian calendar, of the first day of each Japanese month from Taikwa 1st year to Mei-ji 6th year (648 A.D. to 1873 A.D.) with an introductory essay on Japanese chronology and calendars," Transactions of the Asiatic Society of Japan, 37.3 (1910), 1-131.
   An easily available work by virtue of its publication by the Asiatic Society of Japan. It is now superseded by Tsuchihashi's tables (Entry 342).

342. Paul Yachita Tsuchihashi, Japanese chronological tables, Tōkyō, Sophia University Press, 1952, 128 pp.
   The latest and most accurate of the comparative tables of the lunar and solar calendars. This work supersedes the volumes by Bramsen (Entry 341) and Kanda (Entry 343) upon which it is based.

343. Kanda Shigeru 神田茂, Nendai taishō benran narabini in'yoreki taishōhyō 年代対照便覧並陰陽暦対照表 (Handbook of comparative regnal years and lunar and solar calendars), Tōkyō, Kokon Shoin, 1932, 1 v.

344. Morimoto Kakuzō 森本角藏, Nihon nengō taikan 日本年号大觀 (General study of Japanese era names), Tōkyō, Meguro Shoten, 1933, 850+3+16 pp.
   An extremely detailed study of the history, practice, and meaning of Japanese nengō (era names). The work explains the origin of the system in China, relationship between Chinese and Japanese practice, Japanese era name changes and their significance, and the actual procedure used in changing them.

345. Naimushō Chirikyoku 内務省地理局 (Ministry of Home Affairs, Geographical Office), Sansei sōran 三正綜覽 (Handbook of three chronologies), Tōkyō, Teito Shuppansha, 1932, 424 pp.
   This work compares in tabular form the Japanese and Chinese lunar calendar with the Western solar and Mohammedan calendars. While year equivalents can be told at a glance, equivalent days cannot be arrived at without some interpolation. Covers 214 B.C. to 1903. Japan adopted the solar system in 1872.

b. General Historical Chronologies

   Most chronologies, in addition to providing visual comparison between calendar systems, contain a great deal of other information in tabular form. Such works are of two types, the general chronology and specialized. General chronologies afford data on Japanese and Chinese regnal years and on the names and terms in office of chief ministers. They also list under each year a variety of significant events taking place in Japan and sometimes in China and the West. For most accurate coverage of pre-Restoration history, Tsuji Zennosuke's Dai Nihon nempyō (Japanese chronological table) (Entry 346) is recommended. This work also has a number of special features which are noted below. For post-Restoration Japan the Tōyō Keizai Kenkyūsho's Sakuin seiji keizai dainempyō (Chronology of politics and economics with index) (Entry 352) is outstanding.

346. Tsuji Zennosuke 辻善之助, Dai. Nihon nempyō 大日本年表 (Japanese chronological table), Tōkyō, Dai Nihon Shuppan K.K., 5th rev. ed., 1943, 390+84 pp.
   Perhaps the most useful to the historian of the numerous chronologies. Arrangement is similar to others in that the standard calendrical comparisons are made for each year. An added feature is the inclusion of information which makes it possible to compute the exact day-to-day equivalents between lunar and solar calendars. Information is given on emperors, court officials, shogun, feudal officials, and modern cabinets. In each case length of reign or office is indicated by lines to which beginning and terminal dates are affixed. Additional information includes chief events and deaths of prominent persons. For events up to 1868 code words indicate the source from which information was taken. This last feature provides a valuable guide to standard primary sources. There is no index.

347. Yashiro Kuniharu 八代国治, Hayakawa Junzaburō 早川純三郎, and Inobe Shigeo 井野辺茂雄, Daizōtei kokushi dainempyō 大増訂国史大年表 (Revised chronology of Japanese history), Tōkyō, Yoshikawa Kobunkan, 1936, 233 pp.
   A separate appendix to the Kokushi daijiten (Entry 229) by the same authors. Small but packed with information.

348. Sanseidō Henshūjo 三省堂編輯所 (Sanseidō Office of Compilation), Mohan saishin sekai nempyō 模範最新世界年表 (A model chronology of the world, recently compiled), Tōkyō, Sanseidō, 1934.
   A very popular chronology because of its conveniently small size. Its coverage and format is similar to the one by Ōmori and Takahashi (Entry 353).

349. Kiyohara Sadao 清原貞雄, Kaisen Nihon bunkashi nempyō 改撰日本文化史年表 (Revised chronology of Japanese cultural history), Tōkyō, Chūbunkan Shoten, rev. ed., 1931, 387+137+3+2+2+3 pp.
A chronological table divided vertically by years and horizontally according to subjects as follows: government, economics, religion, education, art and science, literature, and crafts. Coverage is to 1927. There is a useful index.

350. Heki Shōichi 日置昌一, Kokushi dainempyō 国史大年表 (Chronology of Japanese history), Tōkyō, Heibonsha, 1935-36, 7 v.
By far the most detailed of the numerous chronologies of Japanese history. Historical events are recorded in tabular form from the mythical origins of Japan to 1934. The usual comparison between Japanese, Chinese, and Western calendars is provided. Volumes 1-3 cover the period to 1868; volumes 4-6 the period from 1868 to 1934; volume 7 is a general index.

351. Kuroita Katsumi 黒板勝美, Kōtei kokushi kenkyū nempyō 更訂国史研究年表(Revised chronology for the study of Japanese history), Tōkyō, Iwanami Shoten, 1936, 13+227+61 pp.
One of the best known standard chronological tables, its listing of events is rather sketchy. There is a separate index for persons and one for events and places.

352. Tōyō Keizai Kenkyūsho 東洋經濟研究所 (Oriental Economic Research Institute), Sakuin seiji keizai dainempyō 索引政治經濟大年表 (Chronology of politics and economics with index), Tōkyō, Tōyō Keizai Shimpōsha, 1943, 2 v.
Invaluable to the student of post-Restoration history. Volume 1 is arranged as a standard chronology covering the period 1841 to 1943. Listing of events is extremely detailed. Volume 2 is an exhaustive index to the chronology proper. Appendices list events from 1941 through 1942 and provide tabular data on governmental officials, elections, etc.

353. Ōmori Kingorō 大森金五郎 and Takahashi Shōzō 高橋昇造, Zōho saishin Nihon rekishi nempyō 増補最新日本歴史年表(Revised latest chronology of Japanese history), Tōkyō, Sanseidō, rev. ed., 1939, 7+14+457+108+177 pp.
One of the most complete of the one-volume chronologies, it covers events up to 1933. Marginal and tabular notes provide the usual comparison between Eastern and Western calendars. Under each year the following information is given: reigning emperor, names of court ministers, dates of office, reigning shogun, chief shogunal officers (after 1868, identity of premier, cabinet ministers, chairmen of both houses of the diet, etc.). A series of appendices provide divine, imperial, and shogunal genealogies, tables showing composition of the Tokugawa rōjū (Councilors) and post-Restoration cabinets, etc. A great variety of indices by emperors, regnal years, subjects and ideographs makes for easy use.

c. Specialized Chronological Tables

The Japanese have prepared chronological tables for nearly every conceivable subject. A standard feature of many historical publications is an appended chronology. The following items have been selected to provide as great a variety of subject matter as possible.

354. Mochizuki Shinkō 望月信亨, Bukkyō dainempyō 佛教大年表(Chronological chart of Buddhism), Tōkyō, Mochizuki Hakase Kanreki Kinenkai, 1930, 450 pp.
This work serves as an appendix to Mochizuki's famous dictionary of Buddhism (Entry 317). Each page is divided into three parts listing Buddhist events in India, China, and Japan from Sakyamuni's birth to 1929. The section on Japan is most complete. Appendices list genealogies and charts of transmission of various doctrines and sects.

355. Okayama Taishi 岡山泰四, Dai Nihon senshi nempyō 大日本戰史年表 (Chronological table of Japanese military history), Tōkyō, Sankyō Shoin, 1941, 6+167 pp.

356. Saitō Shōzō 斉藤昌三, Gendai Nihon bungaku dainempyō 現代日本文学大年表 (A chronology of contemporary literature), Tōkyō, Kaizōsha, 1932.
An exhaustive chronological history of Japanese literature from 1868 to the time of writing. Over 33,000 literary works are mentioned together with a record of the major political and social events which formed a background for the works cited.

357. Yuasa Mitsutomo 湯淺光朝, Kaisetsu kagaku bunkashi nempyō 解説科学文化史年表 (An annotated chronology of the history of science), Tōkyō, Chūō Kōronsha, 1950, 250 pp.

358. Shirai Kōtarō 日井光太郎, Kaitei zōho Nihon hakubutsugaku nempyō 改訂増補日本博物学年表 (A chronological history of the study of natural history in Japan, revised and enlarged), Tōkyō, Ōokayama Shoten, 1934, 437 pp.

359. Shigakukai 史学会, Nempyō Nihonshi teiyō 年表日本史提要(A chronological manual of Japanese history), Tōkyō, Yamakawa Shuppansha, 1950, 165+30 pp.

360. Kobayashi Tsuyoshi 小林剛 and Fujita Tsuneyo 藤田經世, Nihon bijutsushi nempyō 日本美術史年表 (Chronological tables for the history of Japanese art), Tōkyō, Sōgensha, 1952, 398 pp.

361. Minamoto Toyomune 源 豊 宗, Nihon bijutsushi nempyō 日本美術史年表 (Chronology of the history of Japanese art), Tōkyō, Hoshino Shoten, 1940, 9+290+102 pp.
    Contains the usual comparative calendrical tables. Factual information is divided as follows: works, artists, events of importance to the art world, miscellaneous. There are appended charts and genealogies and a full index.

362. Akabori Matajirō 赤堀又次郎, Nihon bungakusha nempyō 日本文学者年表 (Chronological table of Japanese men of letters), Tōkyō, Musashino Shoin, rev. ed., 1926, 242 pp.
    Covers the period up to 1185, listing some 840 writers in order of their dates of death. Each entry contains a short biography with bibliographical references and a list of the author's major works. This work was first published in 1905 and is continued in the following entry.

363. Mori Kōzō 森 洽蔵, Nihon bungakusha nempyō zokuhen 日本文学者年表續篇 (Chronological table of Japanese men of letters, continued), Tōkyō, Dai Nihon Tosho K.K., 1919, 588 pp.
    This work continues the chronology begun by Akabori (see previous entry) and covers the period 1186 to 1882. A supplement brings the coverage up to 1911. Altogether some 1090 names are included.

364. Yamamoto Kunihiko 山本邦彦, Nihon Jugaku nempyō 日本儒学年表 (A chronological table of Japanese Confucian studies), Tōkyō, Hakubunkan, 1922, 449 pp.

365. Terajima Masashi 寺島征史, Nihon kagakushi nempyō 日本科学史年表 (Chronology of the history of science in Japan), Tōkyō, Kasumigaseki Shobō, 1942, 442+100 pp.
    Science is interpreted in extremely broad fashion to include economic and technological developments. There is an elaborate index. (See also the work by Yuasa Mitsutomo, Entry 194.)

366. Hashikawa Masashi 橋川正, Shinsen Nihon Bukkyō nempyō 新撰日本佛教史年表 (A new chronological chart of Japanese Buddhism), Tōkyō, Naigai Shuppan K.K., 1927, 464 pp.
    Covers events related to Buddhist sects, temples, priests, and writings in Japan from c. 700 to 1927.

367. Ōtsuki Nyoden 大槻如電, Shinsen yōgaku nempyō 新撰洋学年表 (A newly compiled chronology of Western learning in Japan), Tōkyō, Rikugokan; Ōsaka, Kaiseikan, 1927, 158+16 pp.
    A detailed chronological listing of events related to the history of Western learning in Japan. One column deals with political events, another with personalities. After 1788 one column is devoted to annotated bibliographical items.

368. Tochiuchi Sōjirō 栃内曽次郎, Zōho Yōjin Nihon tanken nempyō 増補洋人日本探險年表 (A chronology of Western explorations of Japan, revised), Tōkyō, Iwanami Shoten, 1934, 179 pp.

III. HISTORICAL SOURCES

The source materials of Japanese history can be found in three general locations. The vast majority, naturally, lies unknown or unused in storage places long forgotten or largely inaccessible. It is the work of professional Japanese historians and governmental or scholarly institutions to uncover such materials and prepare them for general use. The Western student of Japanese history will rarely need to concern himself with such undiscovered materials, and then only after a period of research in Japan proper. For this reason this guide does not attempt to cover the subject of locating new materials.

A second source of materials are the private or official archives or collections of manuscripts and old block printed books. Such collections are accessible to the Western scholar, and custodians generally permit the copying or microfilming of individual works. The scholar who wishes to pursue his subject fully will need to know the types and holdings of such collections, a task made particularly difficult because of the lack of any general guide to Japanese manuscript collections.

A third form in which historical sources exist is in modern printed collections. Fortunately, the Japanese have been prolific compilers of documentary and historical collections. Furthermore, adequate indices to these collections are available, so that the Western scholar may find his way to printed sources without much difficulty. Naturally such printed collections are limited in subject matter by the intentions of the editors and by the historiographical styles of the times in which they were printed. Thus many historical subjects in which the contemporary scholar is interested cannot be adequately studied by reference to collections published to date. On the other hand, it should be pointed out that even the Japanese have not made adequate use of many of the great printed collections of source materials which now exist.

1. ARCHIVES AND SPECIAL COLLECTIONS

Japan has no national archives comparable to those found in Europe. There exist, however, a large number of specialized collections of original or manuscript materials. Pre-modern collections of this type were created for the most part by the former court or feudal nobility or by ecclesiastical institutions. Long closed to all but privileged individuals, they have now been converted to public use or incorporated into one or another of the modern public libraries. Supplementing such traditional collections, a number of modern organizations are now engaged in collecting historical materials. Unfortunately, no adequate guide to these collections is available, and so the following information, though fragmentary and not strictly of a bibliographic nature, has been included.

While it is difficult to categorize the many special collections of historically important materials, it will be convenient to divide them into three general groups: 1) the so-called bunko or traditional libraries, 2) the monjo or traditional documentary collections, and 3) currently expanding collections. The first two categories are termed traditional in that they refer to collections which were brought together at some time in the past and hence are presently maintained in static form.   The specialist in Japanese history will wish to know the location of such collections together with their special features.   The following is a list of some of the best known traditional libraries.

Ashikaga Gakkō, Iseki Toshokan 足利学校, 遺蹟図書館 (Ashikaga City, Tochigi Prefecture). One of the oldest and most famous of the bunko, this collection has been preserved from the time it was patronized by the Ashikaga shogun.   It contains many works of the Kamakura and Ashikaga periods.

Hōsa Bunko 蓬左文庫 (Nagoya, Aichi), established by the first of the Owari daimyō, Tokugawa Yoshinao 德川義直 (1600-50).   This collection contains part of the Tokugawa Suruga Bunko 駿河文庫, a repository of many pre-seventeenth century books and manuscripts.

Jingū Bunko 神宮文庫 (Kuradayama, Mie), established in 1915 by the Jingūshichō (Department of Shrine Affairs).   This collection based upon earlier collections held by the Ise Shrine, is of special importance for the study of Japanese Shinto.

Kanazawa Bunko 金澤文庫 (Yokohama, Kanagawa), important for its collection of manuscripts dating from the thirteenth century.

Kunaichō Shoryōbu 宮内庁書陵部 (Imperial Household Ministry, Library Department).   Originally called the Zushoryō 図書寮, this collection was first established as a function of the imperial government in 701.   It was officially removed to Tokyo in 1884 where it remains the single most important repository of books and documents on the imperial family and the early imperial government.   Since the Restoration several significant additions have been made to the original collection.   These include the Seisokudō Bunko 捷息堂文庫 of the Mōri 毛利 family (daimyō of Tokuyama), the Shōheikō 昌平黌 library, and part of the Momijiyama Bunko 紅葉山文庫 of the Tokugawa shogunate.   The Momijiyama Bunko contains, in addition to copies of rare works held in the Ashikaga Gakkō and Kanazawa collections, a great deal of primary documentation on the Tokugawa shogunate.

Naikaku Bunko 内閣文庫 (Cabinet Library).   Located within the Imperial Palace, this collection was established in 1911 upon the foundation of the materials gathered by the Shūshikan 修史館, the historiographical office of the early Meiji government.   The collection includes most of the former Momijiyama Bunko 紅葉山文庫 of the Tokugawa shogunate, one of the most important repositories of primary source materials concerning the Tokugawa administration.   In addition it contains many original records of the Meiji period.

Nanki Bunko 南葵文庫. Originally the library of the Tokugawa daimyō of Kii, it is now deposited in the Library of the University of Tokyo.

Onkodō Bunko 温故堂文庫. The library of the famous nineteenth century bibliographer, Hanawa Hokiichi 塙保己一 (1746-1821).   This collection, which became the basis for Hanawa's monumental Gunsho ruijū 群書類従, is now held by the Ueno Public Library.

Seikadō Bunko 静嘉堂文庫 (Tokyo).   The library of the well known zaibatsu Iwasaki Yanosuke 岩崎彌之助, it contains numerous collections of famous Chinese and Japanese scholars such as Lin Shin-yüan 陸心源, Kariya Ekisai 狩谷掖齊, Yashiro Kōken 屋代弘賢, and Ban Nobutomo 伴信友.

Shōkōkan Bunko 彰考館文庫 (Mito, Ibaragi).   The library of the Mito branch of the Tokugawa family, it was built up by Tokugawa Mitsukuni and his successors as the basis of their project for compiling the Dai Nihonshi 大日本史.

Sonkeikaku Bunko 尊經閣文庫 (Meguro, Tokyo).   A great collection of old and rare books and manuscripts built up during the Tokugawa period by the Maeda family, daimyō of Kaga.

Tōyō Bunko 東洋文庫 (Komagome, Tokyo).   The library of Iwasaki Kyuya 岩崎久彌, it is built around the Asiatic Library of George Ernest Morrison.   Though it contains many works of interest to the student of Japanese history, its chief attraction is to the orientalist.

Yōmei Bunko 陽明文庫 (Kyōto).   A collection of tenth century diaries and documents produced by the Kyoto court nobility.

While the above libraries contain a great deal of historically important material, they are not primarily repositories of records and documents.   Raw documentary collections are naturally less accessible and more scattered.   Since Japan has so long been politically decentralized, documentary records are found dispersed among a large number of temples and monasteries or in the possession of descendants of the court or feudal nobility.   Such collections of monjo are constantly being made public, however, and an increasing number are being gathered into central collections or being edited and published.   For the period before the seventeenth century published collections should be sufficient for nearly all purposes.   The remaining documents of this early period are relatively few and hence the percentage published is high.

Documentation for the post-seventeenth century period is a vastly more complicated problem, since so many records remain and so few have been made available in printed editions.   Monjo collections for the Tokugawa period are mostly of two types: daimyō records and village records.   Both types have been comparatively neglected until recently when interest in local history has encouraged many civic or educational organizations to collect and preserve documents concerning their regional heritage. A list of such collections would be out of place in this general guide. Instead, it should be pointed out that documents of the above type are now finding their way to a number of centrally located archival libraries which should be utilized as the starting point of any search for the raw materials of Tokugawa and Restoration history. The following four such libraries are outstanding.

Kenseishi Shiryōshitsu 憲政史資料室 (Archives on constitutional history) in the National Diet Library, Tokyo. A special library engaged in collecting original manuscripts by men of the Restoration period.

Nihon Jōmin Bunka Kenkyūsho 日本常民文化研究所 (Institute for the Study of the Culture of the Common People), Tokyo. This institute, now incorporated into the Fisheries Section of the Ministry of Agriculture and Forestry (Nōrinshō, Suisanchō 農林省水産庁), has taken over the functions of the former Attic Museum (Achikku Myūzeamu アチック・ミューゼアム) established by Shibusawa Keizō 澁澤 敬三. The institute is engaged in the collection, by purchase or by copy, and publication of documents concerning Japan's fishing population. Most of the documents are of the Tokugawa period.

Shiryō Hensansho 史料編纂所 (Historiographical Institute), Tokyo University. This institute stands at the head of historiographical scholarship in Japan. It was established in 1888 as a function of the Tokyo Imperial University (now University of Tokyo) and at that time took over the functions of the Historiographical Section in the Cabinet Bureau. In 1890 it inherited the functions of the Local History Office of the Home Ministry. In 1907 it took over from the Foreign Office the Bakumatsu gaikoku kankei monjo 幕末外国関係文書 (Documents concerning foreign relations at the end of the shogunate) and in 1949 the Ishin shiryō 維新史料 (Restoration documents) from the Ministry of Education. The institute is actively engaged in the collection by purchase or by copy of materials covering all periods of Japanese history. Materials so collected have been the basis of much of the historical research of members of the Tokyo University Department of History. Since 1951 the institute has been formally organized as a research center. The Shiryō Hensansho is engaged in the publication of the following basic documentary series:

> Dai Nihon shiryō (see Entry 382)
> Dai Nihon komonjo (see Entry 380)
> Dai Nihon kokiroku
> Dai Nihon Ishin shiryō (see Entry 379)

Shiryōkan 史料館 (Archives), Tokyo. Now under the supervision of the Ministry of Education, this institution is engaged in collecting daimyō and village documents of the Tokugawa period. Founded on the manuscript collection of the old Mitsui Bunko 三井文庫 (Mitsui Library), it contains much basic material for the study of the merchant class in Tokugawa Japan.

The scholar who would inquire more fully into the history of Japanese library collections is referred to the following list of books on the subject.

369. Mori Junzaburō 森潤三郎, Momijiyama Bunko to Shomotsu Bugyō 紅葉山文庫と書物奉行 (The Momijiyama Library and the Commissioner of Books), Tōkyō, Shōwa Shobō, 1943, 800 pp.

370. Ono Noriaki 小野則秋, Nihon bunkoshi kenkyū 日本文庫史研究 (A study of the history of Japanese libraries), Kyōto, Daigadō, 1944, vol. 1 of 2, 5+6+714 pp.
 Volume 2 seems not to have been completed. Volume 1 is a detailed discussion of pre-seventeenth century libraries and book collections. The work by Takebayashi Kumahiko (Entry 374) continues the treatment of this subject into the modern period.

371. Ono Noriaki 小野則秋, Nihon bunkoshi 日本文庫史 (History of Japanese libraries), Kyōto, Kyōiku Tosho K.K., 1942, 434 pp.
 A survey of a more general nature than Ono's book noted above.

372. Ono Noriaki 小野則秋, Nihon toshokanshi 日本図書館史 (History of Japanese libraries), Tōkyō, Ran Shobō, 1952, 329 pp.
 An authoritative survey of Japanese libraries and their historical development. Appendices provide a bibliography, chronology, and index.

373. Seki Yasushi 関靖, Kanazawa Bunko no kenkyū 金澤文庫の研究 (A study of the Kanazawa Library), Tōkyō, Kōdansha, 1951, 758 pp.

374. Takebayashi Kumahiko 竹林熊彦, Kinsei Nihon bunkoshi 近世日本文庫史 (A history of libraries in modern Japan), Kyōto, Daigadō, 1943, 436 pp.
 Covers libraries and collections in Japan from 1600 to 1912. It is especially useful for its discussion of the history of post-Restoration libraries and the collections which went into them.

375. Tōkyō Daigaku Shiryō Hensansho yōran 東京大学史料編纂所要覧 (The University of Tokyo Historiographical Institute), Tōkyō, Published by the Institute, 1952, 45 pp. + charts.
 A convenient summary of the publication and research program of the Historiographical Institute.

376. Tōyō Bunko 東洋文庫 (Oriental Library), Tōyō Bunko jūgonenshi 東洋文庫十五年史(Fifteen years of the Tōyō Bunko), Tōkyō, Tōyō Bunko, 1939, 883 pp.

2. PUBLISHED MATERIALS

While the Japanese have been somewhat remiss about the cataloguing of manuscript collections and providing public facilities for the utilization of these materials, they have been extremely active in the preparation of printed collections of primary and secondary historical sources. Since the Restoration, organizations, both national and local, have energetically published documentary materials drawn from the relatively inaccessible collections of special libraries and private archives. Through such printed collections, the historian is given a fairly complete documentary coverage of Japanese history up to approximately the beginning of the twentieth century.

Naturally these printed sources have their limitations. In the case of both local and national collections, material tends to be of a public nature concerning the government and upper classes. Documents which reveal the personal side of history or relate the affairs of the lower classes are largely neglected. Also the documentation of twentieth century Japanese history is seldom found in easily accessible printed series, but must be sought out by painstaking search.

Classification of Japanese historical materials presents certain problems. A number of precise terms have been devised by Japanese historians for the handling of written documentary sources. These are generically termed shiryō 史料 and are further subdivided into komonjo 古文書 (public documents and papers) and kiroku 記録 (private records). The great mass of historical materials which occur in published form are not of the above nature, however, and yield to no clear-cut categorization. Such materials, which the Japanese lump under the heading of shiryō 資料, contain documentation of the broadest type: records, personal documents, secondary sources, and even fictional works. Because of the mixed nature of most collections it has been found most practical to divide the following entries by subject rather than by the type of material contained in each collection.

In addition, certain limitations have of necessity been applied in the following choice of entries. For instance, the collected works of historical individuals which, especially if they contain letters or diaries, are of much importance in the reconstruction of Japanese history, have been omitted because of their great volume. Most collections of post-Meiji materials such as government documents, collected laws, letters, treaties and statistical literature have also been excluded. These have been partially covered in the bibliography of political science materials prepared for this series by Robert E. Ward and will be further dealt with in future bibliographies covering the several fields of modern Japanese studies. Within these limitations, this chapter contains a selective list of composite collections of historical materials with emphasis on pre-twentieth century Japanese history.

While collections such as those listed in this section are certainly the chief source of documentation used by the historian, it should be remembered that two important documentary sources are available in somewhat more accessible form. First are the archival encyclopedias such as the Koji ruien and the Kōbunko (Entries 207 and 206) which consist largely of quotations from primary sources. The other is the great mass of histories written in the Chinese tradition of extensive quotation. This category includes most of the histories of prefectures or cities compiled by local historical societies and the official histories of Japanese institutions compiled during the early Meiji era by government committees.

Entries in the following sections of this chapter have been arranged in alphabetical order of title, not by compiler or editor.

a. General Collections

The modern tradition of providing printed collections of important historical materials goes back to the mid-Tokugawa period to the blind bibliographer Hanawa Hokiichi 塙保己一(1746-1821). His great classified library of Japanese works entitled Gunsho ruijū (Classified collection of Japanese classics) (Entry 384) was completed in 1819 and was followed shortly after his death by a continuation (Zoku gunsho ruijū) (Entry 385). Hokiichi's son continued his father's work and began the Shiryō 史料 (Historical documents), a chronological collection of documents beginning with 887, the year in which the last of the Rikkokushi 六国史 (Six national histories) terminated. It was this project which became the basis of the work of the present Shiryō Hensansho (Historiographical Institute) of Tokyo University and its publication, the Dai Nihon shiryō (Japanese historical materials) (Entry 382). When finished, this vast collection will provide as completely as possible a day-to-day documentation of events in Japanese history from 887 to 1867. Two other serial publications of the Shiryō Hensansho are the Dai Nihon komonjo 大日本古文書 (Ancient documents of Japan) (Entry 380), in which are published documents grouped by institution or subject and the Dai Nihon Ishin shiryō 大日本維新史料 (Historical materials relating to the Japanese Restoration)(Entry 379), another chronologically arranged series of documents of a smaller chapter in Japanese history, the period from 1846 to 1871.

The above officially sponsored collections provide the most minute and comprehensive documentation of pre-modern Japanese history. Unfortunately, they are all far from complete; at the present rate of progress it will be many decades before they will approach completion. The historian will thus need to acquaint himself with several other general collections of documents and early historical sources. Of most direct use to the historian are: the Gunsho ruijū and its continuation mentioned above, which bring together several thousand works, generally of a secondary historical nature, from all periods of Japanese history; the Kokushi taikei (Compendium of Japanese history) (Entry 397), which provides the most reliable versions of standard pre-modern historical writings, such as diaries and official histories; the Shiryō taisei (Complete historical materials) (Entry 408), which collects historical diaries from the eleventh through fifteenth centuries; and the Shiseki shūran (Collection of historical works) (Entry 410), which complements the two works just listed by including a large number of lesser known works of historical importance from the fourteenth to the eighteenth centuries.

It is also essential to know of the activities of two publishing organizations which have been printing Japanese historical materials. First is the Kokusho Kankōkai (Society for the Publication of Japanese Texts), which has brought out over 260 volumes (see Entry 398) of pre-modern documentary collections, collected works, and miscellanies of historical importance. The other is the Nihon Shiseki Kyōkai (Association for Japanese Historical Works), which has printed some 183 volumes of materials of largely biographical nature, covering the late Tokugawa and Meiji Restoration periods (see Entry 403).

Other collections listed below are either more circumscribed in scope or are more literary in content. Of the latter type the zuihitsu, miscellany collections, need some comment. These series, such as the Nihon zuihitsu zenshū (Complete collection of Japanese miscellanies) (Entry 405), are of a definitely literary nature. They contain, nevertheless, a large number of historically useful materials.

377. Tsuboi Kumazō 坪 井 九 馬 ニ and Kusaka Hiroshi 日 下 寛 , Bunka Daigaku shishi sōsho 文 化 大 学 史 誌 叢書 (Series of historical materials held by the Tokyo Imperial University, Faculty of Letters), Tōkyō, Tōkyō Teikoku Daigaku, 1908, 27 v.
A collection of diaries and records of the court aristocracy, military families, temples, and shrines during the twelfth to sixteenth centuries. Each volume has a bibliographical introduction containing notes on the works contained in it. Commentaries explain the reading of difficult terms and phrases.

378. Kuroita Katsumi 黒 板 勝 美 and Shimomura Miyokichi 下 村 三四吉, Chōkomonjo 徴 古 文 書 (Selected historical documents), Tōkyō, Nihon Shūshikyoku, Shiryō Hensangakari, 1896-98, 2 v.
These are the only two completed volumes of a contemplated series of ten volumes of collected documents compiled by locality. Volume 1 covers the Kinai region and volume 2 the Tōkaidō. Within each volume documents are grouped by the family supplying them.

379. Tōkyō Daigaku Shiryō Hensansho 東 京 大 学 史 料 編 纂 所 , Dai Nihon Ishin shiryō 大 日 本 維 新 史 料 (Historical materials relating to the Japanese Restoration), Tōkyō, Shiryō Hensansho, 1938—.
The foremost collection of primary materials on domestic affairs during the Restoration period. It was formerly published by the Ishin Shiryō Hensan Jimukyoku, a group of scholars working within the Ministry of Education. Documents will eventually be assembled to cover the years 1846-71 and are being published in eight series as follows: 1) 1846-53, 2) 1854-57, 3) 1858-60, 4) 1861-63, 5) 1864, 6) 1865-67, 7) 1868, 8) 1869-July, 1871. Documents are chronologically arranged. Each volume of approximately 800 pages covers from three weeks to three months. Nineteen volumes have appeared by 1952. For a summary index to this material see the Ishin shiryō kōyo (Entry 13).

380. Tōkyō Daigaku Shiryō Hensansho 東 京 大 学 史 料 編 纂 所 (University of Tokyo Historiographical Institute), Dai Nihon komonjo 大 日 本 古 文 書 (Ancient documents of Japan), Tōkyō, Shiryō Hensansho, 1901—.
Companion publication to the Dai Nihon shiryō (Entry 382), this publication of the Historiographical Institute is comprised of three basic series. The Hennen monjo (Entry 381) contains materials of the eighth century. The Iewake monjo (Entry 416) is comprised of a number of collections of documents dealing with single institutions or famous families. The Jiken monjo (Documents concerning events) assembles documents related to some important historical period. In this series the Bakumatsu gaikoku kankei monjo (Official documents of the later Tokugawa era concerning foreign relations) (Entry 445) is currently being published. For fuller annotation of the Dai Nihon komonjo see under the three separate series referred to above.

381. Tōkyō Daigaku Shiryō Hensansho 東 京 大 学 史 料 編 纂 所 (University of Tokyo Historiographical Institute), Dai Nihon komonjo, hennen monjo 大 日 本 古 文 書. 編 年 文 書 (Ancient documents of Japan, chronological documents), Tōkyō, Shiryō Hensansho, 1901—.
A collection of basic primary documents of the eighth century, most of them from the famous Shōsōin repository. Documents are arranged chronologically. The first five volumes contain appended glossaries of archaic words found in the texts. Twenty-five volumes had been published by 1940.

382. Tōkyō Daigaku Shiryō Hensansho 東 京 大 学 史 料 編 纂 所 (University of Tokyo Historiographical Institute), Dai Nihon shiryō 大 日 本 史 料 (Japanese historical materials), Tōkyō, Shiryō Hensansho, 1901—.
Companion publication to the Dai Nihon komonjo (Entry 380), this is a monumental collection of primary material chronologically arranged. Beginning with the year 887, the last date covered by the last of the Rikkokushi (Six national histories), the work will eventually reach the year 1867. The compilers have divided the intervening period into 16 sections, and publication is continuing independently in the first 12 of these sections. By 1952 a total of 176 volumes had been published with the following distribution.

Section	Completed to:		Section	Completed to:	
	Volume	Date		Volume	Date
1(887-986)	11	967	8(1467-1508)	21	1488
2(986-1086)	8	1016	9(1508-1568)	7	1518
3(1086-1185)	10	1110	10(1568-1582)	7	1571
4(1185-1221)	16	1221	11(1582-1603)	8	1584
5(1221-1333)	13	1241	12(1603-1680)	34	1620
6(1333-1397)	29	1368	13-16(1680-1867)	not yet begun.	
7(1397-1466)	10	1415			

Each volume is over 900 pages in length. There is a complete table of contents at the front and marginal tabs point up the gist of important documents. There are numerous facsimile reproductions. Use of these materials is facilitated by a summary index, Shiryō sōran (Entry 48).

383. Dajōkan 太 政 官 , <u>Fukkoki</u> 復 古 記 (Records of the Restoration), Tōkyō, Naigaishoseki K.K., 1930-31, 15 v.

A basic collection of materials covering the single year from the tenth month of 1867 to the tenth month of 1868. It was compiled under the auspices of the old Dajōkan and completed in 1889 by the predecessor to the present Tokyo University Historiographical Institute. Volumes 1-8 comprise the chronological narrative of events during the crucial year of the Restoration. Volume 9 is a supplement, while volumes 10-14, entitled <u>Fukko gaiki</u> 復 古 外 記 (Further records of the Restoration), cover individual battles. Volume 15 contains a summary of the contents of the set and a full index.

384. Hanawa Hokiichi 塙 保 己 一 , <u>Gunsho ruijū</u> 群 書 類 従 (Classified collection of Japanese classics), Tōkyō, Keizai Zasshisha, 1897-1902, 19 v.

Originally completed in 1819 by the Tokugawa scholar Hanawa Hokiichi (1746-1821), this is a collection of over 1200 miscellaneous writings brought together from all over Japan. Materials are arranged under 25 headings including the following: Shinto deities, emperors, genealogies, biographies, official posts, law, government, literary works, poetry, narratives, diaries, travel accounts, battles, military houses, Buddhist affairs. The work is divided into 530 chapters (kan). The present printing is the most satisfactory modern edition, having been thoroughly edited by Kuroita Katsumi. Chinese passages are punctuated. Volume 1 is a detailed table of contents and index to titles of works. Most indexes to series and collections give detailed coverage to this work and its successors. A more recently edited edition was published in 1928-31 (Naigai Shoseki K.K., 18 v.). For a supplement to this collection see the next entry.

385. Hanawa Hokiichi 塙 保 己 一 , <u>Zoku gunsho ruiju</u> 續 群 書 類 従 (Classified collection of Japanese classics—second series), Tōkyō, Zoku Gunsho Ruijū Kanseikai, 1923-30, 72 v.

A supplement to the <u>Gunsho ruijū</u> (see previous entry) prepared after the death of Hanawa Hokiichi by his son Tadatomo (1807-62). This collection includes approximately 2300 items arranged under the same 25 headings and divided into 100 chapters. Volume 1 is an index to titles in both series.

386. Kosho Hozonkai 古 書 保 存 会 (Society for Preservation of Historical Works), <u>Zoku zoku gunsho ruijū</u> 續 々 群 書 類 従 (Classified collection of Japanese classics—third series), Tōkyō, Kosho Hozonkai, 1903-04, 5 v.

A collection of 16 historical works considered worthy of inclusion in the <u>Gunsho ruijū</u> series. This work should be distinguished from the much more voluminous one of the same title issued by the Kokusho Kankōkai (see next entry).

387. Kokusho Kankokai 国 書 刊 行 会 (Society for Publication of Japanese Texts), <u>Zoku zoku gunsho ruijū</u> 續 々 群 書 類 従 (Classified collection of Japanese classics—third series), Tokyo, Kokusho Kankōkai, 1906-09, 16 v.

Compiled by a group of scholars working for the Kokusho Kankōkai, this work contains over 300 items, largely of the early Tokugawa period, not included in the previous collections of the <u>Gunsho ruijū</u> series or in other similar collections. Material is arranged under 10 headings: Shinto deities, historical biography, records, laws and institutions, geography, education, religion, poetry, songs, miscellaneous. Each volume devotes its introductory pages to bibliographical notes on its contents.

388. Takeuchi Rizō 竹 内 理 三 , <u>Heian ibun</u> 平 安 遺 文 (Documents of the Heian period), Tōkyō, Tōkyōdō, 1947-.

The first of a multiple-volume series which proposes to publish over 4000 heretofore unpublished documents of the Heian period (794-1185). Volume 1 includes nearly 300 items chosen for their social, economic, or legal importance.

389. Takeuchi Rizō 竹 内 理 三 , <u>Nara ibun</u> 寧 樂 遺 文 (Remaining documents of the Nara period), Tōkyō, Tōkyōdō, 1943-44, 2 v.

A classified collection of basic documents of the Nara period (710-794). Documents deal with administration, census, taxation, religion, economics, slavery, military conscription, and literature. Short explanatory notes are appended.

390. Itō Hirobumi 伊 藤 博 文 , ed., <u>Hisho ruisan</u> 秘 書 類 纂 (Classified collection of secret documents), Tōkyō, Ruisan Kankōkai, 1933-36, 25 v.

A basic collection of documents drawn from government files covering all aspects of governmental activity during most of the Meiji period. Originally compiled under the editorship of Prince Itō, the present edition has been revised by Kurino Shin'ichirō and Hiratsuka Atsushi. The work brings together documents, texts and drafts of laws, plans, rescripts, ordinances, treaties, etc., under the following broad categories: Imperial household (2 v.), foreign affairs (3 v.), legal affairs (2 v.), governmental organization (1 v.), the Diet (2 v.), finance (3 v.), commerce and industry (1 v.), Formosa (1 v.), Korean affairs (3 v.), military affairs (1 v.), Sino-Japanese war (1 v.), the constitution (3 v.), miscellaneous (4 v.).

391. Yoshikawa Kōbunkan 吉 川 弘 文 館 , <u>Hyakke setsurin</u> 百 家 說 林 (Collected works of numerous authors), Tōkyō, Yoshikawa Kōbunkan, 1905-07, 7 v.

A collection of 87 miscellanies and treatises written by prominent scholars of the Tokugawa period. Subject matter is primarily limited to the period in which the authors lived, but there are a number of works of antiquarian and historical interest. Volume 7 consists of title and subject indices.

392. Kokusho Kankokai 国書刊行会 (Society for Publication of Japanese Texts), <u>Hyakke zuihitsu</u> 百家 随筆 (Collected miscellanies of numerous authors), Tōkyō, Kokusho Kankōkai, 1917, 3 v.
   Miscellaneous writings of 22 Confucian and Kokugaku scholars of the Tokugawa period covering a variety of antiquarian subjects.   The preface to the collection includes bibliographical notes on the contents.

393. Tanabe Katsuya 田邊勝哉, <u>Hyakke sōsetsu</u> 百家叢説 (Collected essays of numerous authors), Tokyo, Kokusho Shuppan Kyōkai, 1911-12, 3 v.
   Subtitled <u>Chinsho bunko</u> 珍書文庫 (Library of rare books), this collection includes essays on history, religion, literature, and thought by prominent scholars of the Tokugawa period.

394. Hashimoto Hiroshi 橋本博, <u>Ishin nisshi</u> 維新日誌 (Restoration diaries), Shizuoka, Shizuoka Kyōdo Kenkyūkai, 1932-35, 20 v.
   Published in 2 series.   Series I (10 v.) consists of the diary of the Dajōkan from 1868 to 1876.   Series II (10 v.) consists of a number of private diaries of the Restoration years plus documents on the Meiji Constitution.   The last volume contains bibliographic notes and an index.

395. Kichō Tosho Eihon Kankokai 貴重図書影本刊行会 (Society for Publication of Copies of Important Works), <u>Kichō Tosho Eihon Kankōsho</u> 貴重図書影本刊行会刊行書 (Published works of the Kichō Tosho Eihon Kankōkai), Kyōto, Kichō Tosho Eihon Kankōkai, 1930—, 14 v.
   Facsimile reproductions of rare manuscripts prepared for limited distribution.   Most of the works are of literary interest but some, such as the <u>Nagasaki kembunshi</u> (Record of visit to Nagasaki), will be of interest to the historian.   Detailed commentaries are provided.

396. Kurokawa Masamichi 黒川眞道 and Yano Tarō 矢野太郎, <u>Kokushi sōsho</u> 国史叢書 (Japanese historical series), Tōkyō, Kokūshi Kenkyukai, 1914-18, 51 v.
   A collection of 62 works written from the late Heian through the Tokugawa periods.   Volumes 1-36, edited by Kurokawa, consist primarily of military epics (i. e., <u>Gempei seisuiki</u>, <u>Soga monogatari</u>, etc.).   Volumes 37-51, edited by Yano, contain materials on local history and include the six volume <u>Ukiyo no arisama</u>.   Each volume contains a bibliographical preface.

397. Kuroita Katsumi 黒板勝美, <u>Shintei zōho kokushi taikei</u> 新訂増補国史大系 (Revised and supplemented compendium of Japanese history), Tōkyō, Yoshikawa Kōbunkan, 1929—.
   One of the most generally useful of the great collections of historical materials, this series provides collated and edited copies of the chief works used by modern Japanese historians in their study of pre-Restoration Japanese history.   This revised edition begun in 1929 combines two earlier series edited by Taguchi Ukichi entitled <u>Kokushi taikei</u> and <u>Zoku kokushi taikei</u> (Keizai zasshisha, 1897-1902, 32 v.) and adds other works from time to time. Fifty-eight volumes had been published by 1939.   The following are some of the important works included in this series: <u>Rikkokushi</u>, <u>Kojiki</u>, <u>Ruijū kokushi</u>, <u>Fusō ryakki</u>, <u>Eiga monogatari</u>, <u>Mizukagami</u>, <u>Ōkagami</u>, <u>Engishiki</u>, <u>Azuma kagami</u>, <u>Nochi kagami</u>, <u>Tokugawa jikki</u>, <u>Zoku Tokugawa jikki</u>, and <u>Kugyō bunin</u>.   All works are given an extensive bibliographical preface. There are no commentaries or indices, but individual pages are provided with numerous subject tabs to make easy the task of skimming works in search of subject matter.

398. <u>Kokusho Kankōkai sōsho</u> 国書刊行会叢書 (Kokusho Kankōkai series), Tōkyō, Kokusho Kankōkai, 1906-22, 260 v.
   The Kokusho Kankōkai (Society for the Publication of Japanese Texts) under the chairmanship of Count Okuma Shigenobu published a great quantity of useful historical texts.   Many of the individual titles in this series are themselves collections and are listed separately in this chapter.   Volumes were published in eight series with no special subject control for each series.   Aside from the collected works of numerous Tokugawa scholars, this series is a convenient source for printed texts of such works as <u>Zoku zoku gunsho ruijū</u>, <u>Shin gunsho ruijū</u>, <u>Tokugawa bungei ruijū</u>, <u>Kokon yōranko</u>, <u>Shiseki zassan</u>, <u>Jijitsu sōsho</u>, <u>Honchō tsugan</u>, and numerous smaller collections of bibliographies, genealogies, and literary works compiled by members of the society.   Most of the indices to collections and series listed in Part I, Chapter 2e cover the contents of this series.

399. Koten Hozonkai 古典保存会 (Society for Preservation of Classics), <u>Koten Hozonkai kankōsho</u> 古典保存会刊行書 (Publications of the Koten Hozonkai), Tōkyō, Koten Hozonkai, 1923—, 56 v.
   This is a series of de luxe collotype reproductions of manuscript copies of Japanese classics.   Works singled out for reproduction are generally rare manuscripts of well-known classics such as the <u>Tosa nikki</u>, <u>Hōjōki</u>, <u>Jōei shikimoku</u>, etc., though a few texts of greater historical interest are included.

400. Yoshino Sakuzō 吉野作造, <u>Meiji bunka zenshū</u> 明治文化全集 (Complete collection on Meiji culture), Tōkyō, Nihon Hyōronsha, 1928-30, 24 v.
   A comprehensive collection of documents and essays on all aspects of Meiji culture.   Each volume covers one subject and includes introductory notes, reprints of important documents, newspaper and magazine articles, and specialized articles by leading Japanese scholars.   A valuable source of documentation for the Meiji period.

401. Mitamura Engyo 三田村鳶魚, <u>Mikan zuihitsu hyakushu</u> 未刊随筆百種 (Collection of unpublished miscellanies), Tōkyō, Yoneyamadō, 1927-29, 23 v.
   Collected miscellaneous writings of authors chiefly of the Tokugawa period.   The collection is of interest primarily to the student of Tokugawa history and social conditions.   Each volume contains a bibliographical preface.   Volume 23 contains an index to titles of works.

402. Kyōto Daigaku Nihonshi Kenkyūkai 京都大学日本史研究会 (Kyoto University, Society for the Study of Japanese history), Nihonshi kenkyū shiryō 日本史研究資料 (Materials for the study of Japanese history), Tōkyō, Haneda Shobō, 1949—.
The first volume of a series of selected documents on Japanese history.

403. Nihon Shiseki Kyōkai 日本史籍協会 (Association for Japanese Historical Works), Nihon Shiseki Kyōkai kankōsho 日本史籍協会刊行書 (Books published by Nihon Shiseki Kyōkai), Tōkyō, Nihon Shiseki Kyōkai, 1915—, 183 v.
Primarily a collection of biographical materials on individuals prominent in the Meiji Restoration, this series constitutes a valuable source for the study of late Tokugawa and early Meiji history. Materials include diaries, correspondence, collected private documents, and the like.

404. Nihon zuihitsu taisei 日本随筆大成 (Collection of Japanese miscellanies), Tōkyō, Yoshikawa Kōbunkan, 1927-31, 37 v.
A collection of 108 miscellanies written by Tokugawa authors, some are duplicated by the Nihon zuihitsu zenshū series (see following entry). Useful primarily for commentaries which they provide on the life and thinking of the Tokugawa period. Publication was in three series of 11, 12, and 13 volumes each. Small print and the lack of furigana make this series less desirable to use than the following.

405. Kokumin Tosho Kabushiki Kaisha 国民図書株式会社, Nihon zuihitsu zenshū 日本随筆全集 (Complete collection of Japanese miscellanies), Tōkyō, Kokumin Tosho K.K., 1927-30, 20 v.
Contains over 90 miscellanies by Tokugawa writers. The subjects covered range from purely literary matters to antiquarian studies, Shinto studies, and observations of the life and affairs of the time. Useful primarily for the study of Tokugawa history. Each volume contains an excellent bibliographical preface. Printing is excellent and kana readings are provided in difficult spots. Volume 20 provides a subject index to the contents of the other volumes.

406. Nakayama Yasumasa 中山保誠, Shimbun shūsei Meiji hennenshi 新聞集成明治編年史 (Chronological history of the Meiji era compiled from newspapers), Tōkyō, 1935, 15 v.
An extremely valuable coverage of Meiji history as seen through contemporary newspapers. Detailed day-by-day accounts are given in the form of reprints of articles, editorials, cartoons, etc., from a large number of newspapers. The last volume contains a detailed subject and proper name index.

407. Takagami Chūzō 高頭忠造, Shiryō taikan, kirokubu 史料大観記録部 (General survey of historical materials—private records), Tetsugaku Shoin, 1898-1900, 4 v.
Contains the diary of Fujiwara Yorinaga (1120-56) and other early materials.

408. Yano Tarō 矢野太郎, Shiryō taisei 史料大成 (Complete historical materials), Tōkyō, Naigaishoseki K.K., 1934—.
This collection absorbed Sasagawa Taneo's Shiryō tsūran (see next entry) and carried on the plan of publication begun by the earlier work. Thirty-nine volumes had appeared by 1940. These reproduced the diaries of court nobles covering the interval from 1194 to 1469.

409. Sasagawa Taneo 笹川種郎, Shiryō tsūran 史料通覧 (Survey of historical materials), Tōkyō, Nihon Shiseki Hozonkai, 1915-18, 18 v.
This work represents an ambitious plan to publish in chronological arrangement the diaries of court nobles whose observations would span the late Heian through the Ashikaga periods. The 18 volumes completed by Sasagawa carried the coverage only to 1194. However, the project has been continued by the Shiryō taisei series (see previous entry). Printing is extremely readable, and each volume has an extensive bibliographical preface.

410. Kondō Heijo 近藤瓶城, Kaitei shiseki shūran 改定史籍集覧 (Collection of historical works, revised), Tōkyō, Kondō Kappansho, 1900-02, 33 v.
A revised and enlarged edition of a collection first published between 1881 and 1885. This work constitutes an extremely valuable source of primary and secondary historical materials. Not all works included in the original edition were reprinted. The revised collection comprises 464 documents, diaries, records, narratives, private and official letters, and historical studies covering the fourteenth through eighteenth centuries. Included are such important works as: Gukanshō, Jinnō shōtōki, Nihon meisō den, Zenrin kokuhōki, Meiryō tairoku, En'eiroku, Haizetsuroku. The last volume is a general index and annotated bibliography to the set.

411. Kondō Heijo 近藤瓶城, Zoku shiseki shūran 続史籍集覧 (A collection of Japanese historical works—second series), Tōkyō, Kondō Shuppambu, rev. ed., 1930, 10 v.
A supplement to the Shiseki Shūran (see previous entry) containing 70 titles of ancient records and historical works written during the Tokugawa period.

412. Kokusho Kankōkai 国書刊行会 (Society for Publication of Japanese Texts), Shiseki zassan 史籍雑纂 (Miscellaneous collection of historical works), Tōkyō, Kokusho Kankōkai, 1911-12, 5 v.
A collection of 40 basic historical materials gathered from religious institutions and feudal and court families and covering the twelfth through eighteenth centuries.

413. Yūtoku Zaidan 有 徳 財 團 (Yūtoku Foundation), Sonkeikaku sōkan 尊 經 閣 叢 刊 (Sonkeikaku Library series), Tōkyō, Yūtoku Zaidan, 1926, 36 v.
    Facsimile reproductions of rare manuscript editions contained in the famous Sonkeikaku Library of the Maeda family. Most of the works are of purely literary interest, but a few historical texts such as the Joei Shikimoku and Ruijū kokushi have been reproduced. Commentaries on some of the texts have been provided by outstanding Japanese scholars.

414. Kondō Heijō 近 藤 瓶 城, Zonsai sōsho 存 採 叢 書 (Selected series), Tōkyō, Kondō Kappansho, 1885-88, 130 v.
    A collection of historical records gathered by Tokugawa scholars together with historical writings of out-standing Tokugawa scholars. Much of the material covers non-Tokugawa subjects. Volume 130 is a general index to the set.

b. Specialized Collections

1) Family and Institutional Collections

    A large number of formerly important families or religious and craft institutions have published collec-tions of the documents in their possession. The following items are but a small selection of this type of ma-terial. One problem with documents published by private families is that they are often too carefully selected or that they present only materials relating to certain important events. Thus the published documents of many of the Tokugawa daimyō families cover only the important but limited Restoration period (c. 1853-1871). However, the collections contained in the Dai Nihon komonjo, iewake monjo (Ancient documents of Japan, docu-ments arranged according to ownership) (Entry 416), edited by the Historiographical Institute of Tokyo Uni-versity, are generally quite complete. So also are the published documents of the Maeda family (Kaga-han shiryō) (Entry 417) and of the Kii branch of the Tokugawa house (Nanki Tokugawashi) (Entry 419). It should be remembered that the various series published by the Nihon Shiseki Kyōkai (see Entry 403) contain a large num-ber of family and personal documents limited largely to the Restoration period. These collections have not been individually mentioned below.

415. Kōshaku Hosokawa-ke Hensansho 侯 爵 細 川 家 編 纂 所 (Compilation Office of the House of Mar-quis Hosokawa), Kaitei Higo-han kokuji shiryō 改 訂 肥 後 藩 国 事 史 料 (Historical materials on the political affairs of Higo domain, revised), Kōshaku Hosokawa-ke Hensansho, 1932, 10 v.
    An amalgamation of an earlier work by this name and another collection entitled Kumamoto-han kokuji shiryō. This work presents original documents in full or in condensed form to provide chronological historical coverage for the 19 years from 1853 to 1871. Materials are drawn from domain records and contain imperial decrees, shogunal directives, memorials, reports, and correspondence between daimyō and domain officials. The work thus provides a detailed record of the activity of the important Higo domain during the Restoration years.

416. Tōkyō Daigaku Shiryō Hensansho 東 京 大 学 史 料 編 纂 所 (Tokyo University Historiographical Insti-tute), Dai Nihon komonjo, iewake monjo 大 日 本 古 文 書 ，家 わ け 文 書 (Ancient documents of Japan, documents arranged according to ownership), Tōkyō, Shiryō Hensansho, 1904—.
    One of the three divisions under which the Tokyo University Historiographical Institute has been publish-ing old Japanese documents. To date 54 volumes have appeared containing primary documents related to the following institutions and families: Kōyasan (8 v.), Asano-ke (1), Date-ke (10), Iwashimizu (6), Sagara-ke (2), Kanshinji (1), Kongōji (1), Mori-ke (4), Yoshikawa-ke (3), Tōji (4), Kobayakawa-ke (2), Uesugi-ke (2), Aso (3), Kumagaya-ke, Miura-ke, Hiraga-ke (1), Yamanouchi-ke (1), Shimazu-ke (1), Daitokuji (2), and Tōnan'in (2). Each collection contains old family records or documents generally chronologically arranged. The editors provide a large number of photographic reproductions. For let-ters, both envelopes as well as contents are reprinted. Marginal tabs indicate the nature of documents and major subjects of interest.

417. Maeda Kōshaku-ke 前 田 侯 爵 家 (The House of Marquis Maeda), Kaga-han shiryō 加 賀 藩 史 料 (Historical materials of the Kaga domain), Tōkyō, Ishiguro Bunkichi, 1929—.
    The published documents of the famous Maeda family, next in importance to the Tokugawa during the Edo period. Arrangement of materials is chronological and format is similar to that of the Dai Nihon shiryō (Entry 382). Coverage begins with the year 1538 and will continue to 1871. By 1943, fifteen volumes had been completed, covering the years to 1847. A supplementary volume contains genealogical charts and chronological tables. The importance of the Maeda family makes this one of the basic source ma-terials for the pre-Restoration history of Japan.

418. Mito-han shiryō 水 戸 藩 史 料 (Historical documents of the Mito han), privately distributed, 1915-17, 5 v.
    The collected records of the important Mito branch of the Tokugawa family covering the years 1853-71.

419. Horiuchi Makoto 堀 内 信, Nanki Tokugawashi 南 紀 徳 川 史 (History of the Tokugawa branch family in Kishū), Wakayama, Nankai Tokugawashi Kankōkai, 1930-33, 18 v.
    Though primarily a history of the Kii branch of the Tokugawa family, this work contains a great deal of documentary material. Volumes 1-4 constitute a chronological history of the family from 1607 to 1871. Volumes 5-17 contain biographical materials and documents on various domain institutions. Primarily historical materials are extensively quoted in both sections. Volume 18 is a general index.

420. Ressei Zenshū Hensankai 列聖全集編纂会 (Society for Compilation of the Complete Works of the Successive Emperors), Ressei zenshū 列聖全集 (Complete works of the successive emperors), Tōkyō, Ressei Zenshū Hensankai, 1815-17, 25 v.

The collected rescripts, records, letters, poems, and other writings of all Japanese emperors down to the emperor Meiji (1868-1912).

2) Local Historical and Geographical Materials

Pre-modern Japan, especially the late Tokugawa period, produced a vast quantity of writings on local history and geography. These consisted of histories of daimyō families, local gazetteers, travel guides, and records of local habits and customs. These materials, together with actual local documents, have formed the basis of literally hundreds of modern prefectural, district, and city histories. As a by-product of such historical efforts, local historical associations have frequently prepared for publication collections of local materials. These vary considerably from mere series of secondary writings by local scholars to collections of primary documents. A few of the larger and more important of such collections have been listed below.

421. Akita sōsho 秋田叢書 (Akita series), Akita, Akita Sōsho Kankōkai, 1928—.

Collected historical works related to the Satake daimyō family and the pre-modern history of Akita prefecture in northern Honshu. Ten numbered volumes and six supplementary volumes had been published by 1940. Materials are mostly of a secondary nature relating to outstanding historic figures, religious affairs, customs, battles, and political affairs.

422. Bōsō sōsho 房總叢書 (Series of materials on Awa, Kazusa, and Shimōsa provinces), Chiba, Bōsō Sōsho Kankōkai, 1940, 14 v.

Volumes contain: 1) old documents, 2) military annals, 3-5) biographies, 6-7) geographical gazetteers, 8) diaries and travelogues, 9) feudal documents, 10-11) miscellaneous tables and indices.

423. Ishino Akira 石野暎, ed., Busō sōsho 武相叢書 (Series of materials on Musashi and Sagami provinces), Busō Kōkokai, 1929-36, 6 v.

Contains a number of pre-modern works and documentary collections concerned with the old Musashi and Sagami provinces. Of special interest are materials on Odawara and Hakone.

424. Dai Nihon Rekishi Chiri Gakkai 大日本歴史地理学会 (Historical Geography Society of Japan), Dai Nihon chishi taikei 大日本地誌大系 (Compendium of Japanese geographical gazetteers), Tōkyō, Dai Nihon Chishi Taikei Kankōkai, 1914-17, 14 v. 1929—, 40 v.

A voluminous collection of local gazetteers written during the Tokugawa and early Meiji periods. The collection covers all major areas of Japan. Gazetteers give geographical information, detailed notes on local produce, taxation and local government and other data of use in reconstructing local history. There is no general index, though each work is given a bibliographical preface.

425. Harada Miki 原田幹, Dai Nihon meishozue 大日本名所図会 (Illustrated gazetteers of Japan's famous sites), Tōkyō, Dai Nihon Meishozue Kankōkai, 1918-22, 20 v.

Modern printed reproductions of 12 famous illustrated gazetteers compiled during the late Tokugawa period. They cover in detail well-known sites of the major cities (Edo, Kyoto, Osaka) and the great public thoroughfares (notably the Tōkaidō). Pictures provide a wealth of material on the life and customs of late Tokugawa Japan.

426. Edo sōsho 江戸叢書 (Edo series), Tōkyō, Edo Sōsho Kankōkai, 1916-17, 12 v.

A collection of works, charts, and illustrations portraying the history, life, customs, and geography of old Edo. One of its most valuable items is the Bukō nempyō by Saitō Yukinari (1804-1878), a chronological history of events occurring in Edo during the period 1590-1873.

427. Takahashi Yoshihiko 高橋義彦, Essa shiryō 越佐史料 (Historical materials of Echigo and Sado), Niigata, 1925-31, 6 v.

Modeled after the Dai Nihon shiryō, this collection presents documents on the history of the two provinces of Echigo and Sado in chronological order from ancient times to 1569.

428. Etchū shiryō 越中史料 (Historical materials of Etchū province), Toyama, Toyama-ken, 1909, 4 v. + 1 v.

Historical documents concerning the history of Etchū province cut up and distributed chronologically. Coverage is from ancient times to 1878. A supplementary volume contains illustrations and a revised index of works used in the compilation.

429. Ina shiryō sōsho 伊那史料叢書 (Series of historical materials relating to Ina district), Nagano, Shinano Kyōikukai Shimoina Bukai, 1914-32, 11 v.

Historical documents relating to Ina district of Shinano province. Many are of a primary nature and offer information on feudal institutions, local administration, and economic aspects of the Tokugawa period.

430. Kagawa sōsho 香川叢書 (Kagawa series), Takamatsu, Kagawa-ken, 1939-43, 3 v.

Materials collected for the compilation of the history of Kagawa prefecture. Volume 2 is especially valuable for the primary material it presents on feudal institutions and on the Takamatsu, Marugame, and Kompira domains.

431. Hagiwara Yorihira 荻原頼平, Kai shiryo shusei 甲斐史料集成 (Collected historical materials on Kai province), Kofu, Yamanashi-ken, Kai Shiryo Kankokai, 1932-35, 12 v.
>   A classified collection of materials on the history and geography of Kai province. Materials are distributed under the following headings: diaries, travel accounts, gazetteers, histories, education, religion, biography, arts. and miscellaneous.

432. Kibi gunsho shusei 吉備群書集成 (Collected works on the Kibi area), Okayama, Kibi Gunsho Shusei Kankokai, 1921-31, 10 v.
>   A valuable collection of old histories, biographical works, gazetteers, etc., covering the area of old Bizen, Bitchu, Bingo, and Mimasaka. Of special interest is the Kibi onko (Vol. 5-9) which gives detailed information on the Okayama domain.

433. Kyoto sosho 京都叢書 (Kyoto series), Kyoto, Kyoto Sosho Kankokai, 1914-17, 16 v.
>   A collection of old gazetteers, illustrated travel guides and descriptions of the life and customs of Kyoto. Volume 1 is an index.

434. Kondo Heijo 近藤瓶城, Shiryo tsushin soshi 史料通信叢誌 (Series of historical materials collected by correspondence), Tokyo, Shiryo Tsushin Kyokai, 1893-97, 29 v.
>   A collection of over 1500 records and documents brought together from all parts of Japan. Materials are grouped by locality and relate to all aspects of Japanese history from ancient times to 1853. The compilers have added reproductions of pictures and descriptions of folk tales. The historical value of some of the materials is rather small. Volume 29 is a general index to the set.

435. Nambu sosho 南部叢書 (Nambu series), Aomori, Nambu Sosho Kankokai, 1927-31, 11 v.
>   Collected records and local gazetteers dealing with the old Mutsu province, domain of the Nambu family. There is a good deal of important material on local administration, peasant uprisings, commerce and trade, etc. Volume 11 contains an index, chronological tables, and a table of contents for the set.

436. Funagoshi Seiichiro 船越政一郎, Naniwa sosho 浪速叢書 (Naniwa series), Osaka, Naniwa Sosho Kankokai, 1926-30, 17 v.
>   Materials on the history of Naniwa (Osaka) beginning approximately with the year 1615. The collection is especially rich in its coverage of the merchant class and commercial practices.

437. Sendai sosho 仙台叢書 (Sendai series), Sendai, Sendai Sosho Kankokai, 1922-26, 16 v.
>   A valuable collection of materials concerning the old Sendai, domain of the Date daimyo. There are records, genealogies, collections of laws, notes on taxation, currency, local production, etc. Twelve volumes make up the main body of the collection: 4 volumes are supplementary. Volume 12 has a general index to all 16 volumes.

438. Shinano shiryo sosho 信濃史料叢書 (Series of materials on Shinano province), Nagano, Shinano Shiryo Sosho Hensankai, 1913-14, 5 v.
>   Contains historical and geographical material on pre-modern Shinano province. These include documents relating to Suwa, Matsumoto, Ueda, Matsushiro, Takato, Iida, and other domains and several temples (Zenkoji etc.) and shrines (Suwa jinja etc.).

439. Shizuoka-ken shiryo 静岡縣史料 (Historical materials relating to Shizuoka Prefecture), Shizuoka, Shizuoka-ken, 1932—, 5 v.
>   Historical documents relating to Shizuoka arranged chronologically by geographic area. Coverage begins with the Heian period.

440. Suwa shiryo sosho 諏訪史料叢書 (Series of historical materials related to Suwa county), Nagano, Suwa Shiryo Sosho Kankokai and Shinano Kyoikukai Suwa Bukai, 1932—.
>   Documents relating to the Suwa domain and Suwa shrine arranged topically. By 1950, volumes published in this series numbered 36.

441. Yamato shiryo 大和志料 (Materials relating to Yamato province), Nara, Nara-ken Kyoikukai, 1914, 2 v.
>   Pre-modern historical materials of Yamato province arranged geographically by county.

3) Foreign Relations Documents

     No single collection covers the entire range of Japanese foreign relations. Beginning with the renewal of Japanese intercourse with China in the early fourteenth century, however, fairly complete documentary coverage of the official relations of Japan with other foreign countries is to be had by putting together a number of separate works. These include the Zenrin kokuhoki (Entry 452), which with its sequels covers the fourteenth through sixteenth centuries; the Tsuko ichiran (Survey of foreign relations) (Entry 451), which covers most of the Tokugawa period; the Dai Nihon komonjo, bakumatsu gaikoku kankei monjo (Ancient documents of Japan, official documents of the later Tokugawa era concerning foreign relations) (Entry 445), which covers the years 1853-67; and the Dai Nihon gaiko bunsho (Documents on Japanese foreign relations) (Entry 444), which carries on from 1868. For the period prior to the Tokugawa (1600-1867), and even for certain aspects of Tokugawa foreign relations, the most convenient source is the Gaikobu (Foreign relations) section of the Koji ruien (Entry 207). This work should always be consulted when working in pre-Meiji foreign relations, since its pages not only contain a great deal of information but help to lead the historian to other fruitful sources.

442. Bakumatsu Ishin gaikō shiryō shūsei 幕末維新外交史料集成 (Classified historical records on foreign relations: 1853-68). Tōkyō, Gaimushō, 1942-44, 6 v.
A collection of basic foreign relations documents covering the years 1853-68 and classified under broad encyclopedic headings. A total of twenty volumes were planned.

443. Asakura Musei 朝倉無聲, Bummei genryū sosho 文明源流叢書 (Series on the sources of Japanese civilization), Tōkyō, Kokusho Kankōkai, 1913-14, 3 v.
A collection of accounts of travels and of foreign countries recorded by Japanese who went abroad before the Restoration. Many were shipwrecked. There are bibliographical prefaces, supplementary charts and an index to the title of works.

444. Gaimushō 外務省, Dai Nihon gaikō bunsho 大日本外交文書 (Documents on Japanese foreign relations), Tōkyō, Nihon Kokusai Kyōkai, 1936—.
Basic foreign relations documents released for publication by the Japanese Ministry of Foreign Affairs. Materials are arranged chronologically beginning with 1868; each volume covers a year. This series thus carries on where the Dai Nihon komonjo series (see next entry) will leave off. Arrangement and format is similar. Appendices provide tables of important public officials concerned with foreign affairs. Each volume contains an index. By 1952 some 21 volumes had been published covering the period 1868 to 1888. Post-World War II volumes carry the title Nihon gaikō bunsho. A supplementary series of 6 volumes dealing with the treaty revision problem was published between 1941 and 1950.

445. Tōkyō Daigaku Shiryō Hensansho 東京大学史料編纂所 (Tokyo University Historiographical Institute), Dai Nihon Komonjo, bakumatsu gaikoku kankei monjo 大日本古文書・幕末外国関係文書 (Ancient documents of Japan, official documents of the later Tokugawa era concerning foreign relations), Tōkyō, Shiryō Hensansho, 1910—.
One of the three divisions under which the Tokyo University Historiographical Office has been publishing old Japanese documents. Arrangement is chronological and will cover the period 1853-67. Material includes state papers of the shogunate, correspondence with the imperial court, between daimyō, and with foreign powers, reports and advisory memorials, texts of treaties, and the like. Marginal tabs point to major subject matters. Twenty-seven volumes published by 1939 covered the period up to 1863.

446. Ikoku sōsho 異国叢書 (Series of writings by foreigners), Tōkyō, Sunnansha, 1927-31, 13 v.
A collection of 13 works by foreign visitors to Japan describing the country and their impressions of it. Accounts begin with the Jesuits, include Kaempfer, Thunberg, von Siebold, Kreutzenstern, and other later travellers. The works are translated and extensively annotated. There is a detailed subject index. A collection of pre-Restoration correspondence between Japan and various foreign countries entitled Ikoku ōfuku shokanshū 異国往復書翰集 is contained in volume 11.

447. Gaimushō Jōyakukyoku 外務省條約局, (Foreign Office, Treaty Division), Joyaku isan 條約彙纂 (Classified collection of treaties), Tōkyō, Gaimushō Jōyakukyoku, 1926-29, 9 v.
A collection of current treaties arranged in three parts. Part 1 (vols. 1-3) consists of treaties and notes signed between Japan and various foreign powers. Part 2 (vols. 4-6) includes general international agreements to which Japan was a party. Part 3 (vols. 7-9) deals with the Versailles peace treaty and the many agreements which resulted from it.

448. Shimmura Izuru 新村出, Kaihyō sōsho 海表叢書 (Series of writings on Japan's contact with foreigners), Tōkyō, Kōseikaku, 1927-28, 6 v.
A valuable collection of Japanese works dealing with Westerners and Western relations beginning with accounts of the Portuguese and ending with the Dutch. Each volume begins with an extensive bibliographical preface. Volume 6 includes a general table of contents. This series was republished in 1930 under the title Namban kōmō shiryō 南蠻紅毛史料 (Materials for the study of the relations with the West.)

449. Sumida Shōichi 住田正一, Kaiji shiryō sōsho 海事史料叢書 (Series of historical materials on maritime affairs), Tōkyō, Ganshodō, 1929-31, 20 v.
An important collection of materials, laws, documents, reports, and correspondence, concerning Japan's foreign relations from the sixteenth century to the Meiji period. Volume 20 contains a table of contents and general index to the set.

450. Sumida Shōichi 住田正一, Nihon kaibō shiryō sōsho 日本海防史料叢書 (Series of historical materials on Japanese coastal defence), Tōkyō, Kaibō Shiryō Kankōkai, 1932—.
A companion work to the Kaiji shiryō sōsho (see previous entry) compiled by the same editor. It contains works dealing strictly with the problem of Japanese national defence by middle and late Tokugawa writers. By 1940, ten volumes had been published.

451. Hayashi Kō 林煒, Tsūkō ichiran 通航一覽 (Survey of foreign relations), Tōkyō, Kokusho Kankōkai, 1913, 8 v.
A basic collection of documents on foreign relations compiled by shogunal order during the last days of the Tokugawa shogunate. Subject matter is divided by foreign country: China, Korea, countries of Southeast Asia, Portugal, Spain, Holland, and Russia. For each country the origins of intercourse between that country and Japan are traced, and basic laws and documents governing the relations between the two countries are quoted.

452. Nakajima Shō 中島 竦 , ed., <u>Shintei zenrin kokuhōki</u> 新 訂 善 隣 国 宝 記 (Newly edited <u>Zenrin kokuhōki</u>), Tōkyō, Bunkyōdō, 1932, 200 pp.

The basic text for foreign relations, primarily with China and Korea, of the early Ashikaga period (14th and 15th centuries) prepared by Zuikei Shūhō 瑞 溪 周 鳳 , a monk of the Shōkokuji temple in 1466. This text plus several works which continue the work of the monk Shūhō are included in volume 21 of the revised <u>Shiseki shūran</u> (Entry 410).

4) Collected Laws

The following collections of legal materials deal only with pre-Meiji Japan. Modern collections of laws and ordinances are so numerous and voluminous that they have been omitted from this section. Those who would consult post-Restoration materials of this type are referred to Robert E. Ward's bibliography of political science prepared for this bibliographical series.

Of the items listed below, Kimura Shōji's <u>Kempō shiryō</u> (Historical materials on administrative law) (Entry 454), Takayanagi and Ishii's <u>Ofuregaki kampō shūsei</u> (Collection of Tokugawa laws of the Kampō era) (Entry 455), and the Ministry of Justice's <u>Tokugawa kinreikō</u> (Survey of Tokugawa laws) (Entry 456) are most useful. Together they cover the entire space of pre-Restoration administrative law. In the last collection the historian must, unfortunately, be on his guard against corrupted texts.

453. Takigawa Masajirō 瀧 川 政 治 郎 , ed., <u>Hōsei shiryō komonjo ruisan</u> 法 制 史 料 古 文 書 類 纂 (Classified collection of documentary materials on the history of law), Tōkyō, Yūhikaku, 1927, 707 pp.

A select collection of some 460 collections of laws and documents covering the history of Japanese legal development from the eighth through nineteenth centuries. Classification is under four headings: 1) official documents, 2) semi-official documents, i. e., legal documents of feudal lords, estates, and religious institutions, 3) private documents, 4) documents concerning foreign affairs.

454. Kimura Shōji 木 村 正 辞 , <u>Kempō shiryō</u> 憲 法 志 料 (Historical materials on administrative law), Tōkyō, Shihōshō, 1877, 37 v.

A classified collection of legal materials covering Japanese history from ancient times to the seventeenth century. It was compiled for the Ministry of Justice. Classification is under four broad categories: civil and military law, Shinto affairs, the Buddhist priesthood, agriculture and commerce. Within each category laws are arranged chronologically. An index is appended. This collection takes its place as the basic source for pre-Tokugawa legal systems. It is followed by the <u>Tokugawa kinrei kō</u> series listed below (Entry 456).

455. Takayanagi Shinzō 高 柳 真 三 and Ishii Ryōsuke 石 井 良 助 , <u>Ofuregaki kampō shūsei</u> 御 觸 書 寛 保 集 成 (Collection of Tokugawa laws of the Kampō era), Tōkyō, Iwanami Shoten, 1934, 1356 pp.

This is a modern collated edition of the first major official collection of Tokugawa laws and injunctions compiled by the Tokugawa Hyōjōsho (Supreme Court of Justice). The work contains some 3500 laws issued from 1615 to 1743. Laws issued after 1743 were periodically brought together by the Tokugawa government and these have been published by the same editors as follows:

Ofuregaki	Hōreki	shūsei	(covers to 1760) - 1935.
"	Temmei	"	(" " 1787) - 1936.
"	Tempō	"	(" " 1836) - 1937-41.

Together these works provide a definitive coverage of Tokugawa government legislation. The lack of index or convenient classification makes them difficult to use. For this reason the classified collection of Tokugawa laws listed below is of more general service, though not as complete.

456. Shihōshō 司 法 省 (Ministry of Justice), <u>Tokugawa kinreikō</u> 徳 川 禁 令 考 (Survey of Tokugawa laws), Tōkyō, Yoshikawa Kōbunkan, 1931-32, 6 v. Second series 1931-32, 6 v.

A classified collection of Tokugawa laws compiled by Kikuchi Shunnosuke and, first published in the present form in 1894. The 1931-32 edition is a photolithograph version of the earlier printing. The first series consists of general administrative and civil laws. These are classified under broad headings such as court nobles, military houses, temples, shrines, commoners, and foreign affairs, and a number of subheadings. Laws are listed chronologically within each section. This is not an official edition of Tokugawa laws. Many of the texts are corrupt and the coverage is not complete. But it is the most conveniently arranged of such collections. Series II (<u>Tokugawa kinreikō kōshū</u> 後 聚) consists of criminal laws classified by offences. The last volume contains records of trials and sentences.

5) Collected Materials on Social and Economic History

Next to the general collections of historical materials listed above, the most valuable to the historian are the great compendia of materials on Japanese social and economic history listed in this section. Undoubtedly, the best known of these works are Honjō Eijirō's <u>Kinsei shakai keizai sōsho</u> (Documentary series on modern society and economics) (Entry 458) and Takimoto Seiichi's <u>Nihon keizai taiten</u> (Compendium of Japanese economics) (Entry 460). Both of these collections deal primarily with the Tokugawa period, and their contents complement the more formal documentary collections which deal largely with the affairs of the ruling class. In both these works economics is interpreted in its broadest sense to include almost all aspects of the material life of the people. One problem of the Honjō and Takimoto collections is that they do not contain much primary material. Their volumes are filled largely with treatises by Tokugawa scholars on economic and social problems and secondary materials on agrarian affairs, village administration, mercantile affairs, and other similar matters.

More strictly collections of primary source materials than the above two series are such multivolume works as Ono Takeo's Kinsei jikata keizai shiryō (Materials relating to early-modern local economy) (Entry 457) and Nihon nōmin shiryō shūsui (Collected materials on the history of the Japanese peasantry) (Entry 462), Ōuchi Hyōe's Meiji zenki zaisei keizai shiryō shūsei (Collected historical materials relating to finance and economy during the early Meiji period) (Entry 459), and the Ministry of Finance's Nihon zaisei keizai shiryō (Source materials on Japanese financial and economic history) (Entry 465). These works contain a great deal of raw historical material covering Japan's economic development especially during the Tokugawa and Meiji eras.

In the following list only the works published by the Attic Museum (Entries 467 and 469) are solely concerned with primary records. These works present in printed form a number of collections of village records, which, though they are somewhat limited in their subject content, are useful for the examples they offer of materials not found in other collections.

457. Ono Takeo 小野武夫, Kinsei jikata keizai shiryō 近世地方經濟史料 (Materials relating to early-modern local economy), Tōkyō, Kinsei Jikata Keizai Shiryō Kankōkai, 1931, 9 v.
A valuable collection of laws, memoranda, reports, and diaries giving primary documentation to the land-tax system of the Tokugawa period together with secondary discussions and treatises on land problems. Volume 9 contains materials on the land system in the Ryūkyūs.

458. Honjō Eijirō 本庄榮治郎 and others, Kinsei shakai keizai sōsho 近世社会經濟叢書 (Documentary series on modern society and economics), Tōkyō, Kaizōsha, 1926-27, 12 v.
Like the Nihon keizai taiten (Entry 460) this series brings together numerous texts on the social and economic life of the Tokugawa period. Its contents have been extensively used by the Kyoto school of contemporary economic historians.

459. Ōuchi Hyōe 大内兵衛 and Tsuchiya Takao 土屋喬雄, Meiji zenki zaisei keizai shiryō shūsei 明治前期財政經濟史料集成 (Collected historical materials relating to finance and economy during the early Meiji period), Tōkyō, Kaizōsha, 1932, 21 v.
An exhaustive collection of basic materials on the development of national and private finance during the Meiji period. Essential for any study of Japan's post-Restoration economic development.

460. Takimoto Seiichi 瀧本誠一, Nihon keizai taiten 日本經濟大典 (Compendium of Japanese economics), Tōkyō, Shishi Shuppansha, Keimeisha, 1928-30, 54 v.
A monumental collection of pre-modern works on economic affairs. This edition combines two previous series by the same editor, the Nihon keizai sōsho and its supplement. The series contains primary source materials and treatises written by Tokugawa scholars on all aspects of pre-modern economics, finance, agrarian affairs, village administration, mercantile affairs, and the like. Works in this series have formed the basis of a great portion of recent scholarship on pre-modern Japan. Each volume contains extensive bibliographical prefaces on the works contained in it. Most works either refer to or were written during the Tokugawa period, though a few touch on the pre-Tokugawa economic scene. A large quantity of materials contained in the series is of general historical value.

461. Nihon kōtsū shiryō shūsei 日本交通史料集成 (Collected materials for the history of transportation in Japan), Tōkyō, Kokusai Kōtsū Bunka Kyōkai, 1938-39, 3 v.
Basic texts and materials on the history of communications and transportation in Japan. Volume 1 covers post stations on the five main thoroughfares in Japan, volume 2 contains laws dealing with post stations and horse relays, and volume 3 covers inns, transport guilds, etc.

462. Ono Takeo 小野武夫, Nihon nōmin shiryō shūsui 日本農民史料聚粹 (Collected materials on the history of the Japanese peasantry), Tōkyō, Ganshōdō, 1941, 7 v.
The completed volumes of this series are numbers 2, 4, 6, 8A, 8B, 9 and 11. Contents include basic primary materials on the Japanese peasantry during Tokugawa times plus secondary accounts and treatises by Tokugawa writers. Materials cover local laws and admonitions governing the peasantry, problems of land improvement, agriculture, technology, and peasant uprisings.

463. Norinshō Sanrinkyoku 農林省山林局 (Ministry of Agriculture and Forestry, Bureau of Forestry), Nihon rinseishi shiryō 日本林制史資料 (Source materials on the history of Japanese forest administration), 1929-33, 30 v.
A collection of materials for the study of forest administration in Japan from early times to the Meiji Restoration. The documents are arranged chronologically. Volume 1 covers the pre-Tokugawa period. Volume 2 deals with imperial estates and lands of religious institutions. Volume 3 contains laws on forest administration issued by the Tokugawa shogunate. Volume 4 contains material on shogunal lands. The remaining volumes cover forest lands of the several daimyō during the Tokugawa period. Subject indices are provided for each of the main sections of the series.

464. Takimoto Seiichi 瀧本誠一 and Mukai Shikamatsu 向井鹿松, Nihon sangyō shiryō taikei 日本産業資料大系 (Compendium of materials on Japanese industry), Tōkyō, Chūgai Shōgyō Shimpōsha, 1926-27, 13 v.
An imposing collection of materials consisting of historical surveys, documents, extracts from industrial reports, and government studies relating to the growth of modern Japanese industry. The materials cover the pre-modern origins and Meiji development of the commercial production of such commodities as fertilizer, silk, cement, and sugar as well as the development of fisheries, mines, and modern industrial and trading firms. Volume 13 is a detailed subject index.

465. Ōkurashō 大藏省 (Ministry of Finance), Nihon zaisei keizai shiryō 日本財政經済史料 (Source materials on Japanese financial and economic history), Tōkyō, Zaisei Keizai Gakkai, 1922-25, 11 v.
    This invaluable collection is the result of the work of a committee established by the Ministry of Finance to prepare materials on the history of economy and finance in Japan.   The original work was completed in 1886.   Documents are classified under the following headings: finance, economy, civil engineering, transportation, population, island territories, and police systems.   Each category is further subdivided and materials are arranged chronologically within the subdivisions.   Volume 11 contains an index.

466. Kuroha Heijirō 黒羽兵治郎, Ōsaka shōgyō shiryō shūsei 大阪商業史料集成 (Collected historical materials relating to commerce in Osaka), Osaka, Ōsaka Shōka Daigaku Keizai Kenkyusho, 1934-40, 6 v.
    A basic collection of primary and secondary materials relating to the pre-Meiji development of commerce and finance in Osaka.

467. Shakai keizai shiryō zassan 社会經済史料雜纂 (Miscellaneous materials on social and economic history), Tōkyō, Achikku Myūzeamu, 1938, 2 v.
    Collected primary records concerning fishing and agricultural villages of northern and central Japan.

468. Tsūzoku keizai bunko 通俗經済文庫 (Popular economics library), Tōkyō, Nihon Keizai Shōsho Kankōkai, 1916-17, 12 v.
    A collection of materials, mostly from the Tokugawa period, dealing with the economic life of the people.   Subjects treated include commercial ethics, management, agrarian methods, frugality measures, lives of merchants, etc.

469. Shibusawa Keizō 澁澤敬三, Zushū Uchiura gyomin shiryō 豆州内浦漁民史料 (Historical materials relating to the fishing population of Uchiura in Izu), Tōkyō, Achikku Myūzeamu, 1937-38, 2 v.
    Materials held by the Ōkawa family of the Izu peninsula.   They relate to the fishing and agrarian population of the Uchiura area during Tokugawa times.   Unfortunately, the series is not yet complete.   If completed it will stand as perhaps the only printing of a representative collection of village records.

6) Collected Educational Materials

470. Kurokawa Masamichi 黒川眞道 and Odaki Jun 小瀧淳, Nihon kyōiku bunko 日本教育文庫 (Japanese education library), Tōkyō, Dōbunkan, 1910-11, 13 v.
    A collection of 424 works on educational and instructional matters selected from pre-Restoration Japanese literature.   Classification is by broad subject category: for example, house codes, injunctions, instructions for women, filial piety, schools, textbooks, morals, hygiene, etc.   The editors have provided aids to the reading of difficult passages.

471. Mombushō 文部省 (Ministry of Education), Nihon kyōikushi shiryō 日本教育史資料 (Source materials on the history of Japanese education), Tōkyō, Fuzambō, 1890-92, 9 v. + 2 supplements.
    A collection of documents and reports prepared for the Ministry of Education by the several prefectures on the history of education in their local areas.   It provides material for the study of educational systems developed in the chief daimyō domains of the Tokugawa period.   Supplements provide illustrations and drawings of pre-modern schools and Confucian temples.   Volume 9 contains biographies of prominent educators.

7) Collected Materials on Religion, Ethics, and Thought

    One of the largest categories of Japanese printed series deals with the broad field of thought and religion. Although the general historian may find such works somewhat too specialized, it is nonetheless essential that he have access to the basic writings in this field.   The following items have been selected for their general usefulness.   In the section on Buddhism the various editions of the Tripitaka are listed in chronological order.

a) General

472. Adachi Shirōkichi 足立四郎吉, Dai Nihon fūkyō sōsho 大日本風教叢書 (Series on public morals of Japan), Tōkyō, Dai Nihon Fūkyō Sōsho Kankōkai, 1919-21, 10 v.
    Collected works on morals and ethics selected from all periods in Japanese history.   The compilation begins with the writings of Shōtoku Taishi, makes selections from the writings of great Buddhist priests and Shinto and Confucian scholars, and concludes with the works of Tokugawa townspeople and leaders in the Shingaku school.

473. Uemura Katsuya 上村勝彌, Dai Nihon shisō zenshū 大日本思想全集 (Complete collection on Japanese thought), Tōkyō Dai Nihon Shisō Zenshū Kankōkai, 1932-34, 17 v.
    This work brings together selections from 173 books, essays, and miscellanies by over fifty scholars and thinkers of the Tokugawa period representing the Confucian, Kokugaku, Shingaku, and Dutch studies schools of thought.   The original texts are paralleled by translations into modern Japanese.   Glossaries of difficult words are provided after each work.   Each volume contains biographical sketches of the authors whose works are found in the volume.

474. Kinsei shakai keizai gakusetsu taikei 近世社会經済学説大系 (Compendium of early-modern social and economic theories), Tōkyō, Seibundo, 1935-37, 18 v.
    A valuable series of collected works of prominent Tokugawa social and economic theorists.   Each volume contains a selection of work by one or two authors.   Lengthy introductory prefaces are provided by foremost Japanese economic historians.   The collection begins with Kumazawa Banzan and ends with Fukuzawa Yukichi.

475. Fujita Tokutarō 藤 田 德 太 郎 and Fujisawa Chikao 藤 澤 親 雄 , Nihon seishin bunka taikei 日 本 精 神 文 化 大 系 (Compendium of Japanese spiritual culture), Tōkyō, Kinseidō, 1934—, 9 v.
A chronologically arranged anthology of works expressive of Japan's spiritual culture. Each volume covers a major period of Japanese history and begins with a preface on the characteristics of the age. There follows a series of quotations illustrative of the general spiritual currents of the period. Marginal notes aid in the reading of the quoted texts.

476. Date Mitsuyoshi 伊 達 光 美 , Nihon shukyō seido shiryō ruiju kō 日 本 宗 教 制 度 史 料 類 聚 考 (Classified and annotated collection of historical source materials on Japanese religious institutions), Tōkyō, Ganshōdō, 1930, 758 pp.
A brief collection of basic materials for the study of religious institutions in Japan from the sixth to the twentieth centuries. Part 1 contains classified historical materials; part 2 contains laws dealing with religious institutions. The major emphasis is on Buddhism.

b) Shinto, the Emperor System, and Patriotism

477. Inoue Tetsujirō 井 上 哲 次 郎 and Arima Sukemasa 有 馬 祐 政 , Bushidō sōsho 武 士 道 叢 書 (Series on Bushidō), Tōkyō, Hakubunkan, 1905, 3 v.
A collection of 63 essays and writings on Bushidō and the code of the warrior, dating from early times to the end of the Tokugawa period. Each work is given a bibliographical preface containing a brief biography of the author. The last volume contains a bibliography of contemporary writings on Bushidō.

478. Kurita Kan 栗 田 寬 , Jingi shiryō 神 祇 志 料 (Historical materials on Shinto), Tōkyō, Kōchō Hikyū Kankōkai, 1926-27, 4 v.
A collection of texts and materials gathered for the preparation of the essay on Shinto for the Dai Nihonshi. Volumes 1 and 2 were first published in 1876. Volumes 3 and 4 are later supplements.

479. Nakajima Hakkō 中 島 博 光 and others, Shintō sōsho 神 道 叢 書 (Series on Shinto), Tōkyō, Jingū Kyōin, 1896-98, 8 v.
Collected historical materials on Shinto selected from Japanese writings of the ninth through nineteenth centuries.

480. Saeki Ariyoshi 佐 伯 有 義 , ed., Jingi zensho 神 祇 全 書 (Complete collection of Shinto affairs), Tōkyō, Kōten Kōkyūsho Jingū Hōsaikai, 1906-08, 5 v.
A collection of over 90 works on Shinto shrines and Shinto affairs in general selected from pre-Restoration literature.

481. Nihon kokusui zensho 日 本 国 粋 全 書 (Complete collection of Japanese patriotic writings), Tōkyō, Nihon Kokusui Zensho Kankōkai, 1915-18, 24 v.
A collection of works selected from all periods of Japanese history, including post-Restoration Japan, expressing patriotic sentiment. The emphasis is on writings of the Tokugawa Kokugaku school.

482. Mozume Takami 物 集 高 見 , Shinchū kōgaku sōsho 新 註 皇 学 叢 書 (Newly annotated series on the emperor system), Tōkyō, Kobunko Kankōkai, 1927-31, 12 v.
An annotated collection of 70 texts basic to the study of Japanese nationalism and the imperial tradition. Beginning with such works as the Kojiki and the Engishiki, the collection places its main emphasis on the writings of the members of the Tokugawa Kokugaku school. Each volume contains a bibliographical preface.

c) Buddhism

483. Bukkyō taikei 佛 教 大 系 (Compendium of Buddhist works), Tōkyō, Bukkyō Taikei Kanseikai, 1918-30, 130 v.
A collection of Buddhist literature considered most important from the point of view of Japanese Buddhism. Works are classified by sect and subject and hence are conveniently arranged for the student of Japanese Buddhism.

484. Bussho Kankōkai 佛 書 刊 行 会 (Society for Publication of Buddhist Texts), Dai Nihon Bukkyō zensho 大 日 本 佛 教 全 書 (Complete collection of Japanese Buddhism), Tōkyō, Dai Nihon Bukkyō Zensho Hakkōsho, 1913-22, 151 v. Supplement 10 v.
A great compendium of over 1300 sutras, commentaries, histories, and records relating to the history of Buddhism in pre-Restoration Japan. It includes the collected writings of a large number of Japanese priests. Materials are grouped by sects and general subject headings. This series affords an exhaustive coverage of the religious and institutional development of the Buddhist church in Japan, materials on doctrines, iconography, the lives of priests, and the like. An elaborate set of indices to the series and to personal names and the titles of writings is provided.

485. Washio Junkei 鷲 尾 順 敬 , Kokubun Tōhō Bukkyō sōsho 国 文 東 方 佛 教 叢 書 (Series of Eastern Buddhist Books in Japanese), Tōkyō, Kokubun Tōhō Bukkyō Sōsho Kankōkai and Tōhō Shoin, 1925—, 18 v.
A chronological anthology of 281 works by pre-Meiji Japanese Buddhists written in Japanese. The editor has provided explanatory notes to aid in the reading of difficult passages. Publication is still in progress.

486. Iwano Shin'yū 岩野眞雄, ed., <u>Kokuyaku Issaikyō</u> 国譯一切經(The Tripitaka in Japanese translation), Tōkyō, Daitō Shuppansha, 1915—.
A partially complete translation into Japanese of the Chinese Tripitaka. One hundred fifty-five volumes have been published so far covering the original Indian portion of the Tripitaka.

487. <u>Kōsō meicho zenshū</u> 高僧名著全集(Complete works of important priests), Tōkyō, Heibonsha, 1931, 18 v.
The collected biographies and works of famous pre-modern Buddhist priests such as Dengyō Daishi, Kōbō Daishi, Hōnen, Shinran, Rennyō, Ikkū, etc.

488. Nihon Daizōkyō Hensankai 日本大藏經編纂会 (Society for Compilation of the Japanese Tripitaka), <u>Nihon Daizōkyō</u> 日本大藏經 (Japanese Tripitaka), Tōkyō, Nihon Daizōkyō Hensankai, 1914-21, 51 v.
A collection of 759 sutras and writings considered basic to the various Japanese Buddhist sects. Two hundred Japanese priests are represented by their selections of texts, their commentaries, and writings on doctrine. Coverage is from the sixth century to c. 1890. The series concludes with two volumes of annotated bibliography of the works contained in the collection. These volumes constitute a reasonably complete and valuable bibliographical dictionary (Entry 174) for the understanding of Buddhist texts most frequently referred to in Japan. There is a volume devoted to table of contents and other lists.

489. <u>Dai Nihon kōtei Daizōkyō</u> 大日本校訂大藏經, (Japanese collated edition of the Tripitaka), Tōkyō, Kōkyō Shoin, 1880-85, 419 v.
The first modern Japanese reproduction of the Chinese Tripitaka, sometimes referred to as the "Tōkyō" or "Shukusatsu zōkyō 縮刷藏經(Reduced size Tripitaka)" edition. The text is punctuated and well collated.

490. <u>Dai Nihon kōtei Daizōkyō</u> 大日本校訂大藏經(Japanese collated edition of the Tripitaka), Kyōto, Zōkyō Shoin, 1902-06, 347 v.
The "Kyōto" or "Manji (卍)" edition of the Tripitaka.

491. <u>Dai Nihon zoku Zōkyō</u> 大日本續藏經 (Supplement to the Japanese edition of the Tripitaka), Kyōto, Zōkyō Shoin, 1905-12, 75 v.
A collection of Buddhist works by Chinese monks which were preserved in Japan. This collection supplements the Chinese version of the Tripitaka. Referred to as the "Manji (卍) zokukyō" or the "Zoku issaikyō (續一切經)."

492. Takakusu Junjirō 高楠順次郎, Watanabe Kaikyoku 渡辺海旭, and Ono Gemmyō 小野玄妙, ed., <u>Taishō shinshū Daizōkyō</u> 大正新修大藏經 (Newly revised Tripitaka of the Taisho era), Tōkyō, Daizō Shuppan K.K., 1924-32, 100 v.
Referred to as the "Taishō Issaikyō" or the "Shōwa hōbō 昭和法宝 (Buddhist treasures of the Showa era)" edition. This is the most modern edition of the Chinese Tripitaka well collated and punctuated. It contains select items from the "Zoku Issaikyō" (see previous entry).

d) Confucianism

493. Hattori Unokichi 服部宇之吉, ed., <u>Kambun taikei</u> 漢文大系 (Compendium of Chinese classics), Tōkyō, Fuzambō, 1910-16, 22 v.
A conveniently arranged collection of the standard Chinese classics and their chief commentaries. Annotations in Japanese aid in the reading of difficult passages.

494. Kokumin Bunko Kankōkai 国民文庫刊行会, <u>Kokuyaku kambun taisei</u> 国譯漢文大成 (Compendium of Japanese translations of Chinese classics), Tōkyō, Kokumin Bunko Kankōkai, 1920-24, 40 v.
The major Chinese classics in Japanese translation. Each Chinese passage is punctuated and a translation appended. Difficult passages have explanatory notes.

495. Seki Giichirō 関儀一郎, ed., <u>Nihon jurin sōsho</u> 日本儒林叢書 (Series of Japanese Confucian writings), Ōsaka, Tōyō Tosho Kankōkai, 1927-29, 6 v. Second series, 1930-33, 4 v.
A collection of 167 works by Japanese Confucian philosophers of the Tokugawa period. Each volume has an introductory bibliographical section. The selected works themselves are presented without commentaries or annotation. The second series contains 46 similar works.

496. Inoue Tetsujirō 井上哲次郎 and Kanie Yoshimaru 蟹江義丸, ed., <u>Nihon rinri ihen</u> 日本倫理彙編 (Collected works on Japanese Confucianism), Tōkyō, Ikuseikai, 1901-03, 10 v.
A collection of 77 works by Tokugawa Confucian scholars. Arrangement is by philosophical school, i.e., Sung school, Wang Yang-ming school, Ku Hsüeh school, etc. The editors have provided bibliographical and biographical prefaces together with aids to the Japanese readings of Chinese passages.

497. Waseda Daigaku Henshūbu 早稲田大学編輯部 (Editorial Office, Waseda University), <u>Sentetsu isho kanseki kokujikai zensho</u> 先哲遺書漢籍国字解全書 (Complete collection of Japanese commentaries on the Chinese classics by former scholars), Tōkyō, Waseda Daigaku Shuppambu, 1909-20, 53 v.
An exhaustive collection of Japanese commentaries on Chinese classics prepared by Tokugawa Confucianists. All passages are punctuated and translated into modern Japanese with annotations for difficult words and phrases.

8) Collected Literary Works

While belles-lettres are not to be confused with historical sources, they are, nevertheless, of great importance to the historian. First of all, the Japanese include in their general collections of literary works many classical histories or diaries which are admittedly historical in nature. Furthermore, any literature is primary evidence of its own content, revealing many facts about the thoughts, feeling, and customs of the people producing it. Thus the cultural historian, in particular, will need to be familiar with the works included in the modern collections of literary works.

The following list includes the basic multi-volume series of Japanese prose and poetry available today. It should be used in conjunction with the general indices to series contained in Part I, 2, e of this bibliography. The scholar will naturally find a great deal of overlapping in content between the various series listed below. In his selection of texts, therefore, he will wish to pay special attention to authenticity, availability, readability, and the nature and quality of explanatory notes. The annotations for the following items have attempted to provide information so that a wise selection of texts may be made.

Since World War II, with the great changes which took place in the publication world, a number of new publishing houses have begun the issuing of literary series. The author does not have sufficient acquaintance with these series to offer annotated entries below but offers the following list of such new series for the reader's information:

Atene bunko	アテネ文庫
Kadokawa bunko	角川文庫
Mikasa bunko	三笠文庫
Shinchō bunko	新潮文庫
Sōgen bunko	創元文庫
Shun'yō bunko	春陽文庫

498. Dai Nihon bunko 大日本文庫 (The Japanese library), Tōkyō, Shun'yōdō, 1934-38, 93 v.
A collection of standard Japanese classics printed in very convenient form. Type is excellent, and all works are rendered into modern Japanese with furigana and commentaries added. The works are divided into 5 main groups: Confucian, Buddhist, Shinto, history and belles-lettres. Each volume begins with a lengthy bibliographical preface.

499. Kaizōsha 改造社, Gendai Nihon bungaku zenshū 現代日本文学全集 (Complete collection of contemporary Japanese literature), Tōkyō, Kaizōsha, 1927-31, 63 v.
A great series of collected works of over 100 contemporary Japanese writers. Volume 63 is a chronological table of contemporary Japanese literature. This series is being continued by the Kaizōsha's Nihon bungaku daizenshū (Entry 512).

500. Heibonsha 平凡社, Gendai taishū bungaku zenshū 現代大衆文学全集 (Complete collection of contemporary popular literature), Tōkyō, Heibonsha, 1927-32, 60 v.
The collected works of over 50 popular Japanese authors active during the first quarter of the twentieth century. This series contains numerous authors not included in the Kaizōsha series (Entires 499 and 512).

501. Iwanami Shigeo 岩波茂雄, Iwanami bunko 岩波文庫 (The Iwanami library), Tōkyō, Iwanami Shoten, 1927—.
A series of paper-bound pocket-size reprints of classical Japanese works in literature, philosophy, and the social sciences. Each volume is devoted to a single classic or a part thereof. Introductory comments are provided by authorities in Japanese literature. Many of the more obscure works such as the Kojiki are rendered into modern Japanese. Annotations have also been provided. Coverage attempts to be all-inclusive.

502. Kaizōsha 改造社, Kaizō bunko 改造文庫 (The Kaizō library), Tōkyō, Kaizōsha, 1930—.
A library of inexpensive reprints of Japanese classics and standard modern monographs published in two series. Series I contains reprints of recent scholarly studies of Japanese history and society: works by Honjō Eijirō, Takimoto Seiichi, etc. Series II consists of reprints of early classics with annotations and commentaries by modern scholars.

503. Kokumin Tosho K.K. 国民図書株式会社, Kindai Nihon bungaku taikei 近代日本文学大系 (Compendium of early-modern Japanese literature), Tōkyō, Kokumin Tosho K.K., 1926-29, 25 v.
A comprehensive series of collected works of the major writers of the early-modern period in Japan (1600-1868) together with collections of various popular genres such as ukiyo zōshi, kyakuhon, senryū, kyōka, etc. Volume 25 contains a chronological table of the early Japanese novel, biographical sketches, and indices.

504. Kokusho Kankōkai 国書刊行会, Kinsei bungei sōsho 近世文藝叢書 (Series of literary works of the early-modern period), Tōkyō, Kokusho Kankōkai, 1910-12, 12 v.
A classified collection of popular and vulgar literature of the early-modern period in Japan (1600-1868). This collection was compiled to succeed the Shin gunsho ruijū (Entry 516) and contains examples of short stories, comical poems, ballads, guide books, and diaries written for popular consumption. This series is followed by the Tokugawa bungei ruisan (1914-16, 12 v.) and the Edo jidai bungei shiryō (1916, 5 v.),

both compiled and published by the Kokusho Kankōkai. These series all have more than literary interest since they represent the tastes and sentiments of the Tokugawa common people. The editors have provided lengthy prefaces explaining the material contained in each volume.

505. Kokumin Tosho K.K. 国民図書株式会社 Kōchū kokka taikei 校註国歌大系 (Annotated compendium of Japanese songs and poetry), Tōkyō, Kokumin Tosho K.K., 1927-31, 28 v.
A collection of 190 poetical anthologies and books on poetics written from ancient times through the Meiji period. Each anthology is provided with a bibliographical preface and the poems are annotated. Volumes 24-28 consist of an elaborate phrase index to the poems contained in the series. This makes it possible to identify quotations or to locate poems when the first lines are given.

506. Kokumin Tosho K.K. 国民図書株式会社, Kōchū Nihon bungaku taikei 校註日本文学大系 (Annotated compendium of Japanese literature), Tōkyō, Kokumin Tosho K.K., 1925-28, 25 v.
A collection of 558 chronologically arranged literary works written from ancient times through the Tokugawa period. Each work is provided with a bibliographic note and marginal annotations explain difficult passages. Volume 25 contains indices to literary works and poems included in the set.

507. Matsushita Daizaburō 松下大三郎 and Watanabe Fumio 渡辺文雄, Kokka taikan 国歌大観 (A comprehensive survey of Japanese poetry), Tōkyō, Dai Nihon Tosho K.K., 1903, 2 v. Second series, Kigensha Shoten, 1924-25, 2 v.
A standard collection of the chief classical anthologies of Japanese poetry. An elaborate phrase index makes it possible to locate poems when only one line is known.

508. Origuchi Shinobu 折口信夫, Kokubungaku chūshaku sōsho 国文学註釋叢書 (Series of commentaries on Japanese literature), Tōkyō, Meicho Kankōkai, 1929-30, 19 v.
A collection of commentaries on Japanese classics written for the most part by Tokugawa scholars. Literary works are largely those of the Heian period. Volumes 18 and 19 consist of subject indices for the works contained in the series.

509. Muromatsu Iwao 室松岩雄, Kokubun chūshaku zensho 国文註釋全書 (Complete commentaries on Japanese literature), Tōkyō, Kokugakuin Daigaku Shuppambu, 1907-10, 20 v.
A collection of pre-modern commentaries, mostly of the Tokugawa period, on Japanese classical works of literature.

510. Kokumin Bunko Kankōkai 国民文庫刊行会, Kokumin bunko 国民文庫 (People's library series), Tōkyō, Kokumin Bunko Kankōkai, 1909-12, 36 v. Second series, 1912-13, 18 v.
One of the more conveniently printed collections of standard Japanese classical works. Series I covers well-known works and anthologies from early times through the Tokugawa period. Series II contains a few lesser known works and collections of popular works of the Tokugawa period. Kana are added to characters to facilitate reading.

511. Shun'yōdō 春陽堂, Meiji Taishō bungaku zenshū 明治大正文学全集 (Complete collection of Meiji and Taisho literature), Tōkyō, Shun'yōdō, 1928-32, 60 v.
A series of collected works of Japanese authors active from 1868 to 1925.

512. Kaizōsha 改造社, Nihon bungaku daizenshū 日本文学大全集 (Complete collection of Japanese literature), Tōkyō, Kaizōsha, 1931-.
A continuation of the great series of collected works of contemporary Japanese authors published as the Gendai Nihon bungaku zenshū (Entry 499). It adds new authors and supplements the collected works of those authors still actively writing.

513. Katsumine Shimpū 勝峰晋風, Nihon haisho taikei 日本俳書大系 (Compendium of Japanese haiku), Tōkyō, Nihon Haisho Taikei Kankōkai, 1926-28, 17 v.
An exhaustive collection of haiku anthologies, mixed prose and haiku journals, and essays covering the great haiku masters of the Tokugawa period. Explanatory notes are appended to each volume. Volume 15 contains genealogical tables and biographical notes. Volume 16 consists of 3 indices: personal names, place names, and poems of Bashō, Buson, and Issa. Volume 17 is a supplement.

514. Takano Tatsuyuki 高野辰之, Nihon kayō shūsei 日本歌謡集成 (Collection of Japanese songs and ballads), Tōkyō, Shunjūsha, 1927-29, 12 v.
A valuable collection of Japanese folk songs, religious songs, and ballads grouped by period and by type within each period. The collection begins with songs of ancient times and concludes with a compilation of currently preserved folk songs. The editor has written introductory chapters to the various sections. An index is appended.

515. Masamune Atsuo 正宗敦夫, Nihon koten zenshū 日本古典全集 (Complete series of Japanese classics), Tōkyō, Nihon Koten Zenshū Kankōkai, 1925-, 183 v.
A collection of the most representative classical texts of pre-modern Japan printed in pocket-size editions. Many volumes are photolithographic reproductions of early woodblock editions. Original illustrations are thus retained. A number of early works of historical importance are contained in the series. Editors have provided a minimum of marginal annotations. In general the small size of the volumes makes this series inconvenient to use.

516. Kokusho Kankōkai 国書刊行会 , Shin gunsho ruijū 新群書類従 (New collection of classics arranged by subjects), Tōkyō, Kokusho Kankōkai, 1906-08, 10 v.
    A collection of popular works of literature, poetry, and drama written during the Tokugawa period. This collection was followed by several other similar series all compiled by the Kokusho Kankōkai to provide material for the study of the culture of the popular masses during the Tokugawa period (see Entry 398).

517. Hakubunkan 博文館 , Teikoku bunko 帝国文庫 (Imperial library), Tōkyō, Hakubunkan, 1893-97, 50 v. Second series, 1898-1903, 50 v.
    An old but extremely complete and useful collection of Japanese classical texts covering the entire pre-Restoration period of Japanese literary history. Single classics as well as collections of short works, poems, songs, dramatic scripts, diaries, and travelogues are included. Kana have been added to characters in difficult spots.

518. Yūhōdō 有朋堂 , Yūhōdō bunko 有朋堂文庫 (Yūhōdō library), 1911-27, 121 v.
    A standard collection of pre-Meiji literary classics and anthologies conveniently printed with furigana and marginal annotations. Volume 121 consists of a general index and provides bibliographical annotations for the nearly 500 works in the series.

9) Collected Materials on Art and Architecture

    The Japanese have published a remarkable number of fine illustrated books on art, architecture, and crafts. While many of these are compiled for purely aesthetic reasons, others present valuable visual documentation for the history of Japanese art or the development of architectural forms and social customs. The following is but a small selection of art books selected to provide the widest possible coverage of the subject for the general historian.

519. Nezu Art Museum, Illustrated catalogue of the Nezu Collection, Tōkyō, Nezu Art Museum, 1939-43, 10 v.
    The catalogue of one of the finest private art collections in Japan. It embraces both Chinese and Japanese art, though the emphasis is on Japan. Many plates are in color.

520. Meiji-Taishō-Shōwa sandai meisaku bijutsu tenrankai zuroku 明治大正昭和三代名作美術展覧会図録 (Catalogue of the exhibit of masterpieces of art of the Meiji, Taisho, and Showa eras), Tōkyō, Asahi Shimbunsha, 1937, 3 v.

521. Nanto jūdaiji ōkagami 南都十大寺大鏡 (Survey of the art of the ten great temples of Nara), Tōkyō, Ōtsuka Kōgeisha, 1932-35, 27 v.
    A comprehensive pictorial coverage of the architectural monuments and art objects of the great temples of Nara. This work combines the collection on the Hōryuji (Hōryuji ōkagami) with a former coverage of seven Nara temples (Nanto shichidaiji ōkagami) published by the Tōkyō Bijutsu Gakkō in 1919-29. Photographs of buildings, sculpture, painting, and documents are accompanied by explanatory notes.

522. Bijutsu Shiryō Kankōkai 美術史料刊行会 , Nihon bijutsushi shiryō 日本美術史資料 (Materials on the history of Japanese art), Nara, Asukaen, 1935-36, 15 folders.
    Each folder contains over 30 large photographic reproductions of Japanese art through the ages.

523. Nihon emakimono shūsei 日本絵巻物集成 (Collection of Japanese emakimono), Tōkyō, Yuzankaku, 1930, 22 v.
    An extensive collection of Japanese narrative scroll paintings, which are especially valuable for their illustrations of Japanese life.

524. Amanuma Toshiichi 天沼俊一 , Nihon kenchikushi zuroku 日本建築史図録 (Pictorial records of the history of Japanese architecture), Kyōto, Hoshino Shoten, 1934-39, 6 v.
    A pictorial history of Japanese public architecture. The series is arranged by periods and covers to the end of the Tokugawa period. Each plate is provided with an explanatory note.

525. Mombushō Shukyōkyoku 文部省宗教局 (Ministry of Education, Religions Section), Nihon kokuhō zenshū 日本国宝全集 (Complete collection of national treasures), Tōkyō, Nihon Kokuhō Zenshū Kankōkai, 1923-38, 84 v.
    A comprehensive collection of collotype reproductions of Japanese national treasures. All plates are accompanied by explanatory comments. Unfortunately, there is no systematic order to the way the material is presented.

526. Ishihara Kenji 石原憲治 , Nihon nōmin kenchiku 日本農民建築 (Japanese peasant architecture), Tōkyō, Shūrakusha, 1934-43, 16 v.
    A comprehensive collection of photographic views of house exteriors and interiors and of general and detailed studies of peasant architecture. Excellent as a source for the study of house types and material environment of Japanese farm communities.

527. Shigemori Sanrei 重森三玲 , Nihon teienshi zukan 日本庭園史図鑑 (Pictorial history of Japanese gardens), Tōkyō, Yūkōsha 1936-39, 26 v.
    A comprehensive pictorial survey of Japanese gardens, past and present. The collection is arranged chronologically. Each volume contains an introductory chapter, and individual plates are accompanied by explanatory notes.

528. Sakado Miichirō 坂戸彌一郎, ed., *Ukiyoe taika shūsei* 浮世絵大家集成 (Collection of paintings by <u>ukiyoe</u> masters), Tōkyō, Taihokaku Shobō, 1932, 20 v. Supplement 1933, 6 v.
> A comprehensive survey of the lives and works of <u>ukiyoe</u> masters. Each volume deals with one artist. Biographical sketches are provided as well as explanatory notes for the many reproductions.

3. DIPLOMATICS

The study of historical sources, their types, transmission, and deciphering, in other words, the science of diplomatics, is termed <u>komonjogaku</u> in Japan. Numerous works are devoted to this subject, but few of them are of much value to the Western scholar. The majority of Japanese works on diplomatics are overly theoretical in their approach or are limited to a narrow facet of the subject. Few such works, for instance, treat the documentary sources of the Tokugawa period. The majority deal only with the difficult problems confronting the historian of the Nara through Kamakura periods. Again the foreign scholar will find little guidance in the practical problems of reading old documents. To the native scholar the possibility of explaining by paraphrasing is so easy that seldom is enough information given for the more precise needs of the translator. The reading of old documents of whatever period is still largely a craft which is becoming more and more specialized as those trained in such work die off.

529. Aida Jirō 相田二郎, <u>Nihon no komonjo</u> 日本の古文書 (Old Japanese documents), Tōkyō, Iwanami Shoten, 1949–.
> The latest and one of the best works on Japanese diplomatics but covering only up to 1600. Two volumes are scheduled. The author discusses types of documents and gives examples and explanations of each.

530. Igi Juichi 伊木壽一, <u>Nihon komonjogaku</u> 日本古文書学 (Japanese diplomatics), Tōkyō, Yūzankaku, 1930. [<u>Dai Nihonshi kōza</u> 大日本史講座 (Japanese history lecture series), v. 13.]
> An excellent introduction to the study of old documents. The author discusses types, writing materials, forms, signatures, and vocabulary used in ancient documents.

531. Katsumine Gekkei 勝峯月溪, <u>Komonjogaku gairon</u> 古文書学概論 (An introduction to the study of diplomatics), Tōkyō, Meguro Shoten, 1930, 787+16 pp.
> One of the most complete studies of old documents, and one of the few to cover documents of the Tokugawa period. The author discusses types and the problems of reading pre-modern materials. His classification is systematic and usable.

532. Kawase Kazuma 川瀬一馬, <u>Nihon shoshigaku no kenkyū</u> 日本書誌学之研究 (The study of Japanese books and writings), Tōkyō, Dai Nihon Yūbenkai Kōdansha, 1943, 1983+46 pp.
> A voluminous study of early Japanese manuscripts, printed works, and general bibliography. Pages 72-82 contain a history of bibliographical research in Japan. An appendix contains a glossary of terms used in the book collecting trade. There is an index.

533. Kyōto Teikoku Daigaku Kokushi Kenkyūshitsu 京都帝国大学国史研究室 (Kyoto Imperial University, Department of National History), <u>Kyōto Teikoku Daigaku Kokushi Kenkyūshitsu-zō shiryōshū</u> 京都帝国大学国史研究室蔵史料集 (Collection of historical materials held by the Kyoto Imperial University, Department of National History), Kyōto, Hoshino Shoten, 1933, 67 plates + 66 pp.
> A collection of 55 photographic reproductions of old documents chosen for their historical importance and their illustration of documentary styles. Commentaries are provided by Professor Nishida Naojirō.

534. Nakamura Naokatsu 中村直勝, <u>Komonjogaku</u> 古文書学 (Diplomatics), Tōkyō, Bunken Shoin, 1929, [in <u>Kokushi kōza</u> 国史講座 (Lectures in Japanese history)].
> A brief introduction to the study of old documents by a foremost expert on medieval history. The work begins with an introduction on general diplomatics and then proceeds to a detailed discussion of pre-Kamakura official and semi-official documents, describing their types, uses, and reading. Unfortunately, the discussion does not go into later types of document.

535. Shiryō Hensansho 史料編纂所 (Historiographical Institute), <u>Komonjo jidai kagami</u> 古文書時代鑑 (Survey of old documents by periods), Tōkyō, Shiryō Hensansho, 1925-27, 4 v.
> A collection of over 400 collotype reproductions of significant historical documents selected in order to illustrate the handwriting of important individuals. The four volumes are divided into two series of two volumes each. Each series covers the period from ancient times to the Meiji era. Each volume is provided with a supplement which reproduces the manuscripts in modern print and adds necessary annotations. One of the best collections of its kind.

536. Shūshikyoku and Shiryō Hensangakari 修史局 史料編纂掛 (Bureau of Historical Compilation and Office of Historiography), <u>Shichō bokuhō</u> 史徴墨宝 (A treasury of historical handwritings), Tōkyō, Taiseikan, 1887-94, 196 plates. Commentaries 1887-94, 6 v.
> Lithographic reproductions of 167 historical documents selected on the basis of the importance of the document or of the individuals writing them. Detailed commentaries are provided separately.

537. Uematsu Yasushi 植松安, <u>Hompō shoshigaku gaiyō</u> 本邦書誌学概要 (An introduction to Japanese bibliography), Tōkyō, Toshokan Jigyō Kenkyūkai, 1929.
> A scientific inquiry into the problems of pre-modern bibliography in Japan. The work is divided into: 1) a general introduction, 2) a study of early manuscripts and their transmission to the present, and 3) a study of early printed copies of books.

538. Yoshimura Shigeki 吉村茂樹, <u>Komonjo no hanashi</u> 古文書の話 (Talks on old documents), Tōkyō, Nihon Shuppan Haikyū K.K., 1943, 238 pp.
   A popular discussion of the problems of handling and reading old documents. The author presents a great deal of useful and interesting material on the general nature, materials, and shapes of old documents.

539. Yūzankaku Henshūkyoku 雄山閣編輯局 (Editorial Office, Yūzankaku), <u>Komonjo no kenkyūhō</u> 古文書の研究法 (Methods for the study of old documents), Tōkyō, Yūzankaku, 1938, 245 pp.
   A collection of essays by over 20 experts on the problems of handling and reading ancient documents.

540. Yūzankaku 雄山閣, <u>Nihon meihitsu zenshū</u> 日本名筆全集(Complete collection of famous Japanese calligraphy), Tōkyō, Yūzankaku, 1930-33, 16 v.
   Photographic reproductions of Japanese writings from ancient to Restoration times chosen primarily for the beauty of their calligraphic style. Writings are classified according to subject matter. Volumes 13-15 contain historical documents and letters. Each volume contains an appendix in which the documents are translated and annotated by a prominent authority on literature or diplomatics.

541. Yūzankaku 雄山閣, <u>Shiryō kenkyū no jitsurei to sono hōhō</u> 史料研究の実例と其方法 (Examples of the study of historical materials and the methodology for such study), Tōkyō, Yūzankaku, 1939, 3+ 386 pp.
   A number of actual examples showing the techniques of using ancient documents in historical research. Most examples are taken from the pre-seventeenth century period.

IV. PERIODICALS

   A great deal of the most significant research of Japanese historians is published in scholarly journals. This is especially true of the period since 1930. By that time the number of historical journals had greatly increased, and Japanese scholarship had matured to the point where the investigation of refined and detailed problems had taken the place of broad survey type studies. In general, the student of Japanese history will find articles in periodicals better organized and better documented than the usual run of historical literature in book form.
   The number of journals carrying articles of historical interest in Japan is truly amazing. Honjō Eijirō in his <u>Nihon keizaishi shin'bunken</u> (Entry 11) cites bibliographical references from some 400 journals. So also does the Shigakkai's <u>Shigaku bunken mokuroku</u> (Entry 41). The Ōtsuka Shigakkai's <u>Kokushi rombun yōmoku</u> (Entry 101) draws from over 160. Naturally many of these journals are of extremely limited interest or have had short publication lives. In actuality the general historian will find that a rather small handful of major publications carries the greater portion of articles in which he is interested. It is only as he becomes more specialized in his interest that the more unusual journals need be consulted.
   One of the encouraging yet exasperating developments of the postwar period is the mushroom growth of academic journals published by the newly established prefectural universities (<u>shinsei daigaku</u>). Such journals are generally of an interdisciplinary nature and hence contain historical articles in combination with those on many other extremely unrelated subjects. No single such journal can be considered of special interest to the historian. Furthermore, such publications have a limited circulation, so that for all practical purposes many excellent articles published by local historians are unavailable to the scholar who does not have access to the larger libraries.
   The following section presents a selective list of journals useful to the non-specialist student of Japanese history. Emphasis has been placed on those periodicals which are strictly in the historical field, but a selection of the most outstanding journals in each of the fields of geography, government, economics, sociology, religion, literature, and art has also been made. The preparation of even this selective list has been a matter of considerable difficulty, chiefly because of the inadequacy of periodical files even in Japan. In general, the publication history of journals is not well documented. Practically all scholarly periodicals were forced to abandon publication as a consequence of the Pacific War. Most of them ceased operations during 1944 and resumed at the earliest in 1946 but more generally not until 1947 or 1948. Some have failed to reappear. In the following list the author has designated with asterisks those journals which are definitely being published today.
   Note that where Japanese editors have provided their own English titles, these have been retained and enclosed in quotation marks.

1. GENERAL

   The student of Japanese history will often find material of interest to him in the files of some of the better journals of general coverage such as <u>Chūō kōron</u> (The central review) (Entry 543), <u>Kaizō</u> (Reconstruction) (Entry 544), or <u>Bungei shunjū</u> (Literary annals) (Entry 542). These magazines are semi-popular but of high quality, containing articles by leading authorities in a great variety of fields. Most of Japan's better known historians have contributed to such periodicals; their articles often consist of interpretive summaries of research appearing in more scholarly form elsewhere.

542. *Bungei shunjū 文藝春秋 (Literary annals), Tōkyō, Bungei Shunjūsha, 1923—. Monthly.
   A semi-popular magazine of general coverage. Since World War II, its pages have included a high percentage of articles on political affairs and current opinion.

543. *Chūō kōron 中央公論 (The central review), Tōkyō, Chūō Kōronsha, August, 1887—. Monthly.
   A semi-popular monthly journal of general coverage. Articles are of a high quality and range in subject matter from current political discussions to matters of art and literature. Authors are frequently men of high academic reputation. A few articles during the year deal with historical subjects, though the general slant of the journal is contemporary. There is no cumulative index.

544. *Kaizō 改 造 (Reconstruction), Tōkyō, Kaizōsha, April 1919–.   Monthly.
A monthly journal of general coverage similar to Chūō kōron (Entry 543).   Occasional articles of a historical nature appear, though the chief emphasis of the journal is on contemporary political affairs. Kaizō
had a reputation for expressing liberal views before World War II.

545. "Nippon hyōron" 日 本 評 論 (Japan review), Tōkyō, Nihon Hyōronsha, May, 1936-51.   Monthly.
First published as Keizai ōrai 經 濟 往 来 in 1926.   This is a popular journal of general coverage
emphasizing current economic and political problems.

546. *Sekai 世 界 (The world), Tōkyō, Iwanami Shoten, Jan., 1946–.   Monthly.
A post World War II journal similar to Chūō kōron (Entry 543).   Coverage is of a general nature, though
contemporary political problems predominate.   Occasional articles by outstanding Japanese historians appear in its pages.   These tend to be on controversial subjects such as the early Meiji liberal movement
or interpretations of the Meiji Restoration.

547. Tembō 展 望 (Survey), Tōkyō, Chikuma Shobō, Jan., 1946-Sept., 51.   Monthly.
A short-lived semi-popular monthly journal of general coverage with emphasis on thought and literature.
Articles are somewhat more scholarly than those in Chūō kōron or Kaizō and the incidence of works of
an historical nature relatively high.   These are by reputable historians, generally on problems of contemporary interest.

2. HUMANISTIC SCIENCE

    Postwar Japan has seen the appearance of a number of scholarly journals devoted to the humanistic sci-
ences (jimbun kagaku).   In actuality the field represented by the Japanese term "jimbun kagaku" is a combination of the humanities and social sciences, so that it is perhaps more accurately translated as "the cultural
sciences."   Journals in this field often contain a great deal of historical material.   This is especially true of
Jimbun gakuhō (Entry 548) which has published outstanding articles on the history of Japan's modernization.

548. *Jimbun gakuhō 人 文 学 報 ("Journal of Humanistic Science"), Kyōto, Kyōto Daigaku Jimbun Kagaku
Kenkyūsho, Dec., 1950–.
A scholarly journal published by the Japanese section of the Institute of Humanistic and Social Sciences
at Kyoto University.   This group headed by Sakata Yoshio is concentrating on the study of the modernization of Japan.   Articles so far have dealt with interpretations of the Meiji Restoration and early Meiji
political movements.   Contributors are especially distinguished by the freshness and independence of their
thought.

549. *Jimbun kagaku 人 文 科 学 ("Quarterly Journal of Humanistic Science"), Kyōto, Jimbun Gakkai, July,
1946–.   Quarterly.
Organ of the Society of Humanistic Science, Research Institute of Humanistic Science, Kyoto University.
Articles are of a general nature and are written from a social science approach.   A few articles appear
on Japanese cultural history.

550. *Jimbun kenkyū 人 文 研 究 ("Studies in the Humanities"), Ōsaka, Ōsaka Shiritsu Daigaku Bungakkai,
1950–.
Journal of the Literary Association of Osaka City University.   Individual issues are apparently edited in
rotation by several departments.   Thus each year a number of issues are devoted to historical or economic studies.   Articles are scholarly and many utilize the field study approach.

551. *"Zinbun" 人 文 ("The Cultural Sciences"), Tōkyō, Jimbun Kagaku Iinkai, 1947-50; Nihon Jimbun Kaga-
kukai, 1951–.
See Entries 14 and 684 for annotations of this journal during its period of publication by the government
sponsored Jimbun Kagaku Iinkai.   Since 1951 it has passed into private hands and is edited by the Japan
Cultural and Human Science Society.   The first issue was devoted to field studies on the island of
Tsushima.

3. GENERAL HISTORY

    The field of history has been dominated by a few major journals.   Senior in this group have been the
organs of the historical associations of Japan's two leading universities, the Shigaku zasshi (Journal of historical science) (Entry 578) of Tokyo University and Shirin (Journal of history) (Entry 580) of Kyoto University.
Both journals have maintained high scholarly standards in publishing articles by the political and cultural historians of their respective institutions.   It was largely in protest over what was felt to be their overly academic approach that Rekishigaku kenkyū ("Journal of the Historical Science Society")(Entry 568) was begun in
1933.   Since that year Shigaku zasshi and Rekishigaku kenkyū have represented two rival schools of historical
research in Japan, the "academic" and "progressive."   Since the war another "progressive" journal, Nihonshi
kenkyū (Journal of Japanese history) (Entry 563) has begun publication in Kyoto.
    Aside from such major journals, there are a large number of university publications similar to Shigaku
zasshi, all more or less limited in their scope and seldom publishing more than a few articles a year of interest to the general historian.   Furthermore, each of the rival historical schools has also produced journals
of more popular appeal.   Such are "Nippon-rekishi (The Journal of the Japanese History)" (Entry 562), sponsored by Tokyo and Kokugakuin University members, and Rekishi hyōron (Historical review) (Entry 566), published by the Minshushugi Kagakusha Kyōkai (Association of Democratic Scientists), representing the right and
left respectively.   Though the historian must keep in mind the political slants of these periodicals, he will
find a great deal of useful material in them.

552. *Bunkashigaku 文 化 史 学 ("Studies in the Cultural History"), Kyōto, Bunkashi Gakkai, 1950—. Semi-annually.
Published largely through the single efforts of Ishida Ichirō of the Faculty of Letters, Dōshisha University, this journal represents an attempt to balance the overly materialistic approach of so much of recent Japanese historical scholarship. Articles cover both European and Japanese subjects. Ishida himself is a specialist on art and intellectual history.

553. *Bunkashi kenkyū 文 化 史 研 究 (Cultural history review), Tōkyō, Hokuryūkan, Sept. 1947—. 3 times a year.
A popular journal largely devoted to non-Japanese subjects and seldom containing articles of scholarly worth.

554. Chūō shidan 史 央 史 壇 (Central historical review), Tōkyō, Kokushi Kōshūkai, May, 1910-June, 1928. Monthly.
A popular historical journal of wide coverage. Few of the articles are of a scholarly nature and most are undocumented. One feature of this journal was its many special issues devoted to single topics in Japanese history such as the imperial enthronement ceremonies, archeology, biographies of Meiji statesmen, etc. One important series of articles lists damage to libraries and loss of historical materials as a result of the 1923 Tokyo earthquake and fire.

555. *Denki 傳 記 (Biography), Tōkyō, Denki Gakkai, Oct., 1934—. Monthly.
Features articles on Tokugawa and recent Japanese historical figures with frequent bibliographical articles. Important also for its printing of biographical sources.

556. Gunjishi kenkyū 軍 事 史 研 究 (Studies in military history), Tōkyō, Gunjishi Kenkyūkai, Mar. 1936—. Bimonthly.
Organ of the Society for the Study of Military History, this journal contains a large proportion of scholarly articles useful to the historian. Publication was discontinued during the war.

557. *Historia ヒ ス ト リ ア (Historia), Ōsaka, Ōsaka Rekishi Gakkai, 1950—.
A somewhat popular journal patronized by scholars of the Osaka-Kobe area.

558. Kamigata 上 方, Ōsaka, Kamigata Kyōdo Kenkyūkai, Jan., 1931—. Monthly.
Organ of the Society for the Study of the Kamigata (Kyoto-Osaka) Area. Generally contains articles on the cultural history and folklore of Kyoto and Osaka. Publication ceased during the war.

559. *Kōkogaku zasshi 考 古 学 雑 誌 (Journal of archaeology), Tōkyō, Yoshikawa Kōbunkan, May, 1896—. Monthly.
The senior archeological journal in Japan, organ of the Japan Archeological Society (Nihon Kōko Gakkai), National Museum, Tokyo. Between 1900 and 1910 the journal changed its name several times but returned to the original title as above. Articles are scholarly and deal with both Japanese and continental Asiatic archaeology.

560. Kokumin no rekishi 国 民 の 圧 史 (People's history), Tōkyō, Kokumin no Rekishi Kenkyūkai, Jan., 1947-49. Monthly.
A short-lived popular journal aimed at teachers of Japanese history in primary and secondary schools and sponsored by the post-World War "old guard" historians and educators. It carries articles by such men as Tsuji Zennosuke, Ōrui Noboru, Nakamura Kōya, and others. Articles are of a general nature and undocumented.

561. *Kokushigaku 国 史 学 (Japanese history), Tōkyō, Kokugakuin Daigaku Kokushi Gakkai, Nov., 1929—. Quarterly.
Organ of the Japanese History Society of the Faculty of Letters, Kokugakuin University. Pre-World War II issues featured articles on Shinto and national polity. Since the war the scope of the journal has expanded considerably.

562. *"Nippon-rekishi" 日 本 圧 史 ("The journal of the Japanese history"), Tōkyō, Jikkyo Shuppan K.K., 1946—. Monthly.
A somewhat popular journal with a conservative editorial policy similar to Kokumin no rekishi (Entry 560). Articles are short and are generally written to appeal to teachers of history in secondary schools. Contributors are generally members of the Tokyo University Historiographical Institute, for instance, Ienaga Saburō, and Kokugakuin University together with such men as Takeuchi Rizō (Kyūshū U.) and Toyoda Takeshi (Tōhoku U.). A rather large percentage of articles deals with local history and folklore. There are book reviews but no scholarly annexes.

563. *Nihonshi kenkyū 日 本 史 研 究 (Journal of Japanese history), Kyōto, Nihonshi Kenkyūkai, 1946—. Quarterly.
Organ for the Society for the Study of Japanese History of Kyoto, a post-World War II counterpart of the Rekishigaku Kenkyūkai (see Entry 568) of Tokyo. Active in this group are such scholars as Naramoto Tatsuya and Hayashiya Tatsusaburō (Ritsumeikan U.). Articles tend to be somewhat popular and often contain a Marxist bias.

564. <u>Rekishi</u> 圧 史 (History), Tōkyō, Rekishibunka Kenkyūkai, Nov., 1926—. Monthly.
A pre-World War II journal by this name, organ of the Society for the Study of Japanese Culture, was published by Hakuyōsha. Editorial policy tended to be nationalistic. The journal ceased publication during the war.

565. *<u>Rekishi</u> 圧 史 (History), Sendai, Tōhoku Shigakkai, 1949—. Monthly.
Journal of the Tōhoku Historical Association, Faculty of Letters, Tōhoku University, Sendai. Articles on Tokugawa local history are especially good.

566. *<u>Rekishi hyōron</u> 圧 史 評 論 (Historical review), Tōkyō, Minshushugi Kagakusha Kyōkai, May, 1946—. Monthly.
Published by the Association of Democratic Scientists, the chief organization of the Marxist school of historians in Japan. Leading contributors are such men as Hayashi Motoi, Ishimoda Masashi, Tōma Seita, and Matsumoto Shimpachirō. After the first year of publication articles tended to become more scholarly. Many of them concern technical problems of Marxist interpretation of Japanese history. Issues contain a large number of reviews and periodic surveys of the year's historical scholarship as viewed by the Marxist historian.

567. *<u>Rekishigaku geppō</u> 圧 史 学 月 報 (Historiographical monthly), Tōkyō, Rekishigaku Kenkyūkai, Oct., 1950—. Monthly.
A small pamphlet (from 10 to 15 pages) which contains short notes by the leading contributors to <u>Rekishigaku kenkyū</u> on matters of historical interpretation, recent trends in historical scholarship at home and abroad, and critical reviews. Frequent features are a list of newly published books in the historical field and a list of leading articles in current historical journals.

568. *<u>Rekishigaku kenkyū</u> 圧 史 学 研 究 ("Journal of the Historical Science Society"), Tōkyō, Rekishigaku Kenkyūkai, Nov., 1933—, monthly; June, 1946—, bimonthly.
One of the leading historical journals in Japan, organ of the independent Historical Science Association. This association was organized by young historians in protest against the overly academic approach of the Historical Association (Shigakkai) of Tokyo University. Up to 1939 the <u>Rekishigaku kenkyū</u> represented only a more vigorous variation of the mother organization, containing articles written from a more social science point of view. In 1939, with the disbanding of the Rekishi Kagakkai (Historical Science Society), members of this Marxist oriented group entered the Rekishigaku Kenkyūkai and strongly influenced its editorial policies. Since World War II this organization and its journal have been extremely active. Leading members of the group include Hani Gorō, Mishima Hajime, Inoue Kiyoshi, Ishimoda Masashi, Tōma Seita, Tōyama Shigeki, Matsushima Eiichi, and Fujita Gorō. Many are concurrently members of the Minshushugi Kagakusha Kyōkai (Association of Democratic Scientists); on the other hand, a large number are concurrently members of the conservative Shigakkai. <u>Rekishigaku kenkyū</u> contains articles of excellent quality, well documented. There are a number of valuable scholarly features which include bibliographical lists (<u>Rombun yōmoku</u>), surveys of scholarship in various fields (<u>Gakkai dōkō</u>), and a yearly summary of historiography in Japan (see Entries 35 and 36). <u>Rekishigaku kenkyū</u> covers Japanese, Chinese, and Western history, but the emphasis is on Japan.

569. <u>Rekishi kagaku</u> 圧 史 科 学 (Historical science), Tōkyō, Hakuyōsha, June, 1933-39. Monthly.
A scholarly journal featuring interpretative articles by historians of the Marxist school. There are a large number of excellent articles on Japanese national and local history. A journal of this name is now published by the Historical Science Society of Meiji University.

570. <u>Rekishi kōron</u> 圧 史 公 論 (Historical review), Tōkyō, Yūzankaku, 1932—. Monthly, then bimonthly.
A somewhat popular historical journal in the <u>Chūō shidan</u> tradition. It contains a number of specialized articles on Japanese history of high quality as well as interpretive articles by leading historians. It ceased publication during the last war.

571. <u>Rekishi kyōiku</u> 圧 史 教 育 (Teaching of history), Tōkyō, Rekishi Kyōiku Kenkyūkai, November, 1925—. Monthly.
A journal slanted to the interest of teachers of history in primary and secondary schools. Articles are general and undocumented but are written by many of Japan's foremost historians.

572. <u>Rekishi to seikatsu</u> 圧 史 と 生 活 (History and life), Tōkyō, Keiō Gijuku Keizaishi Gakkai, 1938—. Triannual.
Contains stimulating articles on economic history and local institutions.

573. *<u>Shichō</u> 史 潮 (Currents of history), Tōkyō, Tōkyō Bunrika Daigaku Ōtsuka Shigakkai, Feb., 1931—. Triannual and later quarterly.
Organ of the Ōtsuka Historical Association of the Tokyo Bunrika University (now Tōkyō Kyōiku Daigaku). Articles are rather general in nature and cover Japanese, Oriental, and Occidental history. Each number carries a review section and notes on recent events in the historical world. The first number of each year carries a brief survey of the previous year's major historiographical developments. Publication has been irregular since the war.

574. *Shien 史 苑 (Journal of history), Tōkyō, Rikkyō Daigaku Shigaku Kenkyūkai, April, 1928—. Quarterly.
Organ of the Historical Research Association of Rikkyō (St. Paul's) University. Articles cover Japanese,
Oriental, and Occidental history with a strong emphasis on the Occidental. The journal has been active
in making available to Japanese Western views on historiography.

575. *Shien 史 淵 ("Journal of History"), Fukuoka, Kyūdai Shigakkai, 1929—. Irregular.
Organ of the Historical Society of Kyūshū University. Articles cover Japanese, Oriental, and Occidental
history. Those on Japan tend to deal with topics of local interest. Fifty numbers had been published by
Dec., 1951.

576. *Shigaku 史 学 (History), Tōkyō, Keiō Gijuku Daigaku Mita Shigakkai, Oct., 1921—. Quarterly.
Organ of the Mita Historical Association of Keiō University. Coverage is general and includes a large
percentage of works on non-Japanese history. There is an extensive review section. Historians will find
the articles by Nomura Kanetarō of special value and the chief attraction of this journal. An index to
volumes 1-15 was published in 1937.

577. *Shigaku kenkyū 史 学 研 究 ("Review of Historical Studies"), Hiroshima, Hiroshima Bunrika Daigaku
Shigaku Kenkyūkai, Oct., 1929—. Triannually and quarterly.
Organ of the Historical Society, Hiroshima University, it covers Japanese, Oriental, and Occidental history. Occasional articles of significance appear in the field of Japanese history. The chief pre-war feature of this journal is its excellent bibliographical section, entitled "Saikin shikai 最近 史 界 (The
recent historical world)," a classified list of books and articles published during the previous third of a
year. Up to 1942 this section provided one of the most complete bibliographical coverages of historical
literature in Japan. Publication ceased from 1942 to 1948. An index to volumes 1-10 was issued in
1930. Postwar issues deal more fully with Japanese history, especially local history.

578. *Shigaku zasshi 史 学 雑 誌 ("Journal of Historical Science"), Tōkyō, Tōkyō [Teikoku] Daigaku
Shigakkai, Dec., 1889—. Monthly.
The senior historical journal in Japan, organ of the Institute of Historical Science of Tokyo University.
This journal has carried on the scholarly tradition begun by the German historian, Ludwig Riess. Articles deal largely with Japanese history, though Chinese and Western subjects are also treated. A
tendency to academic scholarship was especially noticeable during the 1930s and early 40s. Recent
issues contain more articles written from a social science point of view. Special features of this journal
are an extensive review section, a section devoted to notes and news of the field, and a bibliographical
section. From 1889 to 1916 each issue contained an unclassified bibliographical survey entitled "Saikin
naikoku shikai 最近 内 国 史 界 (The recent Japanese historical world)" which offered a selective
coverage of Japanese historiography. Later, this feature was replaced by two somewhat irregular sections entitled "Shinkan shomoku 新刊 書 目 (List of newly published works)" and "Shincho zasshi
shin'yōmoku 新著 雑 誌 新要 目 (Selected index to newly issued journals)." During the years of
World War II these features were discontinued. Since the war Shigaku zasshi has compiled a yearly survey of historiography in Japan entitled "Sen kyūhyaku [ ] nen no rekishi gakkai 19[ ] 年 の 歴 史
学 界 or "Historical studies during the year 19[ ]." Beginning with 1950 the journal brought out several new annexes besides the regular review section. These include a review of scholarly articles entitled "Kokunai shikai" or "Historiography in Japan," notes on academic society meetings, a selected
index to the content of journals received, and English summaries of leading articles of each number. An
index to volumes 1-60 was published in 1953.

579. *Shikan 史 観 (Historical review), Tōkyō, Waseda Daigaku Shigakkai, Feb., 1931—. Irregular.
Organ of the Historical Society of Waseda University. Coverage is given to Japanese, Oriental, and Occidental history. Articles on Japanese history are rather few. Publication has been at the rate of 2 or
3 numbers a year with a complete lapse from 1944 to Oct., 1949.

580. *Shirin 史 林 (Journal of history), Kyōto, Kyōto Teikoku Daigaku Shigaku Kenkyūkai, Jan., 1916—.
Quarterly.
Organ of the Historical Research Society, Kyoto University. It has the best reputation as a "University"
journal after the Shigaku zasshi of Tokyo University. Coverage is extremely broad, including Japanese,
Oriental, and Occidental history, archaeology, and geography. Hence relatively few articles are on Japanese history proper. Between 1916 and 1930 this journal carried a valuable yearly survey of publications
in the field of history, archeology, and geography (see Entry 37). Since 1950 it has featured an extensive bibliographical list of recent Japanese books and articles on Japanese, Chinese, and Western history.
An index to volumes 1-20 was published in 1935.

581. Shizengaku zasshi 史 前 学 雑 誌 (Journal of prehistory), Tōkyō, Shizen Gakkai, 1929-35. Bimonthly.
A leading archeological journal.

582. *Tōhō gakuhō 東 方 学 報 (Journal of Oriental studies), Kyōto, Tōhō Bunka Kenkyūsho, 1931—. 3 times
a year.
Organ of the Kyoto Institute of Oriental Culture (Tōhō Bunka Kenkyūsho), an organization which has since
been incorporated into the Kyoto Institute of Humanistic and Social Sciences (Jimbun Kagaku Kenkyūsho).
Articles are of a scholarly nature and occasionally touch on subjects of Japanese history or Japanese relations with the continent. The separately published bibliography of Oriental history is extremely complete and can be of value to the historian working in Japanese relations with the continent.

583. *Toho gakuhō 東方学報 (Journal of Oriental studies), Tōkyō, Tōhō Bunka Gakuin, Mar., 1931-. 3 times a year.
Organ of the Tokyo Academy of Oriental Culture (Tōhō Bunka Gakuin), an organization since incorporated into the Institute for Research in Oriental Culture (Tōyō Bunka Kenkyūsho). Articles are of a scholarly nature and occasionally touch on subjects of Japanese history or Japanese relations with the continent.

584. *Tōyō bunka 東洋文化 (Oriental culture), Tōkyō, Tōyō Gakkai, Jan., 1950-. Quarterly.
Organ of the Oriental Society, it was published from 1946 to 1950 under the title Tōyō bunka kenkyū. Contains scholarly articles, a very few of which concern Japanese history.

585. *Tōyō gakuhō 東洋学報 ("Report of the Oriental Society"), Tōkyō, Tōyō Gakujutsu Kyōkai, 1911-. Quarterly.
Organ of the Research Department of the Oriental Library (Tōyō Bunko). Articles are primarily sinological and technical.

586. *Tōyōshi kenkyū 東洋史研究 (Journal of Oriental research), Kyoto, Ibundo Shoten, Oct., 1935-. Bimonthly.
Organ of the Oriental History Research Center, Kyoto University. Exclusively sinological in its approach. Features a yearly survey of Japanese sinological literature.

587. *Yuibutsuron kenkyū 唯物論研究 (Studies in materialistic philosophy), Tōkyō, Yuibutsuron Kenkyū-kai, Nov., 1932-Mar., 1938, monthly; Yuibutsuron Kenkyūsho, Oct., 1947-, monthly.
The post-World War II journal claims not to be a successor to the earlier publication, but it is backed by the same names and carries identical material. Articles are largely interpretations of current and historical problems from the intellectual Marxist point of view. In 1951 the name of the journal was changed to Yuibutsuronsha 唯物論者.

4. LOCAL HISTORY

Interest in local history has given rise to a large number of journals devoted to regional subjects. In prewar Japan, such journals were largely of a non-scholarly nature, concerned primarily with local legend and folklore. Few of them were of national significance or contained the work of trained historians. Most such journals had short publication lives, and few survived the last war. For this reason the earlier prewar local publications have not been included in the following list. The historian should be aware of their existence, however. And if the subject of his investigation has local roots, he should not be content with the organs of centralized scholarship published in Tokyo or Kyoto.
Since the war, local history has entered a new and more scholarly phase of development. This has been due first of all to the decentralization of scholarly personnel brought about by the creation of the new prefectural universities and secondly to a new-found interest in local history among centrally located historians. The establishment of a new journal, Chihōshi kenkyū (Local history) (Entry 588), has done much to encourage and coordinate the activities of local historians. The following list of journals is a selection of locally published periodicals which have demonstrated more than local importance.

588. *Chihōshi kenkyū 地方史研究 (Local history), Tōkyō, Chihōshi Kenkyū Kyōgikai, Mar., 1951-. Three times a year.
A new journal, organ of the Committee for the Study of Local History, a group of Tokyo scholars under the leadership of Nomura Kanetarō. The prime purpose of the journal is to stimulate and coordinate the activities of local historians. Its pages are packed with a great deal of valuable information: short articles by leading historians on the state of local historical research, news of local historical institutions, and bibliographies of recently published books and articles on local history.

589. *Iwate shigaku kenkyū 岩手史学研究 (Iwate history), Morioka, Iwate-ken, Iwate Shigakkai, 1947-. Biannual.
A journal containing scholarly articles on subjects connected with the northern frontier region of Japan.

590. *Nishi Nihon shigaku 西日本史学 (The Western Japan historical review), Fukuoka, Nishi Nihon Shikai, Sept., 1949-. Three times a year.
Organ of the Western Japan Historical Society associated with Kyushu University. This journal contains studies of local history and Japan's early relations with the continent and the West.

591. *Shinano 信濃 ("The Shinano"), Matsumoto, Nagano-ken, Shinano Kyōdo Kenkyūkai, 1932-. Monthly.
One of the most active journals specializing in local history and archeology. Contains a high percentage of historical field studies. Since its origin the journal has passed through three publication series. The present series began in 1949.

5. GEOGRAPHY

The Japanese have long linked geography and history together in their bibliographical categories. Hence a number of journals exist which combine the two subjects. Of these, only Rekishi chiri (Historical geography) (Entry 597) survives today. This periodical, one of the oldest in modern Japan, is as much a journal of history as of geography.
Journals of purely geographical coverage are of less interest to the historian but frequently contain materials on local history or historical geography. Of these, the Chirigaku hyōron (Geographical review of Japan) (Entry 593) is the oldest and most respected. The newly organized Jimbun chiri (Cultural geography) (Entry 596), however, is more in touch with current developments in the geographic field.

592. *Chiiki 地 域 (Regionalism), Tōkyō, Nihon Shoin, 1952—. Monthly.
A recent journal inspired by the example of American geographers.

593. *Chirigaku hyōron 地 理 学 評 論 (Geographical review of Japan), Tōkyō, Nihon Chiri Gakkai, 1925—.
Monthly.
One of the foremost academic geographical journals in Japan, organ of the Association of Japanese Geo-graphers, Faculty of Science, Tokyo University. Occasional articles deal with subjects of local historical interest. A general index to volumes 11-20 (1935-44) was issued in 1951.

594. *Chirigaku ronsō 地 理 学 論 叢 (Geographical studies), Kyōto, Kyōto Teikoku Daigaku Bungakubu Chirigaku Kyōshitsu, Nov., 1932—. Semiannual.
Organ of the Geographical Institute, Faculty of Letters, Kyoto University. This journal was replaced after World War II by Jimbun chiri (Entry 596).

595. Chiri to rekishi 地 理 と 歴 史 (Geography and history), Tōkyō, Kyōiku Chiri Rekishi Remmei, 1919—.
Monthly.
Contained some scholarly articles on local history and biography. Publication ceased during World War II.

596. *Jimbun chiri 人 文 地 理 (Cultural geography), Kyōto, Jimbun Chiri Gakkai, May, 1948—. Quarter-ly.
The post-World War II journal of the Institute of Human Geography, Faculty of Letters, Kyoto University. Contains occasional articles on local history. This journal is now considered the foremost geographical publication in Japan because its pages have kept up with the latest developments in the field of geography.

597. *Rekishi chiri 歴 史 地 理 (Historical geography), Tōkyō, Nihon Rekishi Chiri Gakkai, Oct., 1899—.
Monthly.
One of the first historical publications of modern Japan, this journal may be thought of as a sister publi-cation to the Shigaku zasshi (Entry 578). It contains a high percentage of scholarly articles on Japanese history; volumes 40-60 are especially significant. In addition each number has several editorial features of great value. These include a list of newly published books, a list of significant new articles, and a section on local historical materials. An index to volumes 1-66 was published in 1936.

598. Rekishi to chiri 歴 史 と 地 理 (History and geography), Kyōto, Kyōto Shigaku Chirigaku Dōkōkai,
Nov., 1917-Nov., 1934. Monthly.
Contains a large number of stimulating articles on Japanese local history. An index to numbers 1-53 was published in 1935.

6. GOVERNMENT AND POLITICS

Although a large number of journals are published by the law departments of Japanese universities, the contents of these are generally too specialized to warrant inclusion in this section. Articles on political and administrative history are to be found in historical journals rather than those in the legal or political science field. Those who are interested in problems of contemporary political science and law are referred to the section on periodicals in Robert E. Ward's A Guide to Japanese Reference and Research Materials in the Field of Political Science.
The following journals have been selected for their special interest to the historian. Among them the Hōshakaigaku (Sociology of Law) (Entry 599) represents a new departure in the study of legal institutions. The historian should welcome its studies of the sociological background to the development of legal institutions in Japan.

599. *Hōshakaigaku 法 社 会 学 (Sociology of law), Tōkyō, Nihon Hōshakai Gakkai, 1951—.
A recent journal of irregular appearance sponsored by such men as Kawashima Takeyoshi and Kaino Michitaka. Articles deal with the mutual interaction of law and society.

600. *Jurisuto ジュリスト (Jurist), Tōkyō, Yuhikaku, Jan. 1952—. Twice a month.
A new journal devoted to contemporary problems of jurisprudence.

601. *Kokka gakkai zasshi 国 家 学 会 雑 誌 ("Journal of the Association of Political Science"), Tōkyō,
Kokka Gakkai, Mar., 1887—. Monthly.
The senior political science journal in Japan, organ of the Political Science Association of the Faculty of Law, Tokyo University. Articles tend to be highly legalistic, and since World War II a rather large portion deal with Western law. Occasional articles deal with the history of Japanese legal or political institutions.

602. Toshi mondai 都 市 問 題 (Municipal problems), Tōkyō, Tōkyō Shisei Chōsakai, May, 1925-42.
Monthly.
The foremost journal devoted to local administration and municipal problems. Its coverage was primari-ly contemporary and only occasionally included articles of historical interest.

603. *Waseda seiji keizaigaku zasshi 早 稲 田 政 治 經 済 学 雑 誌 (Waseda journal of political science and economics), Tōkyō, Waseda Hōgakkai, Oct., 1922—. Irregular.
An excellent journal with a social science approach to the problems of politics and government; contains occasional articles of historical interest.

7. ECONOMICS

Two journals listed below are of special interest to the historian. These are Keizaishi kenkyū (Studies in economic history), (Entry 606) and Shakai keizaishigaku ("Journal of the Social and Economic History Society") (Entry 612). These periodicals contain scholarly articles on Japanese social and economic history and rank along with Shigaku zasshi and Rekishigaku kenkyū as the most valuable in the entire field of history. Unfortunately Keizaishi kenkyū is no longer published and Shakai keizaishigaku has lost a good deal of its pre-war vitality. But even the early issues of these journals contain articles of lasting value.

Another journal apt to be overlooked by the general historian is Nōgyō sōgō kenkyū ("Quarterly Journal of Agricultural Economy") (Entry 609). This journal is published by one of the most active research organizations in Japan today and contains a wide variety of articles on the economic history of Japan and other Asiatic countries.

604. *Keizaigaku ronshū 經濟学論集 (Collected essays on economics), Tōkyō, Tōkyō [Teikoku] Daigaku Keizai Gakkai, Series 2, 1931—. Monthly.
Organ of the Tokyo University Economic Society, the journal began publication in 1923. Its interests are primarily contemporary, though a few articles of an historical nature are sometimes included.

605. *Keizai ronsō 經濟論叢 ("Economic Review"), Kyōto, Kyōto Daigaku Keizai Gakkai, 1951—. Monthly.
Organ of the Kyoto University Economic Society. Most articles are on contemporary subjects, but a few deal with historical problems.

606. Keizaishi kenkyū 經濟史研究 (Studies in economic history), Kyōto, Nihon Keizaishi Kenkyūsho, 1929-44. Monthly.
Organ of the Institute of Japanese Economic History of Kyoto University and the journal through which such men as Honjō Eijirō, Kokushō Iwao, Nakamura Naokatsu, Horie Yasuzō, and Miyamoto Mataji published many of their articles. This journal together with Shakai keizaishigaku (Entry 612) is outstanding in the field of economic history. Articles are scholarly and are almost exclusively devoted to the study of Japanese problems. The excellent bibliographical sections of Keizaishi kenkyū became the basis for Honjō's three bibliographies on Japanese economic history (Entries 10-12). The regular feature "Saikin no keizaishi gakkai 最近の經濟史学界" or "Recent developments in the field of economic history" continued to 1944 and is of great value in supplementing these bibliographies. The journal has not been revived since 1944. An index to numbers 1-100 was published in 1938.

607. Kōtsū bunka 交通文化 (Communication culture), Tōkyō, Kokusai Kōtsū Bunka Kyōkai, Jan., 1938—. Quarterly.
Contains some excellent articles on cultural exchange between the West and Japan.

608. *Mitagakkai zasshi 三田学会雑誌 (Journal of the Mita Institute), Tōkyō, Keiō Gijuku Daigaku Rizai Gakkai, Jan., 1909—. Monthly.
Carries occasional articles of interest to the economic historian, especially those by Nomura Kanetarō.

609. *Nōrinshō, Nōgyō Sōgōkenkyūsho 農林省農業綜合研究所 (National Research Institute of Agriculture, Japanese Ministry of Agriculture and Forestry), Nōgyō sōgō kenkyū ("Quarterly Journal of Agricultural Economy"), Tōkyō, Nōgyō Sōgō Kenkyūsho, 1947—. Quarterly.
An excellent scholarly journal containing a wide variety of articles on Japanese agricultural economics. A large percentage deals with the historical development of Japanese economy. Articles on comparative developments in Japan and the United States, China, or Soviet Russia are particularly interesting. An English language Summary Report of Researches issued irregularly by the Institute provides summaries of leading articles in this journal.

610. Rōnō 労農 (Workers and farmers), Tōkyō, Rōnōsha, Dec., 1927—. Monthly.
A journal which carried as its subtitle "Sentō-teki Marukushisuto riron zasshi (A fighting journal of Marxist theory)." A number of leading Japanese economic historians, among them Tsuchiya Takao, wrote for this journal, developing their theories of the economic causes of the Meiji Restoration. Hence this journal has given its name to the Rōnō school of historians.

611. *Nōgyō keizai kenkyū 農業經濟研究 (Studies in agrarian economy), Tōkyō, Nōgyō Keizai Gakkai, 1924—. Quarterly.
Organ of the Association for the Study of Agrarian Economy, Agricultural Department, Tokyo University, it contains scholarly articles on agrarian problems. A high percentage deals with the historical aspects of Japanese agrarian economy.

612. *Shakai keizaishigaku 社会經濟史学 ("Journal of the Social and Economic History Society"), Tōkyō, Shakai Keizaishi Gakkai, May, 1931—. Monthly.
Organ of the Tokyo Social and Economic History Society, organized under the leadership of Ono Takeo. This journal ranks along with Keizaishi kenkyū (Entry 606) as the foremost scholarly publication in the field of social and economic history. It features well-documented studies of local and national social or economic institutions by the best Japanese scholars in the field. During the years 1933-36 the journal carried a regular bibliographical section devoted to a classified list of recent books and articles in social and economic history. After a wartime lapse from 1944 to 1949 the journal has returned to publication but it has lost a great deal of its prewar vitality.

8. SOCIOLOGY, ANTHROPOLOGY, AND FOLKLORE

Journals in this field tend to be of two types, the technical journals of sociology and the more general folkloristic publications. Of the former, the Shakaigaku hyōron (Sociological review) (Entry 618) is perhaps the most respected. Its offerings, however, are somewhat too technical for the general historian. In the latter category the Minkan denshō (Folklore) (Entry 615) published by the group led by Yanagita Kunio is the best known.

Recently two new journals, Hōshakaigaku (Sociology of law) (Entry 599) and Shakaigaku (Sociology) (Entry 617), have adopted the social science approach to problems of Japanese society. These journals are unfortunately not well established and have had considerable difficulty in maintaining publication.

613. Fūzoku kenkyū 風 俗 研 究 (Studies in Japanese customs), Kyōto, Fūzoku Kenkyūsho, Mar., 1916-33. Monthly.
A popular journal of antiquarian studies, historical costumes, and folklore under the sponsorship of Ema Tsutomu. Publication has now ceased.

614. *Jinruigaku zasshi 人 類 学 雑 誌 ("Journal of the Anthropological Society of Japan"), Tōkyō, Nihon Jinrui Gakkai, 1886—. Monthly.
The leading journal in the field of general anthropology, organ of the Japan Anthropological Society, Tokyo University. It emphasizes studies in physical anthropology and archeology of Japan.

615. *Minkan denshō 民 間 傳 承 (Folklore), Tōkyō, Minkan Denshō no Kai, Sept., 1935—. Monthly.
The central journal of folklore studies in Japan. It is representative of the group of folklorists led by Yanagita Kunio. The journal emphasizes reviews, notes, and reports on the activities of folklore studies organization in Japan.

616. *Minzokugaku Kenkyū 民 族 学 研 究 (Japanese journal of enthnology), Tōkyō, Nihon Minzoku Gakkai, Oct., 1935—. Monthly.
This journal succeeded Minzokugaku (July, 1929—) when the Minzoku Gakkai became the Nihon Minzoku Gakkai (Japanese Society of Ethnology). It is the chief ethnological journal in Japan today, featuring scholarly articles, reviews, notes, correspondence, news of field studies, etc. Leading members of the group are Oka Masao and Ishida Eiichirō.

617. *Shakaigaku 社 会 学 (Sociology), Tōkyō, Tōkyō Shakai Kagaku Kenkyūsho, Oct., 1948—. Biannually.
Organ of the Tokyo Institute of Social Science. A technical journal of sociology but useful for bibliographies on various broader sociological subjects such as the family system, village life, etc. The journal is called a quarterly but to date only two issues have appeared annually.

618. *Shakaigaku hyōron 社 会 学 評 論 (Sociological review), Tōkyō, Nihon Shakaigakkai, 1924—.
Organ of the Japan Sociological Association, Sociological Institute, Tokyo University.

9. THOUGHT AND RELIGION

Journals published by Japanese religious organizations or seminaries are often of a limited sectarian nature. It will be found, however, that such institutions have sometimes organized historical associations which publish journals of a more general appeal to the historian. The following list of periodicals in the field of thought and religion has been selected with the interests of the historian in mind.

619. *Bukkyō shigaku 佛 教 史 学 (Buddhist history), Tōkyō, Taishō Daigaku Shigakkai, Sept. 1949—.
Formerly the Ōdai shihō 鴨 台 史 報 (1933—), organ of the Taishō University (Tendai) Historical Society.

620. *Kirisutokyō bunka 基 督 敎 文 化 (Christian culture), Tōkyō, Shinkyō Shuppansha, 1946—. Monthly.

621. *Ryūkoku shidan 龍 谷 史 壇 (Ryūkoku University historical review), Kyōto, Ryūkoku Daigaku Shigakkai, June, 1928—. Semiannual.
Organ of the Historical Society, Ryūkoku (Buddhist) University. Articles are on Japanese and Chinese history with an emphasis on Buddhist subjects.

622. *Ryūkoku Daigaku ronshū 龍 谷 大 学 論 集 (Ryūkoku University review), Kyōto, Ryūkoku Gakkai, 1932—. Bimonthly.
Journal of one of the leading Shinshū sect seminaries in Japan.

623. *Shibun 斯 文 (Confucian culture), Tōkyō, Shibunkai, Feb., 1919—. Monthly.
The foremost journal of Confucian studies. Emphasis is on philosophical and ethical problems. An increasing number of articles gave Confucian sanction to Japan's nationalistic slogans after the late 1930s. Since the war the journal has begun a new series.

624. *Shintō shigaku 神 道 史 学 (Shinto history), June, 1949—.
Contains articles of a general interpretive nature on Shinto history.

625. Shintō shūkyō 神 道 宗 敎 (Shinto religion), Tōkyō Kokugakuin Daigaku, Shintō Shūkyō Kenkyūshitsu.

626. *Shisō 思 想 (Ideas), Tōkyō, Iwanami Shoten, Oct., 1921—. Monthly.
A journal of general cultural coverage emphasizing matters of philosophical interest and contemporary problems of interpretation. Frequent articles deal with historical problems. Contributors are often scholars of high reputation.

627. *Shisō no kagaku 思 想 の 科 学 (The science of thought), Tōkyō, Senkusha, May, 1946—. Irregular.
A scholarly journal dealing with problems of thought and popular opinion from the survey analyst's point of view. Articles analyze popular trends, discuss mass communication problems, social myths, and general climates of thought.

628. *Shūkyō kenkyū 宗 教 研 究 (Journal of religion), Tōkyō, Tōkyō Daigaku Shūkyōgaku Kenkyūkai, 1916—. Bimonthly.
Academic studies in religious problems, the history of religion, folk religion, myths, etc. Organ of the Institute of Religious Studies, Tokyo University.

629. *"Yamato bunkwa" 日 本 文 化 (Yamato culture), Tambaichi, Nara-ken, Tenri Toshokan, Aug., 1934—. Quarterly.
Contains studies in Japanese religion and philosophy. A special feature of pre-World War II numbers of this journal was an extensive classified bibliography of articles in the field of religion.

10. LITERATURE

The study of Japanese literature is essential to the historian not only for what it reveals about the Japanese people in terms of their life and ideals, but also because so many early literary works are the only written sources remaining for the early history of Japan. The following journals put out by various scholarly literary societies, while containing a large percentage of articles of a purely interpretive nature, also deal with literary history and the analysis of historically important literary works.

630. *Bungaku 文 学 (Literature), Tōkyō, Iwanami Shoten, Apr., 1931—. Monthly.
Organ of the Nihon Bungaku Kyōkai (Japan Literary Association), this journal carries a large number of articles by young scholars. Of special value are the survey and bibliographical sections. The March issue of 1950 contains a classified bibliography covering the period Sept., 1948-Dec., 1949. A rather large percentage of articles are of interest to the historian or the general social scientist.

631. *Bunka 文 化 (Culture), Tōkyō, Iwanami Shoten, Jan., 1934—. Monthly.
Organ of the Literary Society, Tōhoku University. Articles treat of religion, philosophy, and literature in both East and West. Only a few deal with the history of these fields in Japan.

632. *Kokugakuin zasshi 国 学 院 雑 誌 (Journal of the Kokugakuin College), Tōkyō, Kokugakuin Daigaku, Dec., 1894—. Monthly.
One of the early professional journals of Japan, this organ of the Kokugakuin College emphasizes Japanese literary history and Shinto studies.

633. *Kokugo kokubun 国 語 国 文 (National language and national literature), Kyōto, Kōbundo Shobō, Apr., 1931—. Monthly.
Successor to Kokugo kokubun no kenkyū (1926-30), this journal is the organ of the Japanese language and literature departments at Kyoto University. It is one of the foremost scholarly journals of Japanese literature and language.

634. *Kokugo to kokubungaku 国 語 と 国 文 学 (National language and literature), Tōkyō, Shibundō, Apr., 1924—. Monthly.
Journal of the Japanese language and literature departments, Tokyo University, this is one of the foremost professional journals of Japanese language and literature. Articles tend to be exclusively literary in scope. But a number of professional features such as bibliographical lists and news of the field make this journal important to the historian.

11. ART AND SCIENCE

The Japanese are famous for their many beautifully illustrated journals of fine arts and crafts. The few titles which follow have been selected for their scholarly quality. It should be pointed out that almost every field of Japanese art and drama is supplied by numerous journals of a more popular nature. Recently, profusely illustrated journals of drama and architecture have increased in numbers and quality. They have not been listed here because of their rather popular slant.

635. *Bijutsu kenkyū 美 術 研 究 (Journal of art studies), Tōkyō, Bijutsu Kenkyūjo, Jan., 1932—. Monthly.
This journal, published by the Tokyo Institute of Art Research, is, along with Kokka (Entry 639), the best of the illustrated art journals. It carries numerous full color reproductions together with technical articles on art evaluation and museum techniques. Much of each issue is of historical interest.

636. *Bijutsushi 美 術 史 (Art history), Tōkyō, Bijutsushi Gakkai, 1949—.
A new publication of the Tokyo Institute of Art Research, this journal carries numerous excellent articles by younger writers in the field.

637. <u>Bukkyō Bijutsu</u> 佛教美術 (Buddhist art), Nara, Bukkyō Bijutsusha, 1924-35.   20 issues.

638. <u>Kōgei</u> 工藝 (Industrial art), Tokyo, Nihon Mingei Kyōkai, 1931—.   Monthly.
Published by the Japan Folk Art Association.   This journal features articles and illustrations of Japanese folk art.

639. *<u>Kokka</u> 国華 ("Kokka"), Tōkyō, Kokkasha, 1889—.   Monthly.
World famous for its excellent large reproductions of Japanese art masterpieces, this is the foremost art journal of Japan.   It was long edited by Taki Seiichi.   An index was published in 1933.

640. *<u>Shiseki to bitjutsu</u> 史迹と美術 (Historic remains and art), Kyōto, Shiseki Bijutsu Dōkōkai, 1930—.
Monthly.
Contains articles on art monuments by foremost scholars in the fields of archeology, Buddhist iconography, and general fine arts.

641. *<u>Kagakushi kenkyū</u> 科学史研究 (Studies in the history of science), Tōkyō, Nihon Kagakushi Gakkai, 1942—.   Bimonthly.
Organ of the Japan History of Science Society, Institute of Technological History, Tokyo Industrial University.

12. LIBRARY SCIENCE

The following journals, though largely of a technical nature, are of some importance to the historian for the information which they publish on library collections and bibliography.

642. <u>Toshokan kenkyū</u> 図書館研究 (Library research), Ōsaka, Mamiya Shoten, Jan., 1928—.   Quarterly.
Organ of the Seinen Toshokan'in Remmei (League of Young Librarians).   It contains general articles on cataloguing, bibliographical technique, and a regular list of works of bibliographical interest accessioned to the Mamiya Library.

643. *<u>Toshokan zasshi</u> 図書館雑誌 (Library journal), Tōkyō, Nihon Toshokan Kyōkai, Oct., 1907—.
Monthly.
The organ of the Japanese Library Association.   It regularly carries a classified list of new publications.

644. *<u>Shomotsu tembō</u> 書物展望 (Bibliographic survey), Tōkyō, Shomotsu Tembōsha, July, 1931—.
Monthly.
Carries a regular index of articles relating to books and bibliography.

645. <u>Shoshigaku</u> 書誌学 (Bibliography), Tōkyō, Nihon Shoshigakkai, 1933-41.   Monthly.
A journal of literary and antiquarian interest, it carried occasional articles on historical sources and surveys of current bibliographical literature.

V. SURVEY HISTORIES

So much has been written by the Japanese even in the nature of surveys of their national history, that the Western historian is faced with an overwhelming problem of orientation and selection.   As a first step in acquiring some basis for intelligent selection, he will do well to learn something of the tradition of historiography in Japan and its contemporary development.

Historical works produced in Japan prior to the advent of modern scientific historiography were largely the product of Chinese methodology.   It was this tradition of rigorous presentation of historical data in chronological order that produced the <u>Rikkokushi</u> (Six national histories, 720-901), the <u>Nihon kiryaku</u> (Records of Japan, c. 1050-1100), the <u>Azuma kagami</u> (Mirror of the East, 1266), <u>Nochi kagami</u> (Later mirror, c. 1843), and the <u>Tokugawa jikki</u> (True records of the Tokugawa, 1849).   Such works rank even today as major repositories of historical fact on early and feudal Japan.   Out of the Chinese tradition, also, came the <u>Honchō tsugan</u> (Complete mirror of Japan, 1670), the <u>Dai Nihonshi</u> (History of Japan, 1709), and other works which were to form the starting point of modern historical scholarship.

With the opening of Japan to Western intellectual influence after the middle of the nineteenth century the Japanese rapidly absorbed Western historical theory and methodology.   The turn into the Meiji period (1868-1911) saw Japanese historiography enter her modern era.   Since that time Japanese historical scholarship has passed through a number of distinct phases of development each of which should be recognized by the historian who would use Japanese materials.   The first phase, embracing the first thirty years of the Meiji period, was largely a time of transition.   During it the state-sponsored historical bureaus, and such scholars as Shimizu Seiken and Kurita Kan continued to produce histories in the old Chinese style.   Concurrently other men led by Fukuzawa Yukichi and Taguchi Ukichi began to experiment with the new methodology imported from the West.   With the 1890s these historiographical techniques were put on a firm foundation by the establishment under German tutelage of a chair of history at Tokyo Imperial University and the organization of the Shigakkai (Institute of Historical Science), Japan's first and foremost scholarly historical association.   The addition to Tokyo University of the Historiographical Institute (Shiryō Hensansho) established the university as the center of historical research in Japan.

During the interval between the Sino-Japanese war of 1894 and the end of World War I, Japanese historiography as a modern science reached maturity.   A new generation of historians began the combination of factual material drawn from the many old-fashioned, but well-documented, historical works of the early Meiji period with new ideology and methodology.   Leading interpretative scholars of this period, such as Hara

Katsurō, Miura Hiroyuki, and Uchida Ginzō, succeeded in developing the general cultural survey history of Japan, while on a more rigorously academic level, Kuroita Katsumi in his Kokushi no kenkyū (Study of Japanese history) laid the methodological foundation for his own and succeeding generations of Japanese historians. During these years Tokyo University emerged as the fountainhead of "academic" historiography, while Kyoto University became the center of the "cultural history" approach.

World War I gave rise to a deep change in the Japanese intellectual atmosphere. The war had stimulated Japan's industrialization. Termination of the war plunged Japan into a series of periods of prosperity and depression. Social and economic problems became uppermost in the minds of Japanese intellectuals. The period from roughly 1920 to 1940 thus marks a third phase in the development of modern Japanese historical science. During these years the academic and cultural historians were overshadowed by new men working in the fields of economic and social history. This shift in interest had already been evident in some of the earlier historians, notably Uchida and Miura, but it remained for such men as Honjō Eijirō, Ono Takeo, Kokushō Iwao, Tsuchiya, and Yanagida Kunio to bring to fruition the new schools of economic and social historiography. The establishment of three new scholarly organizations during the 1930s, the Nihon Keizaishi Kenkyūsho (Institute of Japanese Economic History) of Kyoto, the Rekishigaku Kenkyūkai (Historical Science Society) of Tokyo, and the Shakai Keizaishi Gakkai (Social and Economic History Society) of Tokyo, marked the ascendancy of this new trend. Toward the 1930s Marxism also made its impact on the Japanese academic world, and a fringe of writers began the active analysis of Japan's modern history under the Marxist formula.

The war years (c. 1937-45) constitute a fourth phase of historical development. These, as can be imagined, were circumscribed years for all scholars. Historians were obliged to trim their writings to the nationalistic tone of the times or keep silent. Many of Japan's ablest historians including Hiraizumi Chō and Akiyama Kenzō took the former choice, and were subsequently purged by the Allied Occupation. Of those who remained silent, many became more radical in their thinking.

The post-World War II phase of Japanese historical scholarship has naturally been one of great flux. Many of the old guard historians were purged and have been replaced by younger men of ability and enthusiasm. The new freedom of expression has invited the revaluation of many controversial aspects of Japan's history, while new methodology, especially in the social science fields, has improved the quality of research work done by native scholars. The first few years after the war saw most Japanese historians groping for new methods and philosophies of history. The most enthusiasm and the greatest volume of work came from the Marxist writers who led the way in revisionist literature. Since about 1950, however, their dominance appears to have given way to more balanced scholarship.

By keeping the above periods in mind the historian will obtain some clue to the quality of the books he finds at his disposal. It is not necessarily true that only the most recent works are of value to him. Each period mentioned above has its specialties. Many of the works of Chinese inspiration prepared during the early Meiji period are of lasting value today. This is especially true of the government-sponsored histories of administrative and legal institutions, the encyclopedias such as the Koji ruien (Encyclopedia of ancient matters) (Entry 207) and the local histories of this and later periods. Such works are old fashioned in their structure, but are accurate and usable. The period from 1895 to 1920 produced some of the best political and cultural histories we have. In particular, the Sōgō Nihonshi taikei (Synthetic survey of Japanese history) (Entry 748) has yet to be surpassed for factual content and excellence of documentation. Characteristic of the period of the 20s and 30s are the great joint enterprises which resulted in such works as the Iwanami kōza: Nihon rekishi (Iwanami series on Japanese history) (Entry 725), the Sekai rekishi taikei (Comprehensive survey of world history) (Entry 739), and the Nihon bunkashi taikei (Survey of Japanese cultural history) (Entry 731), works which are standard even today. Thus the historical scholarship of pre-World War II Japan has still a great deal to offer us. On the other hand, the books coming out of postwar Japan frequently have to be watched for excessive ideological content either in the form of artificial "democratic" sentiment or for doctrinaire Marxism.

This problem of historical ideology and bias thus adds another dimension to the historian's basis for evaluating his materials. It will be found, for instance, that certain university departments of history or certain academic associations have reputations for conservatism or liberalism, for sound scholarship or amateurishness. Thus the historical societies of Tokyo and Kyoto Universities, of Kokugakuin University and the Tokyo University of Education are known for their conservative adherence to the "academic" and "cultural" schools while the Rekishigaku Kenkyūkai (Historical Science Society) of Tokyo and the Nihonshi Kenkyūkai (Society for the Study of Japanese History) of Kyoto generally uphold the so-called "progressive," or intellectual Marxist tradition. Even the names of publishing houses offer clues to the quality of books, for it is a matter of common knowledge that certain houses tend to handle works with strong political bias either to the right or left. Familiarity with general problems of historical interpretation and of the development of historical studies in Japan thus constitutes an important introductory step towards orientation in Japanese history. The works listed below under Historiography will aid in acquiring this familiarity.

As explained in the preface, the following section on survey histories comprises a highly selective list of secondary materials in the various fields of Japanese history. In selecting materials for this section the author decided against the adoption of some rigid scheme advocated by either Japanese or Western bibliographers, but permitted categories to evolve as material was collected. This has resulted in a somewhat unorthodox grouping of subjects but one which reflects the major divisions under which modern Japanese historians have published.

As to the material itself, a number of limitations have necessarily been applied. Excluded from consideration were all works written before 1868 and works on archeology, natural science, and Japan's former continental and island possessions. In general, works of recent publication were selected over those of early publication unless the living value of the earlier works could be demonstrated. Generally, the individual volumes of historical series have not been mentioned singly.

In each of the fields of history an attempt has been made to select a minimum number of the most essential surveys which will cover the subject from earliest times to the present. As a rule those books dealing with only a limited time span were eliminated. But this was not always practicable, since in many fields few survey works were found to cover pre-Restoration and post-Restoration periods equally well. This disparity has necessitated the selection, in a number of instances, of works limited to the pre-Restoration period together with those limited to post-Restoration coverage, the two groups serving to complement each other.

In selecting representative publications in the postwar period it has also been extremely difficult to avoid inclusion of works of a limited monographic nature. One reason for this is the increasing specialization evident among contemporary Japanese historians. Present day Japanese historical scholarship tends furthermore to concern itself with limited, albeit complicated problems rather than with broad fields. For instance studies of village life, feudalism, manufacturing, capitalism, or imperialism are now more common than general studies of Japanese political, social, or economic history. Strictly speaking, such subjects are limited ones and hence should not be included in this bibliography. However, because of the fact that so much recent scholarship has taken the form of problem studies, it was determined to provide space for these subjects. Justification may be found in the fact that these problems are often treated in broad survey fashion.

1. HISTORIOGRAPHIES AND GUIDES TO HISTORICAL RESEARCH

The following selection of books on historiography and research techniques has been divided for convenience into three parts. The first includes works on historical theory in general. Such works will be of only secondary interest to the Western student since many of them merely repeat theories derived from Western literature. Nevertheless, they are important for what they reveal of the degree to which Japanese historians rely on Western theories and for their indication of the articles of faith of many of Japan's leading historians or historical schools. Thus Imai Toshiki's pamphlet, Rekishigaku kenkyūhō (Historical methodology) (Entry 647), represents the German-oriented thinking of the Tokyo University "academic" group, while Ishimoda Tadashi's article "Rekishigaku no hōhō ni tsuite no kansō (Thoughts on historical methodology)" (Entry 648), reveals the creed of the intellectual Marxists.

In the second section are listed studies of the history of Japanese historiography with an emphasis on the pre-Restoration period. These works describe and evaluate the major historical writings upon which the Japanese have based their research. Most of the works in this section are fairly standard, but Kuroita Katsumi's Kōtei kokushi no kenkyū (Revised study of Japanese history) (Entry 664) is outstanding.

The third group contains works on practical methodology and on the contemporary development and present state of historiography in Japan. Among the most complete and practical guides to research in Japanese history are the previously mentioned works by Kuroita (Entry 664) and Kurita (Entry 24). These works must be supplemented, however, both for more up-to-date coverage and for information on several recently developed historical fields. For the first purpose the Tōkyō Daigaku Kyōdō Kumiai Shuppambu's Nihonshi kenkyū nyūmon (Introduction to the study of Japanese history) (Entry 683) is most useful. This in turn may be supplemented for more current information by reference to the annual evaluations of the previous year's academic accomplishments published by a number of scholarly journals. The reader is referred to the series now carried in Shigaku zasshi (Entry 39) and Rekishigaku kenkyū (Entry 36).

For more specialized information on the development of social and economic history, the Shakai Keizaishi Gakkai's Shakai keizaishigaku no hattatsu (Social and economic history of Japan, its recent development) (Entry 40) and the Tōkyō Shōka Daigaku's Keizaigaku kenkyū no shiori (Guide to the study of economics) (Entry 162) are of special value.

Information on the present status of academic institutions is not easily available. An extremely handy though limited guide to this subject is the Kyōto Daigaku Shimbunsha's Gakkai no jiten (Dictionary of the academic world) (Entry 674). It should be supplemented by the Ministry of Education's Gakukyōkai ichiran (List of scholarly organizations) (Entry 675). For research recently completed, the same ministry's Mombushō chokkatsu oyobi kokuritsu daigaku kenkyūsho kenkyū gyōseki yōran, 1950 (List of research completed by Ministry of Education and National University research organs) (Entry 676) is most exhaustive.

a. Historical Theory

646. Hani Gorō 羽仁五郎, Rekishigaku hihan josetsu 歴史学批判叙説 (An introduction to historical criticism), Tōkyō, Kindai Shisōsha, 1948, 181 pp.
This is a reissue of a group of essays first written between 1929 and 1932 and published shortly thereafter. They concern general historical philosophy and represent the thinking of an influential contemporary Japanese scholar who has absorbed concepts from both Croce and Marx.

647. Imai Toshiki 今井登志喜, Rekishigaku kenkyūhō 歴史学研究法 (Historical methodology), [in case 18 of Iwanami kōza, Nihon rekishi 岩波講座日本歴史 (Iwanami series on Japanese history)], Tōkyō, Iwanami Shoten, 1935, 82 pp.
A discussion of major Western schools of historical theory, especially the German, together with basic problems of historical criticism and the evaluating of materials. The author concludes with a short illustrative problem taken out of Japanese history.

648. Ishimoda Tadashi 石母田正, "Rekishigaku no hōhō ni tsuite no kansō 歴史学の方法について の感想 (Thoughts on historical methodology), in Rekishi hyōron, v. 4 (1950), nos. 7, 8.
A discussion of theory and historical approach by one of the most active contemporary historians in the intellectual Marxist school.

649. Kaba Toshio 樺俊雄, Rekishi no riron 歴史の理論 (Historical theory), Tōkyō, Tōkō Shoin, 1941, 375 pp.
Discussion of historical theory and periodization by a leading historical philosopher. The author has translated numerous German works on historical theory.

650. Matsui·Hitoshi 松井等 and Ōrui Noboru 大類伸, ed., Gendai shigaku taikei 現代史学大系 (Survey of contemporary historiography), Tōkyō, Kyōritsusha, 1931-32, 15 v.
    A series of studies of problems of contemporary historiography. Most of the series is made up of works on Western historical theory or translations of Western historiographical literature. A few of these volumes have been listed in this section.

651. Nonomura Kaizō 野々村戒三, Shigaku gairon 史学概論 (General treatise on historiography), Tōkyō, Waseda Daigaku Shuppambu, 1929, 394 pp.
    A general discussion of historiography, its theory and methodology largely from the point of view of the west-German school.

652. Ōrui Noboru 大類伸, Shigaku gairon 史学概論 (Introduction to historiography), Tōkyō, Kyōritsusha, 1932, 274 pp.
    One of the Gendai shigaku taikei series (Entry 650). A general discussion of modern historiography by one who has been influenced by Ernst Bernheim. This work has been extremely influential in Japan.

653. Ōtsuka shigaku hihan 大塚史学批判 (A critique of the Ōtsuka view of history), Tōkyō, Daigaku Shimbun Remmei Shuppambu, 1948, 197 pp.
    A series of articles by Hattori Shisō, Izu Kimio, Inoue Kiyoshi, and others of the intellectual Marxist school criticizing Ōtsuka Hisao and his use of the theories of Max Weber in his interpretation of the modern capitalist revolution.

654. Rekishi no shomondai 歴史の諸問題 (The problems of history), special number of Shisō, v. 30, April, 1932.
    A special number of the journal Shisō containing articles by leading Japanese historians on history and historical theory.

655. Tsuboi Kumazō 坪井九馬三, Kaitei zōho shigaku kenkyūhō 改訂増補史学研究法 (Historical methodology, revised and enlarged), Tōkyō, Kyōbunsha, 1926, 430 pp.
    A revised edition of one of the first noteworthy modern studies of historiography in Japan. Tsuboi Kumazō, pupil of Ludwig Reiss, was professor at Tokyo University. His theories were based largely on those of Ernst Bernheim.

656. Tsuda Sōkichi 津田左右吉, Rekishi no mujunsei 歴史の矛盾性 (The inconsistency of history), Tōkyō, Tōyōdō, 1947, 132 pp.
    A provocative essay by one of the foremost experts on Japanese intellectual history. Tsuda is generally described as an independent liberal.

657. Uchida Ginzō 内田銀蔵, Shigaku riron 史学理論 (The theory of historiography), Tōkyō, Dōbunkan, 1922, 340+119 pp.
    A series of eleven essays by one of Japan's senior historians. The author deals with theory, methodology, contributing sciences such as geography, biography, etc. A product of the Taisho and early Showa periods, the author is especially influenced by the British historical tradition.

658. Yanagida Kunio 柳田国男, Kokushi to minzokugaku 国史と民俗学 (Japanese history and ethnology), Tōkyō, Rokininsha, 1948, 243 pp.
    A discussion by a leading ethnologist of the relationship between history and ethnology.

b. History of Japanese Historiography

659. Chiyoda Ken 千代田謙, Matsumoto Hikojirō 松本彦次郎, and Matsui Hitoshi 松井等, Shigaku meicho kaidai 史学名著解題 (An annotated bibliography of famous books on history), Tōkyō, Kyōritsusha, 1931, 137+149+75 pp.
    Volume 15 of the Gendai shigaku taikei (Entry 650). The central section by Matsumoto Hikojirō constitutes an historiography of Japan as seen through the major pre-Restoration works of history.

660. Izu Kimio 伊豆公夫, Nihon shigakushi 日本史学史 (A history of Japanese historiography), Tōkyō, Getsuyō Shobō, rev. ed., 1949, 398 pp.
    First published in 1936, this work, now considerably revised, is a critical evaluation of Japanese historiography written from the materialist point of view. The work begins with a survey of Japanese historiography and contemporary scholars, and then proceeds to analyze the various periods of Japanese historical scholarship in reverse chronological order.

661. Kawaguchi Hakuho 川口白浦, Nihon kokushigaku hattatsushi 日本国史学発達史 (History of the development of historical studies in Japan), Tōkyō, Kembunsha, 1936, 309 pp.
    A standard survey of Japanese historical studies from early times down to the 1930s. The work is arranged by periods. An introductory statement describes the spirit of each period and is followed by a detailed study of the major historical works produced during the period.

662. Kiyohara Sadao 清原貞雄, Nihon shigakushi 日本史学史 (A history of Japanese historiography), Tōkyō, Chūbunkan, rev. ed., 1944, 342+24 pp.
    This work, first published in 1928, is by one of the best known pre-World War II historians. The work is divided into two parts. Part 1 treats the development of Japanese historical studies from ancient times to the Meiji Restoration. Part 2 discusses the development of modern historiography during the

Meiji era outlining the major problems faced by the modern historian and the various solutions advanced by Meiji scholars. The work contains a great deal of bibliographic information, and an index is appended.

663. Konakamura Kiyonori 小中村 清矩 , Kokushigaku no shiori 国史学 の 栞 (Guide to Japanese historiography), Tōkyō, Benkyōdō, 1900, 162 pp.
An early guide to the chief materials necessary for the study of pre-Meiji Japanese history.

664. Kuroita Katsumi 黒板 勝美 , Kōtei kokushi no kenkyū. Sōsetsu 更訂国史 の 研究. 總説 (A study of Japanese history—revised. General introduction), Tōkyō, Iwanami Shoten, 1931, 500 pp.
This is the introductory volume on general historiography of Kuroita's work, which was first published in 1909 and is undoubtedly the single most famous product of modern historiography in Japan. The introductory volume begins with the discussion of diplomatics, historical geography, chronology, genealogy, archeology and other subsidiary sciences. The main portion of the work is devoted to a chronological analysis of the chief sources for the study of pre-Meiji history. It concludes with a chronological list of major contributions in the field of Japanese history between the years 1868-1930. This is followed by a discussion of topical problems: periodization and period histories, local histories, history of law, culture, economics, art, customs, religion, etc. For each of these special fields the author lists important sources, early and recent, and describes their uses. (See also Entry 695.)

665. Miura Kaneyuki 三浦 周行, "Nihon shigakushi gaisetsu 日本史学史概説 (An introduction to the history of Japanese historiography)," in Nihonshi no kenkyū 日本史 の 研究 (The study of Japanese history), Second series, Tōkyō, Iwanami Shoten, 1930, 1338+71 pp.
A survey of Japanese historiography treated by periods.

666. Ōkubo Toshiaki 大久保 利謙 , Nihon kindai shigakushi 日本近代史学史 (History of recent Japanese historiography), Tōkyō, Hakuyōsha, 1940, 277 pp.
A detailed analysis of the emergence of modern historiography in Japan. The author traces the background of Japanese historical studies into Tokugawa times, describes the impact of Western thought on Japan, and concludes with a discussion of the formation of the various schools of modern Japanese historiography.

667. Shigakkai 史学会 , Hompō shigakushi ronsō 本邦史学史論叢 (Essays on the history of Japanese historiography), Tōkyō, Fuzambō, 1939, 2 v.
An important collection of essays on historiography and historical works by top level Japanese historians. The first article by Tsuji Zennosuke gives a concise résumé of the development of historiography in Japan up to contemporary times. The work concludes with studies of the influence of Dutch studies on Japanese historiography, the development of library science, etc. The bulk of the work consists of excellent critical studies of individual works of Japanese history from the Kojiki to Taguchi's Nihon kaika shōshi.

c. Methodology and Guides to Contemporary Historical Research in Japan

668. Akiyama Kenzō, "Orientation in the Study of Japanese History," in A Guide to Japanese Studies, Tōkyō, Kokusai Bunka Shinkōkai, 1937, pp. 3-54.
Though in English, this work was considered of sufficient merit to include in this bibliography. Not all essays in this volume will be of help to the historian. This one by Akiyama Kenzō, however, provides excellent orientation for the beginner in the field of Japanese history.

669. Endō Motoo 遠藤 元男, Nihon rekishi nyūmon 日本歴史入門 (Introduction to Japanese history), Tōkyō, Mikasa Shobō, 1941, 369 pp.
An excellent series of introductory essays on Japanese history by competent experts in the field. Part 1 presents a survey of Japanese history. Part 2, entitled "Problems and methodology for the study of Japanese history," contains essays by Nakamura Kichiji, Kaba Toshio, Ōkubo Toshiaki, and Endō Motoo on the history and contemporary problems of Japanese historiography.

670. Kawai Eijirō 河合 榮治郎, ed., Gakusei to rekishi 学生と歴史 (The student and history), Tōkyō, Nihon Hyōronsha, rev. ed., 1946, 399 pp.
A revised and somewhat shortened version of a work first published in 1940. In its present form the work contains sixteen articles by leading authorities on historiography, historical methodology, historians, and the special characteristics of Western and Oriental history. Meant for Japanese university students, it provides a handy summary of the general field of historical theory and methodology for the beginner in Japanese history.

671. Konakamura Kiyonori 小中村 清矩, Kokushigaku no hōhō 国史学 の 方法 (Methodology for the study of Japanese history), Tōkyō, Tōgakusha, 1936, 233 pp.
A simply written introduction to the chief sources used by modern historians in their study of Japanese history. Chapters deal with general history, law, survey histories, the emperor system, bureaucracy, genealogy and biography, local history, and geography.

672. Kurita Motoji 栗田 元次, Sōgō kokushi kenkyū 綜合国史研究 (General guide for research in Japanese history), Tōkyō, Dōbun Shoin, 1935, 3 v.
Strictly speaking, an annotated bibliography of Japanese history, this work nevertheless contains a great deal of historiographical information. Volume 1, pp. 1-134, presents a general survey of Japanese premodern historical sources, while the prefaces to each section discuss the major primary materials in each field.

673. "Kyōdoshi wa ika ni kenkyū subeki ka 郷 土 史 は 如 何 に 研 究 す べ き か (How should local history be studied?)," in Rekishi kyōiku 歴 史 教 育 (The teaching of history), Tōkyō, Rekishi Kyōiku Kenkyūkai, 1930.

    A special issue of Rekishi Kyōiku devoted to the problems of studying local history.

674. Kyōto Daigaku Shimbunsha 京 都 大 学 新 聞 社, Gakkai no jiten 学 界 の 事 典 (Dictionary of the academic world), Tambaichi, Nara-ken, Yōtokusha, 1951, 220 pp.

    An extremely useful guide to academic fields and institutions. Part 1 provides brief résumeś of scholarly activity, trends and factions in the fields of law, government, literature, history, economics, the natural sciences, and geography and agriculture. Part 2 is a list of universities by location with pertinent information on history, specialties, chief officers, etc. Part 3 lists academic associations and research groups. Part 4 lists principal faculty members with information on specialties, degrees, present position, major publications, etc.

675. Mombushō Daigaku Gakujutsukyoku 文 部 省 大 学 学 術 局, (Ministry of Education, University Research Bureau), Gakukyōkai ichiran 学 協 会 一 覧 (List of scholarly organizations), Tōkyō, Mombushō, 1951, 59 pp.

    A list of academic and research organizations classified by field. For each organization the following information is provided: name, address, telephone number, number of members, name of president, and name of publication organ.

676. Mombushō Shokan Kenkyushochō Kaigi Chōsa Iinkai 文 部 省 所 管 研 究 所 長 会 議 調 査 委 員 会, (Investigating Committee for the Council of Directors of Research Organization Under the Ministry of Education), Mombushō chokkatsu oyobi kokuritsu daigaku kenkyūsho kenkyū gyōseki yōran, 1950 文 部 省 直 轄 及 び 国 立 大 学 研 究 所 研 究 業 績 要 覧 一 九 五 〇 (List of research completed by Ministry of Education and National University research organs, 1950), National University, Tokyo,

    Since much recent research is subsidized by the Ministry of Education, this pamphlet is of considerable value as an index to current Japanese scholarship.

677. Nihon Rekishi Chiri Gakkai 日 本 歴 史 地 理 学 会 (Japanese Society of Historical Geography), Kyōdoshi kenkyū no chōsa to hohō 郷 土 史 研 究 の 調 査 と 方 法 (Research and methodology for the study of local history), Tōkyō, Chijin Shokan, 1944, 369 pp.

    A series of excellent articles on methodology and source materials for the study of local history. The book contains a great deal of bibliographical information.

678. Ono Takeo 小 野 武 夫, Kyōdo keizaishi kenkyū teiyō 郷 土 經 済 史 研 究 提 要 (Manual for study of local economic history), Tōkyō, Asano Shoten, 1932 285 pp.

    A guide to the study of local economic history by one of Japan's foremost scholars in the field of village economic history.

679. Rekishi Kyōiku Kenkyūkai 歴 史 教 育 研 究 会 (Society for Historical Education), Meiji igo ni okeru rekishigaku no hattatsu 明 治 以 後 に 於 け る 歴 史 学 の 発 達 (Development of historical studies since Meiji), Tōkyō, Yonkai Shobō, 1933, 680 pp.

    A survey of historical studies in Japan from 1868 to c. 1925. The work consists of a series of articles by major historians on various aspects of historical research including economic history, thought, law, foreign affairs, government, and Japanese studies of other Oriental countries.

680. Shakai keizaishigaku no hattatsu 社 会 經 済 史 学 の 発 達 (Social and economic history of Japan, its recent development), special issue of Shakai keizaishigaku 社 会 經 済 史 学 (Social and economic history), v. 10, no. 9-10 (Jan. 1941), 272 pp.

    A survey of the development of social and economic history in Japan roughly up to 1940. For a full annotation see Entry 40.

681. Takamura Shōhei 高 村 象 平 and Komatsu Yoshitaka 小 松 芳 喬, Nihon ni okeru keizai shigaku no hattatsu 日 本 に 於 け る 經 済 史 学 の 発 達 (The development of the study of economic history in Japan), Tōkyō, Kaname Shobō, 1949, 148 pp.

    Volume 2 of the Jimbun kagaku kenkyū sōsho (Cultural sciences research series) edited by the Committee on Cultural Sciences attached to the Ministry of Education. It surveys the development of the study of economic history in Japan from 1868 to the time of writing.

682. Tamura Eitarō 田 村 榮 太 郎, Kyōdoshi kenkyū no tebiki 郷 土 史 研 究 の 手 引 (Handbook for the study of local history), Tōkyō, Hakuyōsha, 1938, 428 pp.

    A guide to the solution of the chief difficulties met in the study of local history. Chapters deal with the reading of documents, study of names, labor service, taxation, farm villages, homes, shrines, social organization, customs and yearly festivals.

683. Tōkyō Daigaku Kyōdo Kumiai Shuppambu 東 京 大 学 協 同 組 合 出 版 部 (Tōkyō University Cooperative Publication Department), Nihonshi kenkyū nyūmon 日 本 史 研 究 入 門 (Introduction to the study of Japanese history), Tōkyō, Tōkyō Daigaku Kyōdo Kumiai Shuppambu, rev. ed., 1951, 384 pp.

    One of the most useful introductory surveys to come out of post-World War II Japan. This book, first published in 1949 under the editorship of Tōyama Shigeki, is now augmented by an extensive selective bibliography of books and articles covering all phases of Japanese history. The main body of the work consists of essays by members of the Shiryō Hensansho and the Minshushugi Kagakusha Kyōkai (Society of Democratic Scientists) on various aspects of Japanese historiography. Each essay introduces books and theories concerning a field or period of Japanese history. While it is sometimes necessary to discount the doctrinaire materialism of some of the writers, in general this work provides one of the best introductory guides for the student of Japanese history.

684. "Zinbun" (The cultural sciences), Tōkyō, Jimbun Kagaku Iinkai, March, 1947-50.
This journal regularly carried articles on the state of scholarship in various academic fields. These included surveys of recent research, lists of outstanding scholars, and similar information. A special issue of Zinbun in 1949 was devoted exclusively to a survey of the cultural sciences in Japan.

2. GENERAL HISTORICAL SURVEYS

The great era of general survey histories of Japan was unquestionably the period of the late 1920s and 30s. It was during these years that there appeared the chief multi-volume series upon which we rely today: the Iwanami kōza: Nihon rekishi (Iwanami series on Japanese history) (Entry 725), the Sōgō Nihonshi taikei (Synthetic survey of Japanese history) (Entry 748), the Sekai rekishi taikei (Survey of world history) (Entry 739), the Nihon bunkashi taikei (Survey of Japanese cultural history) (Entry 731) and the Shinkō Dai Nihonshi (New lectures on Japanese history) (Entry 744). These works, while emphasizing the political or cultural side of Japanese life, also included the latest findings of the social and economic historians. Because of their broad approach they are still of great use to the student with a general interest in Japanese history.

Since 1946 the Japanese have been actively producing two types of general historical writings. Most numerous have been the short surveys of the "Shin Nihonshi (New Japanese history)" type which seek to reinterpret Japanese history in the light of the new-found freedom of expression which came to Japan with the end of the war. Perhaps the most widely mentioned of these "new histories" is the Kuni no ayumi (The progress of our country) prepared for primary school use by a group under the direction of Ienaga Saburō. Its publication set off an immediate controversy between leftist and rightist groups in Japan. The split between the self-styled "progressives" and the so-called "academicians" continues to divide the historical field. In this context nearly every major historian and each of the major historical factions in Japan have written "new" histories. These have often been prepared for popular appeal, but others have been substantial enough to list below.

Another feature of postwar publication in the historical field has been the various series dealing with socio-economic systems. The Shin-Nihonshi kōza (New series on Japanese history) (Entry 746) issued by the Chuō Kōronsha and the Nihon rekishi kōza (Japanese history series) (Entry 734) are obviously patterned after the earlier Iwanami series (Entry 725). These new publications differ from the old in that they treat Japanese history primarily through a study of political institutions and socio-economic systems such as ancient slavery, feudalism, capitalism, etc. The swing from political and cultural history to social and economic history noticeable in the prewar decade is thus complete. Today few survey histories divide their chapters to conform with the conventional political turning points but according to the development of economic or social patterns.

The following selective list of general survey works on Japanese history includes both the category of general history (ippanshi) and cultural history (bunkashi) as distinguished by Japanese historians. So many worthwhile works are to be found among this list that the author has hesitated to single out any for special consideration. It is hoped the annotations will provide a sufficient basis for selection. It should be pointed out, however, that not all of the works listed below have been singled out for their excellence. Some have been included because they represent the work of an important historian or of an active historical school. In the first instance, the works may now be completely superseded; in the second, they may be of an extremely biased nature. It will be noticed that in the following list a distinction has been drawn between works of 1) single authorship or those which consist of collected essays by a limited number of authors and 2) the great multi-volume series of multiple authorship. The latter type should be thought of more as reference histories.

a. Single Authorship

685. Akiyama Kenzō 秋 山 謙 蔵, Nihon no rekishi 日 本 圧 史 (Japan's history), Tōkyō, Iwanami Shoten, 1941, 411 pp.
A standard survey of Japanese history by an historian who made his name in prewar days by his scholarly studies of Japanese foreign relations of the fourteenth and fifteenth centuries. His wartime writings tended to be nationalistic.

686. Hagino Yoshiyuki 萩 野 由 之, Nihonshi kōwa 日 本 史 講 話 (Lectures on Japanese history), Tōkyō, Meiji Shoin, 1920, 2 v.
Based on the author's lectures in history at Tokyo University. Professor Hagino (d. 1924) was well known for his analysis of Japan's political history.

687. Haga Kōshirō 芳 賀 幸 四 郎, Nihonshi shin-kenkyū 日 本 史 新 研 究 (A new study of Japanese history), Tōkyō, Ikeda Shoten, 1950, 358 pp.
A survey history written for non-scholars and instructors in secondary schools. Useful for its short classified bibliography of works on Japanese history.

688. Hayakawa Jirō 早 川 二 郎, Yuibutsushikan Nihon rekishi tokuhon 唯 物 史 觀 日 本 圧 史 讀 本 (A reader of Japanese history from the materialistic point of view), Tōkyō, Kōbunsha, 1948, 489 pp.
Reprint of a work first published in 1937. It represents one of the pioneer attempts to fit Japanese history into the Marxist formula. The work is weak on facts.

689. Higo Kazuo 肥 後 和 男, Saishin Nihonshi 最 新 日 本 史 (Latest history of Japan), Tōkyō, Yuhōdō, 1950, 259+25 pp.
A postwar history of Japan by an expert on Japanese thought and folk religion

690. Ienaga Saburō 家永三郎, Shin-Nihonshi 新日本史 (New history of Japan), Tōkyō, Fuzambō, 1948, 10+326 pp.
> A simplified survey of Japanese history by the man credited with editing the new "purged" textbook of history for elementary schools, the Kuni no ayumi. This work thus reveals the "official" approach to the rewriting of Japanese history.

691. Inoue Kiyoshi 井上清, Nihon no rekishi 日本の歴史 (The history of Japan), Tōkyō, Naukasha, 1950, 452 pp.
> A revised edition of a work which appeared in 1947 under the title "Kuni no ayumi" hihan (Critique of "Kuni no ayumi"). This work injects a strong note of political bias to the usual intellectual Marxist attack on the new official elementary school textbook of Japanese history.

692. Izu Kimio 伊豆公夫, Nihon bunkashi kenkyū 日本文化史研究 (Studies in Japanese cultural history), Tōkyō, Getsuyō Shobō, 1948—.
> Volume 1 of a projected series presenting miscellaneous articles on Japanese culture by an active leftist historian and poet. Chapters deal with Japan's world position, art, music, nō drama, the society of the Manyō period, Edo society, haiku, etc.

693. Kawakami Tasuke 川上多助, Nihon rekishi gaisetsu 日本歴史概説 (Introduction to Japanese history), Tōkyō, Iwanami Shoten, 1937-40, 2 v.
> A detailed political history of Japan from ancient to contemporary times written with a minimum of reference to economic and social development. The work is sometimes referred to as the best in the immediate prewar academic tradition and largely replaces Omori Kingorō's more voluminous history (Entry 708).

694. Kurita Motoji 栗田元次, Sōgō Nihonshi gaisetsu 綜合日本史概説 (Synthetic introduction to Japanese history), Tōkyō, Chūbunkan, 1926-28, 2 v.
> A detailed cultural history of Japan. Volume 1 covers the field from ancient times to 1600. Volume 2 deals with the Tokugawa period. The author's interpretations are often stimulating. A unique feature of this work is its extensive classified bibliography of works on Japanese history. Though now seriously outdated, this bibliography represents one of the first attempts at systematic classification of secondary sources. The work has had numerous reprints most of which combine the two volumes in one.

695. Kuroita Katsumi 黒板勝美, Kōtei kokushi no kenkyū 更訂国史の研究 (A study of Japanese history—revised), Tōkyō, Iwanami Shoten, 1931-36, rev. ed., 4 v.
> This work, first published in 1909 and extensively revised several times, stands as a monument to the influence of the German school of historiography in Japan. Volume 1 (general introduction) deals with historical methodology and is annotated separately (Entry 664). The next two volumes constitute a detailed political history of Japan from ancient times to approximately 1918. The historical narrative is rigorously divided into periods and sub-periods. The author cites the titles of primary sources used throughout the study. Volume 4 is a standard historical chronology.

696. Kuroita Katsumi 黒板勝美, Kyoshin bunshū 虚心文集 (The collected works of Kyoshin), Tōkyō, Yoshikawa Kōbunkan, 1939-40, 8 v.
> The collected works of Kuroita Katsumi, one of the best known of the pre-World War II historians and an outstanding representative of the Tokyo University academic school of historiography.

697. Maruyama Jirō 丸山二郎, Saishin Nihon rekishi 最新日本歴史 (Latest history of Japan), Tōkyō, Yoshikawa Kōbunkan, 1950, 329 pp.
> A "new" history by a leading contemporary follower of Kuroita Katsumi and specialist on the early written histories of Japan.

698. Matsumoto Hikojirō 松本彦次郎, Nihon bunkashiron 日本文化史論 (Essays on the cultural history of Japan), Tōkyō, Kawade Shobō, 1942, 12+466+32 pp.
> A collection of 23 essays by one of Japan's foremost cultural historians. The author is a professor emeritus of Tokyo Bunrika University.

699. Miura Kaneyuki 三浦周行, Nihonshi no kenkyū 日本史の研究 (Studies in Japanese history), Tōkyō, Iwanami Shoten, 1922-30, 2 v.
> The collected historical essays of one of the leading historians of the last generation. These essays are surprisingly pertinent today and cover a remarkable diversity of subjects. The following are but a few examples: . studies of agrarian uprisings; popular assemblies in the Sengoku period; Ōmi in economic history; the Tenryūji ships; the development of medieval cities; the ports of Sakai, Kohama, and Hyōgo; social history of Japan; medieval culture; modern culture; studies of historical individuals; studies of foreign relations.

700. Muraoka Maretsugu 村岡典嗣, Nihon bunkashi gaisetsu 日本文化史概説 (Introduction to Japanese cultural history), Tōkyō, Iwanami Shoten, rev. ed., 1949, 141 pp.
> A work first published in 1938 by the foremost specialist on the history of Japanese thought.

701. Naitō Konan 内藤湖南, Nihon bunkashi kenkyū 日本文化史研究 (Studies in Japanese cultural history), Kyōto, Kōbundō Shobō, rev. ed., 1930, 420 pp.
> Essays on Japanese culture, largely in art, thought, religion, and Chinese influence during the Nara and Heian periods by a well-known expert on Chinese history. He is more commonly known as Naitō Torajirō.

702. Nakamura Kōya 中村孝也, <u>Shin-kokushikan</u> 新国史観 (A new view of Japanese history), Tōkyō, Yūzankaku, 1947-49, 10 v.
   A cultural history of Japan up to contemporary times written in the post-World War II "new history" tradition. The author, an officer of the Tokyo University Historiographical Institute and professor at Meiji University, attempts to place Japanese history in proper world perspective and to give due emphasis to the development of the lower classes in Japan.

703. Naramoto Tatsuya 奈良本辰也, <u>Shin-Nihonshi gaisetsu</u> 新日本史概説 (New introductory history of Japan), Kyōto, Ran Shobō, 1949, 322 pp.
   An excellent short survey of Japanese history from ancient times to the present. Naramoto has edited the entire work but individual chapters are written by others. A short list of suggested reading is provided. Naramoto is one of the leading "progressive" historians of the Kyoto area.

704. Nezu Masashi 禰津正志, <u>Atarashii Nihon rekishi</u> 新しい日本歴史 (New history of Japan), Tōkyō, Minshu Hyōronsha, 1949, 2 v.
   A "new history" written from the intellectual Marxist point of view by a specialist in archeology. The emphasis is on social development and the approach is strongly anti-authoritarian.

705. Nishida Kitarō 西田幾多郎, <u>Nihon bunka no mondai</u> 日本文化の問題 (Problems in Japanese culture), Tōkyō, Iwanami Shoten, 1940, 151 pp.
   A philosophical discussion of the meaning and characteristics of Japanese culture. The essay has been extremely influential among Japanese thinkers.

706. Nishida Naojirō 西田直二郎, <u>Nihon bunkashi josetsu</u> 日本文化史序説 (An introduction to the history of Japanese culture), Tōkyō, Kaizōsha, 1932, 645 pp.
   One of the best known cultural histories. The first part consists of a discussion of the meaning of cultural history. The remainder of the work is an interpretive coverage of Japanese history era by era down to the end of the Meiji period. Each chapter catches the spirit of a period of Japanese history. The author's interpretations of Nara, Heian, Ashikaga, and Tokugawa cultures are particularly brilliant.

707. Nishimura Shinji 西村真次, <u>Nihon bunkashi gairon</u> 日本文化史概論 (General survey of Japanese cultural history), Tōkyō, Tōkyōdō, 1930, 548 pp.
   This work consists of a collection of scholarly essays covering such subjects as the Japanese race, the nation, historical periods, language, religion, technology, economics. Emphasis is on the Nara and Heian periods. Articles are heavily documented. An index is provided.

708. Ōmori Kingorō 大森金五郎, <u>Dai Nihon zenshi</u> 大日本全史 (A complete history of Japan), Tōkyō, Fuzambō, 1921-22, 3 v.
   A textbook of Japanese history written for a non-academic public. The emphasis is primarily political, and a great deal of attention is given to periodization. <u>Kana</u> are affixed by the side of proper names to aid in their reading. This work is of value as a reference history because of the quantity of factual information it contains and for the index provided in volume 3. A fourth volume entitled <u>Gendai Nihonshi</u> (History of recent Japan), issued in 1937 by the same publisher, continues the historical treatment down to 1890.

709. Sano Manabu 佐野学, <u>Nihon rekishi kenkyū</u> 日本歴史研究 (Studies in Japanese history), Tōkyō, Kibōkaku, 1930, 381 pp.
   This is volume 2 of Sano's collected works and consists of two parts: "History of Japan" and "Outline of Japanese economic history." Both present a doctrinaire Marxist interpretation of Japanese history through various stages of social and economic development, primitive communities, patriarchal—slave state, feudalism, and the Restoration. These works have become classics of the Marxist historical school in Japan. Sano Manabu was active politically until his bolt from the Communist party in 1933.

710. Sakamoto Tarō 坂本太郎, <u>Nihonshi gaisetsu</u> 日本史概説 (Introduction to Japanese history), Tōkyō, Shinbundō, 1950—, 2 v.
   A postwar history of Japan by the leading contemporary scholar in the Tokyo University academic tradition. His specialty is the Taika period. He is now director of the Shiryō Hensansho.

711. Shiroyanagi Shūko 白柳秀湖, <u>Minzoku Nihon rekishi</u> 民族日本歴史 (History of the Japanese people), Tokyo, Chikura Shobō, 1935, 5 v.
   A somewhat popular narration of the origin and development of the Japanese people. The volumes are divided as follows: 1) the Plain of High Heaven to the establishment of the Yamato state; 2) the conquest of Honshū to the Taika Reform; 3) problems of reform, the Nara and Heian periods; 4) the rule of the Hōjō to that of Oda Nobunaga; 5) Hideyoshi, Tokugawa and the period of inflationary finance.

712. Taguchi Ukichi 田口卯吉, <u>Nihon kaika shōshi</u> 日本開化小史 (A short history of Japanese civilization), Tōkyō, 1877-82; 35th ed. Keizai Zasshisha, 1917, 457 pp.
   Recognized as the first history of Japan to be written under the influence of Western historiographical and economic theories, this work marked a new era in Japanese historical scholarship. Its continued popularity as a classic is attested to by the large number of popular editions.

713. Tamaki Hajime 玉城肇, <u>Nihon rekishi</u> 日本歴史 (Japanese history), Kyōto, Taigadō, 1948-49, 2 v.
   One of the better post-World War II "new histories." The work is a general survey of Japanese history from early to recent times written in non-technical style by a historical materialist.

714. Takekoshi Yosaburō 竹越與三郎, Shin-Nihon rekishi 新日本歴史 (New history of Japan), Tōkyō, Tōkyō Taimususha 東京タイムス社 1947-49, 2 v.
A postwar work by a somewhat unconventional scholar well known to Western readers. This work is based on the same author's monumental economic history of Japan. In it he succeeds in maintaining a position apart from any of the major schools of historiography in Japan today.

715. Toyoda Takeshi 豊田武, Gaisetsu Nihon rekishi 概説日本歴史 (An outline history of Japan), Ōsaka, Ōsaka Kyōiku Tosho K.K., 1947-49, 2 v.
A "new history" by one of the non-Marxist school of historians. The work is written as a textbook and is somewhat over-simplified. Toyoda gives as his guiding principle the writing of a history with balance between political, social, economic, and religious aspects of society. He attempts to place Japan in proper world perspective. Citation of reference works is given throughout, thus enhancing the usefulness of the work.

716. Tsuji Zennosuke 辻善之助, Nihon bunkashi 日本文化史 (Cultural history of Japan), Tōkyō, Shun-jūsha, 1950, 7 v.
A voluminous cultural history of Japan by one of Japan's most respected historians, formerly head of the Tokyo University Historiographical Office and Historical Society. The writing, however, lacks the brilliance of the author's more scholarly studies of Buddhism and foreign influence on Japan. The work is organized along standard chronological lines and there is no citation of reference.

717. Uchida Ginzō 内田銀蔵, Kokushi sōron 国史總論 (General survey of Japanese history), Tōkyō, Dōbunkan, 1921, 189 pp.
An important general survey by one of the most influential historians of the Taisho era.

718. Wakamori Tarō 和歌森太郎, Shinkō Nihonshi 新稿日本史 (Newly drafted history of Japan), Tōkyō, Yūseidō, 1949.
A "new history" by a specialist in Japanese social customs and religious practices.

719. Yashiro Kuniharu 八代国治, Kokushi sōsetsu 国史叢説 (Collected essays on Japanese history), Tōkyō, Yoshikawa Kōbunkan, 1925, 518 pp.
The collected historical essays of one of the foremost historians of the last generation. Subjects include the detailed study of medieval manors, imperial estates, the imperial family, Shinto deities, and festivals. Most of the essays are of a technical and scholarly nature.

b. Series Under Multiple Authorship

720. Waseda Daigaku Shuppambu 早稲田大学出版部 (Waseda University Publications Dept.), Teisei zōho Dai Nihon jidaishi 訂正増補大日本時代史 (History of Japan by periods, revised and enlarged), Tōkyō, Waseda Daigaku Shuppambu, 1915-16, 12 v.
This series was republished in 1926-27 under the title Nihon jidaishi (History of Japan by periods) in 14 volumes. It is a collaborative effort of history professors at Waseda University. The approach is popular and by now somewhat outdated. But the series can be of value for the somewhat original interpretations of political and cultural affairs which it contains.

721. Yūzankaku 雄山閣, Dai Nihonshi kōza 大日本史講座 (Japanese history series), Tōkyō, Yūzankaku, 1928-30, 18 v.
One of the less satisfactory of the multiple-volume series on Japanese history. Ten volumes are devoted to a period analysis of Japanese history, the remainder to topical histories covering foreign relations, diplomatics, religion, customs, thought, Japanese history through Chinese sources, and a chronology. Each volume is by a different author. The general approach and the style of writing are overly formal.

722. Gendai Nihon bummeishi 現代日本文明史 (History of contemporary Japanese civilization), Tōkyō, Tōyō Keizai Shimpōsha, 1940-44, 18 v.
A series of topical histories covering the development of Japan from the Restoration period to the time of publication (roughly 1853-1940). Each volume is written by an expert in a particular field of history. The general level of the entire series is high despite the fact that it came out during a period of limited academic freedom.

723. Yanaihara Tadao 矢内原忠雄, ed., Gendai Nihon shōshi 現代日本小史 (Short history of modern Japan), Tōkyō, Misuzu Shobō, 1952, 2 v.
These two volumes edited by the president of Tokyo University present six chapters on Japanese history, politics, economics, law, labor, and education from the Meiji Restoration to the present. Writing is of a high quality and the treatment is well balanced. Chapters are undocumented but reading lists are appended.

724. Honda Tatsujirō 本多辰次郎, Hanami Sakumi 花見朔己, and Sakai Yuzuru 酒井譲, Isetsu Nihonshi 異説日本史 (Divergent theories on Japanese history), Tōkyō, Yūzankaku, 1931-33, 25 v.
An extremely useful series worthy of more general recognition than it has received to date. It is especially valuable for Western students of Japanese history. The contents of the volumes are arranged as follows: 1-12) biographies; 13) historical monuments and temples; 14) myths; 15-16) battles; 17) government; 18) economics; 19) society; 20-21) religion; 22) arts; 23) historical documents; 24) general interpretation; 25) index. Each volume consists of a series of articles each of which is devoted to some controversial aspect of Japanese history. The editors cite major theories and theses, quoting from books and

articles to present various sides of each controversy. Each article thus consists of a résumé of the chief scholarship concerning some important figure or incident in Japanese history.

725. Iwanami kōza: Nihon rekishi 岩波講座 日本歴史 (Iwanami series on Japanese history), Tōkyō, Iwanami Shoten, 1933-35, 18 cases.
   The most ambitious of the "lecture series" publications. The work was prepared under the general editorship of Professor Kuroita Katsumi. Each case contains between five and ten pamphlets written on specific problems of Japanese history by selected specialists. The entire range of Japanese history from early times to the end of the Meiji period is covered. Generally for each period of history one pamphlet provides a survey, others deal with more limited topics. Contributors are well-established historians of the academic school. Social and economic developments receive scant attention. The general level of scholarship is high. Unfortunately, there is no general table of contents or index. Thus it is extremely difficult to locate material. Articles are unannotated. As a reference history, however, it is of great value.

726. Nihon Kindaishi Kenkyūkai 日本近代史研究会, Kindai hyakunenshi 近代百年史 (History of the last hundred years), Tōkyō, Kokusai Bunka Jōhōsha, 1951—.

727. Kindai Nihon rekishi kōza 近代日本歴史講座 (Series on contemporary Japanese history), Tōkyō, Hakuyōsha, 1939-40, 6 v.
   A series of general political histories covering Japan's development from 1868 to the 1920s. Volumes include: The Korean problem and the Satsuma rebellion (Tanaka Sōgorō); The liberal movement and the parties (Suzuki Yasuzō); The first Diet and treaty reform (Shizutani Hakuji); The Sino-Japanese war (Matsushita Yoshio); The Russo-Japanese war (Hori Makoto); and The Taisho political shift (Kyoguchi Motoyoshi).

728. Shigeno Yasutsugu 重野安繹, Kume Kunitake 久米邦武, and Hoshino Hisashi 星野恒, Kōhon kokushigan 槁本国史眼 (Draft survey of Japanese history), Tōkyō, Tōkyō Teikoku Daigaku Shigakkai, 1890, 7 v.
   An historically important work by three pioneer historians of modern Japan.

729. Waseda Daigaku Shuppambu 早稲田大学出版部 (Waseda University Publications Dept.), Kokumin no Nihonshi 国民の日本史 (A popular history of Japan), Tōkyō, Waseda Daigaku Shuppambu, 1922-23, 12 v.
   More popularly written than the other Waseda history series (Entry 720), this work is nevertheless of value for the rather free interpretations given to Japanese history by its several authors. Kana are supplied at the side of characters to aid in reading.

730. Nihon bunkashi 日本文化史 (Cultural history of Japan), Tōkyō, Daitōkaku, 1922, 12 v.
   An outdated but still valuable survey of Japanese cultural history by twelve outstanding scholars. The volumes are divided according to standard period divisions as follows: 1) Ancient period (Ando Masatsugu); 2) Nara (Nishimura Tamenosuke); 3) Early Heian (Ōta Akira); 4) Mid-Heian (Nishioka Toranosuke); 5) Late Heian (Takeoka Katsuya); 6) Kamakura (Ryō Susumu); 7) Namboku (Nakamura Naokatsu); 8) Muromachi (Uozumi Sōgorō); 9) Azuchi and Momoyama (Hanami Sakumi); 10) Early Edo (Shirazawa Kiyoto); 11) Late Edo (Kiyohara Sadao); 12) Meiji (Tokinoya Tsunezaburō). The volumes are of unequal quality but the series stands as one of the best interpretive surveys of Japanese history. The series was republished in 1941-42 by the Naigai Tosho K. K. under the title Nihon shin-bunkashi.

731. Nihon bunkashi taikei 日本文化史大系 (Survey of Japanese cultural history), Tōkyō, Seibundō Shinkōsha, 1937-42, 12 v.
   The most useful general history of Japan for the survey historian. The series covers Japanese history from early times to the end of the Taisho period (1925). Each volume treats a period in Japanese history and is divided into sections dealing with politics, economy, society, religion, literature, customs, and foreign relations. Each of these sections is written by an expert on the subject. A large number of high-ranking historians contributed to the series, and while individual articles are unannotated each is quite authoritative. The work is profusely illustrated.

732. Nihon gendaishi zensho 日本現代史全書 (Complete series on contemporary Japanese history), Tōkyō, Mikasa Shobo, 1941-45.
   This series complements the Nihon rekishi zensho (Entry 737) series issued by the same publisher. Sixteen volumes were projected. At least nine were issued before the war intervened to stop publication. These cover the following subjects: Meiji Restoration, contemporary politics, economics, continental policy, agricultural policy, southward expansionism, religion, education. Each volume is separately titled and is by an expert in his field.

733. Tōdai Rekishigaku Kenkyūkai 東大歴史研究会 (Tokyo University Historical Research Society), Nihon rekishigaku kōza 日本歴史学講座 (Lectures in Japanese history), Tōkyō, Gakusei Shobō, 1950, 284 pp.
   Based on a series of lectures given during 1947 at Tokyo University under sponsorship of the Rekishigaku Kenkyūkai, this volume supplements the work entitled Nihon shakai no shiteki kyūmei (Entry 738). Writers are mostly the same, but individual essays differ.

734. Nihon rekishi kōza 日本歴史講座 (Japanese history series), Tōkyō, Kawade Shobō, 1952—.
   A postwar series of short essays on Japanese history similar to the Iwanami series (Entry 725). Eight volumes are contemplated. These cover: 1) historical theory; 2) archaic history; 3,4) middle ages;

5,6) modern history; 7) contemporary history; and 8) the teaching of history. Each volume contains a general survey essay, several essays on particular aspects of the period, and a series of biographies of leading historical figures. Writers are leading "progressive" historians of the postwar period. Most essays are well documented.

735. Endō Motoo 遠 藤 元 男 , ed., Nihon rekishi no kōsei to tenkai 日 本 歴 史 の 構 成 と 展 開 (The structure and development of Japanese history), Tōkyō, Koronasha, 1948, 315 pp.
    An introduction to the study and analysis of Japanese history edited by Endō Motoo. Chapters deal with periodization, social and economic structure, structure of the state and politics, Japan's world view, Japanese ideology, and Japanese characteristics. Each chapter is plentifully documented.

736. Endō Motoo 遠 藤 元 男 , Nihon rekishi nyūmon 日 本 歴 史 入 門 (Introduction to Japanese history), Tōkyō, Mikasa Shobō, 1941, 369 pp.
    A guide to the study of Japanese history consisting of chapters contributed by a number of competent scholars. Part 1 discusses major turning points in Japanese history with chapters by Nakamura Kichiji, Ōkubo Toshiaki, Matsumoto Shimpachirō and others. Part 2 deals with historical methodology (see Entry 669). Part 3 discusses Japan's place in world history. This work is credited with giving birth to much of recent Japanese historical scholarship.

737. Mikasa Shobō 三 笠 書 房 , Nihon rekishi zensho (Complete series on Japanese history), Tōkyō, Mikasa Shobō, 1939—.
    Twenty-four volumes were planned in this series, though the war prevented the publication of the last three or four. Each volume covers a period of Japanese history or some specific field. The following are some of the outstanding volumes: General cultural history of Japan (Endō Motoo), Japanese medieval history (Watanabe Tamotsu), Japanese modern history (Kitajima Masamoto), The shōen system (Imai Rintarō), The refeudalization of Japan (Nakamura Kichiji), and Japanese Confucianism (Mampa Masatomo). Other volumes cover archeology, capitalism, arts, thought, the contemporary period, technology, and foreign affairs. The series as a whole is of high quality. Individual volumes carry extensive lists of suggested readings.

738. Rekishigaku Kenkyūkai 歴 史 学 研 究 会 (The Historical Science Society), Nihon shakai no shiteki kyūmei 日 本 社 会 の 史 的 究 明 (Historical study of Japanese society), Tōkyō, Iwanami Shoten, 1949, 340 pp.
    This volume contains eight essays by postwar materialist scholars such as Nezu Masashi, Ishimoda Tadashi, Hayashi Motoi, Hani Gorō, and others. Articles by Furushima Toshio on "Feudal characteristics of Japanese agriculture" and Maruyama Masao on "The ideology of the Meiji state" are outstanding. The last fifty pages are devoted to a bibliographical essay on Japanese social, economic, and intellectual history.

739. Nihonshi 日 本 史 (History of Japan), Tōkyō, Heibonsha, 1935-36, 3 v.
    These are volumes 12, 13A, and 13B of the Sekai rekishi taikei (Survey of world history). The three volumes present a running history of Japan. Volume 1, edited by Nishioka Toranosuke, covers ancient times to the Kamakura period; Volume 2, edited by Akiyama Kenzō, the middle ages; Volume 3, edited by Inobe Shigeo, Tokugawa and Meiji Japan. Each volume brings together chapters by a number of scholars dealing with the political, cultural, social, and economic aspects of Japan's history. Quality of scholarship is high and the social and economic development of the Japanese people is well handled. Chapters conclude with lists of recommended reading. One of the best of the general surveys of Japanese history.

740. Shigakkai 史 学 会 (Institute of Historical Science), Nihonshi gaikan 日 本 史 概 観 (Outline of Japanese history), Tōkyō, Yamakawa Shuppansha, 1950, 347+17 pp.
    Written by Sakamoto Tarō, Hōgetsu Keigo, and eight other members of Tokyo University's historical association, this work represents the "new history" views of the conservative faction of Tokyo University historians. The work, prepared for middle school use, is simply but well written. An index is provided.

741. Izu Kimio 伊 豆 公 夫 , Nihonshi nyūmon 日 本 史 入 門 (Introduction to Japanese history), Tōkyō, Seikisha, rev. ed., 1950, 270 pp.
    First published in 1947, this work presents seven introductory essays on Japanese history from primitive times to the present. Writers are all of the Marxist school and include Tōma Seita, Ishimoda Tadashi, Shinobu Seizaburō, and Moriya Fumio. The last is a member of the Communist party. Emphasis is on socio-economic development. There is an appended annotated bibliography of reference works.

742. Nijisseiki Nihon bummeishi 廿 世 紀 日 本 文 明 史 (The history of Japanese civilization during the twentieth century), Tōkyō, Jiji Tsūshinsha, 1950—, 10 v.
    A series covering the last fifty years of Japanese history from ten different aspects. The first volume entitled Seiji gojūnen (Politics during the last fifty years) is by Ōyama Ikuo. Other similarly titled volumes cover: economics (Sakisaka Itsuro), social thought (Maruyama Masao), literature (Kataoka Yoshikazu), education, art, science, music, drama, and sports. The general quality is high.

743. Tōyama Shigeki 遠 山 茂 樹 and others, Sekai no rekishi, Nihon 世 界 の 歴 史, 日 本 (History of the world, Japan), Tōkyō, Asahi Shimbunsha, 1949, 3+352+10 pp.
    A short survey of Japanese history from early to recent times by several members of the Minshushugi Kagakusha Kyōkai (Association of Democratic Scientists). The emphasis is on interpretation of the major problems of Japan's social development such as the structure of Nara society, feudalism, the nature of the Tokugawa control system, etc. There is an index.

744. Nakamura Kōya 中 村 孝 也 , ed., <u>Shinkō Dai Nihonshi</u> 新 講 大 日 本 史 (New lectures on Japanese history), Tōkyō Yūzankaku, 1941-43, 11 v.

Of much more value than the earlier series published by Yūzankaku (Entry 721), this series assembles contributions by some of the ablest of pre-World War II historians. Unfortunately, only 11 out of 18 projected volumes were completed. Five volumes cover the history of Japan by periods from ancient times to 1926. Each of these is by an individual author. The remaining volumes present collaborative coverage of the history of Japanese legal institutions, economy, thought, literature, and art.

745. <u>Shin-Nihonshi</u> 新 日 本 史 (History of new Japan), Tōkyō, Manchōhōsha, 1926-27, 5 v.

An encyclopedic history of Japan from 1868 to 1925. Volumes are devoted to: 1) politics, law, foreign affairs, military affairs, communications; 2) trade, commerce, industry; 3) education, religion, literature, art; 4) the sciences, labor, sports, amusements, etc. Each volume contains essays covering a multitude of subjects by individual experts.

746. Nishioka Toranosuke 西 岡 虎 之 助 , ed., <u>Shin-Nihonshi kōza</u> 新 日 本 史 講 座 (New series on Japanese history), Tōkyō, Chūō Kōronsha, 1947—.

A new lecture series comparable to the older Iwanami series (Entry 725). In comparison with the prewar work, this one draws on contributions from the younger so-called "progressive" historians. Titles of pamphlets are not dictated by the old political and cultural categories but originate in the newly popular theories of class structure and economic development. Problems of ancient slavery, Asiatic absolutism, feudal development, growth of capitalism, the modern revolution, the emperor system, modern absolutism, feudal remnants in modern Japan, etc., are some of the points of departure for the individual pamphlets. By summer, 1952, 12 cases containing over 60 pamphlets had been published. This series gives excellent coverage of the new theories developed in recent years by the younger Japanese historians. It can be used to good advantage to complement the older Iwanami series.

747. <u>Shin-Nihonshi taikei</u> 新 日 本 史 大 系 (New survey of Japanese history), Tōkyō, Asakura Shoten, 1952—.

Six volumes are projected for this series which will cover: 1) emergence of the Japanese state; 2) ancient society; 3) middle ages; 4) modern society; 5) the Meiji Restoration, and 6) contemporary society. Each volume contains four or five lengthy essays on general aspects of the period. Writers are drawn from the conservative school and include Wakamori Tarō, Takeuchi Rizō, Toyota Takeshi, Kodama Kōta, Horie Yasuzō, Ienaga Saburō, and Ōkubo Toshiaki. This series is especially valuable for its balanced writing. Essays are documented. Each volume contains a chronology of main events and an index.

748. <u>Sōgō Nihonshi taikei</u> 綜 合 日 本 史 大 系 (Synthetic survey of Japanese history), Tōkyō, Naigai Shoseki K.K., 1926, 8 v.

The most scholarly of the multi-volume surveys of Japanese history. It is regrettable that the volumes covering the pre-Nara, Kamakura, Muromachi, and Restoration periods were never published. The eight completed volumes deal with the following periods: Nara (Nishioka Toranosuke), Early Heian (Kawakami Tasuke), Late Heian (Sakurai Hide), Namboku (Uozumi Sōgorō), Azuchi Momoyama (Hanami Sakumi), Early Edo (Kurita Mototsugu), and Late Edo (Tatsui Matsunosuke). Emphasis is on political and cultural history with little attention to social or economic affairs. Each volume is unusually well annotated with references to primary and secondary materials.

749. <u>Taikan Nihon bunkashi sensho</u> 大 觀 日 本 文 化 史 薦 書 (Survey of Japanese cultural history series), Tōkyō, Chijin Shokan, 1940, 19 v.

A valuable series written by top-ranking cultural historians of the immediate prewar period. The following are some of the titles and authors of the individual volumes: Outline of cultural history (Nakamura Kōya), Thought (Kiyohara Sadao), Confucianism (Takahashi Shinji), Christianity (Shimmura Izuru), Agriculture (Ono Takeo), Bushidō (Hashimoto Minoru), Customs (Ema Tsutomu). Most of the volumes carry valuable lists of suggested reading. The general quality is high and many of the individual volumes constitute the best introductory survey available on the subject.

c. Illustrated Histories

750. Kishiro Shūichi 木 代 修 一, Nihon bunkashi zuroku 日 本 文 化 史 圖 録 (Illustrations of Japanese cultural history), Tōkyō, Shikai Shobō, 1938, 28+240+221 pp.

The most useful one-volume illustrated history of Japan. Plates cover archeological objects, architectural monuments, art objects, and documents. The end of the book contains a brief but stimulating outline of Japanese cultural history with plate numbers integrated with the text. Plates are somewhat small but clear.

751. Kokushi daizukan 国 史 大 図 鑑 (Illustrated compendium of Japanese history), Tōkyō, Yoshikawa Kōbunkan, 1932-34, 6 v.

Representing the collaborative efforts of a number of foremost historians this series brings together an impressive collection of illustrative material on Japanese history. Volumes 1-5 each cover a major period of Japanese history. Plates include historic sites, buildings, art and craft objects. Each plate is followed by an explanatory page. Volume 6 deals with customs and clothing. Each volume contains an index to plates.

752. Nishioka Toranosuke 西 岡 虎 之 助 , <u>Shin-Nihonshi zuroku</u> 新 日 本 史 圖 録 (New illustrated history of Japan), Tōkyō, Chūō Kōronsha, 1952, 2 v.

The latest and most satisfactory of the illustrated histories.

753. Tōkyō Daigaku Shiryō Hensansho 東京大学史料編纂所 (Tokyo University Historiographical Institute), E de miru Nihonshi 絵で見る日本史 (Japanese history seen through pictures), Tambaichi, Naraken, Yōtokusha, 1949, 2 v.

A carefully edited selection of illustrations covering all aspects of Japanese history. Volume 2 contains lucid explanations and interpretations of the illustrations contained in volume 1.

754. Tōyō Bunka Kyōkai 東洋文化協会 (Oriental Culture Association), Rekidai bunka kōkokushi taikan 歴代文化皇国史大観 (A visual survey of Japanese cultural history through the ages), Tōkyō, Tōyō Bunka Kyōkai, 1934, 94+720+116 pp.

This work presents in chronological order photographs of historical relics and of reconstructed scenes from the past. A number of plates reproduce the annual Jidai Matsuri (Festival of History) of Kyoto. Coverage is from ancient times through the Meiji period. Each plate is given a full annotation on the facing page. There is an index.

d. Source Books

755. Haga Kōshirō 芳賀幸四郎, Shiryō ni yoru Nihonshi kenkyū 史料による日本史研究 (The study of Japanese history through primary sources), Tōkyō, Ikeda Shoten, 1951, 124 pp.

This work written for beginning Japanese students is of special value because of its careful explanations of the materials presented. The author selects primary sources from documentary collections as well as from the popular literature of each period. These are translated into modern Japanese, annotated, and explained.

756. Kuroita Katsumi 黒板勝美, Shiryō tekiroku kokushi gaikan 資料摘録国史概観 (Documentary survey of Japanese history), Tōkyō, Yoshikawa Kōbunkan, 1936, 381 pp.

The right-hand pages of this survey reproduce selected historical documents used by Professor Kuroita in the preparation of his Kokushi no kenkyū. The selection is overly restricted, and there are no explanatory comments.

757. Maruyama Jirō 丸山二郎, Kyōju shiryō Nihonshi yōsetsu 教授資料日本史要説 (An outline history of Japan with instructional documentary materials), Tōkyō, Yoshikawa Kōbunkan, 1949, 425+10 pp.

The author worked with Kuroita Katsumi in editing the Kokushi taikei (Entry 397) and aided in the preparation of the Shiryō tekiroku kokushi gaikan (Entry 756). This work is arranged similarly to Kuroita's with running text on odd pages and documents on even. The selection is much more satisfactory, however. The author provides a bibliographical index to the primary sources quoted.

758. Ōkubo Toshiaki 大久保利謙 and others, Shiryō ni yoru Nihon no ayumi 史料による日本の歩み (A documentary history of Japan), Tōkyō, Yoshikawa Kōbunkan, 1951—.

The first volume of a proposed multi-volume documentary history of Japan. This volume covers the post-Restoration period. It presents selected documents on the development of the modern Japanese state, the constitution, capitalistic expansion, international affairs, internal political movements, cultural affairs, etc. Marginal tabs indicate important facts found in the documents.

759. Tōkyō Daigaku Shigakkai 東京大学史学会 (Tokyo University Institute of Historical Science), Shiryō Nihonshi 資料日本史 (A source book of Japanese history), Tōkyō, Yamakawa Shuppansha, 1951-52, 2 v.

A useful, chronologically arranged collection of Japanese historical documents for use by college instructors.

3. LOCAL HISTORY AND HISTORICAL GEOGRAPHY

Material on Japanese local history is extremely voluminous but is seldom of a general survey variety. The bulk of such writing occurs in two specialized forms: either as 1) scholarly articles in such journals as Rekishi chiri, Rekishi to chiri, Shakai keizaishigaku, and other localized journals; or as 2) prefectural, district, city, or village histories. Such local histories have a long tradition in Japan beginning with the fudoki 風土記 (local gazetteers) of the eighth century. During the Tokugawa period (1600-1868) nearly every major feudal domain ordered the writing of official local histories and gazetteers. Besides these, large numbers of histories, descriptions of customs, guides to famous spots, and records of local production or topography were prepared privately by local scholars or publishers. After the Meiji Restoration these Tokugawa works became the basis of modern histories and gazetteers produced by various local historical associations. Today nearly every pre-modern province, every modern prefecture, every major city, gun (district) and even an occasional village has a history or gazetteer to its credit. Such works are somewhat old fashioned in their methodology, but they nevertheless remain as important repositories of factual information not only on local institutions in general but on such diverse subjects as Japanese foreign relations, the life of special groups such as merchants or minorities, and pre-modern feudal administration and economic organization. When used properly they can be of considerable use to even the general historian. Because of the great volume of such material, only a few of the most significant local histories have been listed below. The reader is referred to the bibliographies of Honjō Eijirō (Entries 10 to 12) for a more complete list.

Since World War II the establishment of prefectural universities and the government's attempt to decentralize education in Japan have stimulated new activity in the local history field. On the one hand several series of local histories for higher school use have made their appearance. The Shakaika kyōdo shiriizu (Social science local community series) (Entry 778) is published under Ministry of Education sponsorship and proposes to print 46 volumes on local communities in Japan. On the other hand, professors in the new prefectural universities are applying the skills of centrally trained historians to the study of local materials. The result has been the publication of numerous local studies of high technical quality. The founding in 1950 of the Committee for the Study of Local History (Chihōshi Kenkyū Kyōgikai) illustrates the growing importance of local history in Japan today.

760. Aichi-ken 愛知縣 (Aichi Prefecture), Aichi kenshi 愛知縣史 (History of Aichi Prefecture), Tōkyō, Yoshikawa Kōbunkan, 1935-40, 5 v.
    A detailed history of the important prefecture of Aichi which has Nagoya as its central city. Edited by Kuroita Katsumi and Endō Masao, it maintains a high standard of scholarship. Volume 1 covers the early history up to 1600. Volume 2 deals with the Tokugawa period (1600-1868). Volumes 3-4 treat the post-Restoration period up to 1926. The last volume contains historical sources.

761. Chiri Kyōiku Kenkyūkai 地理教育研究会 (Society for the Study of the Teaching of Geography), Shūraku chirigaku rombunshū 聚落地理学論文集 (Collected essays on village geography), Tōkyō, Chirikyōiku Kenkyūkai, 1935, 5 v.
    A collection of articles by recognized Japanese authorities on such topics as: The nature of the Japanese village, castle towns and villages, Tokushu buraku, cities and geography, etc.

762. Fujita Motoharu 藤田元春, Nihon chirigakushi 日本地理学史 (History of geographical studies in Japan), Tōkyō, Tōkō Shoin, 1932, 442+50 pp.
    A collection of individual essays on early local gazetteers, maps, and the development of geographical knowledge in Japan.

763. Fukushima shigaku kenkyū 福島史学研究 (A study of the history of Fukushima), Fukushima, Fukushima-ken Shigakkai, 1951.
    A scholarly history of the Fukushima area.

764. Hokkaidō-chō 北海道庁 (Hokkaido Territorial Office), Shinsen Hokkaidōshi 新撰北海道史 (New history of Hokkaido), Sapporo, Hokkaidō-chō, 1936-37, 7 v.
    Volume 1 is a general survey of Hokkaido history. Volumes 2-6 contain a more detailed history and original documents. Volume 7 is made up of genealogies, chronologies, and an index. This work is extremely important for the study of early Japanese relations with the Russians.

765. Ishikawa-ken 石川縣 (Ishikawa Prefecture), Ishikawa kenshi 石川縣史 (History of Ishikawa Prefecture), Kanazawa, Ishikawa-ken, 1927-33, 5 v.
    A local history of the area around Kanazawa. The area is of special significance as headquarters of the Kaga domain in feudal times. This history, used in conjunction with the Kaga-han shiryō (Entry 417), affords a most complete coverage of one of the key geographical areas of Japan. Volume 1 covers the pre-Tokugawa era. Volumes 2-3 deal with Tokugawa government, economics, and culture. Volume 4 treats the Meiji period. The last volume deals with geography and contains reprints of ancient local gazetteers.

766. Kagoshima-ken 鹿兒島縣 (Kagoshima Prefecture), Kagoshima kenshi 鹿兒島縣史 (History of Kagoshima Prefecture), Kagoshima, Kagoshima-ken, 1939-43, 5 v.
    An historical survey of an important area of feudal Japan and one which gave leadership to the Meiji Restoration. This work was edited by Kuroita Katsumi, senior historian of the last generation in Japan. Volume 1 covers the period up to 1600. Volumes 2-3 offer a detailed description of political, economic and cultural institutions of the period from 1600 to 1877. Volume 4 completes the historical coverage to 1935. Volume 5 contains charts, tables, and historical sources.

767. Kōda Shigetomo 幸田成友, Edo to Ōsaka 江戸と大阪 (Edo and Osaka), Tōkyō, Fuzambō, 1934, 333+14 pp.
    A lively description of the cities of Edo and Osaka and the trade which flourished between them during the 17th through 19th centuries. Several chapters of this book have been translated by Neil S. Smith, Tokugawa Japan, Tokyo, 1937.

768. Kyōto no kenkyū 京都の研究 (Studies of Kyoto), Tōkyō, Nihon Hyōronsha, 1931, 116 pp.
    [=Keizaishi kenkyū (Studies in economic history), special issue, no. 19]. Scholarly articles deal with the economic development of Kyoto from the fourteenth to twentieth centuries.

769. Kyōto Shiyakusho 京都市役所 (Kyoto City Office), Kyōto shishi 京都市史 (History of Kyoto), Kyōto, Kyōto Shiyakusho, 1944—.
    A detailed chronological and documentary history of Kyoto. Of the volumes published so far the map supplement (1946) is of special interest.

770. Nagasaki shishi 長崎市史 (History of Nagasaki), Nagasaki, Nagasaki Shiyakusho, 1935-38, 3 v.
    Divided into sections on the city, relations with Oriental nations, and relations with Westerners, this work combines both collected source materials and excellent interpretive articles by Japanese scholars. The work is of great importance for the study of Japan's foreign relations from 1568 to the end of the Tokugawa period. Editors included such well-known scholars as Murakami Naojirō and Yano Jin'ichi.

771. Okayama Shiyakusho 岡山市役所 (Okayama City Office), Okayama shishi 岡山市史 (History of Okayama), Okayama, Okayama Shiyakusho, 1936-38, 6 v.
    A standard and detailed history of the Okayama area from early times to the time of writing. The work is heavy on statistics and extracts quoted from local archival materials. Volumes 1-2 deal with place

names and Okayama history up to the seventeenth century.   Volumes 3, 4, and 5 cover the Tokugawa period.   Volume 6 deals with the Meiji period and brings coverage down to approximately 1930.

772. Ōsaka no kenkyū 大阪の研究 (Studies of Osaka), Tōkyō, Nihon Hyōronsha, 1931, 106 pp. [=Keizaishi kenkyū (Studies in economic history), special issue, no. 15].   Scholarly articles deal with the economic development of Osaka since the Restoration.

773. Ōsaka shishi 大阪市史 (History of Osaka), Ōsaka, Ōsakashi Sanjikai, 1911-15, 8 v.
Edited by Kōda Shigetomo, this series consists of two volumes of narrative history, four volumes of documentary materials, one of index, and one of plates.   The historical section covers the development of the city from archaic times through the Tokugawa.   Economic growth of the city is dealt with in great detail. Documents are drawn largely from the Tokugawa period.   Plates depict old maps, charts, plans, and drawings of the old castle, etc.   This work is particularly important for the light it sheds upon the development of the Osaka merchant community.

774. Sakai Shiyakusho 堺市役所 (Sakai City Office), Sakai shishi 堺市史 (History of Sakai), Sakai, Sakai Shiyakusho, 1929-31, 8 v.
A voluminous history of one of the most important port cities of pre-modern times.   The editor was Miura Kaneyuki, one of the best known scholars of the 1920s.   Volumes 1-3 deal with the history of Sakai from its origins to the time of writing, describing the development of political, economic and cultural institutions.   Emphasis is on the 14th through 19th centuries.   Volumes 4-6 contain historical materials, volume 7 deals with persons and religious institutions, and volume 8 comprises an index and chronology.

775. Sekai chiri taikei, Nihon 世界地理大系，日本 (A survey of world geography, Japan), Tōkyō, Kawade Shobō, vol. 2 of the series, 1951, 5+327+19 pp.
A clearly written synthetic geography of Japan edited by Ishida Tatsujirō and Watanabe Akira.   Part 1 deals with the natural environment of the Japanese people.   Part 2 treats social forces such as population, production, land use, etc.   Part 3 consists of a regional treatment of Japan's geographical, economic, and social problems.   Separate chapters are written by individual specialists.   Each chapter is followed by a bibliographical list.

776. Sendai Shishi Hensan Iinkai 仙台市史編纂委員会 (Committee for the Compilation of the History of Sendai), Sendai no rekishi 仙台の歴史 (History of Sendai), Sendai, Sendai Shiyakusho (Sendai City Office), 1949, 222 pp., separate maps.
Compiled by a group of scholars at work on the voluminous Sendai shishi (next entry), this work is an abridged history of the city of Sendai and its surrounding territory.   One-half of the volume deals with the Tokugawa period, another third with the development of the city since 1868.   The treatment is extremely detailed yet at the same time arranged to give a clear picture of the development of local political, economic, and social institutions.

777. Sendai Shishi Hensan Iinkai 仙台市史編纂委員会, Sendai shishi 仙台市史 (History of Sendai), Sendai, 1949—.
Scheduled to run to ten volumes, this series constitutes one of the best city histories to come out of postwar Japan.   It is being compiled by scholars of excellent repute.   The abridged history (see previous entry) published by the same group gives some idea of the scope of the finished series.

778. Shakaika kyōdo shiriizu 社会科郷土シリーズ (Social science local community series), Tōkyō, Shimizu Shoin, 1949, 46 v.
A series of local community studies covering most prefectures and large cities.   Written for students below the college level, the studies nonetheless contain a great deal of factual material in extremely usable form.   While they are not historical in approach, they describe many local features or peculiarities which have historical origins.   Sections in each volume treat such subjects as geography, demography, rural areas, cities, natural resources, industry, communications, natural disasters, local culture, and political institutions.

779. Tōkyō Shiyakusho 東京市役所 (Tokyo Municipal Office), Tōkyō shishi kō 東京市史稿 (Draft history of Tokyo), Tōkyō, Hakubunkan, 1911—.
Sixty-six volumes of this series had been published by 1940.   The work is divided into several topical sections as follows: the imperial castle, the city, water works, the port and bay, relief, disasters, parks, graveyards, etc.   Each chapter begins with an introduction and then cites original sources in chronological order.   Coverage is from early times to the end of Meiji, but the Tokugawa years are naturally the fullest.   There are a great number of illustrations and charts.

780. Yamaguchi-ken Bunkashi Hensan Iinkai 山口縣文化史編纂委員会(Committee for the Compilation of the Cultural History of Yamaguchi Prefecture), Yamaguchi-ken bunkashi 山口縣文化史 (Cultural history of Yamaguchi Prefecture), Yamaguchi, 1951—.
An excellent history of Yamaguchi Prefecture written with a modern interpretive approach.   Volume 1 (688 pp.) is a general history from prehistoric times to the middle of the Meiji period.   Subsequent volumes will contain historical materials.

781. Yanagida Kunio 柳田国男, Chimei no kenkyū 地名の研究 (A study of place names), Tōkyō, Kokon Shoin, 1936, 368 pp.
  Contains a great deal of miscellaneous information on place name origins. Chapters are entitled: legends and place names, geography and place names, history and place names, place name origins as derived from reclaimed land, branch villages, and shōen. There is an index.

782. Yokohama shishi-kō 横浜市史稿 (Draft history of Yokohama), Yokohama, Yokohama Shiyakusho, 1931-33, 11 v.
  Divided into sections on administration, temples, shrines and churches, customs, education, geography and production, this work assembles a great deal of material vital to the study of early Western trade with Japan. Volume 11 is an index.

783. Yoshida Tōgo 吉田東伍, Chiriteki Nihon rekishi 地理的日本歴史 (Japanese history from the geographic point of view), Tōkyō, Nambokusha, 1914, 476 pp.
  This work treats the history of Japan from early times to the time of writing giving special emphasis to the influence of geography upon the course of history. Each chapter takes a separate phase of Japanese history: political, economic, military, literary, etc. A revision of this work was prepared by Yokoi Haruno in 1929.

784. Yoshida Tōgo 吉田東伍, Nihon rekishichiri no kenkyū 日本歴史地理の研究, (Studies in Japanese historical geography), Tōkyō, Fuzambō, 1923, 1011 pp.
  Selected essays of Japan's foremost historical geographer. Essays deal with: levee work and flood control, Musashi during the Nara period, maritime rights in the Inland Sea, the Kamakura manorial system, and many other subjects.

785. Yūzankaku 雄山閣, Kyōdoshi kenkyū kōza 郷土史研究講座 (Series on the study of local history), Tōkyō, Yūzankaku, 1931-32, 15 v.
  A collection of unscholarly essays on regional history and geography. Essays treat local materials, history of shrines, villages, etc., but tend toward folkloristic subjects.

4. BIOGRAPHICAL HISTORIES

  Biographical literature is plentiful in Japan but exists mostly in the form of individual studies. Because of the limited scope of individual biographies they have been excluded from this bibliography and will be listed in the more detailed historical bibliographies which follow. The present list includes a few modern and pre-modern sources which consists of retsuden, collected biographies.

786. Hotta Masaatsu 堀田正敦, Kansei chōshū shokafu 寛政重修諸家譜 (Kansei collated genealogies), Tōkyō, Eishinsha, 1917, 9 v.
  Prepared at official shogunate request during the years 1799-1812, this work gives genealogies of the families of all daimyō and officers of the Tokugawa government. Of special value are the lengthy notes on the official careers of each individual. An index to this work is provided in Tokushi biyō (Entry 233).

787. Hotta Shōzayū 堀田璋左右 and Kawakami Tasuke 川上多助, ed., Nihon ijin genkō shiryō 日本偉人言行資料 (Materials on the words and lives of eminent Japanese), Tōkyō, Kokushi Kenkyū-kai, 1915-17, 24 v.
  Collected autobiographies, biographies, and writings of daimyō and scholars of the Tokugawa period.

788. Honda Tatsujirō 本多辰次郎 and others, Isetsu Nihonshi 異説日本史 (Divergent theories on Japanese history), Tōkyō, Yūzankaku, 1931-33, 25 v.
  Volumes 1-12 of this series are devoted to divergent interpretations of famous historical individuals. (See Entry 724 for a fuller annotation.)

789. Iida Tadahiko 飯田忠彦, Dai Nihon yashi 大日本野史 (Unofficial history of Japan), 3rd ed., Tōkyō, Zuihitsu Taisei Kankōkai, 1930, 6 v.
  Completed in 1853, this work is an "annals and biographies" style history of Japan from 1392 to the beginning of the nineteenth century. The lives of emperors, consorts, court nobles, feudal lords, priests and scholars are related in great detail. References indicate the use of primary sources. There is an index. The work is written in Kambun.

790. Ruijū denki Dai Nihonshi 類聚傳記大日本史 (A biographical history of Japan), Tōkyō, Yūzankaku, 1934, 15 v.
  This series contains biographies of eminent Japanese from early times to 1926. Volumes are classified as follows: 1) Court nobles, 2) Shogun, 3) Daimyō, 4) Loyalists (largely of the Restoration), 5) Generals, 6) Artists and craftsmen, 7) Priests, 8) Shinto priests, 9) Authors and poets, 10) Men of moral integrity, 11) Meiji political figures, 12) Modern industrialists, 13) Eminent modern naval officers, 14) Eminent modern army officers, 15) Women. Each volume carries lengthy biographies of the most outstanding figures and ends with a short biographical dictionary of lesser known individuals.

791. Saeki Ariyoshi 佐伯有義, Kōtei hyōchū rikkokushi 校訂標註六国史 (The six national histories collated and annotated), Tōkyō, Asahi Shimbunsha, 1931, 11 v.
  The Rikkokushi (Six national histories), written between 712 and 901, cover Japanese history from earliest times to 887. They comprise the most complete source of biographical information for the Nara and early Heian periods. This modern edition has an index.

792. Tōin Kimisada 洞 院 公 定, Sompi bummyaku 尊 卑 文 脈 (Genealogies of main and branch families), Tōkyō, Yoshikawa Kōbunkan, 1903-04, 12 v.

A voluminous collection of genealogies of the chief noble and feudal aristocratic families. Considered the most authoritative reference work on the subject. An index was published by the same publisher in 1924.

793. Tokugawa Mitsukuni 徳. 川 光 圀 and others, Dai Nihonshi 大 日 本 史 (History of Japan), Tōkyō, Yoshikawa Kōbunkan, 1900-17, 13 v.

Known as the Mito history of Japan, this work is written in the Chinese dynastic history style of annals, biographies, and essays. The work covers Japanese history from early times to 1392. In the modern edition volumes 1-5 contain imperial annals and biographies. Text is written in Chinese but a Japanese translation by Yamaji Aizan 山 路 愛 山 entitled Shakubun Dai Nihonshi and published in the Daishisō zenshū (1929-30) is available.

5. GOVERNMENT AND POLITICS

Survey histories of political institutions in Japan are for the most part far from satisfactory. Most works of this type are hardly more than political histories. Their analyses of the development and articulation of Japanese government are rudimentary and generally incomplete. To obtain a picture of the origin and growth of Japanese administrative institutions, the distribution of political power, and the actual functioning of the various organs of Japanese government, the historian must consult a wide variety of works. These should include studies of the various stages of political development from the early clan period, the period of sinicized bureaucracy, the period of feudal-military rule, modern constitutionalism and absolutism, as well as works on various governmental institutions: the state, the emperor, the bureaucracy, administrative and legal devices, etc. It is only through such a composite reading that a satisfactory history of Japanese government and politics may be obtained.

The following section includes selected works in most of the categories which the historian of political institutions will wish to consult. They should be augmented, however, by the listings under socio-economic systems included in Chapter 6, Section c of this part. As usual the emphasis in the following selection has been on works relating to the pre-Restoration period, though certain representative works on the post-Restoration era have been included in each category. Those whose chief interest is modern government and politics will find fuller coverage in Robert E. Ward's A Guide to Japanese Reference and Research Materials in the Field of Political Science.

a. Political History

As stated in the previous paragraphs, much of the survey literature in Japanes history is actually written in the form of political history. Pre-modern works in the Chinese tradition as well as products of the Tokyo University's modern geschichtswissenschaft school of historiography are largely concerned with history as seen through the deeds of rulers and the events of government. For this reason many of the best works in the field of political history are to be found among the general survey histories previously listed in Chapter 2, Sections a and b of this part. Outstanding among early works in this category are Kuroita Katsumi's Kokushi no kenkyū (A study of Japanese history) (Entry 695) and the Sōgō Nihonshi taikei (Synthetic survey of Japanese history) (Entry 748). Both are largely descriptive in their approach but contain a wealth of detail. Later survey histories of the prewar period were less detailed but attempted a greater degree of analysis chiefly through the eyes of the economic historian.

Recent Japanese political historians have been inclined to pay more attention to the problems of political power structure and political movements. Unfortunately, no good general survey has come out of the postwar period, as most contemporary scholars prefer to specialize in limited fields. The collected views of many such specialists will be found, however, in a number of the more recent historical series, particularly in the Shakai kōseishi taikei (Comprehensive outline of the history of social structures) (Entry 1156).

The pioneer attempt to write a history of political institutions rather than a mere political history was made by Imanaka Tsugimaro in his Nihon seijishi taikō (Outline of Japanese political history) (Entry 795). Like most products of prewar scholarship, this work takes a primarily static view of governmental structure. Postwar historians have attempted to analyze more fully the forces behind change and development of Japan's political institutions, often, however, with the aid of Marxist theories of political dynamics. Their views are most readily accessible in the various historical series of recent origin and in the symposium published by the Rekishigaku Kenkyūkai entitled Kokka kenryoku no shodankai (Stages of national power) (Entry 796).

1) General

794. Hosokawa Kameichi 細 川 亀 市, Nihon seijishi 日 本 政 治 史 (History of Japanese politics), Tōkyō, Nankōsha, 1939, 14+286 pp.

A general political history of Japan from early times to 1890. The work is organized by periods; within each period subsections treat political theories, concepts of national polity, political structure, and administrative practices.

795. Imanaka Tsugimaro 今 中 次 麿, Nihon seijishi taikō 日 本 政 治 史 大 綱 (Outline of Japanese political history), Tōkyō, Nankōsha, 1936, 495 pp.

A pioneer attempt to study the history and development of political institutions in Japan. Sections are given the following titles: the clan state, the imperial state, the feudal state, the people's state. There is an index.

796. Rekishigaku Kenkyūkai 歴史学研究会 (Historical Science Society), Kokka kenryoku no shodankai 国家権力の諸段階 (Stages of national power), Tōkyō, Iwanami Shoten, 1950, 144 pp.
   A summary of the 1949 annual meeting of the society, this work contains a large number of brief reports on studies and theories on the various stages of Japanese national development from ancient times through the feudal period until modern times.

797. Satō Kiyokatsu 佐藤清勝, Dai Nihon seiji shisōshi 大日本政治思想史 (History of Japanese political thought), Tōkyō, Dai Nihon Seiji Shisōshi Kankokai, 1939, 2 v.
   An interpretation of the development of Japanese political philosophies with emphasis on the central position of the emperor.

798. Shakaishugi Kyōiku Kyōkai 社会主義教育協会 (Socialist Education Society), Nihon Seiji no henkaku katei 日本政治の変革過程 (The process of change in Japanese government), Tōkyō, Sangensha, 1948, 222 pp.
   [=Shakaishugi kōza (Series on socialism), v. 1]. Contains essays by a number of contributors.

799. Uchida Shigetaka 内田繁隆, Nihon shakai keizaishi 日本社会経済史 (A social and economic history of Japan), Tōkyō, Bun'eidō, rev. ed., 1940, 354 pp.
   This work is actually a political history of Japan with emphasis on governmental structure at various stages of Japanese social and economic development.

800. Watanabe Tamotsu 渡辺保 and Takahashi Shin'ichi 高橋磌一, Nihon no seiji 日本の政治 (Japanese politics), Tōkyō, Keisetsu Shoin, 1940, 16+155+137 pp.
   A standard political history of Japan from early times to the Meiji period.

801. Yoshino Sakuzō 吉野作造, Seijishi 政治史 (Political history), Tōkyō, Bunshinsha, 1926.
   The chief work of one of the pioneer political scientists in Japan. The book is based on the author's lectures in Japanese political history at Tokyo University.

2) The Taika Reform and the Sinicized Bureaucracy

   Prior to the end of World War II the standard interpretations of the Taika Reform (645 A.D.) and the sinicized bureaucracy of the seventh through twelfth centuries were found in the major historical series, particularly in the Iwanami kōza: Nihon rekishi (Iwanami series on Japanese history) (Entry 725) and the Sōgō Nihonshi taikei (Synthetic survey of Japanese history) (Entry 748). Both contain works by accepted prewar authorities such as Nishioka Toranosuke, Kawakami Tasuke, and Sakamoto Tarō. The following list presents a limited selection of works of leading postwar scholars in the field of ancient political institutions. Among them Ishimoda Tadashi and Tōma Seita represent the new school of Marxist interpreters. Recent scholarship in this field has attempted to formulate a more comprehensive explanation, in terms of social, economic, as well as political forces, of the Taika Reform and the bureaucratic government which resulted from it. Thus, while the relationship of state to aristocracy and state to the serf class is dealt with in great detail, comparatively little is written upon the actual articulation of the post-Taika bureaucracy.

802. Inoue Mitsusada 井上光貞, Nihon kodaishi no shomondai 日本古代史の諸問題 (Problems of ancient Japanese history), Tōkyō, Shisakusha, 1949, 358 pp.
   Contains seven essays dealing with the ancient be, the Yamato state and its military policy, the clan system, and the Taika reform.

803. Ishimoda Tadashi 石田田正, "Kodai makki no seiji katei oyobi keitai 古代末期の政治過程及び政治形態 (The development and structure of political institutions during the late ancient period)," in Shakai kōseishi taikei 社会構成史体系 (Series on the history of social structures), Tōkyō, Nihon Hyoronsha, 1950-51.
   The most accessible of the many works by a prolific and influential intellectual Marxist. The work analyzes the political structure of Japanese society during the Heian period as the aristocratic bureaucratic government gave way to feudal institutions.

804. Kitayama Shigeo 北山茂夫, Naracho no seiji to minshū 奈良朝の政治と民衆 (Government of the Nara period and the people), Kyōto, Kōtō Shoin, 1948, 251+30+9 pp.
   Contains five chapters dealing with changes in administration and life of the people occasioned by the Taika reform.

805. Sakamoto Tarō 坂本太郎, Taika kaishin no kenkyū 大化改新の研究 (A study of the Taika reform), Tōkyō, Shibundō, 1938, 606+26 pp.
   The standard analysis of the political, social, and economic history of the Taika Reform by the director of the Tokyo University Historiographic Institute.

806. Tōma Seita 藤間生大, Nihon kodai kokka 日本古代国家 (The Japanese nation in ancient times), Tōkyō, Itō Shoten, 1946.
   An influential work on the early Japanese aristocratic state. The author is primarily interested in the position of the cultivator class which he compares to the slave class of ancient Europe. In Japanese society, however, the village and patriarchal family were the foundations of the state. There was little individual slavery as in Europe but rather a village-centered communalism.

807. Watanabe Yoshimichi 渡部義通, Nihon kodai shakai 日本古代社会 (The society of ancient Japan), Tōkyō, Mikasa Shobō, 1947, 200 pp.
        First published in 1936, this work describes the structure of ancient Japanese society.

3) Military Rule and the Shogunal System

        The period of shogunal rule, from the twelfth to nineteenth centuries, has been studied chiefly in terms of the broader feudal institutions of the times.   Works on Japanese feudalism will be found listed in Chapter 6, Section c 3 below.   Among historians specializing in the feudal period, however, a number have given primary concern to the structure of military government.   Of the older historians, Shimmi Kichiji, Ryū Susumu, Maki Kenji, Nakamura Naokatsu, Takigawa Masajirō, Endō Motoo, Nakamura Kichiji, and Kurita Motoji are the most widely accepted today.   Their works are most readily available in the standard prewar historical series.   Since the war, outstanding contributions to the field of feudal government have been made by Satō Shin'ichi whose specialty is the Kamakura shogunate, Watanabe Seisuke who specializes in the Ashikaga shogunate, and Itō Tasaburō whose chief concern is the Tokugawa shogunal system.

808. Ishimoda Tadashi 石母田正, Chūseiteki sekai no keisei 中世的世界の形成 (Formation of the medieval world), Tōkyō, Itō Shoten, 1950, 475 pp.
        A representative and influential work of the Marxist school which explains the emergence of feudal military rule in Japan through an analysis of the changing pattern of land holding.   The author uses detailed studies of four locales as the basis of his generalizations.

809. Ito Tasaburō 伊東多三郎, "Bakuhan taisei 幕藩体制 (The structure of the bakufu)," in Shin-Nihonshi kōza 新日本史講座 (New series on Japanese history), Tōkyō, Chūō Kōronsha, 1948, v. 1.
        A lucid exposition of the establishment and structure of the Tokugawa system of government by a specialist in the rise of the modern daimyō.

810. Shimmi Kichiji 新見吉治, Buke seiji no kenkyū 武家政治の研究 (Studies in military administration), Tōkyō, Chūbunkan Shoten, 1936, 301+19 pp.
        This work contains three famous works by a pioneer student of Japanese feudal government: 1) "Nihon ni okeru buke seiji no rekishi (The history of feudal military rule in Japan)," originally written in German for the University of Leipzig in 1911; 2) "Kamakura Muromachi jidai no kosaku seido (Tenancy system of the Kamakura—Muromachi periods)"; and 3) "Nanushi no kenkyū (Study of landowners)."   Essays are copiously annotated.   Professor Shimmi's interpretations are based on thorough research, and in many instances have made academic history.

811. Satō Shin'ichi 佐藤進一, "Bakufuron 幕府論 (Treatise on the bakufu)," in Shin-Nihonshi kōza 新日本史講座 (New series on Japanese history), Tōkyō, Chūō Kōronsha, 1949, v. 7.
        The most accessible of the many works by one of the most active medievalists of Japan.   The author describes the establishment and development of the Kamakura bakufu, its political and legal institutions.

812. Watanabe Seisuke 渡辺世祐, Muromachi jidaishi 室町時代史 (History of the Muromachi period), Tōkyō, Sōgensha, 1948.

4) The Meiji Restoration

        Unquestionably no aspect of Japanese history has been more vigorously studied or hotly debated than that of the Meiji Restoration.   Interpretations of the Restoration have differed widely and continue to divide the Japanese scholarly world.   Roughly speaking, it is possible to distinguish three main groups of interpreters: those who emphasize the political nature of the Restoration, those who stress the importance of foreign influence upon Japan, and those who analyze the Restoration as a social and economic revolution.   Each of these groups in turn has developed numerous refinements.
        The officially favored view of the Restoration, prior to the end of World War II, was that of a political restoration of power to the emperor, a view most characteristically expressed in the works emanating from the Office for the Compilation of the Restoration Documents, (see Entry 818).   Emphasizing the political aspects of the Restoration, yet more realistic in its treatment of political movements and motivations, is the work of the great legal and constitutional historian, Osatake Takeshi.   Analysis of the foreign influence upon the Restoration is characteristically handled by Inobe Shigeo (Entry 816).
        Widest divergence has existed among those who see the Restoration as an economic and social revolution.   So great has been the controversy of interpretation among this group that several entire books have been written on the history of the controversy alone.   Early writers in this group were the pioneer economic historians such as Honjō Eijirō, Tsuchiya Takao, Nakamura Kōya, and others who emphasized the economic aspects of the collapse of the Tokugawa regime.   During the late 1920s, however, Japanese historians began to expand the scope of their study of the Restoration to include comparisons with European revolutionary movements and social and economic developments.   The impact of Marxist thought gave impetus to this line of approach and added ideological fervor to the divisions of opinion concerning the nature of the social participation in the Restoration, or of the stage of economic maturity Japan had reached in 1868, or of the nature of the Japanese capitalistic state.   A pioneer writer in the Marxist tradition was Hani Gorō.   After the publication in 1932-33 of the Nihon shihonshugi hattatsushi kōza (Series on the history of the growth of capitalism in Japan) (Entry 1032), the Japanese academic world became divided into two camps.   The rōnō (Farm-labor) group, taking its name from the journal Rōnō (Entry 610) and under the leadership of Tsuchiya, considered the Restoration a bourgeois revolution and explained the authoritarian nature of post-Restoration Japanese society as due to the persistence of feudal remnants.   The kōza (Lecture series) group including Hani, Noro

Eitarō, Yamada Moritarō, Hirano Yoshitarō, Hattori Shisō and others who had published in the above series, advanced the concept that the Restoration was basically a movement towards absolutism and that modern Japanese capitalism was by nature semi-feudal and authoritarian. This basic division in interpretation continues to exist, though fewer adherents of the rōnō group are found today. (For further remarks on this controversy see the preface to Chapter 6, Section c 4 below.)

The outstanding work on the Meiji Restoration to come out of post-World War II Japan is Tōyama Shigeki's Meiji Ishin (Meiji Restoration) (Entry 822). This work not only synthesizes the views of earlier scholars but in its preface and appendix narrates the history of the scholarly controversy on the Restoration and provides excellent bibliographic notes. Toyama's interpretation of the Restoration as a movement towards political absolutism is now fairly generally accepted. Other works bearing on the Meiji Restoration period will be found listed in Section 6, c 4.

813. Hani Gorō 羽 仁 五 郎, Meiji Ishin 明 治 維 新 (Meiji Restoration), Tōkyō, Iwanami Shoten, 1946, 177 pp.
     A reprint of the controversial article first included in the Iwanami historical series (Entry 725).

814. Hattori Shisō 服 部 之 總, Meiji Ishinshi 明 治 維 新 史 (History of the Meiji Restoration), Tōkyō, Ueno Shoten, 1929, 237 pp.
     Reprint of the author's essays contributed to the Marukusu shugi kōza (Series on Marxism), this work has become a classic among the Marxist interpretations of the Restoration.

815. Hirano Yoshitarō 平 野 義 太 郎, Burujoa minshushugi kakumei ブルジョア民主主義革命 (The bourgeois-democratic revolution), Tōkyō, Nihon Hyōronsha, 1948, 324 pp.
     Collected essays on "democratic revolutions" in Europe and Japan by a leading intellectual Marxist. Articles deal with the decline of Tokugawa feudalism, the rise of the early Meiji democratic movement, the rise of Japanese nationalism, etc.

816. Inobe Shigeo 井 野 辺 茂 雄, Ishin zenshi no kenkyū 維 新 前 史 の 研 究 (Studies in the historical background of the Restoration), Tōkyō, Chūbunkan Shoten, 1935, 4+17+546+16 pp.
     A chronological study of Japan's foreign relations from the 1750s to the Restoration.

817. Irimajiri Yoshinaga 入 交 好 脩, Meiji Ishinshi kenkyū no hatten 明 治 維 新 史 研 究 の 発 展 (Development of the study of the Meiji Restoration), Tōkyō, Dōbunkan, 1949, 199 pp.
     A detailed study of the bibliography of the Restoration together with an analysis of the major theories concerning the Restoration.

818. Ishin Shiryō Hensan Jimukyoku 維 新 史 料 編 纂 事 務 局 (Office for the Compilation of the Restoration Documents), Gaikan Ishinshi 概 観 維 新 史 (Introduction to the history of the Restoration), Tōkyō, Meiji Shoin, 1940, 881+65 pp.
     A one-volume abridgement of the same office's six-volume history of the Restoration. This work is extremely detailed in its coverage of political maneuvering behind the Restoration. There is little interpretation but the approach is emperor-centered.

819. Osatake Takeshi 尾 佐 竹 猛, Meiji Ishin 明 治 維 新 (The Meiji Restoration), Tōkyō, Hakuyōsha, 1942-49, 4 v.
     A work terminated by the author's death, this study nevertheless represents one of the most informed and unbiased studies of the Restoration. The author is an academician rather than a theorist. The four volumes were published as part of the Kindai Nihon rekishi kōza (Entry 727).

820. Shibuzawa Eiichi 澁 澤 榮 一, Tokugawa Keiki-kō-den 德 川 慶 喜 公 傳 (Biography of Prince Tokugawa Keiki), Tōkyō, Ryūmonsha, 1918, 8 v.
     More than a biography of the last shogun, this work casts valuable light on the history of the Restoration period.

821. Shigakkai 史 学 会, Meiji Ishinshi kenkyū 明 治 維 新 史 研 究 (Studies on the Meiji Restoration), Tōkyō, Fuzambō, 1929, 823 pp.
     Contains 27 interpretive articles on all aspects of Restoration history by members of the Tokyo University Institute of Historical Science. Most of the well-known "academic" historians are represented. A special feature of this work are the two bibliographical articles, one on Japanese and one on Western sources.

822. Tōyama Shigeki 遠 山 茂 樹, Meiji Ishin 明 治 維 新 (The Meiji Restoration), Tōkyō, Iwanami Shoten, 1951, 7+368+8 pp.
     An outstanding interpretive work on the Meiji Restoration. Emphasis is on political causes underlying the Restoration which the author traces from the time of the Tempō reforms. The driving force of the Restoration, according to the author, is the trend toward political absolutism. The work is copiously documented and concludes with a valuable bibliography and an index.

823. Watanabe Ikujirō 渡 辺 幾 治 郎, Meijishi kōwa 明 治 史 講 話 (Lectures on the history of the Meiji period), Tōkyō, Yoshikawa Kōbunkan, 1936, 373 pp.
     A traditionalist view of the Restoration and early Meiji politics.

5) Constitutionalism and Political Parties

The political history of Japan since 1868 has been abundantly studied in reference to the legal background of the establishment of the constitution and to the public activities of individual parties.   More discerning studies of the actual operation of constitutional government or of the pressure groups or interests behind party activity have been slow to appear.   The following list contains some of the outstanding prewar sources on Meiji and Taisho politics together with representative works of leading postwar scholars in the field such as Oka Yoshitaka, Rōyama Masamichi and Shinobu Seizaburō.   Two men whose names do not appear below, because they have as yet contributed little in the form of book-length publications, are Maruyama Masao and Tōyama Shigeki.   Both have established themselves through their research as outstanding interpreters of recent Japanese politics.   Students of the politics of this period will also find a great deal of useful material in such collections as Shimbun shūsei Meiji hennenshi (Chronological history of the Meiji era compiled from newspapers) (Entry 406) and the Meiji bunka zenshū (Complete collection on Meiji culture) (Entry 400).

824. Aono Gon'emon 青野権右衛門, Nihon seitō hensenshi 日本政党変遷史 (History of changes in Japanese political parties), Tōkyō, Ankusha, 1935, 10+346 pp.
A chronological treatment of the development of modern Japanese political parties from 1874 to 1932. The work assembles texts of party programs, pronouncements, speeches of party leaders, etc.

825. Fujii Jintarō 藤井甚太郎, Nihon kempō seiteishi 日本憲法制定史 (History of the establishment of the Japanese constitution), Tōkyō, Yūzankaku, 1929, 2+6+312 pp.
This work discusses the historical background of the constitutional movement in Japan.   Part 1 covers the subject from early times to the end of the Tokugawa, and describes concepts of the roles of the several social classes in government.   Part 2 covers the Meiji constitutional movement to 1890.

826. Hayashida Kametarō 林田亀太郎, Nihon seitōshi 日本政党史 (History of Japanese political parties), Tōkyō, Dai Nihon Yūbenkai Kōdansha, 1927, 2 v.
A detailed history of the development of political parties in Japan from 1867 to 1926.   A great deal of factual material together with quotations from party literature and political speeches makes this work a valuable reference.   But it is weak on interpretation and critical analysis.   For a work which carries on from 1926 see Entry 833.

827. Oka Yoshitake 岡義武, Kindai Nihon no keisei 近代日本の形成 (The formation of modern Japan), Tōkyō, Kōbundō, 1947.

828. Osatake Takeshi 尾佐竹猛, Nihon kenseishi taikō 日本憲政史大綱 (Outline of Japanese constitutional history), Tōkyō, Nihon Hyōronsha, 1938, 2 v.
The most detailed of Osatake's numerous treatments of the constitutional movement of the Meiji period. The work is based on the extensive use of primary sources and gives a step-by-step analysis of the stages through which Japan's post-Restoration government passed in its movement toward constitutionalism.

829. Ōtsu Jun'ichirō 大津淳一郎, Dai Nihon kenseishi 大日本憲政史 (Constitutional history of Japan), Tōkyō, Hobunkan, 1927-28, 10 v.
A voluminous chronological history of Japanese government and politics from 1867 to 1926.   Each major political or constitutional event is discussed in great detail.   Extensive quotations are made from primary sources.   Statistical tables give information on Diet sessions, rosters of officers, etc.

830. Rōyama Masamichi 蝋山政道, Seijishi 政治史 (Political history), Tōkyō, Tōyō Keizai Shimpōsha, 1940, 476 pp. [=Gendai Nihon bummeishi, v. 2].
This work by one of Japan's foremost political scientists gives a detailed and unbiased coverage of Japanese political history from 1868 to 1932.

831. Shinobu Seizaburō 信夫清三郎, Meiji seijishi 明治政治史 (Political history of the Meiji era), Tōkyō, Kenshinsha, 1951.

832. Shinobu Seizaburō 信夫清三郎, Taishō seijishi 大正政治史 (Political history of the Taisho era), Tōkyō, Kawade Shobō, 1951-53, 4 v.
Volume 4 of this work contains an excellent detailed bibliography covering the author's entire research.

833. Shiroki Masayuki 白木正之, Nihon seitōshi 日本政党史 (History of Japanese political parties), Tōkyō, Chūō Kōronsha, 1949, 327 pp.
An analysis of Japanese political parties and their activities from 1925 to the Suzuki cabinet of 1945.

834. Suzuki Yasuzō 鈴木安蔵, Jiyūminken 自由民権 (Popular rights), Tōkyō, Hakuyōsha, 1949, 494 pp.
An analysis of the "Popular rights" movement during the Meiji period.

835. Suzuki Yasuzō 鈴木安蔵, Kempō no rekishiteki kenkyū 憲法の歴史的研究 (Historical study of the constitution), Tōkyō, Sōbunkaku, 1934, 487 pp.
An interpretive study of the Meiji constitution and its promulgation.   The work discusses influences which helped to shape the constitution, the views of Japanese officials, and popular opinion regarding the constitution, contemporary scholarly views on the constitution, and the actual operation of the constitution.

6) <u>Absolutism, Nationalism, and Fascism</u>

While the politics of Japan's ultra-nationalistic expansion was almost totally neglected prior to the termination of World War II, there has been a rash of material on this subject since the war. Much of this work has appeared as revaluations of the emperor system; these are listed in Section <u>c</u> below. The following list includes a few of the better known analyses of nationalism and fascism in Japan.

836. Asada Kōki 浅 田 光 輝 and Nakamura Hideichirō 中 村 秀 一 郎 , <u>Nihon fuashizumu no shomondai</u> 日本 ファシズム の 諸 問 題 (Problems of Japanese fascism), Tōkyō, Iwasaki Shoten, 1949, 231 pp.

837. Hattori Shisō 服 部 之 總. , <u>Zettaishugi-ron</u> 絶 対 主 義 論 (Essays on absolutism), Tōkyō, Getsuyō Shobō, 1948, 230 pp.
The author, one of the leading interpreters of the Meiji Restoration, develops the thesis that post-Restoration Japan represented a refeudalization of Japanese socio-political structure; after a brief struggle for freedom, the masses of Japanese society were subdued under a new absolutism similar to that of feudal times.

838. Kada Tetsuji 加 田 哲 二 , <u>Nihon kokkashugi no hattatsu</u> 日 本 国 家 主 義 の 発 達 (The development of Japanese nationalism), Tōkyō, Keiō Shobō, 1938, 390 pp.
A scholarly discussion of the origins and growth of nationalism in Japan from Tokugawa times. The author emphasizes the role of the Meiji leaders in consciously fashioning a new emperor-centered patriotism and concludes with the <u>Kokusui</u> (ultra-nationalistic) movement of the thirties.

839. Kainō Michitaka 戒 能 通 孝 , <u>Bōryoku—Nihon shakai no fuasshizumu kikō</u> 暴 力 — 日 本 社 会 の フ ァ ッ シ ズ ム 機 構 (By force—Japanese society and the structure of fascism), Tōkyō, Nihon Hyōronsha, 1950.

840. Kawano Kenji 河 野 健 二 , <u>Zettaishugi no kōzō</u> 絶 対 主 義 の 構 造 (The structure of absolutism), Tōkyō, Nihon Hyōronsha, 1950, 266 pp.
An analysis of Japan's modern absolutist government and the movement towards fascism.

841. Suzuki Takeo 鈴 木 武 雄 and others, <u>Nihon teikoku shugi kōza</u> 日 本 帝 国 主 義 講 座 (Series on Japanese imperialism), Tōkyō, Hakujitsu Shoin, 1949, 8 v.
A rather mediocre series of essays, many of them highly biased, on problems of Japanese imperialism. Some of the titles are as follows: history of Japan's imperialistic government, labor movements and the communist party, nationalism, military diplomacy, general crisis and depression, the imperialist state and finance, credit, land, agriculture, commerce and trade.

842. Nihon Keizai Kikō Kenkyūsho 日 本 經 濟 機 構 研 究 所 (Institute for the Study of Japanese Economic Structure), <u>Nihon kokka dokusen shihonshugi no kōzō</u> 日 本 国 家 独 占 資 本 主 義 の 構 造 (The structure of Japanese national monopoly capitalism), Tōkyō, Aoki Shoten, 1948.

b. <u>The State and National Polity (Kokutai)</u>

The ideological core of Japan's prewar nationalism was found in the concept of national polity (<u>kokutai</u>), the classical expression of which was presented in the Ministry of Education's <u>Kokutai no hongi</u> (The true meaning of national polity) (Entry 849). Prior to the termination of World War II many historians lent their energies to the creation of a historical rationale around the concept of <u>kokutai</u>. Little has been written on the subject of the state and <u>kokutai</u> since the war. Most revisionists have concentrated their attention on the institution of the emperor, for which works see Section <u>c</u> below.

843. Higo Kazuo 肥 後 和 男 , <u>Nihon kokka shisō</u> 日 本 国 家 思 想 (Theories of the Japanese nation), Tōkyō, Kōbundo, 1940, 171 pp.
An historical analysis of the development of Japanese theories of state. Chapters cover the mythological basis, imperial system, influence of Buddhism, feudalism, Meiji and post-Meiji developments.

844. Hiramatsu Ichizō 平 松 市 藏 , <u>Kokkaron</u> 国 家 論 (Essay on the nation), Tōkyō, 1936, 196 pp.
An analysis of the concept of state and nationalism, its theoretical bases, the nature of the state, contemporary theories of state, patriotism, the Japanese empire.

845. Itō Chimazō 伊 藤 干 眞 三 , <u>Nihon kokutai semmeishi</u> 日 本 国 体 闡 明 史 (Explanatory history of the Japanese polity), Tōkyō, Hōbunkan, 1926.

846. Kiyohara Sadao 清 原 貞 雄, <u>Kokutai ronshi</u> 国 体 論 史 (History of the theory of national polity), Tōkyō, Tōyō Tosho K.K., 1939, 8+252 pp.
An historical survey of the development of the Japanese concept of emperor and national polity.

847. Kuroita Katsumi 黒 板 勝 美 , <u>Kokutai shinron</u> 国 体 新 論 (A new essay on national entity), Tōkyō, Hakubundō, 1925, 265 pp.
This is a somewhat nationalistic analysis of the Japanese theory of state by one of Japan's foremost historians. Chapters deal with the establishment of the Japanese people, early theocratic government, divinity of the emperor, the rights of the people, the principle of harmony, Japanization of Buddhism, Bushido, breakdown of the Japanese system, and restoration of "the original work of Emperor Jimmu," i.e. the Meiji Restoration.

848. Maki Kenji 牧 健二, Nihon kokutai no riron 日 本 国 体 の 理 論 (The theory of Japanese national polity), Tōkyō, Yūhikaku, 1944, 20+582+10 pp.

An analysis of the historical background of the development of Japanese ideas of state, the emperor, and the position of the citizen by an expert on feudal law. Chapters deal with national polity as expressed in Japanese history, Japanese characteristics, national polity and the family system, feudal military rule and national polity.

849. Mombushō 文 部 省 (Ministry of Education), Kokutai no hongi 国 体 の 本 義 (True meaning of national polity), Tōkyō, Mombushō, 1937, 156 pp.

The official expression of the ideas of national polity and the duties of the citizen, prepared for use as a school text. Chapters deal with the establishment of the state, imperial virtues, the special nature of the Japanese subject, harmony, truth, unity of religion and state, imperial mission, etc. In a conclusion Japan's special characteristics are contrasted with those of the West. An official commentary by Miura Tōsaku 三 浦 藤 作 entitled Kokutai no hongi seikai 精 解 (Tōkyō, Toyo Tosho, 1937, 387 pp.) is helpful in reading the many difficult passages in the original. An English translation also exists. See R. K. Hall, Kokutai no Hongi, Cambridge, Mass., Harvard University Press, 1949.

c. The Emperor

The aura of mystery and authority built around the emperor since the Restoration of 1868 has given rise to a voluminous literature on the history and institutional status of the Japanese sovereign. Objective analysis of this subject prior to 1945 was naturally taboo, and such a courageous scholar as Minobe Tatsukichi suffered for his advocacy of the theory that the emperor was an organ of constitutional government. Since the lifting of these taboos after 1945, there has appeared a flood of revisionist literature directed at the institution of the emperor. Much of it has come from the pens of Marxist writers and is extremely bitter. The following list attempts to include both the more authoritative and useful of prewar works on the emperor system together with some of the more sober postwar publications.

850. Akamatsu Keisuke 赤 松 啓 介, Tennōsei kigen shinwa no kenkyū 天 皇 制 起 源 神 話 の 研 究 (Study of myths concerning the origin of the emperor system), Tōkyō, Miwa Shorin, 1948, 176 pp.

An iconoclastic study of the mythological traditions of the emperor system by a specialist in Oriental archeology.

851. Meiji Tennō 明 治 天 皇 (Emperor Meiji), Chokuyu 勅 諭 (Imperial rescripts), Tōkyō, Rikugunshō, 1882.

Important utterances of the Meiji emperor which became the basis of much of modern Japanese political development and helped shape Japanese political behavior.

852. Higo Kazuo 肥 後 和 男, Tennōshi 天 皇 史 (History of the emperor), Tōkyō, Fuzambō, 1950, 343+6 pp.

A relatively impartial and factual treatment of the origins and history of the emperor system. Chapters are entitled: origin, the emperor as a court noble, the emperor and the feudal warrior class, the emperor in modern (Tokugawa) times. The author writes in both the fields of history and folklore studies.

853. Ihara Yoriaki 井 原 頼 明, Kōshitsu jiten 皇 室 辞 典 (Dictionary of the imperial house), Tōkyō, Fuzambō, 1938, 64+372+37 pp.

This work is more a series of essays than a dictionary. Such subjects as the emperor, the empress, imperial household, succession, memorials, ceremonies, military powers, festivals, etc., are briefly treated.

854. Ishii Ryōsuke 石 井 良 助, Tennō 天 皇 (The emperor), Tōkyō, Kōbundō, 1950, 250 pp.

An objective analysis of the origin and development of the emperor system in Japan by an authority on institutional and legal history.

855. Izu Kimio 伊 豆 公 夫, Tennōsei no rekishi 天 皇 制 の 歴 史 (The history of the emperor system), Tōkyō, Tamba Shorin, 1947, 178 pp.

The Japanese emperor system analyzed according to the Marxist formula. Chapters are devoted to the emperor system and Asiatic absolutism, the Meiji Restoration and capitalism. The final chapter deals with contemporary problems concerning the nature and position of the emperor.

856. Kamiyama Shigeo 神 山 茂 夫, Tennōsei ni kansuru rironteki shomondai 天 皇 制 に 関 す る 理 論 的 諸 問 題 (Problems concerning the theory of the emperor system), Tōkyō, Minshū Hyōronsha, 1947, 246 pp.

A partisan criticism by a JCP member of the use of the emperor for nationalistic purposes at the time of and following the Meiji Restoration.

857. Kuroita Katsumi 黒 板 勝 美, ed., Kōshitsushi no kenkyū 皇 室 史 の 研 究 (Studies in the history of the imperial household), Tōkyō, Higashifushimi no Miya-ke, 1932, 258 pp.

Collected essays by ranking historians on the cultural contributions of the imperial household in Japan. Essays treat of the imperial household's relationship to Shinto, social welfare, literature, national morals, etc.

858. Minobe Tatsukichi 美濃部達吉, Chikujō kempō seigi 逐條憲法精義(Article-by-article commentary on the constitution), Tōkyō, Yūhikaku, ed. 2, 1928, 739+13 pp.
A fundamental work by one of Japan's greatest students of constitutional law. Professor Minobe developed the theory of the emperor as an organ of constitutional government.

859. Nakamura Naokatsu 中村直勝, Tennō to kokushi no shinten 天皇と国史の進展 (The emperor and the development of Japanese history), Tōkyō, Kembunkan, 1934, 410 pp.
A study of the influence of forceful emperors such as Uda, Daigo, Goshirakawa, and Gotoba upon the course of Japanese history. The work develops the theme that the emperor is central to Japanese national growth. The author is an authority on the medieval period.

860. Rekishigaku Kenkyūkai 歴史学研究会 (Historical Science Association), Rekishika wa tennōsei o dō miru ka 歴史家は天皇制をどう見るか(How does the historian view the emperor system?), Kyōto, San'ichi Shobō, 1949, 187 pp.
A symposium of historians' views on sovereignty and sovereigns. Essays discuss the Japanese, British, French, and other systems. Pages 1-115 are devoted to an essay by Inoue Kiyoshi on the history of the Japanese emperor system. This essay expresses the position of the intellectual Marxist school with respect to the Japanese emperor, outlining the concept that the emperor was used first by the feudal warrior class, then by recent authoritarian groups, as a means of dominating the people.

861. Sakamaki Yoshio 酒巻芳雄, Kōshitsu seido kōwa 皇室制度講話(Lectures on the imperial system), Tōkyō, Iwanami Shoten, 1934, 369 pp.
Discusses the relationship of the imperial house to the people, the state, and to the legal structure of modern Japan, the status of the emperor, court ceremonies, imperial succession, tombs, imperial revenues, special laws and practices of the imperial household, and many other aspects of the emperor system.

862. Shiba Kuzumori 芝葛盛, Kōshitsu seido 皇室制度 (The imperial household system), Tōkyō, Iwanami Shoten, 1934, 61 pp.
An historical discussion of the emperor as an institution. Parts of the book deal with the throne, the imperial heir, empresses, and the imperial household.

863. Takigawa Masajirō 瀧川政次郎, Nihon rekishi kaikin 日本歴史解禁 (Uncensored Japanese history), Tōkyō, Sōgensha, 1950, 260 pp.
The author, an outstanding authority on Japanese social structure, legal history, and slave systems, seeks to dispel the myth surrounding certain aspects of Japanese history. He discusses in objective fashion the formerly taboo subjects of the three sacred treasures, the early slavery system, and the Namboku period, about which traditional attitudes had developed and become part of the nationalistic emperor-centered version of Japanese history.

864. Tanaka Sōgorō 田中惣五郎, Tennō no kenkyū 天皇の研究 (A study of the emperor), Tōkyō, Kawade Shobō, 1951, 318 pp.
An objective study of the nature and development of the emperor system during the Meiji, Taisho, and Showa periods. Considerable attention is given to the emperor's post-World War II status, to the emperor as human rather than divine.

865. Teikoku Gakushiin 帝国学士院 (Imperial Academy), Teishitsu seidoshi 帝室制度史 (History of the imperial system), Tōkyō, Herarudosha, 1938-45, 6 v.
A detailed documentary study of the origin, development, status, and powers of the emperor. Volumes 1 and 2 treat Kokutai (national polity); volumes 3 and 4 deal with the imperial succession; volume 6 concerns the imperial title, honorific names, etc. The general style is chronological and under each subject numerous quotations are cited from primary sources.

866. Teishitsu Rin'yakyoku 帝室林野局 (Office of Imperial Estates), Goryōchi shikō 御料地史稿 (Draft history of imperial estates), Tōkyō, Teishitsu Rin'yakyoku, 1938, 416 pp.
An authoritative history of the origin and development of imperial estates which were the economic bulwark of the imperial house in Japan.

867. Toda Shintarō 戸田慎太郎, Tennōsei no keizaiteki kiso bunseki 天皇制の經濟的基礎分析 (Analysis of the economic base of the emperor system), Kyōto, San'ichi Shobō, 1947, 229 pp.
A Marxist analysis of the Japanese emperor system and its economic supports.

868. Watanabe Ikujirō 渡辺幾治郎, Kōshitsu shinron 皇室新論 (New essays on the imperial household), Tōkyō, Waseda Daigaku Shuppambu, 1929, 342 pp.
A somewhat eulogistic discussion of the place of the emperor in Japanese society. The author believes all major crises in Japanese history and social development were solved by reference to the throne.

869. Yokota Kisaburō 横田喜三郎, Tennōsei 天皇制 (The emperor system), Tōkyō, Rōdō Bunkasha, 1949, 286 pp.
A general discussion of the shifting status of the emperor from the Meiji period to the present. An exposition is given of the emperor's position under the old constitution and the changes which the new constitution forced upon the emperor and upon the concept of national polity (Kokutai).

d. The Court and Bureaucracy

For students of pre-Restoration political history, the intricacies of the court and bureaucratic systems in Japan present a constant problem. However, information on ranks, titles, functions, etc., is not difficult to obtain. For reference purposes the antiquarian dictionaries listed in Part II, Chapter 2 c above, together with the Koji ruien (Encyclopedia of ancient matters) (Entry 207) and the Tokushi biyō (Handbook of history) (Entry 233) provide excellent coverage. Analytical works on court and bureaucracy in Japan are less satisfactory. The pioneer and still standard work in this field is Konakamura Kiyonori's Kanshoku seido enkakushi (History of the bureaucratic system) (Entry 872). For the post-1868 period Tanaka Sōgorō's works (Entries 875 and 876) are as yet the only studies available.

870. Hagino Yoshiyuki 萩野由之 and Konakamura Yoshikata 小中村義象, Nihon seidotsū 日本制度通 (Complete institutions of Japan), Tōkyō, Yoshikawa Kōbundō, 1929, 268 pp.
     First published in 3 volumes, 1889-90, this work is an outline survey of Japanese court, administrative, and military institutions from early times to c. 1890. Besides the usual coverage of bureaucratic systems, the work touches upon official salaries, census, land tax systems, currency, weights and measures, communications. Though outdated, this work is accurate and still useful.

871. Hashimoto Hiroshi 橋本博, Daibukan 大武鑑 (Great military mirror), Tōkyō, Taikōsha, 1935-36, 13 v.
     This work reproduces a number of Bukan (Military mirrors), a type of semi-official register of the feudal bureaucracy during the Kamakura and Tokugawa periods. Volume 1 includes material on the Kamakura period. Volumes up to number 11 cover the period from 1699 to 1869. Volume 12 is an index, and number 13 a supplement. Each Bukan contains rosters of officials arranged in hierarchical order, information on ranks, special privileges, lineage, family crests, domains, fiefs, and various other matters for each official.

872. Konakamura Kiyonori 小中村清矩, Kanshoku seido enkakushi 官職制度沿革史 (History of the development of the bureaucratic system), Tōkyō, Benkyōdō, 1901, 526 pp.
     A standard descriptive survey of Japanese officials and their functions from early times to the Meiji period. A more popular work by the same author was published posthumously under the title Nihon kanshoku seido enkakushi, Tōkyō, Tōgakusha, 1935, 358 pp.

873. Matsudaira Tarō 松平太郎, Edo jidai seido no kenkyū 江戸時代制度の研究 (A study of the Edo period administrative system), Tōkyō, Bukeseido Kenkyūkai, 1919, 1100 pp.
     The most authoritative study of the Tokugawa shogunate and its bureaucratic organization. The author describes minutely the life of the shogun, the administration of the shogun's private and public affairs, etc. Unfortunately, a second volume which was to deal with organs of local government was never completed.

874. Naimushō Keihokyoku 内務省警保局 (Ministry of Home Affairs, Police Office), Chōfuken keisatsu enkakushi 庁府県警察沿革史 (History of the development of the prefectural police), Tōkyō, Naimushō Keihokyoku, 1927, 4 v.
     A detailed history of the modern Japanese police system. Two volumes are devoted to the Metropolitan Police Bureau and the other two to the history of the police force in each of the prefectures.

875. Tanaka Sōgorō 田中惣五郎, Kindai Nihon kanryōshi 近代日本官僚史 (History of the Japanese bureaucracy in recent times), Tōkyō, Tōyō Keizai Shimpōsha, 1941, 479 pp.
     A historical and analytical discussion of the establishment, function, status, and development of Japan's post-Restoration bureaucracy.

876. Tanaka Sōgorō 田中惣五郎, Nihon kanryō seijishi 日本官僚政治史 (History of Japanese bureaucratic government), Tōkyō, Sekai Shoin, 1947, 289 pp.
     Continues the discussion of Japan's modern bureaucracy down to the World War II period.

e. Administration and Law

Studies of Japanese administrative practices as distinct from the laws and ordinances which form their basis are seldom found in Japan. Administration must be viewed, therefore, largely in ideal terms through the histories of legal institutions. For pre-Restoration laws the outstanding pioneer authorities were Miura Kaneyuki and Nakada Kaoru, many of whose studies are still standard. In recent years Ishii Ryōsuke has dominated this field, and his works are to be recommended both for the general and specialized student. Post-Restoration administrative law is such a vast subject that no attempt has been made here to do more than suggest a few standard works. Those whose interest is primarily in the period after 1868 will find fuller coverage in Robert E. Ward's A Guide to Japanese Reference and Research Works in the Field of Political Science.
     The following works have been divided into two groups, those treating Japanese law and administrative ordinances in general fashion and those devoted primarily to laws and practices governing taxation, land tenure, and forest rights. The second category has a voluminous literature in Japanese, since civil administration prior to the twentieth century was largely concerned with governing the agrarian population, stabilizing land tenure, and assuring the steady flow of the land tax. For both of the following groups, the reader should be reminded that several of the volumes of Koji ruien (Encyclopedia of ancient matters) (Entry 207), notably those on Hōroku (Fiefs and stipends) and Seiji (Civil administration), offer valuable material.

1) <u>General</u>

877. Hagino Yoshiyuki 萩 野 由 之 and Konakamura Yoshikata 小 中 村 義 象, <u>Nihon seido tsū</u> 日本 制度 通 (History of Japanese institutions), Tōkyō, Yoshikawa Hanshichi, 1890, 3 v.
 An old but authoritative study of Japanese legal and administrative institutions.

878. Hosokawa Kameichi 細 川 亀 市, <u>Nihon hōseishi taikō</u> 日 本 法 制 史 大綱(An outline history of Japanese legal systems), Tōkyō, Jichōsha, rev. ed., 1942, 22+418 pp.
 An analytical treatment of the development of legal institutions and theory in Japan up to the Meiji period. Emphasis is on the developmental growth and progress of Japanese law. There is an index.

879. Ikebe Yoshikata 池 辺 義 象, <u>Nihon hōseishi</u> 日 本 法 制 史 (History of Japanese law), Tōkyō, Hakubunkan, 1912, 1052 pp.
 A basic study of Japanese legal systems. The author arranges his materials by periods: the period of unwritten law (clan period), sinicised law, feudal military law, and household law. In treating each period he discusses administrative, financial, civil, and criminal law systems. The coverage stops with the end of the Tokugawa period. Emphasis is on pre-Tokugawa systems.

880. Ishii Ryōsuke 石 井 良 助, <u>Nihon hōseishi gaisetsu</u> 日 本 法 制 史 概 説(An introduction to the history of Japanese jurisprudence), Tōkyō, Kōbundō, 1948, 607+58 pp.
 This work is recommended as one of the best introductory works on Japanese legal systems written from a contemporary point of view. The work treats the development of legal systems from early times through the Tokugawa period stressing administrative, social, and economic legislation, the tax systems, and civil and criminal codes. The work is well documented and there are 58 pages of index. It is somewhat weak on local legal institutions.

881. Ishii Ryōsuke 石 井 良 助, <u>Nihon hōseishiyō</u> 日 本 法 制 史要(Essentials of Japanese legal history), Tōkyō, Shibundō, 1949, 17+337 pp.
 Pages 297-337 of this standard text contain an exhaustive classified bibliography of modern studies of Japanese legal history. Both books and articles are listed. The author interprets legal institutions in their broadest sense to include such subjects as the manorial and feudal systems, social class systems, and financial, military, and religious institutions.

882. Kobayakawa Kingo 小 早 川 欣 吾, <u>Meiji hōsei shiron</u> 明 治 法 制 史 論(Essays on the history of Meiji legislation), Tōkyō, Ganshōdō, 1941, 2 v.
 A detailed survey of Meiji laws and the reasons behind their enactment. The work is divided as follows: volume 1, emperor system, hierarchy, and the constitution; volume 2, the Privy Council, administrative law, civil law, criminal law, the military, and foreign affairs. There is an index.

883. Kokugakuin 国 学 院, <u>Hōsei ronsan</u> 法 制 論 纂 (Collected essays on legal systems), Tōkyō, Dai Nihon Tosho K.K., 1903-04, 2 v.
 A collection of essays by experts in legal history on the legal institutions of pre-Meiji Japan. Essays cover official posts and functions, court ceremonies, etc.

884. Kumasaki Wataru 隈 崎 渡, <u>Nihon hōseishi</u> 日 本 法 制 史 (History of Japanese legislation), Tōkyō, Shōkasha, 1936, 431 pp.
 A well-documented survey of Japanese legal institutions through the Tokugawa period.

885. Maki Kenji 牧 健 二, <u>Nihon hōseishi gairon</u> 日 本 法 制 史 概 論 (Outline of Japanese legal history), Tōkyō and Kyōto, Kōbundō, 1948, 542 pp.
 Covers the history of Japanese legal institutions from ancient times to 1950.

886. Minobe Tatsukichi 美 濃 部 達 吉, <u>Nihon gyōseihō</u> 日 本 行 政 法 (Japanese administrative law), Tōkyō, Yūhikaku, 1936-40, 2 v.
 An excellent, detailed study of modern Japanese administrative law. It treats general concepts of administrative law, basic laws, administrative organization, laws of government corporations, local self-government, factory and welfare laws, public works, finance, and military affairs.

887. Miura Kaneyuki 三 浦 周 行, <u>Hōseishi no kenkyū</u> 法 制 史 の 研 究(Studies in legal history), Tōkyō, Iwanami Shoten, 1925, 2 v.
 Volume 1 of this set was first published in 1919. These volumes contain a series of related articles on legal history by one of Japan's most respected historians of the last generation. A pioneer student of legal history, his studies in this field have become deservedly famous. Articles treat household law, census and registers, property laws, commercial law, criminal law, the <u>tokusei</u> (cancellation of debts), <u>za</u> (guilds), <u>goningumi</u> (five-man cooperative groups) and many other subjects. There have been numerous later editions of this work.

888. Miura Kaneyuki 三 浦 周 行, <u>Nihon hōseishi</u> 日 本 法 制 史(History of Japanese legislation), Ōsaka, Sōgensha, 1943, 8+210 pp.
 A survey of Japanese pre-modern legal systems by an acknowledged authority in the field.

889. Naimushō Chihōkyoku 内 務 省 地 方 局 (Local Affairs Office, Home Ministry), Minseishikō 民 政 史 稿 (Draft history of civil administration), Tōkyō, Naimushō Chihōkyoku, 1913-15, 8 v.

A basic documentary history of civil administration in Japan from early times to the Meiji period. Individual volumes treat the following subjects: institutions of civil administration, encouragement of production, manners and customs, relief measures, encouragement of virtuous conduct, rule by moral injunction. The general style is chronological with copious quotations from primary sources.

890. Nakada Kaoru 中 田 薫, Hōseishi ronshū 法 制 史 論 集 (Collected essays on the history of legislation), Tōkyō, Iwanami Shoten, 1926-43, 3 v.

Scholarly studies of Japanese customary law by a pioneer student of legal history. Volumes deal with: 1) family and household law; laws of inheritance and succession; 2) laws of real property; 3) laws of obligation.

891. Nakada Kaoru 中 田 薫, ed., Miyazaki Sensei hōseishi ronshū 宮 崎 先 生 法 制 史 論 集 (Dr. Miyazaki's collected essays on the history of legislation), Tōkyō, Iwanami Shoten, 1929, 698+53+12+11 pp.

The collected essays of Japan's first modern authority on the history of Japanese law. Dr. Miyazaki adopted the German philological approach to the study of law. His analysis of Korean influence on early Japanese law is of special importance.

892. Sumida Shōichi 住 田 正 一, Nihon kaihōshi 日 本 海 法 史 (History of Japanese maritime law), Tōkyō, Ganshōdō, 1928, 462 pp.

A documentary chronological history of laws governing Japan's maritime relations from the twelfth century to the end of the Tokugawa shogunate.

893. Suehiro Izutarō 末 弘 嚴 太 郎, ed., Gendai hōgaku zenshū 現 代 法 学 全 集 (Complete series on contemporary jurisprudence), Tōkyō, Nihon Hyōronsha, 1928-31, 39 v.

A monumental collection of essays by 60 authorities covering all phases of modern Japanese law. Essays treat administrative and constitutional law, civil and criminal procedure, commercial, labor, and insurance laws, and many other related subjects. This series is the best single source of information on modern Japanese law.

894. Takikawa Masajirō 瀧 川 政 次 郎, Nihon hōseishi 日 本 法 制 史 (History of Japanese legal systems), Tōkyō, Yūhikaku, rev. ed., 1930, 42+616+50 pp.

A survey of Japanese legal institutions by an expert on social class structure. The work is divided into four parts: 1) early law, 2) sinicised law, 3) feudal law, 4) Westernized law. Under each period the author discusses origins of legal systems, administrative law, criminal procedure, and popular customary law. Source materials and methodology are discussed but there is no documentation.

2) Land, Taxation, and the Peasantry

895. Inoue Kazuo 井 上 和 夫, Nihon tochihōshi 日 本 地 法 史 (History of Japanese land law), Tōkyō, Nihon Hōri Kenkyūkai, 1943, 373 pp.

A discussion of the origins and development of Japanese land law. The work concludes with a chapter on the problems of contemporary land law.

896. Fujita Gorō 藤 田 五 郎, Kinsei nōsei shiron 近 世 農 政 史 論 (Historical essays on agricultural administration in early modern times), Tōkyō, Ochanomizu Shobō, 1950, 193 pp.

A collection of technical articles on the nature of feudal land tenure in Japan with special emphasis on the stratification of landlord and tenant classes among the peasantry. The author draws many comparisons with European institutions.

897. Jimbunkagaku Iinkai 人 文 科 学 委 員 会 (Cultural Science Committee), Tochi seido no kenkyū 土 地 制 度 の 研 究 (Studies in land systems), Tōkyō, Hakujitsu Shoin, 1948, 176 pp.

A symposium of lectures and field reports on Japanese land systems by a number of authorities. Of special interest are the reports on historical field studies conducted in agricultural and fishing villages and the analysis of land-tax systems in northern Japan.

898. Kamada Masatada 鎌 田 正 忠, Nihon nōchi shōmon no kenkyū 日 本 農 地 證 文 の 研 究 (A study of Japanese agricultural land documents), Tōkyō, Ganshōdō Shoten, 1944, 23+825 pp.

A fundamental study of records of sale and alienation of agricultural land from the Nara through the Tokugawa periods. The work makes extensive use of primary documentary materials. Technical and archaic terms are defined.

899. Katsu Masanori 勝 正 憲, Nihon zeisei kaikakushi 日 本 税 制 改 革 史 (History of Japanese tax reform), Tōkyō, Chikura Shobō, 1938, 395 pp.

A discussion of tax problems and reform measures in Japan from 1868 to the time of writing. The author emphasizes the causes behind the various changes in the tax laws.

900. Nakamura Kichiji 中 村 吉 治, ed., Tochi seidoshi kenkyū 土 地 制 度 史 研 究 (Studies in land systems), Tōkyō, Hōkei Shobō, 1948, 320 pp.

A collection of well-documented essays by several scholars on Japanese land systems from ancient to present times.

901. Nōshōmushō 農商務省 (Ministry of Agriculture and Commerce), Dai Nihon nōseishi 大 日 本 農 政 史 (History of agricultural administration in Japan), Tōkyō, Bungei Shunjūsha, 1932, 866 pp.
　　This work is a reprint of Oda Kanshi's 織田完之 Dai Nihon nōsei ruihen 大 日 本 農 政 類 編 (Classified documents on agrarian administration), published in 1897. Documents are classified under such headings as: census and inspection, festivals, officials, legal systems, taxes, types of field, labor duties, stock raising, forests, fishing, etc. Coverage is chronological from early times through the Tokugawa period.

902. Nonaka Jun 野 中 準, comp., Dai Nihon sozeishi 大 日 本 租 税 志 (History of Japanese taxation), Tōkyō, Chōyōkai, 1926+27, 3 v.
　　Originally published by the Ministry of Finance in 1882-85. This work is largely a chronologically arranged classified collection of documentary excerpts from primary sources covering tax systems from early times to 1880. There are four basic divisions: land systems; land tax and miscellaneous taxes; corvée, labor service; and miscellaneous.

903. Ono Takeo 小 野 武 夫, Chiso kaisei shiron 地 租 改 正 史 論 (History of land tax reform), Tōkyō, Ōyashima Shuppan K.K., 1948, 6+253 pp.
　　A scholarly study of the Meiji land-tax reforms of 1872-73.

904. Shirakawa Tarō 白 川 太 郎, Teikoku rinseishi 帝 国 林 制 史 (History of forest administration in Japan), Tōkyō, Yūrindō, 1902, 265 pp.
　　A chronological history of the administration of forest lands in Japan. Treatment is by periods with emphasis on pre-Restoration history.

905. Tsuchiya Takao 土 屋 喬 雄, Nihon nōchi seidoshiron 日 本 農 地 制 度 史 論 (Essays on the history of Japanese agricultural land systems), Tōkyō, Mainichi Shimbunsha, 1948, 143 pp.
　　Primarily a study of the Tokugawa land system and the effects of reclaimed land on the growth of the new landlord class (shin-jinushi).

906. Yano Tomoichi 矢 野 友 一, Nihon nōseishi 日 本 農 政 史 (History of Japanese agricultural administration), Tōkyō, Bungei Shunjūsha, rev. ed., 1933, 545 pp.
　　This edition has been thoroughly revised since its first appearance in 1915. It is divided into two parts dealing with the pre-feudal age and the feudal age. Each part is divided into sections on: administrative systems, land systems, taxation, water works, famine relief, etc. Treatment is chronological and extensive quotations are made from primary materials.

907. Yokoi Tokifuyu 横 井 時 冬, Nihon fudōsanhō enkakushi 日 本 不 動 産 法 沿 革 史 (History of the development of real estate laws in Japan), Tōkyō, Hakuyōsha, 1925, 277 pp.
　　A study of laws governing the sale, tenure, and use of land in Japan from early times through the Tokugawa period.

908. Yokoyama Yoshikiyo 横 山 由 清, Nihon denseishi 日 本 田 制 史 (History of Japanese land systems), Tōkyō, Ōokayama Shoten, 1926, 364 pp.
　　A detailed but dated exposition of the development of agricultural land rights and land-tax systems in pre-Meiji Japan.

f. Foreign Diplomatic and Cultural Relations

　　The following selection is devoted primarily to works on the pre-1868 phase of Japanese foreign affairs. Of the general surveys of Sino-Japanese relations, Kimiya Yasuhiko's Nisshi kōtsūshi (A history of Sino-Japanese relations) (Entry 920) is excellent for its handling of diplomacy and trade, while Tsuji Zennosuke's Zōtei kaigai kōtsū shiwa (Essays on the history of overseas relations) (Entry 942) deals with cultural contacts. Of a more specialized nature, Akiyama Kenzō's Nisshi kōshō shiwa (Historical essays on Sino-Japanese relations) (Entry 910) and Mori Katsumi's Nissō bunka kōryū no shomondai (Problems of cultural exchange between Sung China and Japan) (Entry 928) are outstanding for their treatment of relations with China up to 1600. Among the works on Western relations, Iwao Seiichi's Nanyō Nihon machi no kenkyū (A history of Japanese settlements in Southeast Asia) (Entry 919), Kōda Shigitomo's Nichi-Ō tsūkōshi (History of Japan's relations with Europe) (Entry 923), and Shimmura Izuru's Namban kōki (Studies of Western relations) (Entry 935) concentrate on the period of the "Christian century" (1549-1650). Shimmura's work also touches on Dutch relations after 1650. The most authoritative study of Japanese contacts with the Russians, British, and Americans after the beginning of the eighteenth century is Tabohashi Kiyoshi's Kindai Nihon gaikoku kankeishi (A history of Japan's foreign relations in modern times) (Entry 938).
　　Satisfactory studies of Japan's diplomatic history after 1868 are hard to come by. This is due, in large part, to the failure of the Japanese government to make public the documents essential for such studies. Furthermore, the academic atmosphere of prewar Japan was not conducive to the study of contemporary politics. Postwar revisionists have not appeared in great numbers and, of those who have, many have written with a marked personal bias.

909. Akiyama Kenzō 秋 山 謙 藏, Nisshi kōshōshi kenkyū 日 支 交 渉 史 研 究 (A study of the history of Sino-Japanese relations), Tōkyō, Iwanami Shoten, 1939, 663 pp.
　　An authoritative and heavily documented study of Japan's trade and diplomatic relations with China from the beginning of the fourteenth century to the middle of the sixteenth century. The author provides an index and bibliography. An introductory chapter discusses methodology and the history of Japanese studies of Sino-Japanese relations.

910. Akiyama Kenzō 秋 山 謙 藏, Nisshi kōshō shiwa 日 支 交 涉 史 話 (Historical essays on Sino-Japanese relations), Tōkyō, Naigai Shoseki K.K., 1935, 575 pp.
Scholarly studies of Japanese trade and diplomatic relations with China with emphasis on the period prior to 1600. Several essays deal with the role of Korea and the Ryukyus in Japan's foreign relations.

911. Fujita Motoharu 藤 田 元 春, Jōdai Nisshi kōtsūshi no kenkyū 上 代 日 支 交 通 史 の 研 究 (Studies in Sino-Japanese relations of the ancient period), Tōkyō, Tōkō Shoin, 1943, 455 pp.
A series of informative essays on Japan's relations with the continent prior to the seventh century.

912. Fujita Motoharu 藤 田 元 春, Nisshi kōtsū no kenkyū 日 支 交 通 の 研 究 (Studies of Sino-Japanese relations), Tōkyō, Fuzambō, 1938, 423 pp.
Contains scholarly studies of Sino-Japanese relations from roughly 1250 to 1640. Essays deal with Japan's relations with Yüan and Ming China, and the Ryukyu islands, Japanese embassies sent to China during the Muromachi era, the shuinbune, Japanese relations with Siam, Japanese shipbuilding, etc.

913. Gaikō shikō 外 交 志 稿 (Draft history of foreign relations), Tōkyō, Gaimushō, 1884, 2 v.
An officially compiled detailed chronological history of Japan's foreign contacts from earliest times to 1868. Sections are devoted to castaways, immigrants, naturalized citizens, scholarly and religious contacts, tribute and trade.

914. Hikasa Mamoru 日 笠 護, Nissen kankei no shiteki kōsatsu to sono kenkyū 日 鮮 關 係 の 史 的 考 察 と 其 の 研 究 (An historical examination of Japanese-Korean relations and studies thereof), Tōkyō, Shikai Shobō, 1930, 250 pp.
A study of Japanese relations with Korea from early times to the twentieth century. The work contains a useful bibliography.

915. Hiraoka Masahide 平 岡 雅 英, Nichi-Ro kōshō shiwa 日 露 交 涉 史 話 (Historical discourses on Russo-Japanese relations), Tōkyō, Chikuma Shobō, 1944, 7+418 pp.

916. Ienaga Saburō 家 永 三 郎, Gairai bunka sesshu shiron 外 來 文 化 攝 取 史 論 (Essays on the importation of foreign culture), Tōkyō, Iwanami Shoten, 1948, 410 pp.
A study of the impact of Western culture and ideas upon the Japanese of the late Tokugawa and Meiji periods primarily as seen through the writings of Japanese travelers and writers. A thorough and well-documented work though somewhat limited in its scope.

917. Ikenaga Hajimu 池 長 孟, Hōsai banka daihōkan 邦 彩 蠻 華 大 宝 鑑 (Illustrations of exotic objects, Japanese and foreign), Ōsaka, Sōgensha, 1933, 2 v. + charts.
Catalogue of the Ikenaga collection of Western-influenced Japanese art and artifacts. The collection deals with the pre-Meiji period and contains early Christian relics, Japanese illustrations of Portuguese missionaries and traders, European goods, illustrations of the Dutch at Deshima, etc. Plates are excellent, but explanatory notes are inadequate and are often whimsically written.

918. Irie Toraji 入 江 寅 次, Hōjin kaigai hattenshi 邦 人 海 外 発 展 史 (History of the overseas expansion of the Japanese people), Tōkyō, Imin Mondai Kenkyūkai, 1936-38, 2 v.
Volume 1 treats Japanese immigration following 1868. Volume 2 deals with the more recent Japanese colonies in Brazil and other South American countries, the Pacific islands, and East Asia.

919. Iwao Seiichi 岩 生 成 一, Nan'yō Nihon-machi no kenkyū 南 洋 日 本 町 の 研 究 (A study of Japanese settlements in South East Asia), Tōkyō, Minami-Ajia Bunka Kenkyūsho, 1940, 367+20 pp.
An important and scholarly study of Japan's 16th century maritime ventures in the seas to her south and of the history of the Japanese settlements in this area. Professor Iwao has written several shorter works and articles on the subject of Japanese relations with Portugal and Holland.

920. Kimiya Yasuhiko 木 宮 泰 彦, Nisshi kōtsūshi 日 本 交 通 史 (A history of Sino-Japanese relations), Tōkyō, Kinseki Hōryūdō, 1927, 2 v.
A well-documented survey of Japanese relations with China up to the middle of the Tokugawa period. The work is best for its treatment of Japanese relations with Sung China. Emphasis is on diplomatic and trade relations.

921. Kin Eiken 金 永 鍵, Indoshina to Nihon to no kankei 印 度 支 那 と 日 本 と の 関 係 (Relations between Japan and Indo-China), Tōkyō, Fuzambō, 1943, 7+315 pp.

922. Kiyosawa Kiyoshi 清 澤 冽, Gaikōshi 外 交 史 (History of foreign relations), Tōkyō, Tōyō Keizai Shimpōsha, 1941, 17+578+12 pp.
Part of the Gendai Nihon bummeishi (Entry 722), this work covers Japanese foreign relations from the end of the Tokugawa period to the China Incident. The author is relatively objective in his treatment. The work itself is heavily documented.

923. Kōda Shigetomo 幸 田 成 友, Nichi-Ō tsūkōshi 日 欧 通 交 史 (History of Japan's relations with Europe), Tōkyō, Iwanami Shoten, 1942, 22+414+40 pp.
A well-documented study of Japanese relations with Westerners during the century from 1540 to 1640. There is an elaborate index.

924. Kokuryūkai 黒龍会, Nisshi kōshō gaishi 日支交渉外史 (Unofficial history of Sino-Japanese relations), Tōkyō, Kokuryūkai, 1938-39, 2 v.
   An important study of modern Sino-Japanese relations by the Amur River (Black Dragon) Society, whose members played active behind-the-scenes roles in shaping Japan's foreign policy.

925. Kuzuu Yoshihisa 葛生能八, Nikkan gappei hishi 日韓合併秘史 (Secret history of the annexation of Korea), Tōkyō, Kokuryūkai, 1930, 2 v.
   A behind-the-scenes history of the diplomacy and intrigue which paved the way for Japan's annexation of Korea. The work was prepared from materials in the files of the Amur River (Black Dragon) Society.

926. Maruyama Kunio 丸山国雄, Nihon kindai gaikōshi 日本近代外交史 (History of Japan's foreign relations in recent times), Tōkyō, Mikasa Shobō, 1940, 284 pp.
   Part of the Mikasa Shobo's Nihon rekishi zensho series (Entry 737). This work gives a detailed analysis of Japanese foreign relations from 1868 to 1910. The author is an authority on Japanese relations with Germany. There is a useful bibliography.

927. Miki Sakae 三木榮, Nissha kōtsū shikō 日暹交通史考 (Historical study of relations between Japan and Siam), Tōkyō, Kokon Shoin, 1934, 398 pp.
   A survey of Japan's relations with Siam from their origin to the gradual cessation of intercourse after 1640. Emphasis is on the sixteenth and seventeenth centuries, the shuinbune, Japanese competition with the Portuguese, Japanese trading communities in Siam, and diplomatic negotiations between Japan and Siam.

928. Mori Katsumi 森克己, Nissō bunka kōryū no shomondai 日宋文化交流の諸問題 (Problems of cultural exchange between Sung China and Japan), Tōkyō, Tōkō Shoin, 1950, 323 pp.
   An exhaustive and technical treatment of the cultural influences of Sung China on Japan. The study is thoroughly documented.

929. Mutō Chōzō 武藤長藏, Nichi-Ei kotsūshi no kenkyū 日英交通史の研究 (Studies in the history of Japanese-British relations), Kyōto, Naigai Shuppan K.K., 1937, 769 pp.
   A carefully documented history of English-Japanese diplomatic and trade relations from their origins to the time of the first modern treaties in 1854. The author has used familiar English sources together with a large number of relatively unfamiliar Japanese materials.

930. Nishimura Shinji 西村眞次, Nihon kaigai hattenshi 日本海外発展史 (History of Japan's overseas development), Tōkyō, Tōkyōdō, 1942, 26+507 pp.
   A detailed study of Japan's foreign adventures from early times to 1640. Emphasis is on the two centuries prior to Japan's seventeenth century seclusion when the wakō and shuinsen were active. The work is undocumented but there is a complete index.

931. Okamoto Ryōchi 岡本良知, Jūrokuseiki Nichi-Ō kotsūshi no kenkyū 十六世紀日欧交通史の研究 (Studies of Japanese intercourse with Europeans during the sixteenth century), Tōkyō, Kobunsō, 1936, 810+46 pp.

932. Saitō Bunzō 齋藤文藏, Nihon gaikōshi 日本外交史 (History of Japanese foreign relations), Tōkyō, Yūzankaku, 1929, 423 pp.
   This work is volume 12 of the Dai Nihonshi kōza. It covers from early times to the 1920s in three major periods: 1) pre-1640 seclusion, 2) 1640-1853, 3) after 1853. The first two periods are given primary emphasis.

933. Saitō Tadashi 齋藤忠, Jōdai ni okeru tairiku bunka no eikyō 上代に拾ける大陸文化の影響 (The influence of continental culture on Japan during the archaic period), Tōkyō, Ōyashima Shuppan K.K., 1947, 226+9 pp.
   A study of Japan's borrowings from continental civilization prior to the seventh century. The author is an expert on early Japanese and Korean folklore.

934. Shida Fudōmaro 志田不動麿, Tōyōshi jō no Nihon 東洋史上の日本 (Japan's position in Oriental history), Tōkyō, Shikai Shobō, 1940, 338 pp.
   An account of Japan's relationship to the rest of the Far East from early times to 1868. The primary emphasis is on Sino-Japanese relations. A bibliography and index are appended.

935. Shimmura Izuru 新村出, Namban kōki 南蠻廣記 (Studies of Western relations), Tōkyō, Iwanami Shoten, 1925, 547+10 pp.
   A revised edition of a work first published in 1919. It has been followed by several succeeding volumes: Zoku Namban kōki (Tōkyō, Iwanami, 1925), Nampō ki (Tōkyō, Meiji Shoin, 1934), and Namban ki (Kyōto, Daigadō, 1943). Each volume consists of a collection of Professor Shimmura's essays on Japanese relations with the Portuguese and Dutch. His studies of the Japanese side of the development of Christianity in Japan, the influence of the early missionary press, the influence of Western art, the growth of Dutch studies, and Japan's intellectual reaction to seclusion are outstanding.

936. Shimomura Fujio 下村富士夫, Meiji ishin no gaikō 明治維新の外交 (Foreign relations of the Meiji Restoration), Tōkyō, Ōyashima Shuppan K.K., 1947, 337 pp.
   An introductory survey of Japan's foreign relations during the critical Restoration period and up to the revision of the early treaties (1853-99). The author gives no annotation but depends upon his experience in the editorial room of the Dai Nihon gaikō bunsho (Entry 444).

937. Shinobu Seizaburō 信夫清三郎, Kindai Nihon gaikōshi 近代日本外交史 (History of recent Japanese foreign relations), Tōkyō, Kenshinsha, 1948, 4+268 pp.
A leftist interpretation of Restoration and post-Restoration Japanese foreign relations.

938. Tabohashi Kiyoshi 田保橋潔, Kindai Nihon gaikoku kankeishi 近代日本外国関係史 (A history of Japan's foreign relations in modern times), Tōkyō, Tōkō Shoin, rev. ed., 1943, 10+8+859 pp.
The outstanding treatment of Japan's modern foreign relations beginning with the seventeenth century Russian penetration of the northern area and ending with the securing of the first modern treaties (1854). The author has accumulated imposing documentation from native and foreign sources.

939. Takamura Shōhei 高村象平, Nippo kōtsūshi 日葡交通史 (History of Japanese-Portuguese relations), Tōkyō, Kokusai Kōtsūbunka Kyōkai, 1943, 6+328 pp.
A well-documented study of the limited period of Portuguese activity in Japan.

940. Tomaru Fukuju 登丸福壽, Mogi Shūichiro 茂木秀一郎, Wakō kenkyū 倭冠研究 (Studies of the wakō), Tōkyō, Chūō Kōronsha, 1942, 262 pp.
A detailed study of the origin and development of the wakō. The authors have not annotated their study.

941. Toyama Usaburō 外山卯三郎, Nichi-Ō kōshō bunkaron 日欧交渉文化論 (Essays on Japanese cultural relations with Europe), Tōkyō, Katsuragi Shoten, 1942, 6+306 pp.
Stimulating studies in the cultural aspects of early Japanese relations with the Portuguese and Spanish.

942. Tsuji Zennosuke 辻善之助, Zōtei kaigai kōtsū shiwa 増訂海外交通史話 (Essays on the history of overseas relations, revised and supplemented), Tōkyō, Naigai Shosekisha, 1930, 816 pp.
An outstanding study of the cultural influences of continental civilization on Japan from early times to the middle of the eighteenth century. Professor Tsuji is especially at home with Buddhist documents. The work is detailed and well-documented.

943. Watanabe Ikujirō 渡辺幾治郎, Nihon kinsei gaikōshi 日本近世外交史 (History of modern Japanese foreign relations), Tōkyō, Chikura Shobō, 9+494 pp.
A clearly written and well-documented survey of Japan's foreign relations from the beginning of the Russian problem to the first modern treaties.

944. Watsuji Tetsurō 和辻哲郎, Sakoku 鎖国 (Seclusion), Tōkyō, Chikuma Shobō, 1950, 8+748+25 pp.
One of the few Japanese studies of the problem of Japanese seclusion from 1640 to 1854. The treatment is primarily analytical. Professor Watsuji, writing after Japan's Pacific War defeat, believes that Tokugawa seclusion cost Japan valuable progress in the scientific field.

g. Military History

Military histories of Japan have flourished along with the growth of Japan's modern military bureaucracy. Factual descriptions of battles and wars abound, the most authoritative being the Nihon senshi (Military history of Japan) series edited by the General Staff (Entry 956). This should be supplemented, for battles prior to the middle of the sixteenth century, by Takayanagi Mitsutoshi's Dai Nihon senshi (Military history of Japan) (Entry 963). Works on castles and medieval defenses will be found listed under architecture (Chapter 11 b below).
Interpretive studies of Japanese armed forces and military policy present a greater problem. From the issuance of the Imperial Rescript on Military Service in 1882 until the termination of World War II, objective study of this subject was next to impossible. Characteristic of the prewar historian's sympathetic approach to the history of military institutions was the Nihon heiseishi (History of military institutions in Japan) (Entry 952), compiled by members of the Japan Historical Geography Society. The first to write from a critical position was Izu Kimio, whose essay in the Nihon shihonshugi hattatsushi kōza (Series on the history of the growth of capitalism in Japan) (Entry 1032) took a Marxist view of modern Japanese military development. In the following list the works of Matsushita Yoshio are recommended for their balanced coverage of the modern period.

945. Iizuka Kōji 飯塚浩二, Nihon no guntai 日本の軍隊 (Japan's fighting forces), Tōkyō, Tōkyō Daigaku Shuppambu, 1950, 3+274 pp.

946. Heki Shōichi 日置昌一, Nihon sōhei no kenkyū 日本僧兵の研究 (Study of Japanese warrior-monks), Tōkyō, Heibonsha, 1934, 12+343+35 pp.

946a. Itō Masanori 伊藤正徳, Kokubōshi 国防史 (History of national defense), Tōkyō, Tōyō Keizai Shimpōsha, 1941.
A carefully compiled and well-documented history of the modern development of Japan's armed forces up to approximately the time of writing. The style is somewhat too statistical, but the approach is remarkably free from bias.

947. Izu Kimio 伊豆公夫 and Matsushita Yoshio 松下芳男, Nihon gunji hattatsushi 日本軍事発達史 (History of Japanese military development), Tōkyō, Mikasa Shobō, 1938, 379 pp.
A general survey of the development of Japan's armed forces. Part 1, by Izu, covers the history of various military systems in pre-modern Japan. Part 2, by Matsushita, deals with Japan's modern war machine. Sections are devoted to the army, navy, and air force.

948. Kaigun Yūshūkai 海軍有終会 (Navy Perfection Society), Taiheiyō nisenroppyakunenshi 太平洋二千六百年史 (2600 years of Pacific history), Tōkyō, Kaigun Yūshūkai, 1940, 1086 pp.
    A detailed and somewhat romantic history of the development of Japanese sea power in the Pacific from remote times to 1937.

949. Kuwaki Sūmei 桑木崇明, Rikugun gojūnenshi 陸軍五十年史 (Fifty years of army history), Tōkyō, Masu Shobō, 1943, 420 pp.

950. Matsushita Yoshio 松下芳男, Kindai Nihon gunjishi 近代日本軍事史 (History of recent Japanese military affairs), Tōkyō, Kigensha Shoten, 1941, 312 pp.
    A survey of military affairs in Japan from 1868 through the warring in Manchuria in the 1930s.

951. Matsushita Yoshio 松下芳男, Nihon gunseishi ronshū 日本軍制史論集 (Collected essays on the history of Japanese military systems), Tōkyō, Ikuseisha, 1938, 338 pp.
    Essays by an expert on Meiji military history. The work treats such subjects as the independence of the army command, political crises and the army and navy ministers, the development of the Imperial Headquarters, the army code and early military law.

952. Nihon Rekishi Chiri Gakkai 日本歴史地理学会 (Japan Historical Geography Society), Nihon heiseishi 日本兵制史 (History of military institutions in Japan), Tōkyō, Nihon Gakujutsu Fukyūkai, 1926, 304+4 pp.
    A symposium by the leading historians of the late 1920s such as Miura Kaneyuki, Ōmori Kingorō, Nishioka Torajirō and Kurita Motoji. The essays cover a wide variety of subjects including: shifts in the center of military power, bushi of the Nara period, monastic armies, the ashigaru, the Korean invasions, the Osaka campaign and the rōnin problem, the peasant armies of the Meiji Restoration period, etc.

953. Ozawa Shigeshi 小澤滋, Nihon heishoku shiron 日本兵食史論 (Historical essays on Japanese military rations), Tōkyō, Hōbunsha, 1938, 3 v.
    A technical and detailed study of the history of military rations in Japan. Volume 1 concludes with the Kamakura period; volume 2 covers the 14th through 19th centuries. Volume 3 is devoted to the theory of the part played by food supplies in the development of military science.

954. Sakanoue Nobuo 坂上信夫, Nihon kaibōshi 日本海防史 (History of Japanese coastal defense), Kyōto, Taikōdō, 1942, 419 pp.
    A survey of the development of Japanese coastal defense from earliest times to 1868. The author discusses both naval and land-based defense measures. The work is illustrated but not annotated.

955. Sakurai Chūon 櫻井忠温, Kokubō daijiten 国防大辞典 (Dictionary of national defense), Tōkyō, Chūō Sangyō Chōsakai, 1933, 860 pp.
    An encyclopedic dictionary covering all phases of military development in Japan. Articles cover the history and contemporary status of various branches of the armed forces, analyses of military law, and explanations of technical terms.

956. Sambō Hombu 参謀本部 (General Staff), Nihon senshi 日本戦史 (Military history of Japan), Tōkyō, Sambō Hombu, 1899-1924, 24 v.
    These official accounts of Japan's major wars are patterned on the famous German campaign histories. The studies are lavishly supplied with maps, charts, tables, and illustrations. The twenty-four volumes published by 1924 cover the major battles of the late sixteenth and early seventeenth centuries including the Korean campaigns of Hideyoshi (1592-98), the battle of Sekigahara (1600), and the Osaka campaigns (1614-15). Later wars are covered in separate series as follows:

    _____, Meiji nijūshichi-hachinen Nisshin sen'eki 明治廿七八年日清戦役 (The Sino-Japanese War of 1894-95), Tōkyō, Sambō Hombu, 1912-14, 20 v.

    _____, Meiji sanjūshichi-hachinen Nichi-Ro senshi 明治卅七八年日露戦史 (History of the Russo-Japanese War of 1904-05), Tōkyō, Kaikōsha, 1912-14.

    _____, Taishō sannen Nichi-Doku senshi 大正三年日独戦史 (History of the German-Japanese conflicts of 1914), Tōkyō, Sambō Hombu, 1916, 4 v.

    Sambō Hombu Rikugunbu Hensanka 参謀本部陸軍部編纂課 (General Staff, Army Section, Compilation Office), Seiseisen kiko 征西戦記稿 (Records of the Satsuma Rebellion), Tōkyō, Rikugun Bunko, 1887, 4 v.

961. Satō Ichiro 佐藤市郎, Kaigun gojūnenshi 海軍五十年史 (Fifty years of navy history), Tōkyō, Masu Shobō, 1943, 425 pp.

962. Satō Kenji 佐藤堅司, Nihon bugakushi 日本武学史 (History of Japanese military science), Tōkyō, Daitō Shokan, 1942, 894 pp.
    A highly idealized discussion of Japan's military virtues and strategy. Chapters deal with Bushido, the spirit of the modern Japanese conscription system, pre-modern military strategists, etc.

963. Takayanagi Mitsutoshi 高柳 光壽, <u>Dai Nihon senshi</u> 大 日 本 戰 史 (Military history of Japan), Tōkyō, Sankyō Shoin, 1938-39 3 v.

    Contains in chronological order detailed accounts of major battles from early times through the first part of the Tokugawa period.

6. ECONOMIC HISTORY

    The Japanese have shown themselves prolific writers of economic history. Characteristic of their work in this field has been an extreme breadth of approach which has linked economics with cultural, social, and political developments. Most survey works written under the heading of economic history are thus more in the nature of socio-economic interpretations rather than strict economic analyses of Japanese history.

    Although it was not until the 1920s that economic historians came into their own in Japan, spadework in the field was begun before the turn into the twentieth century. Important as foundation works upon which the later survey histories were based were the officially inspired histories of finance, taxation, agriculture, and industry compiled during the 1870s and 80s. The next two decades saw the appearance of the first theoretical and synthetic studies. Among the pioneer economic historians of this time were Uchida Ginzō, influenced by the British scholar William Cunningham, and Fukuda Tokuzō, who had studied in Germany under Franz Brentano. Subsequently the pupils of these pioneer scholars brought to maturity the first phase in the development of Japanese economic history. During the 1920s such men as Honjō Eijirō, Kokusho Iwao, Takekoshi Yosaburō, Ono Takeo, Tsuchiya Takao, and Nomura Kanetarō poured out works on the general economic history of Japan in such profusion as to dominate the entire historical field. Under them the general outlines of Japanese economic history became fully established, while their pupils began the investigation of more detailed problems. It was under their inspiration also that two scholarly organizations, the Shakai Keizaishi Gakkai (Social and Economic History Association) of Tokyo and the Nihon Keizaishi Kenkyūsho (Japan Economic History Association) of Kyoto, were founded as headquarters of the new trend in historical research.

    During the late 1920s, Japanese scholars became increasingly concerned with current social and economic problems and the relationship between economics and politics. At the same time the theories of Marx and Lenin came into vogue. The result was the development of a Marxist school of historians pioneered by such men as Noro Eitarō, Hani Gorō, and Hayakawa Jirō. Early attention of the Marxists was concentrated upon the Meiji Restoration (see Section 5, <u>a</u>, 4 above) and the analysis of Japan's modern capitalism (see Section 6, <u>c</u>, 4 below) but it soon moved on to embrace problems of Japan's primitive society, feudalism, the peasantry, and many other historical aspects of Japanese economic development. The story of the vicissitudes of doctrinaire Marxist interpretations of Japanese history is overly technical and need not detain us here. Influence of Marxist concepts on the thinking of traditional economic historians is another matter and of vital importance in our evaluation of works in this field.

    Since the mid-1930s most economic historians have been influenced by Marxist theories in one way or another. At the same time the factual base of economic history has expanded tremendously as monographic studies have made use of more and primary material. Today the field of economic history is divided rather sharply between the "academic" followers of Honjō, represented below by Horie Yasuzō, and the more numerous and prolific "progressive" or Marxist historians, represented below in the work of Naramoto Tatsuya.

    The survey economic histories which follow are but a small selection from a vast field. Among them Horie Yasuzō's <u>Nihon keizaishi</u> (Economic history of Japan) (Entry 967) and Nakamura Kichiji's <u>Nihon keizaishi gaisetsu</u> (An introduction to the economic history of Japan) (Entry 973) are recommended for their balanced approach. Horie's work is especially valuable for the excellent classified bibliography which it contains. As a brief introduction to the field, Honjō Eijirō's <u>Nihon keizaishi sōron</u> (Collected essays on Japanese economic history) (Entry 966) will be found particularly useful, especially for its essays on methodology and bibliography.

a. Survey Histories

964. Honjō Eijirō 本 庄 榮 治 郎 and Kokusho Iwao 黑 正 巖, <u>Nihon keizaishi</u> 日本 經 济 史 (Economic history of Japan), Tōkyō, Nihon Hyōronsha, 1929, 361 pp.

    Volume 6 of the <u>Gendai keizaigaku zenshū</u> (Modern series on economics), this work presents in outline form the development of Japanese economic institutions as affected by the evolution of Japan's political and social structure. Coverage is from early clan economy to post-Restoration "national" economy.

965. Honjō Eijirō 本 庄 榮 治 郎, <u>Kaihan Nihon keizaishi gaisetsu</u> 改 版 日 本 經 濟 史 概 説 (An introduction to Japanese economic history—revised), Tōkyō, Nihon Hyōronsha, 1932, 373 pp.

    A revised edition of Professor Honjō's lectures in economic history delivered at Kyoto University and first published in 1928. Lectures cover chronologically and in outline form major developments in the fields of population, village economy, mining, forestry, marine products, animal husbandry, agriculture, land systems, industry, commerce, currency, finance, and transportation. Each chapter is followed by a selected list of recommended reading.

966. Honjō Eijirō 本 庄 榮 治 郎, <u>Nihon keizaishi sōron</u> 日 本 經 濟 史 總 論 (Collected essays on Japanese economic history), Tōkyō, Ryūginsha, 1948, 222 pp.

    Contains miscellaneous articles on Japanese economic history by a pioneer authority in this field. The chapter on the development of the study of economic history in Japan and the bibliographic section are of particular value.

967. Horie Yasuzo 堀 江 保 藏, <u>Nihon keizaishi</u> 日 本 經 濟 史 (Economic history of Japan), Tōkyō, Tōyō Shokan, 1949, 322 pp.

    Perhaps the most generally useful of the one-volume survey histories of Japanese economic development. The author begins with early clan society and traces the parallel interaction of political, social, and economic institutions down to the 1920s. The style is simple and lucid. The appended bibliographical section is particularly valuable.

968. Kajinishi Mitsuhaya 楫 西 光 速 , Nihon keizaishi 日 本 經 済 史 (Economic history of Japan), Tōkyō, Rōdōbunkasha, 1950, 240 pp.
　　An introductory survey by a specialist in modern Japanese industrial development.　The author covers both ancient and modern Japan.　There is an appended bibliography.

969. Kōda Shigetomo 幸 田 成 友 , Nihon keizaishi kenkyū 日 本 經 済 史 研 究 (Studies in Japanese economic history), Tōkyō, Ookayama Shoten, 1928, 854+61 pp.
　　A series of essays on various aspects of Tokugawa economic history.　The studies of the kurayashiki, fudasashi, shichiya, kabu-nakama, and goyōkin are especially valuable.　Essays are scholarly and well documented.

970. Kokushō Iwao 黒 正 巖 , Nihon keizaishi 日 本 經 済 史 (Japanese economic history), Tōkyō, Nihon Hyōronsha, 1939-40, 5 v.　[=Volumes 1 and 3-6 of the Shin keizaigaku zenshū (New series on economics].
　　This work is an introductory survey of Japanese economic history by an expert on Tokugawa village economy and peasant uprisings.

971. Miyamoto Mataji 宮 本 又 次 , Nihon keizaishi kōwa 日 本 經 済 史 講 話 (Lectures on Japanese economic history), Tōkyō, Daiyamondosha, 1946, 388+18 pp.
　　Consists of broadly interpretive lectures covering the entire range of pre-modern Japanese economic development.　The style is simple.　The final 18 pages consist of a chronologically arranged bibliography.

972. Nakamura Kichiji 中 村 吉 治 , Nihon keizaishi 日 本 經 済 史 (Economic history of Japan), Tōkyō, Kadokawa Shoten, 1949, 349 pp.
　　A recent, abridged survey of Japan's pre-modern economic development.

973. Nakamura Kichiji 中 村 吉 治 , Nihon keizaishi gaisetsu 日 本 經 済 史 概 説 (An introduction to the economic history of Japan), Tōkyō, Nihon Hyōronsha, 1941, 17+603 pp.
　　Perhaps the most useful of the prewar general surveys.　The author is a specialist in feudal institutions.　Coverage of this work is from early times to the Meiji Restoration and emphasis is upon the interplay of political, social, and economic institutions.

974. Nakamura Kōya 中 村 孝 也 and others, Nihon shakai keizaishi 日 本 社 会 經 済 史 (Japanese social economic history), Tōkyō, Yūzankaku, 1939, 329 pp.　[= Volume 11 of the Shinkō Dai Nihonshi (Entry 744)].
　　This work consists of specialized essays by individual experts.　An introductory chapter by Professor Nakamura is followed by contributions by Hōgetsu Keigo (agriculture), Endō Motoo (industry), Toyoda Takeshi (commerce), and Shinjō Tsunemi (communications).

975. Naramoto Tatsuya 奈 良 本 辰 也 , Nihon keizaishi 日 本 經 済 史 (Economic history of Japan), Tōkyō, Mikasa Shobō, 1951, 3+3+200 pp.
　　A brief survey of Japanese economic history up through the early years of Meiji by a leading exponent of the intellectual Marxist school.　The author is especially familiar with the history of the western han of the Tokugawa period.　A brief selected bibliography is appended.

976. Nomura Kanetarō 野 村 兼 太 郎 , Nihon shakai keizaishi 日 本 社 会 經 済 史 (Social and economic history of Japan), Tōkyō, Daiyamondosha, 1950+.
　　An ambitious work, scheduled to go to twelve volumes, by one of the leading economic historians of Japan. Each volume covers a major historical period and deals in general interpretive fashion with its political, social, economic, and cultural development.　Each volume ends with an elaborate set of indices covering places, persons, events, and bibliography.

977. Nomura Kanetarō 野 村 兼 太 郎 , Nihon keizaishi josetsu 日 本 經 済 史 序 説 (Introduction to Japanese economic history), Tōkyō, Yūhikaku, 1948, 252 pp.
　　The first volume of a general survey of Japanese economic history by a recognized leader in the field. This volume covers early times through the middle ages.

978. Sakisaka Itsurō 向 坂 逸 郎 , ed., Keizai gojūnen 經 済 五 十 年 (Fifty years of economic development), Tōkyō, Jiji Tsūshinsha, 1950, 315 pp.
　　This work brings together essays of a somewhat uneven quality on the following aspects of the last fifty years of Japan's economic development: finance, industrial production, agriculture, foreign trade, labor problems, and peasant movements.

979. Takahashi Kamekichi 高 橋 亀 吉 , Nihon keizaishi 日 本 經 済 史 (History of Japanese economics), Tōkyō, Kaizōsha, 1930, 570 pp.
　　This book is the result of the joint efforts of members of the Takahashi Economic Research Institute. Individual specialists cover the economic history of the Meiji Restoration, history of credit in Japan, agriculture, finance, and manufacturing.

980. Takekoshi Yosaburō 竹 越 與 三 郎 , Nihon keizaishi 日 本 經 済 史 (Economic history of Japan), Tōkyō, Nihon Keizaishi Hensankai, 1920, 8 v.
　　One of the pioneer attempts to write a general history of pre-modern Japan with emphasis on its underlying economic factors.　The early sections of this work tend to be more political than economic in interpretation.　Takekoshi is particularly at home in the Tokugawa period and presents a considerable volume of primary data on the financial and commercial institutions of the time.　The whole work is

somewhat disorganized.   An abridged translation of this work has appeared in English as The Economic Aspects of the History of the Civilization of Japan, New York, Macmillan, 1930, 3 v.

981. Tsuchiya Takao 土 屋 高 雄 , Nihon keizaishi gaiyō 日 本 經 済 史 概 要 (An outline of Japanese economic history), Tōkyō, Iwanami Shoten, 1934-39, 2 v.
    An outline history of Japanese economic development.   Volume 1 treats pre-Meiji economy by periods. Within each period the major segments of Japan's economy are separately treated.   Each chapter concludes with a selected bibliographical list.   Volume 2 (zokuhen) discusses post-Restoration capitalistic developments up to the period following World War I.   Volume 1 has been translated into English as "An Economic History of Japan," Transactions of the Asiatic Society of Japan, second series, 15 (1937).

982. Uchida Ginzō 内 田 銀 蔵 , Nihon keizaishi no kenkyū 日 本 經 済 史 の 研 究 (Studies of Japanese economic history), Tōkyō, Dōbunkan, 1921, 2 v.
    Consists of collected essays by one of the pioneer economic historians of modern Japan.   The volumes contain several general survey articles on Japanese economic history, its study, and its main sources. For the most part the articles are of a specialized nature and deal with widely separate subjects including studies of Chinese economic theory, Buddhist economic thought, Okinawan land systems, as well as problems of Japanese economic development.

983. Uchida Ginzō 内 田 銀 蔵 , Nihon keizaishi gaiyō 日 本 經 済 史 概 要 (An outline of Japanese economic history), Tōkyō, Sōgensha, 1939, 134 pp.
    A short survey of Japanese economic history published posthumously with a memorial article on the author by Nishida Naojirō.

b. Economic Thought

    Most of the following works are concerned with the political economists of the Tokugawa period.   This field has been dominated by three men, Takimoto Seiichi, Honjō Eijirō, and Nomura Kanetarō, whose activity in collecting and publishing the works of Tokugawa economists has already been commented upon (see Part III, Chapter 2, b, 4 above).
    Of the following entries, Nomura Kanetarō's Tokugawa jidai no keizai shisō (Economic thought of the Tokugawa period) (Entry 991) is recommended for its analytical treatment of the subject.   Kada Tetsuji's work (Entry 988) is one of the few on post-Restoration economic theory.

984. Azuma Shintarō 東 晋 太 郎 , Kinsei Nihon keizai rinri shisōshi 近 世 日 本 經 済 倫 理 思 想 史 (History of modern Japanese economic theory), Tōkyō, Keiō Shuppansha, 1944, 22+678 pp.
    An excellent study of the economic theories developed during the Tokugawa era.   The author begins with a careful analysis of the basic principles of Confucian social and economic theory and describes the application of these to Tokugawa Japanese society.   The last half of the work is devoted to an analysis of the thinking of Yamaga Sokō, Kumazawa Banzan, Kaibara Ekken, Ogyū Sorai and Dazai Shundai.   The work is annotated and there is an index and a table of primary works consulted.

985. Honjō Eijirō 本 庄 榮 治 郎 , Nihon keizai shisōshi gaisetsu 日 本 經 済 思 想 史 概 説 (An introduction to the history of Japanese economic thought), Tōkyō, Yūhikaku, 1946, 10+280 pp.
    An introductory survey, of special value for its general bibliography of the subject and for its list of writings of Japanese economic philosophers.   Emphasis is on the Tokugawa period.

986. Honjō Eijirō 本 庄 榮 治 郎 , Nihon keizai shisōshi 日 本 經 済 思 想 史 (History of Japanese economic thought), Tōkyō, Ryūginsha, 1948, 279 pp.
    Part 1 is a brief introduction to the economic thought of the Tokugawa period.   Part 2 discusses 20 Tokugawa and 7 Meiji economic theorists.

987. Honjō Eijirō 本 庄 榮 治 郎 , Nihon keizai shisōshi kenkyū 日 本 經 済 思 想 史 研 究 (Studies in the history of Japanese economic thought), Tōkyō, Nihon Hyōronsha, 1942, 466 pp.
    The first half of these essays deals with general economic problems of the Tokugawa and early Meiji periods.   The second half treats individually ten of the Tokugawa economic thinkers from Arai Hakuseki to Ōshima Teieki.   A volume of "further studies" published in 1946 includes a number of general surveys of the field and covers the main currents of Japanese economic thought from the 17th century to the 1920s.

988. Kada Tetsuji 加 田 哲 二 , Ishin igo no shakai keizai shisō gairon 維 新 以 後 の 社 会 經 済 思 想 概 論 (Outline of post-Meiji social and economic thought), Tōkyō, Nihon Hyōronsha, 1934, 275 pp.
    Chapters deal with: economic theory behind the Restoration, laissez-faireism and national policy, economic policy of the Meiji government, liberalism and conservatism, the economic theory of nationalism, economic theories of the jiyū-minken movement and of the labor movement, development of socialism, etc.

989. Kinsei shakai keizai gakusetsu taikei 近 世 社 会 經 済 学 説 大 系 (Outline of social and economic theory in modern times), Tōkyō, Seibundō, 1935-37, 18 v.
    Each volume is devoted to one or two Tokugawa and early Meiji economic thinkers.   Each individual is introduced with a lengthy preface on his work and thought written by a leading contemporary authority. The bulk of each volume is comprised of selected and annotated readings from the individual's works. Among those included in this series are: Kumazawa Banzan, Yamaga Sokō, Kaibara Ekken, Arai Hakuseki, Ogyū Sorai, Miura Baien, Dazai Shundai, Honda Toshiaki, Kaibo Seiryū, Satō Shin'en, Ninomiya Sontoku, and Fukuzawa Yukichi.

990. Nomura Kanetarō 野村兼太郎, Nihon keizai shisō 日本經濟思想 (Japanese economic thought), Tōkyō, Keiō Shuppansha, 1941, 163 pp.

    A brief introduction to Japanese economic thought by the leading authority in the field. Part 1 treats early Tokugawa thinkers and theories, part 2 the late Tokugawa, and part 3 the Meiji period.

991. Nomura Kanetarō 野村兼太郎, Tokugawa jidai no keizai shisō 德川時代の經濟思想 (Economic thought of the Tokugawa period), Tōkyō, Nihon Hyōronsha, 1939, 562 pp.

    A significant analysis of economic theories and theorists of the Tokugawa period. Part 1 consists of a general discussion of the basic premises of economic thought of the period and the split between the advocates of agrarian and commercial economy. Part 2 contains short studies of individual theorists from Kumazawa Banzan to Sato Shin'en.

992. Takimoto Seiichi 瀧本誠一, Nihon keizai shisōshi 日本經濟思想史 (History of Japanese economic thought), Tōkyō, Nihon Hyōronsha, 1929, 303 pp.

    An introduction to the major writers on economic theory during the Tokugawa period by a pioneer writer in the field.

c. Socio-economic Systems

    The following works on socio-economic systems are not specifically economic in nature. They are included at this point, however, because in Japan these subjects have been primarily the concern of the economic rather than the social historian. Today economic histories of Japan are written largely in the broader social and political context of economic development. Hence a great deal of current scholarship attempts to define more sharply the structure of Japan at various stages of economic growth and to compare Japanese institutions with similar ones in continental Asia and in Europe. This emphasis has in turn engendered a number of bitter controversies over interpretation, chiefly between the Marxists and non-Marxists. The following sections cover some of the major divisions under which Japanese economic historians have written.

1) Primitive Economy, Asiatic Absolutism, and Slavery

    Crucial to the study of Japanese economy of the sixth through tenth centuries is the problem of the existence or non-existence of slavery. Standard prewar views on this subject will be found in the general survey histories such as the Sōgō Nihonshi taikei (Entry 748), and Heibonsha's Nihonshi (Entry 739), and in the writings of such specialists as Takigawa Masajirō and Abe Kōzō listed below. Postwar interpretations have come largely from Marxist scholars who view ancient Japan as conforming to the stage of "Asiatic absolutism" in which an aristocratic ruling class rested upon a base of semi-free communal units. Most prolific in their presentation of this view have been Mishima Hajime, Ishimoda Masashi, Tōma Seita, and Watanabe Yoshimichi. A recent arrival in this field, Inoue Mitsusada, has utilized theories developed by Max Weber. His work is as yet limited to articles.

993. Abe Kōzō 阿部弘蔵, Nihon doreishi 日本奴隷史 (History of slavery in Japan), Tōkyō, Shūhōkaku, 1926, 16+447+2+17 pp.

    An analysis of the origin and development of various unfree classes or minorities in Japanese society. The work is authoritative and free from bias. There is an index.

994. Mishima Hajime 三島一, Ishimoda Tadashi 石母田正, and Tōma Seita 藤間生大, Nihon kodai shakai 日本古代社会 (Ancient Japanese society), Tōkyō, Nihon Dokusho Kumiai, 1947-48, 2 v.

    An interpretative survey of the development of early Japanese society by leading specialists in this field. Among those contributors not listed as editors are Inoue Mitsusada and Wakamori Tarō.

995. Takigawa Masajirō 瀧川政治郎, Nihon dorei keizaishi 日本奴隷經濟史 (Economic history of slavery in Japan), Tōkyō, Kangensha, 1948, 553 pp.

    First printed in 1930. This is a detailed and well documented study of early slavery in Japan. The author tends to minimize the existence of slavery as defined in its legal sense. There is an index.

996. Tsuda Sōkichi 津田左右吉, Jōdai Nihon no shakai oyobi shisō 上代日本の社会及び思想 (Society and thought in ancient Japan), Tōkyō, Iwanami Shoten, 1933, 606+8 pp.

    An attempt to reconstruct the pre-seventh century life of the Japanese by a specialist in Japan's ancient literature. The author is not afraid to cast doubts on some of the cherished nationalist folklore of the time.

997. Watanabe Yoshimichi 渡部義通, Kodai shakai no kōzō 古代社会の構造 (The structure of ancient society), Tōkyō, Itō Shoten, 1948, 488 pp.

    An analytical discussion of the political, social, and economic structure of ancient society in Japan.

998. Watanabe Yoshimichi 渡部義通, Hayakawa Jirō 早川二郎, Izu Kimio 伊豆公夫, and Akizawa Shūji 秋澤修二, Nihon rekishi kyōtei 日本歴史敎程 (A manual of Japanese history), Tōkyō, Hakuyōsha, 1936-37, 2 v.

    An early presentation of the Marxist approach to Japanese history. Publication was stopped before completion. These two volumes cover Japanese social and economic institutions from earliest times to the feudal age.

2) The Shōen

Japan has produced a number of able medievalists who have specialized in the study of the shōen (manorial) system. Beginning with Yoshida Tōgo (Entry 1012) the historical geographer, and the legalists, Nakada Kaoru (Entry 1004), Maki Kenji (Entry 1003), Nishioka Toranosuke (Entry 1006), and Nakamura Naokatsu (Entry 1005), a number of scholars have developed in detail the legal framework of the shō and its administrative superstructure. More recent scholars beginning with Shimizu Mitsuo (Entry 1008) have concentrated their attention on the village unit within the shōen system and particularly on the mura-nanushi-bushi complex.

999. Egashira Tsuneji 江頭恒治, Nihon shōen keizai shiron 日本荘園經済史論 (An historical discussion of the Japanese shōen economy), Tōkyō, Yūhikaku, 1942, 12+445 pp.
　　A detailed and carefully documented study.

1000. Endō Motoo 遠藤元男, Nihon hōkensei seiritsushi 日本封建制成立史 (History of the establishment of feudalism in Japan), Tōkyō, Mikasa Shobō, 1939, 233 pp.
　　A study of the breakdown of the Taika system of government and the emergence of feudalistic practices in Japan.

1001. Hosokawa Kameichi 細川亀市, Nōdo shakai shikō 農奴社会史考 (Historical study of serf society), Tōkyō, Hakutōsha, 1932, 314 pp.
　　A detailed study of peasant unrest during the Tokugawa period and movements to liberate the peasantry.

1002. Imai Rintarō 今井林太郎, Nihon shōensei ron 日本荘園制論 (Essays on the Japanese shōen system), Tōkyō, Mikasa Shobō, 1939, 268 pp.
　　A study of the origin and development of the shōen system in Japan. The author is thoroughly grounded in primary materials. Emphasis is on problems of agricultural production and the position of various classes with respect to the land. The work is marred by many typographical errors.

1003. Maki Kenji 牧健二, Nihon hōken seido seiritsushi 日本封建制度成立史 (History of the emergence of feudalism in Japan), Tōkyō, Kōbundō, 1935, 526 pp.
　　A legalistic study of early feudal institutions and feudal law. The author is familiar with both Chinese and European feudal institutions and draws many fruitful comparisons.

1004. Nakada Kaoru 中田薫, Shōen no kenkyū 庄園の研究 (A study of shōen), Tōkyō, Shōkō Shoin, 1948, 5+404+15 pp.
　　An important study of the legal foundations of the shōen in Japan. The author is one of the pioneer students of medieval law in Japan.

1005. Nakamura Naokatsu 中村直勝, Shōen no kenkyū 荘園の研究 (A study of the shōen), Kyōto, Hoshino Shoten, 1939, 11+809 pp.
　　A study of the Tōdaiji shō. The work is exceptionally technical but gives excellent insight into the actual life of a typical shō.

1006. Nishioka Toranosuke 西岡虎之助, Shōensei no hattatsu 荘園制の発達 (The development of the shōen system), Tōkyō, Iwanami Shoten, 1933, 63 pp.
　　One of the Iwanami lecture series pamphlets. It gives a brief description of the origins and development of the shōen system.

1007. Ono Takeo 小野武夫, Nihon shōensei shiron 日本庄園制史論 (An historical treatise on the shōen system), Tōkyō, Yūhikaku, 1943, 555 pp.
　　A detailed and fully documented study of the emergence of the shōen system in Japan by one of the foremost economic historians of prewar Japan. The author was aided in his study by Imai Rintarō.

1008. Shimizu Mitsuo 清水三男, Nihon chūsei no sonraku 日本中世の村落 (The Japanese village in the medieval period), Tōkyō, Nihon Hyōronsha, 1942, 401+41 pp.
　　An important work analyzing the structure and economic state of the village (mura) during the 12th to 14th centuries. This work is largely responsible for shifting the emphasis of Japanese medievalists from a study of the shōen as a legal entity to a consideration of the mura-nanushi-bushi complex.

1009. Shimizu Mitsuo 清水三男, Nihon shōen no kiso kōzō 日本荘園の基礎構造 (The basic structure of the Japanese shōen), Kyōto, Kōtō Shoin, 1948, 359 pp.

1010. Takeuchi Rizō 竹内理三, Jiryō shōen no kenkyū 寺領荘園の研究 (Studies of ecclesiastic shōen), Tōkyō, Unebi Shobō, 1942, 555 pp.
　　A specialized study.

1011. Tōma Seita 藤間生大, Nihon shōenshi 日本庄園史 (History of the Japanese shōen), Tōkyō, Kondō Shobō, 1947, 480 pp.
　　A Marxist synthesis of the recent studies of the emergence of the shōen. Emphasis is upon changes at the local village level and in modes of economic production. The work concludes with a lengthy analysis of the history of shōen studies in Japan.

1012. Yoshida Tōgo 吉田東伍, Nihon shōen seido no taiyō 日本庄園制度の大要 (Outlines of the Japanese shōen system), Tōkyō, Nihon Gakujutsu Fukyūkai, 1916, 254 pp.
　　A pioneer study by a leading historical geographer.

3) Feudalism

No doubt it is because the Japanese have only recently emerged from their period of feudalism that their historians are still actively studying and debating the nature of the feudal past and its legacy to the present. The literature in this field is vast and complicated. Few writers have been equally at home in all three of the major divisions into which the Japanese feudal period falls. Instead they have tended to specialize either in early (Kamakura) or late (Tokugawa) institutions. Until recently the middle period (Ashikaga) has been relatively neglected. Early writers on feudalism came from among the legal historians, whose works have been listed in greater detail in Sections 5 e 1 and 6 c 3 above. During the 1920s and 30s the economic historians took over the major role in the study of Japanese feudalism.

Among the more recent survey histories in this field, Itō Tasaburō's Nihon hōken seidoshi (History of the feudal system in Japan) (Entry 1014) and Nakamura Kichiji's Hōken shakai (Feudal society) (Entry 1019) are outstanding. Specialists in early feudalism correspond largely to those listed in the section under shōen, 6 c 2 above. A large number of historians have concentrated upon the late feudal period. Among them Nakamura and Miyamoto (Entries 1018 and 1017) have contributed chiefly to an understanding of the transition from middle to late feudalism and Tsuchiya and Naramoto (Entries 1025 and 1020) to the nineteenth century decay of feudal institutions. The current trend towards study of the economic life of the feudal peasantry is dealt with later in Section 7 d 4.

1013. Irimajiri Yoshinaga 入交好脩, Hokensei hōkai katei no kenkyū 封建制崩壞過程の研究 (Studies in the decay of feudal institutions), Tōkyō, Waseda Daigaku Shuppambu, 1948, 382 pp.
　　　Studies in the basic problems underlying the decline of feudal institutions of the Tokugawa period. Part 1 deals with the so-called "reestablishment of feudalism" in the seventeenth century; part 2 treats the peasantry and their problems; part 3 deals with problems of land reclamation, the family system, and the development of manufacturing. The author evaluates critically several recent studies of these subjects.

1014. Ito Tasaburō 伊東多三郎, Nihon hōken seidoshi 日本封建制度史 (History of the feudal system in Japan), Tōkyō, Yoshikawa Kōbunkan, 1950, 335 pp.
　　　The most lucid survey of the development of Japanese feudal institutions. It traces these institutions from their origin in the twelfth century to their decline in the nineteenth. The author is a specialist in feudal intellectual history and one of the few students of local history of the Tokugawa period.

1015. Makino Shinnosuke 牧野信之助, Bukejidai shakai no kenkyū 武家時代社會の研究 (Studies in the society of the feudal military period), Tōkyō, Tōkō Shoin, 1928, 630 pp.
　　　An early study of feudal institutions by a specialist in feudal law. Part 1 treats the legal superstructure of early Japanese feudalism; part 2 covers the land system and village organization; part 3 analyzes the social structure.

1016. Matsumoto Shimpachirō 松本新八郎, Hōkenteki tochi shoyū no seiritsu katei 封建的土地所有の成立過程 (On the emergence of feudal land tenure), Tōkyō, Itō Shoten, 1949, 154 pp.
　　　A technical, Marxist analysis of the changing pattern of land tenure which accompanied the breakdown of the public domain system after the eighth century in Japan. The author believes that the increased freedom of the cultivator class plus its greater productivity led to the growth of feudalism.

1017. Miyamoto Mataji 宮本又次, Hōkenshugi no saishuppatsu 封建主義の再出發 (The reemergence of the feudal ideology), Kyōto, Ōyashima Shuppan K.K., 1948, 364 pp.
　　　A clear exposition of the thesis that the emergence of the daimyō in the sixteenth century brought with it a reassertion of feudal controls. This work describes earlier feudal institutions and analyzes the policies of Nobunaga and Hideyoshi. There is an extensive bibliography.

1018. Nakamura Kichiji 中村吉治, Nihon hōkensei saihenseishi 日本封建制再編成史 (History of the reestablishment of the feudal system in Japan), Tōkyō, Mikasa Shobō, 1940, 248 pp.
　　　An early statement of the thesis that the institutions of the Tokugawa period represented a "refeudalization" of Japanese society. The author is an expert on the land survey (kenchi) which laid the foundation for renewed feudal control over the land. There is an appended bibliography.

1019. Nakamura Kichiji 中村吉治, Hōken shakai 封建社會 (Feudal society), Tōkyō, Kawade Shobō, 1943, 398 pp.
　　　An excellent survey introduction to Japanese feudal institutions. The work covers the entire field of feudalism in Japan and makes stimulating comparisons with European history.

1020. Naramoto Tatsuya 奈良本辰也, Kinsei hōken shakai shiron 近世封建社會史論 (Essays on the history of modern feudal society), Kyōto, Kōtō Shoin, 1948, 229 pp.
　　　Based primarily on the study of the Mōri domain (Chōshū) and its economic and administrative reforms of the Tempō period (1830-43). This work has been extremely influential among contemporary "progressive" students of the Meiji Restoration.

1021. Ono Takeo 小野武夫, Nihon heinō shiron 日本兵農史論 (Essays on the history of peasant conscription in Japan), Tōkyō, Yuhikaku, 1938, 394 pp.
　　　A broad historical analysis of the position of the peasant in the fighting forces of Japan. The author describes the military system of eighth century Japan, changes which occurred thereafter, and ends with a discussion of the gōshi (rural samurai) of the Tokugawa period.

1022. Takahashi Kamekichi 高橋亀吉 , Tokugawa hōken keizai no kenkyū 德川封建經済の 研究 (Studies of Tokugawa feudal economy), Tōkyō, Zenshinsha, 1931, 480 pp.

    Detailed and copiously documented studies of the development of commercial farming and handicraft production during the Tokugawa period. Special emphasis is placed on the development of the silk, cotton and sugar industries under government encouragement and monopoly.

1023. Takimoto Seiichi 瀧本誠一 , Nihon hōken keizaishi 日本封建經済史 (History of feudal economy in Japan), Tōkyō, Maruzen, 1930, 451+136+39+4 pp.

    An historical analysis by topics of Tokugawa economy. It covers such subjects as the land system, finance, currency, manufacturing, commerce, cities, uprisings, social classes, economic thought, and feudal laws.

1024. Teikoku Daigaku Shimbunsha Henshūbu 帝国大学新聞社編輯部 (Editorial Office, Imperial University Newspaper), Nihon hōkensei no bunseki 日本封建制の分析 (Analysis of Japanese feudalism), Tōkyō, Teikoku Daigaku Shimbunsha Shuppambu, 1947, 159 pp.

    A collection of articles from the Tōkyō Imperial University Newspaper by fifteen authorities. They discuss the nature of Japanese feudalism, make comparisons with European and Chinese institutions, and analyze the feudal remnants in contemporary Japanese society.

1025. Tsuchiya Takao 土屋喬雄 , Hōken shakai hōkai katei no kenkyū 封建社会崩壊過程の 研究 (A study of the process of decay of feudal society), Tōkyō, Kōbundō, 1927, 729 pp.

    A standard and influential analysis of the economic forces which undermined the feudal structure of nineteenth century Japan. The author emphasizes the financial difficulties of the feudal regime and the growth of government monopolies. He documents his thesis from his studies of the Sendai and Kagoshima domains.

1026. Tsuchiya Takao 土屋喬雄 , Hōken shakai no kōzō bunseki 封建社会の構造分析 (Structural analysis of feudal society), Tōkyō, Keisō Shobō, 1950, 338 pp.

    Collected essays by followers of the Tsuchiya school of economic history on the establishment and development of Tokugawa feudalism. Authors include Imai Rintarō, Naramoto Tatsuya, Abe Makoto, Irimajiri Yoshinaga, and Hattori Shisō. Most essays are documented.

1027. Yasuda Motohisa 安田元久 , Shoki hōkensei no kōsei 初期封建制の構成 (The structure of early feudalism), Tōkyō, Kokudosha, 1950, 219 pp.

    The author uses the "sociology of law" approach in his analysis of the structure of Kamakura feudalism.

4) Capitalism

    The "capitalism problem" has been one of the most bitterly debated subjects in the entire field of Japanese economic history. By now a number of books have appeared on the controversy alone. Of these, three are listed below (Entires 1037 to 1039). Though there is risk of over-simplification, it is possible to discern four broad schools of approach to the problem of interpreting Japanese capitalism. Early writers on the subject included members of the first generation of economic historians such as Honjō, Ono, and Tsuchiya. Their writings were largely of a generalized and descriptive nature and avoided the use of interpretive formulae. Today this school continues and is exemplified in the work of Horie Yasuzō (Entry 1030).

    Marxist theorizers entered the field with Inomata Tsunao. Their chief contribution prior to World War II was the publication of the Nihon shihonshugi hattatsushi kōza (Series on the history of the growth of capitalism in Japan) (Entry 1032). It was the appearance of this series which gave rise to the split between the kōza group and the rōnō group discussed previously in Section 5 a 4 above. In simplest terms the "capitalism controversy" between these two groups hinged on a difference of opinion concerning the degree of economic development which Japan had attained by 1868. The kōza school minimized this development and hence emphasized the necessity of state participation. The rōnō scholars claimed to see progressive economic tendencies at the local level which they believed fashioned the foundation of Japan's modern capitalism. This split continues today. A final school of thought was brought into vogue by Ōtsuka Hisao (Entry 1034), who has used the ideas of Max Weber in his analysis of Japanese capitalism.

1028. Asada Mitsuteru 淺田光輝 and Nakamura Hideichiro 中村秀一郎 , Nihon shihonshugi shakai keiseishi 日本資本主義社会形成史 (History of the establishment of Japanese capitalistic society), Tōkyō, Iwasaki Shoten, 1949, 317 pp.

    An historical survey of the development of Japanese capitalistic society beginning with the origins of modern capitalistic institutions during the Tokugawa period. The author is a postwar adherent of the kōza school.

1029. Hirano Yoshitarō 平野義太郎 , Nihon shihonshugi shakai no kikō 日本資本主義社会の 機構 (The mechanism of Japanese capitalistic society), Tōkyō, Iwanami Shoten, 1934, 388 pp.

    Considered the best work of an influential exponent of the kōza school.

1030. Horie Yasuzō 堀江保蔵 , Nihon shihonshugi no seiritsu 日本資本主義の成立 (The establishment of Japanese capitalism), Tōkyō, Daidō Shoin, 1938, 340 pp.

    One of the best-balanced interpretations of the development of capitalism in Japan by the successor to Professor Honjō Eijirō at Kyoto University.

1031. Moriya Norio 守 屋 興 郎 , Nihon shihonshugi hattatsushi 日本資本主義発達史 (History of the development of capitalism in Japan), Tōkyō, Naukasha, 2nd ed., 1949, 173 pp.

The work of a high ranking member of the Japanese Communist Party, it is written to set forth in simple terms the party's official interpretation of the "capitalism problem."

1032. Nihon shihonshugi hattatsushi kōza 日本資本主義発達史講座 (Series on the history of the growth of capitalism in Japan), Tōkyō, Iwanami Shoten, 1932-33, 48 pamphlets.

One of the most controversial and publicized works in the modern historical field in Japan, this series of articles by members of the early Marxist school of historians made a strong impression by its anti-government interpretation of the Meiji Restoration and the "capitalism problem." Publication of this series was largely responsible for the subsequent effort to suppress academic Marxists in Japan. Many passages in the pamphlets are censored. It is from this series that the kōza school takes its name, the chief writers being Hani Gorō, Hattori Shisō, Hirano Yoshitarō, and Yamada Moritarō.

1033. Noro Eitarō 野 呂 榮太郎 , Nihon shihonshugi hattatsushi 日本資本主義発達史 (History of the growth of Japanese capitalism), Kyōto, San'ichi Shobō, 1949, 270 pp.

First published in 1930, this work is by a former secretary general of the Japanese Communist Party. The work emphasizes the imperialist orientation of post-Meiji capitalist development in Japan.

1034. Ōtsuka Hisao 大 塚 又 雄 , Kindai shihonshugi no keifu 近代日本主義の系譜 (The pedigree of modern capitalism), Tōkyō, Gakusei Shobō, 1947, 320 pp.

A controversial work which attempts to analyze Japan's modern capitalistic development by the aid of parallels drawn from European society. Ōtsuka is chiefly a follower of Max Weber and hence represents an anti-Marxist trend in current scholarship.

1035. Shinobu Seizaburō 信 夫 清 三郎 , Nihon no dokusen shihonshugi 日本の独占資本主義 (Japan's monopoly capitalism), Tōkyō, Aoki Shoten, 1948, 287 pp.

An analysis of Japan's modern capitalism with emphasis on its monopoly aspects. The author, one of the leading young Marxists, is a prolific writer on modern Japanese politics and foreign relations.

1036. Tsuchiya Takao 土 屋 高 雄 and Okazaki Saburō 岡 崎 三 郎 , Nihon shihonshugi hattatsushi gaisetsu 日本資本主義発達史概説 (An introduction to the history of the development of Japanese capitalism), Tōkyō, Yūhikaku, 1937, 550+4 pp.

An analysis of Japanese capitalism by the chief exponents of the rōnō school. Tsuchiya deals with the economics of the Meiji Restoration, Okazaki with developments in the fields of heavy industry and mining. The work concludes with a discussion of the influence of Japan's growing capitalism on farm economy.

1037. Shakai Keizai Rōdō Kenkyūsho 社 会 經 済 勞 働 研 究 所 (Research Institute for Social, Economic and Labor Problems), Nihon shihonshugi rōnsōshi 日本資本主義論争史 (History of the controversy over Japanese capitalism), Tōkyō, Itō Shoten, 1947, 273 pp.

A survey of the "capitalism controversy" by a research group committed to neither of the two conflicting schools of thought on the subject. There is an extensive bibliography.

1038. Tsushima Tadayuki 對 馬 忠 行 , Nihon shihonshugi ronsōshiron 日本資本主義論争史論 (Historical essays on the controversy over Japanese capitalism), Tōkyō, Kōdōsha, 1947, 361 pp.

One of the many works devoted to describing the long and complex controversy in Japanese academic circles over the interpretation of Japanese capitalism. The author is a partisan of the rōnō group.

1039. Uchida Jōkichi 内 田 穰 吉 , Nihon shihonshugi ronsō 日本資本主義論争 (The controversy over the interpretation of Japanese capitalism), Tōkyō, Shinkō Shuppansha, 1949, 2 v.

Perhaps the most detailed description of the bitter "capitalism dispute." Volume 1 covers the prewar period, volume 2 the postwar years. Volume 2 ends with an extensive bibliography on Japanese capitalism. The author is sympathetic to the kōza school.

1040. Yamada Moritarō 山 田 盛 太 郎 , Nihon shihonshugi bunseki 日本資本主義分析 (Analysis of Japanese capitalism), Tōkyō, Iwanami Shoten, 1934.

The chief work of an early leader of the kōza school of economic historians.

d. Agriculture

Most of the prewar generation of economic historians have surveyed the development of Japanese agriculture and agricultural technology. Their views are most accessible in general series such as the Nihon bunkashi taikei (Survey of Japanese cultural history) (Entry 731), the Heibonsha Nihonshi (History of Japan) (Entry 739), the Shinkō Dai Nihonshi (New lectures on the history of Japan) (Entry 744), and in the Nihon keizaishi jiten (Dictionary of Japanese economic history) (Entry 291). Since the war the agricultural economist Furushima Toshio has made brilliant contributions to the study of Japanese agricultural history. His work has unusual vitality owing to its combined use of library and field study techniques.

1041. Furushima Toshio 古 島 敏 雄 , Kinsei Nihon nōgyō no kōzō 近世日本農業の構造 (The structure of modern Japanese agriculture), Tōkyō, Nihon Hyōronsha, 1944, 18+619+26 pp.

Considered the outstanding work on agriculture and agriculturalists of the Tokugawa period. The author treats in detail the formation of the modern agricultural village, land holding, agricultural technology, crops, types of field, and the hikan (bound-tenant) system.

1042. Furushima Toshio 古 島 敏 雄, <u>Nihon hōken nōgyōshi</u> 日 本 封 建 農 業 史(History of Japanese feudal agriculture), Tōkyō, Shikai Shobō, 1941, 338 pp.

    An introductory survey of the development of Japanese agriculture and the life of the peasantry during the feudal period. The author, a specialist on agricultural technology, peasant society, and communal lands, draws his conclusions from numerous field studies.

1043. Furushima Toshio 古 島 敏 雄, <u>Nihon nōgakushi</u> 日 本 農 学 史 (History of Japanese agricultural science), Tōkyō, Nihon Hyōronsha, 1946, 563 pp.

    An authoritative study of the historical development of agricultural technology and theory in Japan up to the end of the Tokugawa period.

1044. Furushima Toshio 古 島 敏 雄, <u>Nihon nōgyō gijutsushi</u> 日 本 農 業 技 術 史 (History of Japanese agricultural technology), Tōkyō, Jichōsha, 1947-48, 2 v.

    The outstanding work on agricultural technology. Volume 1 covers the subject from primitive times to the beginning of the Tokugawa period. Volume 2 covers the Tokugawa period. Treatment is authoritative and extremely broad, embracing development in tools, crops, land use, fertilizers, irrigation, animal husbandry, silk industry, etc.

1045. Hōgetsu Keigo 宝 月 圭 吾, <u>Chūsei kangaishi no kenkyū</u> 中 世 灌 漑 史 の 研 究 (Studies in the history of irrigation during the middle ages), Tōkyō, Meguro Shoten, rev. ed., 1950, 376 pp.

    One of the few studies of the history of the development of irrigation systems in Japan. The author is especially interested in the relationship of feudal political authority and the development of irrigation. A member of the Tokyo University Historiographical Institute, he has used with success the wealth of historical materials in the Institute's library.

1046. Kimura Yasuji 木 村 靖 二, <u>Nihon nōgu hattatsushi</u> 日 本 農 具 発 達 史(The history of the development of agricultural implements in Japan), Tōkyō, Nōgyō to Kikaisha, 1936, 271 pp.

    Covers the history of the development of agricultural implements from prehistoric times to c. 1920.

1047. Kitamura Toshio 喜 多 村 俊 夫, <u>Nihon kangai suiri kankō no shiteki kenkyū</u> 日 本 灌 漑 水 利 慣 行 の 史 的 研 究 (Historical studies of Japanese irrigation and water control practices), Tōkyō, Iwanami Shoten, 1950, 3+6+503 pp.

    An outstanding analysis of the development of water control systems and the attendant problems of water rights and their administration. The author has drawn his material from a wide variety of sources and from extensive field studies. Emphasis is upon the Tokugawa period.

1048. Matsuyoshi Sadao 松 好 貞 夫, <u>Shinden no kenkyū</u> 新 田 の 研 究 (A study of reclaimed land), Tōkyō, Yūhikaku, 1936, 311+7 pp.

    A pioneer study of the relationship of reclaimed agricultural land to previously cultivated areas. Emphasis is on the Tokugawa period. The author develops the thesis that reclaimed land being less encumbered with feudal dues became the basis of capitalistic land ownership.

1049. Miyagawa Chiyozō 宮 川 千 代 蔵, <u>Nihon nōgyō hattatsu shi</u> 日 本 農 業 発 達 史 (History of the development of agriculture in Japan), Tōkyō, Seikatsusha, 1942.

    The author emphasizes the development of intensive fragmented agriculture in Japan.

1050. Morimoto Rokuji 森 本 六 爾, <u>Nihon nōkō bunka no kigen</u> 日 本 農 耕 文 化 の 起 源(The origins of agriculture in Japan), Tōkyō, Iga Shobō, rev. ed., 1946, 303 pp.

    A study of the origins of agricultural economy in Japan. The author bases his conclusions on an extensive analysis of archeological data.

1051. Ono Takeo 小 野 武 夫, <u>Nihon nōgyō kigen ron</u> 日 本 農 業 起 源 論 (On the origin of agriculture in Japan), Tōkyō, Nihon Hyōronsha, 1942, 393 pp.

    An important study of the problem of the origins of agricultural economy in Japan.

1052. Suzuki Naoji 鈴 木 直 二, <u>Beisaku no kenkyū</u> 米 作 の 研 究 (Study of rice production), Tōkyō, Ganshōdō, 1940, 387+16 pp.

    Part 1 covers the history of rice production technology. Part 2 describes recent Japanese technology in rice production. An index is appended.

1053. Takimoto Seiichi 瀧 本 誠 一, ed., <u>Dai Nihon nōshi</u> 大 日 本 農 史(History of Japanese agriculture), Tōkyō, Chūgai Shōgyō Shimpōsha, 1926, 1090 pp.

    This work is a revision of the early "official history" of agriculture compiled under the direction of the Nōshōmushō (Ministry of Agriculture and Commerce) in 1890-91. It is primarily a history of agricultural administration prior to 1868. The work serves mainly to bring together in chronological order a large quantity of documentary material.

e. Production, Industry and Technology

1) General

    The following works consist of two widely different types: 1) standard descriptive surveys of Japanese industrial and technological development, and 2) specialized studies of the so-called "manufacture problem." Among the first variety, the works by Nagusa Yasuhiro (Entry 1064) and Saigusa Hiroto (Entry 1065), when used in combination, should give fairly complete survey coverage of the field. Both are liberal in their citation of recommended reading. The "manufacture problem" is a by-product of the recent attempt of Japanese historians to assess the level of economic development attained by pre-modern Japan and to equate this to European stages of industrial development. Such speculation is chiefly confined to the Marxists such as Fujita Gorō, Hattori Shisō, Shinobu Seizaburō, and Horie Eiichi. Their studies deal primarily with the development of manufacturing in the transition period between Tokugawa and Meiji Japan.

1054. Dai Nihon Sanshikai 大 日 本 蚕 糸 会 (Raw Silk Association of Japan), Nihon sanshigyōshi 日 本 蚕 糸 業 史 (History of the Japanese raw silk industry), Tōkyō, Dai Nihon Sanshikai, 1935-36, 5 v.
A collection of topically arranged documents on the development of silk production in Japan. Volumes cover the following topics: 1) early history of silk culture; 2) silk reeling and trade; 3) silk worms, their types and cultivation; 4) mulberry cultivation, state policy with respect to silk culture; 5) technology, chronological tables, and index.

1055. Doboku Gakkai 土 木 学 会 (Civil Engineering Association), Meiji izen Nihon dobokushi 明 治 以 前 日 本 土 木 史 (History of public works in pre-Meiji Japan), Tōkyō, Doboku Gakkai, 1936, 1745+14 pp.
A monumental study of civil engineering works in pre-Meiji Japan. Chapters deal with waterways and water control, reclamation, irrigation, docks, harbors, roads, cities, castles, and technology. Documents are extensively quoted. The work is well illustrated and there is an extensive bibliography.

1056. Fujita Gorō 藤 田 五 郎, Nihon kindai sangyō no seisei 日 本 近 代 産 業 の 生 成 (The establishment of modern Japanese industry), Tōkyō, Nihon Hyōronsha, 2nd ed., 1948, 380 pp.
A technical analysis, from the Marxist point of view, of the development of modern industrial production in Japan. The introduction carries an analysis of previous studies in the field. An appendix provides an annotated list of source materials.

1057. Hattori Shisō 服 部 之 總 and Shinobu Seizaburō 信 夫 清 三 郎, Nihon manyufakuchua shiron 日 本 マ ニ ュ フ ァ ク チ ュ ア 史 論 (Essays on the history of Japanese manufacturing), Tōkyō, Ikuseisha, 1937, 254 pp.
Contains two technical studies of the development of the textile industry in Akita and Kurume during the late Tokugawa period. This work has served to document many of Hattori's theories concerning the Meiji Restoration.

1058. Horie Eiichi 堀 江 英 一, Nihon no manyufakuchua mondai 日 本 の マ ニ ュ フ ァ ク チ ュ ア 問 題 (The "manufacture problem" in Japan), Kyōto, San'ichi Shobō, 1949, 121 pp.
A Marxist discussion of the problems involved in determining the technological level of manufacturing techniques in pre-Meiji Japan.

1059. Horie Eiichi 堀 江 英 一, Gotō Yasushi 後 藤 靖, Nishijin kigyō no kenkyū 西 陣 機 業 の 研 究 (Studies of the Nishijin weaving industry), Tōkyō, Yūhikaku, 1950, 110 pp.
Significant studies of the craft industry of the Nishijin weavers of Kyoto.

1060. Ikeda Shōfū 池 田 嘯 風, Nihon yakugyōshi 日 本 薬 業 史 (History of the Japanese medicine industry), Kyōto, Kyōto Yakugyō Jironsha, 1929, 415 pp.
A standard survey of the production, sale, and use of drugs in Japan from earliest times to the time of writing. Emphasis is placed on the post-Restoration period.

1061. Kajinishi Mitsuhaya 楫 西 光 速, Nihon kindai mengyō no seiritsu 日 本 近 代 綿 業 の 成 立 (The establishment of Japan's modern cotton textile industry), Tōkyō, Kadokawa Shoten, 1949, 240 pp.
A study of the origins of Japan's modern textile industry. Part 1 deals with early cotton textile production during the middle ages and the Tokugawa period. Part 2 covers the development of machine weaving, Osaka as a textile center, and the penetration of world markets. Coverage is limited to the Meiji period. There is an appended list of selected reference works.

1062. Kōgakkai 工 学 会 (Engineering Association), Meiji kōgyōshi 明 治 工 業 史 (History of industry during the Meiji era), Tōkyō, Kōgakkai, 1925-31, 10 v.
A monumental collection of materials on the development of industry during the Meiji era. Volumes deal with the following subjects: 1) chemical industry, 2) shipbuilding, 3) railroads, 4) building industry, 5) electrical industry, 6) civil engineering, 7) armaments and steel, 8) mining, 9) machinery, 10) summary and index.

1063. Mori Kiichi 森 喜 一, Nihon kōgyō kōseishi 日 本 工 業 構 成 史 (History of Japanese industrial organization), Tōkyō, Itō Shoten, 1943, 5+380+9 pp.
An analysis of the changing patterns of industry and industrial organization in Japan since the Meiji Restoration.

1064. Nagusa Yasuhiro 南 種 康 博, Nihon kōgyōshi 日 本 工 業 史 (History of Japanese industry), Tōkyō, Chijin Shokan, 1942, 419 pp.
Published as part of the Taikan Nihon bunkashi sensho series (Entry 749). This work provides an excellent survey coverage of the entire field of industrial development in Japan. Part 1 deals with the premodern craft period. Part 2 covers recent developments going into such late industrial activities as aluminum and rayon production. There is an extensive list of suggested reading.

1065. Saigusa Hiroto 三 枝 博 音, <u>Gijutsushi</u> 技 術 史 (History of technology), Tōkyō, Tōyō Keizai Shimpōsha, 1940, 370+48 pp.
Published as volume 14 of the <u>Gendai Nihon bummeishi</u> series (Entry 722), this work presents a detailed analysis of the technological development of Japan after 1850. Chapters deal with shipbuilding, iron works, textiles, motive power, machines, railroads, telegraph, lighting, factories, mining, and technical training. Coverage is limited to the Meiji period. There is an excellent appended bibliography.

1066. Mikame Takako 三 瓶 孝 子, <u>Nihon mengyō hattatsushi</u> 日 本 綿 業 発 達 史(History of the development of the cotton textile industry in Japan), Tōkyō, Keiō Shobō, 1941, 514 pp.

1067. Shinobu Seizaburō 信 夫 清 三 郎, <u>Kindai Nihon sangyōshi josetsu</u> 近 代 日 本 産 業 史 序 説 (Introduction to the history of modern Japanese industrial production), Tōkyō, Nihon Hyōronsha, 1946, 359+12 pp.
A study of the development of modern industrial production in Japan from the end of the Tokugawa period through the early Meiji period. The author is a leading scholar of the Marxist school.

1068. Tamura Eitarō 田 村 榮 太 郎, <u>Nihon kōgyō bunkashi</u> 日 本 工 業 文 化 史(History of Japanese industrial development), Tōkyō, Kagakushugi Kōgyōsha, 1943, 789 pp.
A detailed description of various craft products and artifacts of the pre-modern period. The work covers vehicles, lamps, mine construction, household implements, cloth, civil engineering works, paper, printing, military implements, and machines of various kinds.

1069. Yamamoto Saburō 山 本 三 郎, <u>Nihon kindai gijutsushi</u> 日 本 近 代 技 術 史(History of Japanese technology in recent times), Tōkyō, Mikasa Shobō, 1940, 293 pp.
A survey of Japan's technological advance from the Tokugawa craft stage of production to the establishment of modern light and heavy industry. Chapters deal with silk, cotton, iron and steel, mining, and other industries. The author emphasizes Japan's success in catching up with the rest of the world in all fields of technology.

1070. Yokoi Isamu 横 井 勇, <u>Nihon chikkōshi</u> 日 本 築 港 史 (History of Japanese harbor construction), Tōkyō, Maruzen Shoten, 1927, 373 pp.
An factual survey of harbor construction in Japan from the twelfth century. Chief attention is given to the post-Restoration period.

1071. Yokoi Tokifuyu 横 井 時 冬, <u>Nihon kōgyōshi</u> 日 本 工 業 史 (History of Japanese industry), Tōkyō, Yoshikawa Kōbunkan, 1898, 359 pp.
A pioneer study of the pre-modern development of the productive crafts in Japan. The author concentrates his attention on technological change while neglecting the problems of production volume and quality.

1072. Zōsen Kyōkai 造 船 協 会 (Shipbuilding Association), <u>Nihon kinsei zōsenshi</u> 日 本 近 世 造 船 史 (History of modern shipbuilding in Japan), Tōkyō, Kōdōkan, 1911, 944 pp.
An early work dealing with the transition of the shipbuilding industry in Japan from the days of the Tokugawa shogunate to the early years of Meiji. It covers naval and civil ship construction, marine transportation, state control of shipping, technological training of workers, etc.

2. <u>Fishing</u>

1073. Habara Yūkichi 羽 原 又 吉, <u>Nihon gyogyō keizaishi</u> 日 本 漁 業 經 済 史(History of fishing economy in Japan), Tōkyō, Iwanami Shoten, 1952–.
Scheduled to run to several volumes, this series will provide the best coverage of the field when complete. The author, a member of the Fisheries Section of the Ministry of Agriculture and Forestry, bases his studies on the documentary collection being compiled by that section. The work provides detailed information on the history and development of fishing and fishing communities in Japan by region. Volume 1 covers the Kyūshū and Setonaikai areas.

1074. Habara Yūkichi 羽 原 又 吉, <u>Shina yushutsu Nihon kombugyō shihonshugishi</u> 支 那 輸 出 日 本 昆 布 業 資 本 主 義 史(A history of the capitalistic production of <u>kombu</u> for export to China), Tōkyō, Yūhikaku, 1940, 299+11 pp.
An important study of the production of dried seaweed for export to China during the Tokugawa and Meiji periods.

1075. Katayama Fusakichi 片 山 彦 吉, <u>Dai Nihon suisanshi</u> 大 日 本 水 産 史 (History of marine production in the Japanese empire), Tōkyō, Nogyō to Suisansha, 1937, 1102 pp.
This work is to date the foremost historical survey of fishing in Japan. Its special value lies in the large number of documentary sources it utilizes. Part 1 deals with the pre-Meiji period, and part 2 with the modern development of the fishing industry. There are nine pages of bibliography.

1076. Shimizu Hiroshi 清 水 弘 and Konuma Isamu 小 沼 勇, <u>Nihon gyogyō keizai hattatsushi josetsu</u> 日 本 漁 業 經 済 発 達 史 序 説(Introduction to the history of the development of fishing economy in Japan), Tōkyō, Chōryūsha, 1949, 284 pp.
An analysis of the development of fishing in Japan and the social and economic position of the fishing population. The authors are concerned primarily with the growth of capitalistic fishing techniques after 1868, the problems of industrial organization, and the condition of the labor force.

1077. Yamaguchi Kazuo 山 口 和 雄 , Nihon gyogyō keizaishi kenkyū 日本漁業經濟史研究 (Studies in the history of Japanese fishing economy), Tōkyō, Hokuryūkan, 1948, 380 pp.
    Collected essays on various aspects of the pre-modern fishing industry in Japan. The author, a former member of the Attic Museum staff, has emphasized the problem of disputes over fishing rights.

1078. Yamaguchi Kazuo 山 口 和 雄 , Nihon gyogyōshi 日 本 漁 業 史 (History of the Japanese fishing industry), Tōkyō, Seikatsusha, 1946, 349 pp.
    An extremely useful survey of the development of Japanese fishing. Emphasis is on the technological aspects of the industry. Chapters deal with individual varieties of fish and describe fishing methods from early times to the present.

3. Mining and Forestry

1079. Endō Yasutarō 遠 藤 安 太 郎 , Nihon sanrinshi 日 本 山 林 史 (History of Japanese mountains and forests), Tōkyō, Nihon Sanrinshi Kankōkai, 1934, 2 v.
    The author, a former member of the historical documents section of the Ministry of Forestry, has brought together a wealth of documentation on Japan's pre-modern protected forests (hogorin). Volume 1 contains documents on the origin and administration of such forests. Volume 2 contains illustrations and maps.

1080. Kōzan Konwakai 鑛 山 懇 話 会 (Mining Association), Nihon kōgyō hattatsushi 日 本 鑛 業 発 達 史 (History of the development of mining in Japan), Tōkyō, Kōzan Konwakai, 1932, 3 v.
    One of the most detailed studies of the recent development of mining in Japan. Chapters deal with metallurgy, iron refining, oil, safety measures, labor problems, and technology.

1081. Kuboyama Yūzō 久 保 山 雄 三 , Sekitan kōgyō hattatsushi 石 炭 鑛 業 発 達 史 (History of the development of coal mining), Tōkyō, Kōronsha, 1942, 468 pp.
    Covers the history of coal mining in Japan and her modern colonial possessions.

1082. Nishio Keijirō 西 尾 銈 次 郎 , Nihon kōgyō shiyō 日 本 鑛 業 史 要 (Principles of the history of Japanese mining), Jūichikumi Shuppambu, 1943, 188 pp.
    A brief survey of Japanese mining up to the Tokugawa period. The author discusses the sources for such a study in his introduction. The body of the work deals with the history and technology of mining during this early period.

1083. Shirakawa Taro 白 河 太 郎 , Teikoku rinseishi 帝 国 林 制 史 (History of the administration of Japanese forests), Tōkyō, Yūrindo, 1902, 265 pp.
    Based on documents submitted to the Ministry of Forestry by the several prefectures in 1881-82, this work is a documentary description of the development of Japanese forests during the Tokugawa period.

1084. Toba Masao 鳥 羽 正 雄 , Nihon ringyōshi 日 本 林 業 史 (History of Japanese forestry), Tōkyō, Yūzankaku, 1951, 238 pp.
    An analysis of forests and forestry in pre-modern Japan by an expert on the Tokugawa period. Sections include a general historical survey, studies of special forest products and their relationship to Japanese economy, government policies towards forest exploitation, etc. There is an appended chronological table and a bibliographical list.

f. Commerce and Trade

1) Merchants and Domestic Commerce

    The early generation of economic historians such as Honjō, Takekoshi, and Tsuchiya contributed a great deal to the general knowledge of commercial development in Japan. The standard economic histories published by these writers are still useful as introductions to the field. In succeeding years the pupils of these men began to work out detailed problems connected with the history of Japanese commerce. The immediate prewar historical series such as Heibonsha's Nihonshi (History of Japan) (Entry 739) and Nihon bunkashi taikei (Survey of Japanese cultural history) (Entry 731) contain the work of these younger specialists and are excellent for survey purposes.
    The following brief list of works is not in any way exhaustive but will serve to supplement the more general material just mentioned. Outstanding for their recent work in this field are Toyota Takeshi, whose specialty is the middle ages, and Miyamoto Mataji, a specialist in Tokugawa commerce. Miyamoto's Nihon shōgyōshi (History of commerce in Japan) (Entry 1089) is recommended as the best one-volume introduction. The appended guide to methodology and sources is particularly valuable.

1085. Kanno Wataro 菅 野 和 太 郎 , Nihon shōgyōshi 日 本 商 業 史 (History of commerce in Japan), Tōkyō, Nihon Hyōronsha, 1930, 352 pp.
    A general survey of the development of commercial activity in Japan from ancient times to the time of writing. Part 1 deals with the period of markets (ichi); part 2, with the period of guides and special privileges; part 3, with merchant economy, and part 4, occupying the last half of the work, covers the post-Restoration period. Emphasis is on domestic trade.

1086. Kanno Watarō 菅野 和太郎, Ōmi shōnin no kenkyū 近江商人の研究 (Study of the Ōmi merchants), Tōkyō, Yūhikaku, 1941, 329 pp.

The basic study of the most significant group of merchants in pre-modern Japan. The work covers the early origin of the Ōmi merchants during the Heian period and concludes with a description of the way in which they became the core of commercial activity during the Tokugawa period.

1087. Kōda Shigetomo 幸田 成友, Edo to Ōsaka 江戸と大阪 (Edo and Osaka), Tōkyō, Fuzambō, 1934, 333+14 pp.

A lively description of the development of Edo and Osaka as commercial centers during the Tokugawa period. Chapters cover municipal organizations, life of the cities, commercial and financial activity centering in the cities, trade in rice and oil, trade between Osaka and Edo, the guild system, etc. Much of this work has been translated in N. Smith, Materials on Japanese Social and Economic History: Tokugawa Japan (1), Tōkyō, The Asiatic Society of Japan, 1937.

1088. Miyamoto Mataji 宮本又次, Kabunakama no kenkyū 株仲間の研究 (Studies of the kabunakama), Tōkyō, Yūhikaku, 1938, 434+8 pp.

A detailed study of the guild system of Tokugawa Japan.

1089. Miyamoto Mataji 宮本又次, Nihon shōgyōshi 日本商業史 (History of commerce in Japan), Tōkyō, Ryūginsha, 1949, 310 pp.

A detailed survey of the commercial history of Japan from ancient times to the time of writing. The appendix (pp. 285-310) is a guide to sources and methodology for the study of Japanese commercial history and provides an excellent introduction to the subject. A 1943 edition of this work contains certain sections on foreign trade which are missing in the 1949 edition.

1090. Rekishi Chiri Gakkai 歴史地理学界 (Historical Geography Society), Nihon shōninshi 日本商人史 (History of Japanese merchants), Tōkyō, Rekishichiri Gakkai, 1925, 372 pp.

A special issue of Rekishi chiri, it contains articles covering the entire span of pre-modern commercial development. Contributions are by such prominent scholars of the 20s as: Miura Kaneyuki (General survey), Nishioka Toranosuke (Heian merchants); Aida Jirō (Merchants in the middle ages), Nakamura Kōya (Tokugawa policy towards merchants), Fujii Jintarō (Early Meiji), Kōda Shigetomo (Hyōgo and Osaka in early Meiji), etc.

1091. Toyota Takeshi 豊田武, Chūsei Nihon shōgyōshi no kenkyū 中世日本商業史の研究 (Studies of the history of commerce in the middle ages), Tōkyō, Iwanami Shoten, 1944, 386 pp.

Basic studies of the guild system of the thirteenth through sixteenth centuries in Japan. A revised edition was published in 1952.

1092. Toyota Takeshi 豊田武, Nihon shōninshi, chūsei-hen 日本商人史, 中世篇 (History of Japanese merchants, the middle ages), Tōkyō, Tōkyōdō, 1949, 282 pp.

A survey of commercial activity during the thirteenth through sixteenth centuries in Japan by the leading authority on the subject.

2) Foreign Trade

The field of foreign trade has remained the domain of rather narrow specialists in Japan. Thus few general surveys of the field are to be found. Perhaps the best sources of general information on foreign trade are contained in the prewar historical series, particularly the Nihon bunkashi taikei (Survey of Japanese cultural history) (Entry 731). The works listed below include a few of the more general monographs on Japanese foreign trade. They should be supplemented in part by the works on foreign relations listed in Section 5 f above.

1093. Ishii Takashi 石井孝, Bakumatsu bōekishi no kenkyū 幕末貿易の研究 (A study of foreign trade during the last days of the shogunate), Tōkyō, Nihon Hyōronsha, 1944, 526+7 pp.

An important study of Japan's foreign trade during the critical years following the opening of Japanese ports in 1858.

1094. Itazawa Takeo 板澤武雄, Nichi-Ran bōekishi 日蘭貿易史 (History of Japanese-Dutch trade), Tōkyō, Heibonsha, 1949, 144 pp.

A slender volume packed with information on the Dutch trade with Japan. The author uses both Dutch and Japanese sources, and presents useful descriptions of the type and volume of goods traded and the trading methods used. He adds little, however, to the descriptions by Kaempfer, Murdoch, and Boxer.

1095. Kaneshiro Yōsuke 金城陽介, Nihon kaizoku shiwa 日本海賊史話 (Historical discussion of Japanese piracy), Tōkyō, Daishinsha, 1937, 267 pp.

1096. Kawashima Motojirō 川島元次郎, Shuinbune bōekishi 朱印船貿易史 (History of shuinbune trade), Tōkyō, Naigai Shuppan K.K., 1921, 616 pp.

A detailed description of the shuinbune period of Japanese trade (late Ashikaga and early Tokugawa). The author describes the system of "red seal" licenses, the ships, their crews and navigation methods, their cargoes, etc. The work terminates with descriptions of the lives and activities of twenty famous shuinbune traders.

1097. Mori Katsumi 森 克己, Nissō bōeki no kenkyū 日宋 貿易の研究 (Studies of trade between Japan and Sung China), Tōkyō, Kokuritsu Shoin, 1948, 574 pp.
   An exhaustive and scholarly study of trade relations between Japan and Sung China. The author treats trade routes, both land and sea, the mechanics of trade, government policies, controls, duties, goods and their volume, social and economic effects of trade. The coverage is from 834 to 1368.

1098. Murakami Naojirō 村上 直次郎, Bōekishijō no Hirado 貿易史上の平戸 (Hirado as a trading center), Tōkyō, Nihon Gakujutsu Fukyūkai, 1917, 131+50 pp.
   The leading study in Japanese of a subject well covered by Western sources.

1099. Murata Shirō 村田 四郎, Bahansenshi 八幡船史 (History of the bahansen), Takamatsu, Sōgabō, 1943, 23+298+10 pp.
   A detailed study of the activity of the Japanese freebooters who operated in the China Seas during the sixteenth century.

1100. Obata Atsushi 小葉田 淳, Chūsei Nankai tsūkō bōekishi no kenkyū 中世南海通交貿易史の研究 (Studies of the trade with the South Seas areas during the middle ages), Tōkyō, Nihon Hyōronsha, 1939, 538+14 pp.
   Part 1 deals with Japan's trade and political relations with the Ryukyu Islands; part 2 covers Ryukyuan relations with Ming China; and part 3 deals with trade to the South Seas. The work is based on primary sources.

1101. Takekoshi Yosaburō 竹越 與三郎, Wakōki 倭寇記 (The story of the wakō), Tōkyō, Hakuyōsha, rev. ed., 1939, 10+384 pp.
   A general account of the origin of the wakō and Japanese participation in freebooting activities during the thirteenth to fifteenth centuries. The work ends with an analysis of the licensed trade with China carried on by the coalition of the Ashikaga forces, the temples, the court, and merchant houses.

1102. Tokumasu Eitarō 德增 策太郎, Nihon bōekishi 日本貿易史 (History of Japanese foreign trade), Kyōto, Genrin Shobō, 1948, 282 pp.
   A survey of Japanese foreign trade from early times to the present.

1103. Toyama Usaburō 外山 卯三郎, Nippo bōeki shōshi 日葡貿易小史 (Short history of Japanese-Portuguese trade), Tōkyō, Wakai Hitosha, 1942.
   A study based largely on the work of Charles Boxer.

1104. Tsurumi Sakio 鶴見 左吉雄, Nihon bōekishikō 日本貿易史綱 (Outline history of Japanese trade), Tōkyō, Ganshōdō Shoten, 1939, 21+732+58 pp.
   Perhaps the best introductory survey of the modern period. The work is divided into five sections: pre-Meiji, 1869-95, 1895-1906, 1906-18, 1918 to c. 1930. Treatment is interpretive with a minimum of tables and figures in the text. Significant tables and graphs are appended. There is an index.

1105. Yamaguchi Kazuo 山口 和雄, Bakumatsu bōekishi 幕末貿易史 (History of foreign trade at the end of the shogunate), Tōkyō, Seikatsusha, 1947, 380 pp.
   An important analysis of the nature and impact of foreign trade during the years immediately after the signing of the first commercial treaties (1858). The author is particularly concerned with the social and political repercussions of the rise in commodity prices and the growth of commercial farming which resulted from the opening of the ports.

g. Finance

   Government publications predominate in the field of public finance and currency. Standard sources for Japan's pre-modern and early modern finance are the semi-official Suijinroku (Entry 1113) and the Ministry of Finance histories of Meiji and Taisho finance (Entries 1115 and 1116). For modern analytical studies of national and local finance the works of Fujita Takeo and Hijikata Seibi used together offer ample coverage.
   Works on currency are numerous and generally well illustrated. The standard source is the Finance Ministry's Dai Nihon kaheishi (History of Japanese money) (Entry 1117), although Kusama's Sanka zui (Illustrated encyclopedia of coinage) (Entry 1119) is more easily used. Both works are chiefly chronologies of government minting operations. Hence, while they provide detailed numismatic data, they offer little information on the actual circulation of coins and their function as currency.

1) General

1106. Fujita Takeo 藤田 武夫, Nihon chihō zaisei seido no seiritsu 日本地方財政制度の成立 (Establishment of local financial institutions in Japan), Tōkyō, Iwanami Shoten, 1941.
   A detailed study of the development of modern local financial organs in Japan between 1850 and 1888.

1107. Fujita Takeo 藤田 武夫, Nihon chihō zaisei hattenshi 日本地方財政発展史 (History of the development of local financial institutions), Tōkyō, Kawade Shobō, 1949, 694 pp.
   This work continues the coverage of the previous entry and brings it up to 1940.

1108. Fujita Takeo 藤田 武夫, Nihon shihonshugi to zaisei 日本資本主義と財政 (Capitalism and finance in Japan), Tōkyō, Jitsugyō no Nihonsha, 1949, 2 v.
   A history of Japan's public finance beginning with the reform of the land-tax laws in 1873 and continuing through the late 1930s.

122   A GUIDE TO JAPANESE REFERENCE AND RESEARCH MATERIALS

1109. Hagino Yoshiyuki 萩野由之, Nihon zaiseishi 日本財政史 (History of finance in Japan), Tōkyō, Hakubunkan, 1890, 274 pp.
A pioneer survey of the finances of the governmental institutions in Japan from early times to the Restoration.

1110. Hijikata Seibi 土方成美, Zaiseishi 財政史 (History of finance), Tōkyō, Tōyō Keizai Shimpōsha, 1940, 595 pp.
Volume 6 of the Gendai Nihon bummeishi series (Entry 722), this work is divided into two parts. Part 1 presents a general survey of the development of Japanese public finance after 1868 under the influence of the policy of military expansion. Part 2 is a non-technical analysis of national expenditures, taxes, public bond issues, and local finance. Presentation is factual and balanced.

1111. Hijikata Seibi 土方成美, Nihon zaisei no hattatsu 日本財政の発達 (The development of Japanese finance), Tōkyō, Tonan Shobō, 1943, 546 pp.
A survey of finance in Japan from the eighth century through the 1930s. Approximately half the book deals with the post-1868 period. The early portion is little more than an economic history with emphasis on taxation and financial institutions. The latter half is more specifically concerned with finance.

1112. Honjō Eijirō 本庄榮治郎, Nihon zaiseishi 日本財政史 (History of Japanese finance), Tōkyō, Kaizōsha, 1926, 285 pp.
A somewhat elementary introduction to the history of public finance in Japan with emphasis on taxation. The author covers the subject from early times to the Meiji period. The work is most useful for its extensive documentation.

1113. Katsu Kaishū 勝海舟, Suijinroku 吹塵録, Tōkyō, Ōkurashō, 1890, 35 v.
An important source of documentation for the study of Tokugawa finances. The work consists of classified documents taken from public and private sources.

1114. Kazahaya Yasoji 風早八十二, Nihon zaiseiron 日本財政論 (A treatise on Japanese finance), Tōkyō, Mikasa Shobō, 1947.
A Marxist analysis of Japan's modern financial structure by a Communist Party member.

1115. Meiji Zaiseishi Hensankai 明治財政史編纂会, Meiji zaiseishi 明治財政史 (History of finance during the Meiji era), Tōkyō, Maruzen Shoten, 1904-5, 15 v.
A work of encyclopedic proportions covering Japanese public finance, budgeting, taxes, national income, government monopolies, public aid and relief currency, banking, etc., from 1868 to 1902. There is an index.

1116. Ōkurashō 大藏省 (Ministry of Finance), Meiji-Taishō zaiseishi 明治大正財政史 (History of finance during the Meiji and Taisho eras), Tōkyō, Hakutōsha, 1936-40, 20 v.
A continuation of the previously listed work covering the years 1903-25. Volumes are devoted to the following subjects: 1) Introduction and financial institutions, 2) the system of accounting, 3-5) budget, 6-7) domestic taxes, 8) customs, 9-10) monopolies, 11-12) state bonds, 13) currency, 14-16) banks, 17) credit, 18-19) finance abroad, 20) miscellaneous.

2) Currency

1117. Honjō Eijirō 本庄榮治郎, ed., Dai Nihon kaheishi 大日本貨幣史 (History of Japanese money), Tōkyō, Chōyōkai, 1925-26, 8 v.
A revision of the standard work on pre-modern currency in Japan. The work was originally published by the Ministry of Finance in 1876-77 and covers the history of Japanese currency from its origins up to 1872. It is elaborately illustrated. The text consists mainly of chronologically arranged quotations from primary documentary sources. Concluding chapters contain materials on investment, finance, commodity prices, and fluctuation in value of gold and silver.

1118. Obata Atsushi 小葉田淳, Nihon kahei ryūtsūshi 日本貨幣流通史 (History of Japanese monetary circulation), Tōkyō, Tōkō Shoin, 1931, 450 pp.
One of the pioneer interpretive studies of monetary circulation in Japan. The author covers only the period from the fourteenth century to the middle of the seventeenth, in other words, the period of Chinese currency in Japan and the establishment of a national currency in the early Tokugawa period. The work is scholarly and copiously documented. A revised edition appeared in 1943.

1119. Kusama Naokata 草間直方, Sanka zui 三貨図彙 (Illustrated encyclopedia of coinage), Tōkyō, Hakutōsha, 1932, 1246 pp.
A much used illustrated history of old Japanese coins. Illustrations are largely rubbings of the surface of coins. Primary descriptive sources are quoted along with each illustration.

1120. Maruyama Kiyoyasu 丸山清廉, Hōken shakai no tsūka mondai 封建社会の通貨問題 (Problems of currency in feudal society), Tōkyō, Hakuyōsha, 1939, 288 pp.
An analytical study of the circulation and use of coins during various stages of development of feudal society in Japan. Chapters deal with currency in early feudal society, the establishment of the shōen and the spread of currency, the development of the use of money and the middle feudal period, late feudalism and the unification of currency. There is an appended bibliography.

1121. Ōsaka Ryōgaeshō Kumiai 大阪両替商組合, ed., Ryōgaeshō enkakushi 両替商沿革史
(History of money-changing houses), Ōsaka, Ōsaka Ryōgaeshō Kumiai, 1903, 2 v.
  A standard documentary treatment.

1122. Takimoto Seiichi 瀧本誠一, Nihon kaheishi 日本貨幣史 (History of Japanese currency),
Tōkyō, Kokushi Kōshūkai, 1923, 238 pp.
  An introductory survey history of old coins, their physical properties, dates of issue, etc. Emphasis is
  upon the Tokugawa period.

1123. Tsukamoto Toyojirō 塚本豊次郎, Nihon kaheishi tsuketari kinzakō 日本貨幣史附金座考
(History of Japanese money with an appended commentary on gold coinage), Tōkyō, Zaisei Keizai Gakkai, 1923,
254 pp.
  A survey history of coinage in Japan. Part 1 of the main section deals with the pre-Restoration period.
  Part 2 covers Meiji and Taisho Japan. Part 3 is a bibliography. The appendix is a detailed analysis of
  the Tokugawa Gold Guild (kinza), its method of operation, and its minting techniques.

3) Banking, Credit, and Exchange

1124. Iibuchi Keitarō 飯淵敬太郎, Nihon shin'yō taikei zenshi 日本信用大系前史 (Background history of the credit system in Japan), Tōkyō, Gakusei Shobō, 1948, 194 pp.
  An analysis of the growth of finance capital in Japan from the late Tokugawa to early Meiji periods and
  the effect of Meiji land reforms on land tenure and capital accumulation.

1125. Ishibashi Tanzan 石橋湛山, Nihon kin'yūshi 日本金融史 (History of Japanese banking), Tōkyō,
Kaizōsha, 1936, 302 pp.
  The history of Japan's modern banking and finance systems. Part 1 deals with the financial troubles of
  the early Meiji period and the establishment of the silver standard. Part 2 covers the period from the
  establishment of the gold standard in 1897 to World War I. Part 3 covers the years from World War I
  to 1927 and the world depression.

1126. Kurusu Takeo 栗栖赳夫, Nihon kinyū seido hattatsu no kenkyū 日本金融制度発達の
研究 (Study of the development of the Japanese financial system), Tōkyō, Keimeisha, 1929, 218 pp.
  A general survey of Japanese financial systems from the eighth century to the time of writing.

1127. Matsuyoshi Sadao 松好貞夫, Nihon ryōgae kinyū shiron 日本両替金融史論 (His-
torical essays on money changing and banking in Japan), Tōkyō, Bungei Shunjūsha, 1932, 447+26 pp.
  The author is an expert on Tokugawa finance.

1128. Nomura Junnosuke 野村順之助, Nihon kinyū shihon hattatsushi 日本金融資本発達史
(History of the development of Japanese finance capital), Tōkyō, Kyōseikaku, 1931, 329 pp.
  A materialistic view of the development of Japan's post-Meiji financial system.

1129. Okada Sumio 岡田純夫, Hompō ginkō hattatsushi 本邦銀行発達史 (History of the development of Japanese banks), Tōkyō, Shibun Shoin, 1932, 253 pp.

1130. Sakairi Chōtarō 坂入長太郎, Nihon kinyū seidoshi 日本金融制度史 (History of credit
and banking in Japan), Tōkyō, Sekai Shoin, 1950, 460 pp.
  Covers the period 1868 to 1950.

1131. Shirai Kiku 白井規矩, Nihon no kinyū kikan—sono seisei to hatten 日本の金融機関—
其の生成と発展 (Japanese credit and banking facilities—their establishment and growth), Tōkyō,
Moriyama Shoten, 1937, 2+2+20+383 pp.
  Covers Japanese banking systems from the beginning of the Tokugawa period. Emphasis is placed upon
  the post-1868 phase of development.

4) Prices

1132. Honjō Eijirō 本庄榮治郎, Tokugawa bakufu no beika chōsetsu 徳川幕府の米価調節
(The control of the price of rice by the Tokugawa shogunate), Kyōto, Kōbundō, 1924, 414 pp.
  An important study of the efforts of the Tokugawa shogunate to control rice prices. The work was first
  published in 1916 under the title Edo bakufu no beika chōsetsu. A table of rice prices during the Tokugawa period is appended.

1133. Morimoto Sō 森本宋, Shika hendō no kenkyū 糸価変動の研究 (Studies in the fluctuation of
silk prices), Yokohama, Yokohama Bōeki Shimpōsha, 1926, 370 pp.

1134. Nakazawa Benjirō 中澤辨次郎, Nihon beika hendōshi 日本米価変動史 (History of fluctuation of rice prices in Japan), Tōkyō, Meibundō, 1933, 552 pp.
  A detailed study of the fluctuation of rice prices together with the factors affecting such changes. Coverage is from earliest times to the time of writing. The second half of the book is devoted to tables.

1135. Ōta Kasaku 太田嘉作, Meiji-Taishō-Shōwa beika seisakushi 明治.大正.昭和.米價政策史 (A history of the policy regarding rice prices during the Meiji, Taisho, and Showa eras), Maruyamasha, 1938, 1287 pp.

Part 1 discusses the fluctuation of rice prices since the beginning of Meiji (1868) and attempts to analyze the causes of such fluctuation. Part 2 discusses government policy with respect to rice prices.

h. Communications

No complete survey of the history of communications in Japan has yet been written. Of the following works Mitsui Takaharu's Nihon kotsu bunkashi (Cultural history of transportation in Japan) (Entry 1139) is recommended as an introduction to the pre-1868 aspects of the subject. For the subsequent development of modern communications in Japan, the lack of adequate survey material presents the scholar with the necessity of referring to a number of detailed specialized works. The following list includes only two of a large number of such works: The Ministry of Communications' Teishin jigyōshi (History of achievements in communications) (Entry 1146) and the Railroad Ministry's Nihon tetsudōshi (History of railroads in Japan) (Entry 1147).

1136. Aida Jirō 相田二郎, Chūsei no sekisho 中世の関所 (Barriers in the middle ages), Tōkyō, Unebi Shobō, 1943, 554+21 pp.

An important collection of studies of the sekisho (barriers) of the Kamakura and Ashikaga periods.

1137. Aoe Shū 青江秀, Dai Nihon Teikoku ekitei shiko 大日本帝国驛遞志稿 (Draft history of Japanese post stations), Tōkyō, Chūgai Shōgyō Shimpōsha, 1926-27. [= Nihon sangyō shiryō taikei (Compendium of materials on Japanese industry), vol. 10].

Originally published in 1881, this work was compiled under government sponsorship. Part 1 covers the history of the development of post stations and roads in Japan from early times to the Meiji period. Part 2 deals with conditions of travel, official communications, etc. The style is old fashioned, the body of the work being largely a chronological ordering of related source materials. Though it is the first modern work on the subject, it is still useful.

1138. Hibata Sekko 干潟畑雪湖, Nihon kōtsū shiwa 日本交通史話 (Historical discussion of transportation in Japan), Tōkyō, Yūzankaku, 1937, 210 pp.

Originally written as part of the Fūzokushi kōza series (Entry 1293), this work describes travelers, travel facilities, and travel conditions from the time of the Taika Reform (645) to early Meiji. Emphasis is on land travel.

1139. Mitsui Takaharu 三井高陽, Nihon kōtsū bunkashi 日本交通文化史 (Cultural history of transportation in Japan), Tōkyō, Chijin Shokan, 1942, 239 pp.

Perhaps the most useful introductory book in the field, this work is a simply written survey of the development of transportation from early times to Meiji. Of special value is the selective annotated bibliography. Published as part of the Taikan Nihon bunkashi sensho (Entry 749).

1140. Nihon Rekishi Chiri Gakkai 日本歴史地理学会 (the Japanese Society of Historical Geography), Nihon kōtsū shiron 日本交通史論 (Essays on the history of Japanese transportation), Tōkyō, Nihon Gakujutsu Fukyūkai, 1925, 686 pp. [Special issue of Rekishi chiri (v. 57, no. 4)].

Contains articles by a number of historians covering the following aspects of the history of sea and land transportation in Japan: road systems in ancient Japan (Sakamoto Tarō), transportation between Japan and China (Kimiya Yasuhiko, Mori Katsumi), Geography and transportation of Ōmi (Nakagawa Senzō), wakō (Akiyama Kenzō), honjin (Katada Eizaemon), Korean railroads (Tabohashi Kiyoshi).

1141. Ōshima Nobujirō 大島延次郎, Nihon kōtsūshi 日本交通史 (History of transportation in Japan), Tōkyō, Shikai Shobō, 1942, 10+400 pp.

A chronological survey of the development of land transport in pre-modern Japan.

1142. Ōshima Nobujirō 大島延次郎, Nihon Kōtsūshi ronsō 日本交通史論叢 (Collected essays on the history of Japanese transportation), Tōkyō, Kokusai Kōtsū Bunka Kyōkai, 1939, 468 pp.

A collection of essays on Japanese land and water transportation. The author is a specialist in the northern (Ōu) region. Essays vary from general survey histories to specific studies of transport, barriers, and post stations. The work ends with a survey of the modernization of transport after the Meiji Restoration.

1143. Ōyama Shikitarō 大山敷太郎, Kinsei kōtsū keizai shiron 近世交通經済史論 (Historical treatise on the economics of modern transportation), Tōkyō, Kokusai Kōtsū Bunka Kyōkai, 1941.

An excellent survey of the growth and development of communications and transportation during the Tokugawa period.

1144. Sakamoto Tarō 坂本太郎, Jōdai ekisei no kenkyū 上代驛制の研究 (A study of post stations in the ancient period), Tōkyō, Shibundō, 1928, 271 pp.

An important monograph on the problem of the origin and development of post-roads in Japan.

1145. Sumita Masaichi 住田正一, Kaijō unsō shiron 海上運送史論 (Essays on the history of marine transportation), Tōkyō, Ganshōdō Shoten, 1925, 230 pp.

A survey of marine transportation, its technological development, and the laws governing it, from early times through the Tokugawa period.

1146. Teishinshō 逓信省 (Ministry of Communications), Teishin jigyōshi 逓信事業史 (History of achievements in communications), Tōkyō, Teishinshō, 1940-44, 7 v.
    The basic source on the development of communications since the end of the Tokugawa period. It combines the work of a large number of experts. Separate volumes deal with the postal service, telegraph, telephone, postal savings, air transportation, etc.

1147. Tetsudōshō 鉄道省 (Railroad Ministry), Nihon tetsudōshi 日本鉄道史 (History of railroads in Japan), Tōkyō, Tetsudōshō, 1921, 3 v.
    The official history of the first fifty years of railroad development in Japan.

1148. Watanabe Eizaburō 渡部英三郎, Nihon rikuun shi 日本陸運史 (History of Japanese land transportation), Tōkyō, Keizai Tosho K.K., 1943, 490 pp.
    A survey of the development of land transportation in Japan from early times to the end of the Tokugawa period.

7. SOCIAL HISTORY

The majority of the works listed below have been written, not by sociologists, but by legal or economic historians. Historians with sociological or anthropological training have only begun to make their appearance in Japan. And as yet no sociologist or ethnologist, of which there are many, has written a general survey of the historical development of Japanese society. The first writers in the field of Japanese social history were legalists such as Miura Kaneyuki, Maki Kenji, and Takigawa Masajirō. To them we owe the systematic differentiation of classes and social groups based on the study of pre-modern laws and administrative codes. These men were followed by the economic historians of the 1920s such as Honjō Eijirō, Tsuchiya Takao, Kokusho Iwao, and Nomura Kanetarō, in whose writings social change was largely linked to economic change. The works of Marxist scholars of the period after 1930 were also socio-economic in nature, although they were rarely published as social histories. For instance, Hayakawa Jirō's history of Japan (Entry 688) differs little in form from the so-called social histories of the economic school, though it departs from them in theory. Since World War II the "progressive" school of Marxist historians has been extremely active in the field of Japanese social history. Their most characteristic work to date is the Shakai kōseishi taikei (Comprehensive outline of the history of social structures) (Entry 1156).

Beginning with the 1930s, ethnologists and sociologists began to move into the historical field. However, most of their work is as yet of a specialized and fragmentary nature. One of the few ethnologists to write a general history of Japan is Wakamori Tarō (Entry 718). Because of this lack of survey literature from a sociological or ethnological point of view, a number of bibliographical sections have been added below to cover such subjects as the history of social structure, family and communal groups, social problems, and the life and pastimes of the Japanese people. The reader will wish also to refer to the sections on socio-economic systems in Chapter 6 c above.

a. Survey Histories

1149. Honjō Eijirō 本庄榮治郎, Nihon shakaishi 日本社会史 (History of Japanese society), Tōkyō, Kaizōsha, 1924, 269 pp.
    An early and overly simplified analysis of the changing social structure of Japan from early times to the first part of the Meiji period. Changes are explained in terms of economic movements. Treatment is by periods. Within each period the author discusses political and social organizations, social classes, and economic and political problems.

1150. Honjō Eijirō 本庄榮治郎, Nihon shakai keizaishi 日本社会経済史 (History of Japanese society and economics), Tōkyō, Kaizōsha, 1928, 634 pp.
    A reprint of the author's Nihon shakaishi (Entry 1149) together with his Nihon zaiseishi.

1151. Kada Tetsuji 加田哲二, Shakaishi 社会史 (History of society), Tōkyō, Tōyō Keizai Shimpōsha, 1940, 493 pp. [= v. 11 of the Gendai Nihon bummeishi (Entry 722)].
    The author, a specialist in modern intellectual history, traces the development of Japanese society since the Tokugawa period. Chapters deal with the nature and collapse of Tokugawa social structure, the emergence of a new class configuration, the formation of capitalistic society, the reestablishment of "Japanese society." The work is primarily a political history of modern Japan with emphasis on class struggles and social forces.

1152. Miura Kaneyuki 三浦周行, Kokushijō no shakai mondai 国史上の社会問題 (Social problems in Japanese history), Tōkyō, Daitōkan, 1920, 364 pp.
    A pioneer work which did much to direct the attention of Japanese scholars to the problems of social history. It is largely a study of economic factors underlying the position of social classes in Japanese history. The work was republished in 1938 by the Sōgensha.

1153. Nakamura Kichiji 中村吉治, Nihon shakaishi gaisetsu 日本社会史概説 (Outline history of Japanese society), Tōkyō, Usui Shobō, 1949, 336 pp.
    One of the best surveys of Japanese socio-political history. The author, a specialist in Japanese feudal institutions, has a more sociological approach than most writers in the field. This work is especially valuable for its analysis of the social structure of the feudal age in Japan.

1154. Takigawa Masajirō 瀧川政次郎, Nihon shakaishi 日本社会史 (Social history of Japan), Tōkyō, Tōkō Shoin, 1929, 377 pp.

A static and legalistic analysis of the class structure of Japanese society from early times to the Meiji period. All classes in existence in each period in Japanese history are examined in detail. The author documents his study extensively. This work created a stir in academic circles. The author's answer to his critics is contained in the following entry.

1155. Takigawa Masajirō 瀧川政次郎, Rekishi to shakaisoshiki 歴史と社会組織 (History and social organization), Ishihama Tomoyuki 石浜知行, Rekishi to keizaisoshiki 歴史と経済組織 (History and economic organization), Tōkyō, Kyōritsusha, 1931, 245 pp.

The first half of this work consists of an interpretive essay in which Takigawa develops his concept of social history, classes and their interrelationships in Japan, the clan nature of Japanese society, etc. In it he also attempts to answer critics of his previous work (see previous entry).

1156. Watanabe Yoshimichi 渡部義通 and others, Shakai kōseishi taikei 社会構成史大系 (Comprehensive outline of the history of social structures), Tōkyō, Nihon Hyōronsha, 1949—.

An ambitious series of essays on the order of the Iwanami Nihon rekishi series (Entry 725). It contains lengthy pamphlets concerning the social, political, and economic problems of Japan, China, and Europe. Contributors are for the most part members of the postwar "progressive" school. More than a third of the essays deal with Japan. Many of them are well documented.

b. Family and Social Organization

The family, its structure, and its position in the community has been of central importance for the understanding of Japanese society. Literature on this subject is quite extensive and results from the work of a number of distinct schools of approach. The works in the following brief list have been selected to illustrate these various approaches. Hozumi Shigetō represents the school of legal historians. Fukuo Takeichirō (Entry 1157) is a product of the folkloristic school which acknowledges Yanagida Kunio as its head. Toda Teizō (Entry 1164), a sociologist, is concerned primarily with the internal structure of the family. Tamaki Hajime (Entry 1162) approaches the subject as an economic determinist. A postwar development in the field is the school of the sociology of law which seeks to combine the disciplines of law and sociology. The works of Kawashima Takeyoshi (Entry 1160) and Wagatsuma Sakae (Entry 1165) are characteristic of this new group.

1157. Fukuo Takeichirō 福尾猛市郎, Nihon kazoku seidoshi 日本家族制度史 (History of the Japanese family system), Tōkyō, Ōyashima Shuppan, 1948, 6+230 pp.

A clearly written descriptive history of the development of the Japanese family from prehistoric times to the twentieth century. The treatment is chronological. The work is unannotated. The 1951 edition published by the Yoshikawa Kōbunkan contains an index.

1158. Furushima Toshio 古島敏雄, Kazoku keitai to nōgyō no hattatsu 家族形態と農業の発達 (Family structure and the development of agriculture), Tōkyō, Gakusei Shobō, 1947, 184 pp.

An important study of the relationship of the family system and agricultural technology by a leading agricultural economist. Coverage is from earliest times to the Meiji period.

1159. Hozumi Shigetō 穂積童遠 and Nakagawa Zennosuke 中川善之助, Kazoku seido zenshū 家族制度全集 (Series on the family system), Tōkyō, Kawade Shobō, 1937, 10 v.

1160. Kawashima Takeyoshi 川島武宜, Nihon shakai no kazokuteki kōsei 日本社会の家族的構成 (The familial structure of Japanese society), Tōkyō, Gakusei Shobō, 1948, 4+207 pp.

A significant study of the nature of Japanese society and its family basis by a pioneer scholar of the "sociology of law" school. Chapters deal with the family system and Japanese society, law as an expression of the family system, conflict between state law and common law, the new Constitution and the family, actual and legal marriage practices, etc.

1161. Sunagawa Kan'ei 砂川寛襯, Nihon kazoku seidoshi kenkyū 日本家族制度史研究 (Historical study of the Japanese family system), Tōkyō, Chūbunkan, 1925, 285+66 pp.

A legalistic description of the evolution of the family system from ancient times to the twentieth century. The author, a sociologist, makes certain comparisons with family systems in Europe and America. The work is well documented; there is an index.

1162. Tamaki Hajime 玉城肇, Kazoku seido no rekishi 家族制度の歴史 (History of the family system), Tōkyō, Itō Shoten, 1946, 65 pp.

A Marxist view of the evolution of the family system in Japan.

1163. Tamaki Hajime 玉城肇, Nihon kazoku seido hihan 日本家族制度批判 (Critique of the Japanese family system), Tōkyō, Fukuda Shobō, 1934, 340 pp.

An analysis of the influence of the Meiji Restoration on the Japanese family system. An appendix carries studies of the economic basis of patriarchy and an analysis of social statistics.

1164. Toda Teizō 戸田貞三, Kazoku kōsei 家族構成 (Family structure), Tōkyō, Kōbundō Shobō, 1942, 606 pp.

A standard work by a leading sociologist on the Japanese family system. The author is particularly concerned with the evolution of the structure of the family.

1165. Wagatsuma Sakae 我 妻 榮 , Ie no seido 家 の 制 度 (The family system), Tōkyō, Kantōsha, 1948, 300 pp.

c. Communal Organizations: Village and Cooperative Life

Beyond the family, various types of communal groups have functioned as fundamental units within Japanese society. Prior to 1935, investigation of the historical aspects of this subject was carried on primarily by legal historians and folklorists. The former tended to confine themselves to the legally enforced cooperative groups, such as the goningumi, while the latter were interested chiefly in groups of a somewhat unusual sociological nature. Over-all consideration of the village community was first undertaken by the great economic historian Ono Takeo. His Nihon sonrakushi gaisetsu (Introduction to the history of Japanese villages) (Entry 1181) still stands as one of the best of the general surveys of the structure, function, and history of the Japanese village.

During and after World War II the outstanding development in this field has been the widespread adoption of field study techniques. Among the scholars using this new methodology is Furushima Toshio, an agricultural economist and historian who has led a number of field expeditions composed primarily of historians. In his Sanson no kōzō (The structure of a mountain village) (Entry 1168) he traces the evolution of social patterns and class tensions within the village. Fukutake Tadashi and Ariga Kizaemon are sociologists working on contemporary village structure and social problems. Rōyama Masamichi (Entry 1184) is a political scientist using the technique of questionnaire surveys to determine changes in the political temper of the village. Yanagida Kunio (Entries 1192 and 1193), a pioneer folklorist, has compiled his data by cooperative field observation of a large number of villages. The Setonaikai Sōgō Kenkyūkai (Joint Society for the Study of the Setonaikai) (Entry 1185) has pioneered in the interdisciplinary study of a single community.

1166. Ariga Kizaemon 有 賀 喜 左 衛 門 , Sonraku seikatsu 村 落 生 活 (Village life), Tōkyō, Kokuritsu Shoin, 1948, 360 pp.
A sociological view of village life. Chapters deal with rice culture and village life, festivals, superstition, fireplaces and the structure of the farm house, etc. The work is full of information derived from field notes.

1167. Fukutake Tadashi 禍 武 直 , Nihon nōson no shakaiteki seikaku 日 本 農 村 の 社 会 的 性 格 (Social characteristics of the Japanese agricultural village), Tōkyō, Tōdai Kyōdo Kumiai Shuppambu, 1949, 298 pp.
An important sociological study of Japanese villages and their characteristics. It is based on contemporary field study. The author distinguishes two basic types of village structure: northeastern and southwestern. Within these he develops several other characteristics based on village origins, location, system of land holding, etc. The work concludes with a discussion of current problems: the village and the city, effects of reform, individualism and the family, etc.

1168. Furushima Toshio 古 島 敏 雄 , ed., Sanson no kōzō 山 村 の 構 造 (The structure of a mountain village), Tōkyō, Nihon Hyōronsha, 1949, 304 pp.
An epoch-making report on the social and economic structure of a Japanese village. The work is the result of an interdisciplinary field study in Yamanashi Prefecture by historians, agricultural economists, legal specialists, and experts on land tenure, agricultural cooperatives, etc. The study traces the evolution of the village from Tokugawa times to the postwar land reform era.

1169. Higo Kazuo 肥 後 和 男 , Miyaza no kenkyū 宮 座 の 研 究 (A study of shrine guilds), Tōkyō, Kōbundō Shobō, 1941, 538 pp.
The standard anthropological study of an important remnant of early social practices in Japanese rural communities: the association of male villagers responsible for the upkeep of village shrines and certain religious observances.

1170. Hosokawa Kameichi 細 川 亀 市 , Rimpo seidoshi 隣 保 制 度 史 (History of neighborhood self-protection groups), Tōkyō, Hakuyōsha, 1939, 249 pp.
A survey of cooperative organizations throughout Japanese pre-twentieth century history. The author, a legal historian, traces the early origin of neighborhood groups, the goho system, and the goningumi system up to their modern dissolution. There is an appended annotated reading list.

1171. Hozumi Nobushige 穗 積 陳 重 , Goningumi seidoron 五 人 組 制 度 論 (Essays on the goningumi system), Tōkyō, Yūhikaku, 1921, 584+24+22 pp.
The first and foremost work on the five-man mutual responsibility groups of the Tokugawa period. The author, an expert in legal history, spent some thirty years preparing this work. It is divided into the following parts: historical introduction, the structure of the five-man group, major laws relative to the system. There is an index.

1172. Hozumi Nobushige 穗 積 陳 重 , Goningumi hōkishū 五 人 組 法 規 集 (Collected regulations relating to the goningumi system), Tōkyō, Yūhikaku, 2nd ed., 1930, 705 pp.
A collection of primary sources from which the author's interpretive work (see previous entry) was drawn.

1173. Kitajima Masamoto 北 島 正 元 , Kinsei Nihon nōson shakaishi 近 世 日 本 農 村 社 会 史 (History of Japanese peasant village society in the early modern period), Tōkyō, Yūzankaku, 1947, 255 pp.
A clearly written survey of the Tokugawa peasant village society. The approach is legalistic. There are lists of suggested reading at the end of chapters.

1174. Makita Shigeru 牧田 茂, <u>Sonraku shakai</u> 村落 社会 (Village society), Tōkyō, Sanseidō, 1948, 147 pp.
> Written as a high school text, this work is of value as a synthesis of the work of the Yanagida school on the subject. The approach is that of the social anthropologist and folklorist.

1175. Nakada Kaoru 中田 薫, <u>Mura oyobi iriai no kenkyū</u> 村及び入会の研究 (Studies of villages and communal rights), Tōkyō, Iwanami Shoten, 1949, 331+6 pp.
> Basic studies of the village as a legal entity and the problems of communal lands and forests. The author begins his analysis in the Tokugawa period and carries his studies into the Meiji period. Emphasis is placed upon the legal status of the village and the rights of villagers especially with respect to forest rights.

1176. Nakayama Tarō 中山 太郎, <u>Nihon wakamonoshi</u> 日本若者史 (History of young men's groups in Japan), Tōkyō, Shun'yōdō, 1930, 218 pp.
> A study of bachelor and youth organizations in Japan, their comparison with similar organizations in Southeast Asia, and their historical development.

1177. Nishimura Seiichi 西村 精一, <u>Goningumi seido shinron</u> 五人組制度新論 (New treatise on the <u>goningumi</u> system), Tōkyō, Iwanami Shoten, 1938, 237 pp.
> An interesting discussion of cooperative groups in Japanese rural society in the 1930s. The author traces the influence of previous cooperative systems upon contemporary practices.

1178. Nomura Kanetarō 野村兼太郎 <u>Goningumichō no kenkyū</u> 五人組帳の研究 (A study of the <u>goningumi</u> register), Tōkyō, Yūhikaku, 1943, 775 pp.
> A scholarly study of village communal life through the "five-man-group" registers of the Tokugawa period.

1179. Nomura Kanetarō 野村兼太郎, <u>Mura meisaichō no kenkyū</u> 村明細帳の研究 (A study of village handbooks), Tōkyō, Yūhikaku, 1949, 1122+136 pp.
> A monumental study of the Tokugawa village, its structure and organization through the medium of the village handbooks kept by village headmen.

1180. Okutani Matsuji 奥谷 松治, <u>Nihon kyōdō kumiaishi</u> 日本協同組合史 (History of Japanese cooperative associations), Tōkyō, Mikasa Shobō, 1938, 286 pp.
> A study of the rural cooperative associations of recent origin in Japan.

1181. Ono Takeo 小野武夫, <u>Nihon sonrakushi gaisetsu</u> 日本村落史概説 (An introduction to the history of Japanese villages), Tōkyō, Iwanami Shoten, 6th ed., 1942, 483 pp.
> The most general of Professor Ono's many works on the Japanese village. This work, first published in 1936, describes the evolution of the agricultural community from the dawn of Japanese history to the twentieth century. Chapters deal with the administrative village, the natural village and its structure, the village and its cooperative life, the culture of the village, and the village since the Meiji Restoration.

1182. Ono Takeo 小野武夫, <u>Nihon sonraku shikō</u> 日本村落史考 (Historical studies of Japanese villages), Tōkyō, Tōkō Shoin, 1941, 25+538 pp.
> Specialized studies of the structure of the Japanese village based primarily on materials drawn from the Tokugawa period. Chapters deal with problems of tenancy, primogeniture, famines, etc.

1183. Ono Takeo 小野武夫, <u>Nōsonshi</u> 農村史 (History of the agricultural village), Tōkyō, Tōyō Keizai Shimpōsha, 1941, 584 pp.
> Part of the <u>Gendai Nihon bummeishi</u> series (Entry 722). This work deals in detailed fashion with the evolution of village life and rural administration from the Meiji Restoration to the end of the Meiji period (1911).

1184. Rōyama Masamichi 蠟山 政道, <u>Nōson jichi no hembō</u> 農村自治の変貌 (Changes in peasant village autonomy), Tōkyō, Nōgyō Sōgō Kenkyū Kankōkai, 1948—.
> A series of detailed field studies of villages in contemporary Japan. The author, a leading political scientist, seeks to trace changes in the strength of local autonomy following the postwar occupation—inspired land reforms and changes in local administrative law. Two volumes had been published by 1951.

1185. Setonaikai Sōgō Kenkyūkai 瀬戸内海總合研究会 (Joint Society for the Study of the Setonaikai), <u>Nōson no seikatsu</u> 農村の生活 (The life of an agricultural village), Okayama, Setonaikai Sōgō Kenkyūkai, 1951, 236 pp.
> An interdisciplinary report on the life of a farming village near the city of Okayama, prepared by members of Okayama University. The work is of special value for its studies of the village's history, irrigation system and related problems, population, economy, cycle of yearly activity, the effects of postwar land reform, and the hygienic standards of the village.

1186. Shimomura Torarokurō 下村虎六郎, <u>Wakamono seido no kenkyū</u> 若者制度の研究 (Studies of youth organizations), Tōkyō, Dai Nihon Rengō Seinenkai, 1936, 508 pp.
> An historical inquiry into the origin and development of youth organizations in Japan.

1188. Takeuchi Toshimi 竹内利美, <u>Chūseimatsu ni okeru sonraku no keisei to sono tenkai</u> 中世末に於ける村落の形成と其の展開 (Formation and development of the village in the late middle ages), Tōkyō, Itō Shoten, 1944, 206 pp.
> An analysis of the formation of the "modern village," the characteristic village community of Tokugawa Japan.

1189. Toda Teizō 戸田貞三 and Suzuki Eitarō 鈴木榮太郎, Kazoku to sonraku 家族と村落 (The family and the village), Tōkyō, Nikkō Shoin, 1939, 323 pp.
A collection of articles by experts in the field of the sociology of the family. Essays deal with the village as a collective social unit, the family system as seen in the census reports of Tokugawa days, status and marriage in feudal Japan, and the social structure of a mountain village. The work concludes with an important bibliographical essay on the sociology of the village.

1190. Wakamori Tarō 和歌森太郎, Chūsei kyōdōtai no kenkyū 中世共同体の研究 (Studies of the cooperative community of the middle ages), Tōkyō, Kōbundō, 1950, 289 pp.
Studies by a social anthropologist of the village communities of the early feudal period in Japan.

1191. Wakamori Tarō 和歌森太郎, Kokushi ni okeru kyōdōtai no kenkyū 国史に於ける協同体の研究 (A study of the communal social unit in Japanese history), Tōkyō, Teikoku Shoin, 1947—.
Volume 1 of a projected series.

1192. Yanagida Kunio 柳田国男, Kaison seikatsu no kenkyū 海村生活の研究 (Studies of maritime villages), Tōkyō, Nihon Minzoku Gakkai, 1949, 472 pp.
Anthropological and ethnological studies of the fishing village in Japan. The work is based on field studies conducted in some 100 localities.

1193. Yanagida Kunio 柳田国男, Sanson seikatsu no kenkyū 山村生活の研究 (Studies of mountain village life), Tōkyō, Iwanami Shoten, 1937, 5+562 pp.
Ethnological studies of the material life, social and family structure, religious beliefs, etc., in mountain villages in Japan. This work is the result of detailed field studies in 66 Japanese mountain communities.

d. Classes and Groups

1) Primitive Society

The following works constitute but a fragment of an extensive field of publication on prehistoric Japan. It is not the intent of this bibliography to cover the fields of prehistory and archaeology; however, the few titles listed below have been included by virtue of their recent publication and the contribution they make to our understanding of Japan's primitive society. They should be supplemented by works listed previously under Section 6 c 1.

1194. Harada Yoshito 原田淑人, Nihon kōkogaku nyūmon 日本考古学入門 (Introduction to Japanese archaeology), Tōkyō, Yoshikawa Kōbunkan, 2nd ed., 1950, 267 pp.
A standard archaeological approach to the origins of the Japanese people and the life of the early Japanese.

1195. Kawakami Tasuke 川上多助, Nihon kodai shakai no kenkyu 日本古代社会の研究 (Studies in the history of ancient Japanese society), Tōkyō, Kawade Shobō, 1947, 500 pp.
Combines 10 articles on ancient and medieval Japanese society by a recognized scholar. It includes his well-known study of the be, ancient Japanese communal corporations.

1196. Kiyono Kenji 清野謙次, Nihon minzoku seiseiron 日本民族生成論 (An essay on the origins of the Japanese people), Tōkyō, Nihon Hyōronsha, 1946, 471 pp.
A technical study of the origins of the Japanese people. The author supports the thesis that the Japanese racial stock took shape as early as the Jōmon period.

1197. Kiyono Kenji 清野謙次, Nihon rekishi no akebono 日本歴史のあけぼの (The dawn of Japanese history), Tōkyō, Chōryūsha, 1947, 252 pp.
A more popular presentation of the author's thesis (see previous entry).

1198. Tōma Seita 藤間生大, Nihon kodai kazoku 日本古代家族 (The family in ancient Japan), Tōkyō, Itō Shoten, 1943, 176 pp.
A study of pre-Taika (645) communal organization.

1199. Tōma Seita 藤間生大, Nihon minzoku no keisei 日本民族の形成 (Establishment of the Japanese people), Tōkyō, Iwanami Shoten, 1951, 306 pp.
An analysis of the origins and development of the Japanese people based on the theories of economic determinism.

1200. Tsuda Sōkichi 津田左右吉, Nihon jōdaishi no kenkyū 日本上代史の研究 (Studies in ancient Japanese history), Tōkyō, Iwanami Shoten, 1947, 502+26 pp.
A selection of stimulating essays by a leading student of ancient Japanese society. The work concludes with a methodological and bibliographical essay.

1201. Tsuda Sōkichi 津田左右吉, Nihon koten no kenkyū 日本古典の研究 (Studies in ancient Japanese classics), Tōkyō, Iwanami Shoten, 1948-50, 2 v.
The author's penetrating studies of the mythology, religious ceremonies, and historical and literary works of the ancient period in Japan form the basis of his historical writings.

1202. Wakamori Tarō 和歌森太郎, <u>Nihon kodai shakai</u> 日本古代社会 (Japanese ancient society), Tōkyō, Shōbunsha, 1949, 158 pp.
    A general survey of early Japanese history from the sociologist's point of view.

1203. Watanabe Yoshimichi 渡部義通, <u>Kodai shakai no kōzō</u> 古代社会の構造 (The structure of ancient Japanese society), Tōkyō, Itō Shoten, 1945, 488 pp.
    Covers Japanese society from the period of primitive communalism to the beginning of the <u>shōen</u>.

2) The Court Aristocracy

    From the seventh through twelfth centuries Japan was dominated politically by the court nobles (<u>kuge</u>). The cultural importance of the courtiers was of even longer duration. Yet there has been an almost total neglect of the sociological history of this classical court society in Japan. Those interested in this subject will find a good deal of information on the life, customs, and court practices of the civil nobility in the general cultural histories such as the <u>Nihon bunkashi</u> (Cultural history of Japan) (Entry 730) and in the works on customs and manners which follow in Section f 1. Aside from the work of Ienaga Saburō listed below, the reader is referred to Takigawa Masajirō's <u>Nihon shakaishi</u> (Social history of Japan) (Entry 1154).

1204. Ienaga Saburō 家永三郎, "Kizokuron 貴族論 (An essay on the nobility)," in <u>Shin-Nihonshi kōza</u>, Tōkyō, Chūō Kōronsha, 1949, v. 6, 36 pp.
    A brief survey of the origin and history of the noble class in Japan.

1205. Kojima Shōgorō 小島小五郎, <u>Kuge bunka no kenkyu</u> 公家文化の研究 (Studies of court culture), Tōkyō, Ikuhōsha, 1943, 305 pp.
    A study of court society, chiefly from the intellectual and religious side.

3) The Feudal Aristocracy

    As the following list indicates, sociological studies of the warrior class as distinct from general institutions of feudal times are few in number. Information on the material life of the feudal aristocracy (<u>buke</u>) will be found in the survey histories of Japanese manners and customs listed below in Section f 1. The legal and official structure of feudal society is treated in considerable detail in the works on legal history listed in Chapter 5 e 1 above and in the survey social histories listed at the beginning of this chapter.

1206. Fuji Naomoto 藤直幹, <u>Chūsei bukeshakai no kōzō</u> 中世武家社会の構造 (The structure of medieval military society), Tōkyō, Meguro Shoten, 1944, 495 pp.
    A detailed study of the political, intellectual and social structure of Japanese society from the 12th century emergence of the <u>bushi</u> to the end of the Ashikaga shogunate in the 16th century.

1207. Nakamura Kichiji 中村吉治, <u>Buke to shakai</u> 武家と社会 (Feudal military houses and Japanese society), Tōkyō, Baifūkan, 1948, 283 pp.
    An historical survey of the rise and fall of the Japanese feudal class.

1208. Ishikawa Tsunetarō 石川恒太郎, <u>Nihon rōninshi</u> 日本浪人史 (History of <u>rōnin</u> in Japan), Tōkyō, Shunjūsha, 1931, 122 pp.
    A brief history of the <u>rōnin</u>, or unattached warriors, of the Tokugawa period. The work treats the forces which created <u>rōnin</u>, the life and social position of <u>rōnin</u>, etc.

1209. Itō Tasaburō 伊東多三郎, "Hōken jidai kōki no bushi no seikatsu 封建時代後期の武士の生活 (The life of the <u>bushi</u> during the late feudal era)," in <u>Shin-Nihonshi kōza</u>, Tōkyō, Chūō Kōronsha, 1948, v. 4, 45 pp.
    A brief but detailed description of the official status, economic position, and spiritual life of the samurai of the Tokugawa period.

1210. Ono Takeo 小野武夫, <u>Gōshi seido no kenkyū</u> 郷土制度の研究 (Studies of the <u>gōshi</u> system), Tōkyō, Ōokayama Shoten, 1925, 201+11+4 pp.
    The basic study of the <u>gōshi</u> (rural samurai) of the Tokugawa period.

1211. Sakata Yoshio 坂田吉雄, <u>Sengoku bushi</u> 戦国武士 (Feudal warriors of the Sengoku period), Tōkyō, Kōbundō, 1952, 217 pp.
    A study of the emergence of the dependent samurai of the later feudal period and the fundamental principles under which they lived.

4) The Peasantry

    Of all the classes the peasantry has been given the most attention by Japanese historians. The following works have been selected as having most general usefulness to the non-specialist. They should be used in conjunction with titles listed above under Communal Organizations (Section 7 c).

1212. Ariga Kizaemon 有賀喜左衛門, <u>Nihon kazokuseido to kosakuseido</u> 日本家族制度と小作制度 (The tenancy system and the family system in Japan), Tōkyō, Kawade Shobo, 1943, 3+732+36 pp.
    This is a revised edition of a work published in 1938 under the title <u>Nōson shakai no kenkyū</u>. The author analyzes the effect of tenancy on peasant society in Japan with special emphasis on the <u>nago</u> (bound tenant) system. Coverage is from the Tokugawa period to the time of writing. The study is based on extensive field work and is well documented.

1213. Honjō Eijirō 本 庄 榮 治郎, Hyakushō chōnin no rekishi 百 姓 町人の歴史 (History of the peasantry and bourgeoisie), Tōkyō, Baifūkan, 1949, 262 pp.
    A brief interpretive essay on the position and life of peasants and chōnin in Japan. The author is largely concerned with the Tokugawa period.

1214. Irimajiri Yoshinaga 入 交 好脩, Nihon nōmin keizaishi kenkyū 日本農民經済史研究 (Economic history of Japanese peasantry), Tōkyō, Kamakura Bunko, 1949, 456 pp.

1215. Kawanishi Seigo 河 西 省五, Nihon nōminshi 日本農民史 (History of Japanese peasantry), Tōkyō, Kokon Shoin, 1930, 453 pp.
    A survey of the development of the Japanese peasantry from ancient times through the Tokugawa period. The author presents a summary of current research on the subject.

1216. Kimbara Seigo 金 原 省五, Nihon nōminshi 日本農民史 (History of the Japanese peasantry), Tōkyō, Kokon Shoin, 1930, 7+453 pp.
    The author, an art historian, emphasizes the development of folk art and peasant architecture.

1217. Kodama Kōta 兒玉幸多, Kinsei nōmin seikatsushi 近 世農民生活史 (History of peasant life in early-modern Japan), Tōkyō, Yoshikawa Kobunkan, 1951, 347 pp.
    An extremely lucid description of the status and life of the peasantry in Tokugawa Japan. Chapters deal with central administration, village administration, taxation, peasant life, problems, etc. There is a list of sources and an index. The author has done extensive field work in the Kantō region of Japan.

1218. Nihon Rekishichiri Gakkai 日本歴史地理学会 (Japanese Historical Geography Society), Nihon nōminshi 日本農民史 (A history of Japanese peasantry), Tōkyō, Nihon Rekishichiri Gakkai, 1924, 375 pp. [Special issue of Rekishichiri (44, 3)].
    This work is devoted to articles on the Japanese peasantry from ancient times to the Meiji period.

1219. Ono Takeo 小 野 武 夫, Nōson shakaishi ronkō 農 村 社 会 史 論 講 (Essays on the social history of peasant villages), Tōkyō, Ganshōdo, 1927, 335 pp.
    Essays on problems affecting the peasantry of the Tokugawa period. The author touches such problems as peasant uprisings, passive resistance, landlordism, tenant disputes, farm laborers, the village and family social status.

1220. Ono Takeo 小 野 武 夫, Nōson kikō no bunretsu katei 農 村 機 構の分裂過程 (The disruption of peasant village organization), Tōkyō, Kaizōsha, 1928, 267 pp.
    An analysis of the disruption of the peasant community in Japan after the Meiji Restoration. Chapters deal with the causes of dislocation, peasant movements, government policies, land reform and the tenancy problem, etc.

1221. Ono Takeo 小 野 武 夫, Nihon heinō shiron 日本兵農史論 (Essays on the history of peasant and soldier in Japan), Tōkyō, Yūhikaku, 1938, 394 pp.
    A survey of the relationship of the peasantry and military forces in Japan from earliest times to the time of the Meiji army. The author treats the Nara-Heian conscript army, the armed peasantry of late Heian and Kamakura, separation of soldier and peasant, the gōshi, and Japan's modern army.

1222. Yanagida Kunio 柳 田 国 男, Nihon nōminshi 日本農民史 (History of Japanese peasantry), Tōkyō, Tōkō Shoin, 1933, 192 pp.
    An ethnological analysis of the historical development of the Japanese peasantry. The work treats the social organization and economic status of the peasantry. Chapters describe village life, peasant families, the peasant and his environment. There is an index.

5) Cities and City Life

1223. Endō Motoo 遠 藤 元 男, Nihon chūsei toshiron 日本中世都市論 (Essays on the Japanese city of the middle ages), Tōkyō, Hakuyōsha, 1940, 247 pp.
    The author treats four problems related to the growth of cities in Japan from the thirteenth through fifteenth centuries: the origin of cities, the causes of their growth, social problems engendered by their growth, and the nature of city life.

1224. Imai Toshiki 今 井 登 志喜, Toshi hattenshi kenkyū 都 市 発 展 史 研 究 (Studies in the development of cities), Tōkyō, Tōkyō Daigaku Shuppambu, 1951, 296 pp.
    A brief descriptive history of urban growth in Europe and Japan. The section on Japan covers the development of cities from Nara to Tokyo.

1225. Isomura Eiichi 磯 村 英 一, Ku no kenkyū 區 の 研 究 (A study of city wards), Tōkyō, 1936, 357 pp.
    A study of the social and administrative aspects of wards (ku) of modern Japanese cities. The chief emphasis is on Tokyo and the problems of ku government and metropolitan controls.

1226. Ōkōchi Kazuo 大 河 内 一男, Sengo shakai no jittai bunseki 戰 後 社 会 の 実 態 分 析 (A field analysis of postwar Japanese society), Tōkyō, Nihon Hyōronsha, 1950, 292 pp.
    A series of articles by specialists in labor problems and social policy on the life of lower class urban groups in postwar Japan. Articles deal with laborers, labor organizations, female workers, and displaced persons. Studies are based on field work.

1227. Okui Fukutarō 奥 井 復 太 郎, Gendai daitoshiron 現 代 大 都 市 論 (An essay on present-day large cities), Tōkyō, Yūhikaku, 1940, 743 pp.
 A study of the Mita district of Tokyo. The author is a specialist in urban problems and social relations.

1228. Ono Hitoshi 小 野 均, Kinsei jōkamachi no kenkyū 近 世 城 下 町 の 研 究 (A study of castle towns in Tokugawa Japan), Tōkyō, Shibundō, 1928, 298 pp.
 A pioneer study of the social and economic aspects of the castle town in Japan. The author treats the origin and development of castle towns, the socio-political organization of castle towns, the relationship of the castle town to the countryside, etc.

1229. Sakata Yoshio 坂 田 吉 雄, Chōnin 町 人 (The urban resident), Tōkyō, Kōbundō, 1939, 158 pp.
 A readable description of the life of the urban population of Edo and Osaka during the Tokugawa period. The author emphasizes the cultural and intellectual life of the bourgeoisie.

1230. Toyota Takeshi 豊 田 武, Nihon no hōken toshi 日 本 の 封 建 都 市 (Feudal cities in Japan), Tōkyō, Iwanami Shoten, 1952, 303+9 pp.
 A concise and lucid description of the development of cities in feudal Japan. Chapters cover the origin of feudal cities, early feudal cities, free cities, cities under the daimyō, size and population, organization and life of the bourgeoisie, cities and commerce and industry, and the dissolution of feudal cities. There is a useful bibliography, a list of major castle towns, and an index.

1231. Yokoyama Gennosuke 横 山 源 之 助, Nihon no kasō shakai 日 本 の 下 層 社 会 (Society of the lower classes in Japan), Tōkyō, Iwanami Shoten, 1949, 348 pp.
 A postwar reprint of a work first published in 1899. This study of the life of the underprivileged city classes of the early Meiji period has become a classic.

6) Women, Professional Groups, and Minorities

1232. Inoue Kiyoshi 井 上 清, Nihon joseishi 日 本 女 性 史 (History of Japanese women), Kyōto, San'ichi Shobō, 1944, 356 pp.
 A Marxist analysis of woman's position in Japanese society and her struggle for emancipation. The subject is treated chronologically by periods from the early clan society through the stages of slave society, feudal society, to the present capitalistic society.

1233. Josei sōsho 女 性 叢 書 (Collected articles on women), Tokyo, Mikuni Shobō, 1942-44, 12 v.

1234. Kikuchi Sansai 菊 池 山 哉, Etazoku ni kansuru kenkyū 穢 多 族 に 関 す る 研 究 (Studies on the eta), Tōkyō, Sanseisha Shoten, 1923, 400 pp.
 Studies concerning the origins and assimilation of the eta minority in Japanese society.

1235. Nakayama Tarō 中 山 太 郎, Nihon mōjinshi 日 本 盲 人 史 (History of the blind in Japan), Tōkyō, Shōwa Shobō, 1934, 453 pp.
 The standard study of the history of the blind in Japan from early times to the twentieth century. The work describes the status afforded the blind, their methods of gaining a livelihood, special functions assigned them, methods for relief, etc. A supplement to this volume published in 1938 extends the coverage and corrects errors in the first volume.

1236. Nakayama Tarō 中 山 太 郎, Nihon mikoshi 日 本 巫 女 史 (History of Japanese female shamans), Tōkyō, Ōokayama Shoten, 1930, 743 pp.
 A detailed scholarly study of the role of priestesses in Japanese religious practices and beliefs.

1237. Sakurai Shōtarō 櫻 井 左 太 郎, Nihon jidō seikatsushi 日 本 兒 童 生 活 史 (History of the life of Japanese children), Tōkyō, Nikkō Shoin, 1949, 279 pp.

1238. Takahashi Sadaki 高 橋 貞 樹, Tokushu buraku issennenshi 特 殊 部 落 一 千 年 史 (A thousand years of the "special community"), Kyōto, Kōseikaku, 1924, 340 pp.
 This work, based on the research of Kida Teikichi, constitutes the most systematic treatment of this difficult problem in prewar times. Part 1 covers the history of outcast communities. Part 2 deals with the present status of such communities and discusses the emancipation movement (suihei undō).

1239. Takamure Itsue 高 群 逸 枝, Nihon josei shakaishi 日 本 女 性 社 会 史 (A social history of Japanese women), Ōsaka, Shin-Nihonsha, 1948, 318 pp.
 Written by an authority on matriarchal systems, this work is a history of Japanese social systems with an emphasis on the position of women throughout.

1240. Tamura Eitarō 田 村 榮 太 郎, Ikki, kumosuke, bakuto 一 揆, 雲 助, 博 徒 (Uprisings, coolies, and gamblers), Tōkyō, Ōhata Shoten, 1933, 471 pp.
 An analysis of the oyabun-kobun (boss—follower) relationship among gamblers of the Tokugawa period, class distinctions among coolies and prostitutes, and the class nature of peasant uprisings.

1241. Uemura Yukiaki 上 村 行 彰, Nihon yūrishi 日 本 遊 里 史 (History of gay quarters in Japan), Tōkyō, Shun'yōdō, 1929, 615 pp.
 A history of prostitution in Japan from the Nara period until the time of writing. The work deals extensively with the Tokugawa period with emphasis on the Genroku era. For the post-Restoration period, the

author gives detailed treatment to laws and practices relating to prostitution, describes the lives and working conditions of prostitutes, etc.

1242. Yamakawa Kikue 山 川 菊 枝, <u>Buke no josei</u> 武 家 の 女 性 (Women of the feudal military houses), Tōkyō, Mikuni Shobō, 1943, 266 pp.

A description of the life of women of the samurai houses of the Tokugawa period based on interviews with women who could remember the pre-Meiji days.

1243. Yanagida Kunio 柳 田 国 男, <u>Kodomo fudoki</u> こ ど も 風 土 記 (A children's gazetteer), Ōsaka, Asahi Shimbunsha, 1946, 93 pp.

A folkloristic description of the life of Japanese children.

e. Social Movements

Japanese writers have tended to bring together under the title of social movements a large number of assorted studies of social unrest and the underprivileged classes of Japanese society. In pre-modern times Japanese society was disturbed by agrarian discontent and its violent manifestation, the peasant uprising. In modern times the chief problems were rural tenancy and industrial labor conditions which helped to engender left-wing political movements. Population, or rather, over-population has also been a constant factor leading to social unrest in Japanese history.

The following works are heavily weighted in favor of the pre-Restoration period of Japanese history. The pioneer authority on peasant uprisings is Kokushō Iwao (Entry 1248). His studies are limited largely to the pre-Restoration period. Those who are interested in the post-Restoration agrarian problem will find additional material listed in Robert E. Ward's A Guide to Japanese Research and Reference Materials in the Field of Political Science. For labor movements and left-wing politics, there exists a voluminous but unorganized literature. Tanaka Sōgorō's documentary history (Entry 1264) is of great value for background purposes. The most convenient historical summary is the one by Akamatsu Katsumaro entitled Nihon shakai undōshi (History of social movements in Japan) (Entry 1256). Further items will be found in Ward's bibliography referred to above.

On population, Takahashi Bonsen's Nihon jinkōshi no kenkyū (A study of the history of population in Japan) (Entry 1270) is most detailed. However, the non-specialist will find Sekiyama Naotarō's Kinsei Nihon jinkō no kenkyū (Studies of population in Tokugawa Japan) (Entry 1268) of much greater usefulness because of its lucid presentation and its coverage of the transition into the Meiji period. No attempt has been made to supply references to the complex field of post-Restoration population studies.

1) <u>Agrarian Unrest</u>

1244. Aoki Keiichirō 青 木 恵 一 郎, Nihon nōmin undōshi 日 本 農 民 運 動 史 (History of the agrarian movement in Japan), Tōkyō, Minshu Hyōronsha, 1948, 18+524 pp.

A Marxist analysis of the agrarian movement in Japan since the Meiji Restoration.

1245. Honjō Eijirō 本 庄 栄 治 郎, Waga kuni kinsei no nōson mondai 我 国 近 世 の 農 村 問 題 (Problems of the agricultural village in early modern Japan), Tōkyō, Kaizōsha, 1930, 265 pp.

A revised edition of the author's previous work Kinsei nōson mondai shiron (Tōkyō, Kaizōsha, 1925). Chapters deal with the land tax, government policy towards the peasantry, hardships of peasant life, population, decline of land productivity, tenancy, famines, peasant uprisings, etc.

1246. Kasahara Kazuo 笠 原 一 男, Nihon ni okeru nōmin sensō 日 本 に お け る 農 民 戰 争 (Peasant wars in Japan), Tōkyō, Kokudosha, 1949, 257 pp.

A study of the religious uprisings (ikko ikki) of the fifteenth and sixteenth centuries.

1247. Kimura Yasuji 木 村 靖 二, Nihon nōmin tōsōshi 日 本 農 民 闘 争 史 (History of the struggles of the Japanese peasantry), Tōkyō, Hakuyōsha, 1930, 544 pp.

A study of peasant resistance to authority under the feudal system and under the post-Restoration capitalistic system.

1248. Kokushō Iwao 黒 正 巌, Hyakushō ikki no kenkyū 百 姓 一 揆 の 研 究 (A study of agrarian uprisings), Tōkyō, Iwanami Shoten, 1928, 474 pp.

A pioneer study of peasant uprisings in Tokugawa Japan. The author records some five hundred uprisings, analyzes their causes, the counter measures of the government, the attitude of Tokugawa economic philosophers, etc. There is a chronological table of uprisings and a regional listing of uprisings.

1249. Kuroda Hisao 黒 田 壽 男 and Ikeda Tsuneo 池 田 恒 雄, Nihon nōmin kumiai undōshi 日 本 農 民 組 合 運 動 史 (History of the farmers' union movement in Japan), Tōkyō, Shinchi Shobō, 1949, 332 pp.

A history of Japan's modern farmers' union movement by men active in the farm-labor political parties.

1250. Nakamura Kichiji 中 村 吉 治, Chūsei no nōmin ikki 中 世 の 農 民 一 揆 (Agrarian uprisings in the middle ages), Tōkyō, Chūō Kōronsha, 1948, 320 pp.

A basic study of the early phase of peasant uprisings in Japan.

1251. Nojiri Shigeo 野 尻 重 雄, Nōmin rison no jisshōteki kenkyū 農 民 離 村 の 実 証 的 研 究 (Studies of rural exodus), Tōkyō, Iwanami Shoten, 1942, 9+569 pp.

A basic study by an agricultural economist into the causes of the abandonment of the farm by Japanese farmers since the Meiji Restoration.

1252. Ono Takeo 小 野 武 夫, Ishin nōmin hōkitan 維 新 農 民 蜂 起 譚(A study of peasant uprisings during the Meiji Restoration), Tōkyō, Kaizōsha, 1930, 623 pp.
An analysis of eleven uprisings in the period immediately after the Meiji Restoration. An appendix carries a list of sources on the subject.

1253. Shakai Keizaishi Gakkai 社 会 經 済 史 学 会 (The Social and Economic History Society), Nōmin kaihō no shiteki kōsatu 農 民 解 放 の 史 的 考 察 (Historical analysis of the emancipation of the peasantry), Tōkyō, Nihon Hyōronsha, 1948, 267 pp.
Collected essays on the subject of peasant resistance to landlordism and feudal controls both in Europe and Japan.

1254. Suzuki Ryōichi 鈴 木 良 一, Nihon chūsei no nōmin mondai 日 本 中 世 の 農 民 問 題(Peasant problems in the medieval age of Japan), Kyōto, Kōtō Shoin, 1948, 272 pp.
A study of the peasant uprisings of the fifteenth and sixteenth centuries.

2) Labor Movements and Left-Wing Politics

1255. Akamatsu Katsumaro 赤 松 克 麿, Nihon rōdō undō hattatsushi 日 本 勞 働 運 動 発 達 史(History of the development of the Japanese labor movement), Tōkyō, Bunka Gakkai, 1925.
A history of the Japanese labor movement since the Restoration. The account is divided into three phases: from 1883 to 1894, the Sino-Japanese War to 1912, and 1912 to 1924.

1256. Akamatsu Katsumaro 赤 松 克 麿, Nihon shakai undōshi 日 本 社 会 運 動 史 (History of social movements in Japan), Tōkyō, Iwanami Shoten, 1952, 330 pp.
A simply written survey of social movements in Japan from the early Meiji period to the outbreak of the Pacific War. The author, a participant in the labor movement, has made extensive use of secondary sources, so that his footnote references are of considerable value. The treatment is divided chronologically into five parts: 1) early political movements and the Socialist Party; 2) the early labor movement and the government; 3) World War I, the labor movement, and the Communist Party; 4) peasant participation; 5) national socialism and the popular mass parties.

1257. Arahata Kanson 荒 畑 寒 村, Nihon shakaishugi undōshi 日 本 社 会 主 義 運 動 史 (History of the socialist movement in Japan), Tōkyō, Mainichi Shimbunsha, 1948, 290 pp.
An inside history of the early activities of the socialist movement in Japan by a participant and subsequent founder of the Communist Party in Japan.

1258. Ichikawa Shōichi 市 川 正 一, Nihon kyōsantō tōsō shōshi 日 本 共 産 党 闘 争 小 史 (Short history of the struggle of the Japan Communist Party), Tōkyō, Gyōmeisha, 1947.
An inside history of the Japan Communist Party in its pre-World War II phase by an active member.

1259. Kikugawa Tadao 菊 川 忠 碓, Gakusei shakai undōshi 学 生 社 会 運 動 史(History of social agitation by students), Tōkyō, Umiguchi Shoten, 1947, 14+475+9 pp.
A detailed and documented study of left-wing activity by students in the period 1918-1931.

1260. Kyōchōkai 協 調 会 (Conciliation Society), Saikin no shakai undō 最 近 の 社 会 運 動(Recent social movements), Tōkyō, Kyōchōkai, 1927, 1422 pp.
An authoritative collection of information on all aspects of social movements in Japan and other nations from roughly 1916 to 1926. The section on Japan covers the labor movement, the farmer cooperative movement, proletarian parties, women's organizations, organizations and procedures for securing cooperation between labor and management, etc.

1261. Matsushita Yoshio 松 下 芳 男, Meiji Taishō hansen undōshi 明 治 大 正 反 戦 運 動 史 (A history of the pacifist movement in Meiji and Taisho Japan), Tōkyō, Sōbisha, 1949, 271 pp.
A history of the pacifist movement in Japan up through World War I.

1262. Suehiro Izutarō 末 弘 嚴 太 郎, Nihon rōdō kumiai undōshi 日 本 勞 働 組 合 運 動 史(History of the labor union movement in Japan), Tōkyō, Nihon Rōdō Kumiai Undōshi Kankōkai, 1950, 256 pp.
A detailed history of the labor union movement in Japan from early Meiji up to 1949 by an authority on labor law.

1263. Tanaka Sōgorō 田 中 惣 五 郎, Nihon shakai undōshi 日 本 社 会 運 動 史(History of social movements in Japan), Tōkyō, Sekai Shoin, 1947-48, 3 v.
A detailed, well-documented history of social and political movements in Japan from 1868 to 1938.

1264. Tanaka Sōgorō 田 中 惣 五 郎, Shiryō Nihon shakai undōshi 資 料 日 本 社 会 運 動 史 (Documentary history of social movements in Japan), Tōkyō, Tōzai Shuppan K.K., 1948-, 3 v.
A valuable collection of selected documents on social movements in Japan beginning with 1866. Each volume begins with a chronological table of events. Documents and sources are taken from government publications, party pronouncements, articles from newspapers, and party publications.

1265. Watanabe Ikujirō 渡 辺 幾 治 郎, Nihon shakai undō shikan 日 本 社 会 運 動 史 観 (An historical view of social movements in Japan), Tōkyō, Dai Nihon Bummei Kyōkai, 1925, 382 pp.
A conservative view of Japan's social movements from early Meiji to the 1920s. The author reflects back to the historic position of the emperor as the solution to class disputes in Japan.

3) Population

1266. Honjō Eijirō 本庄栄治郎, *Jinkō oyobi jinkō mondai* 人口及人口問題 (Population and the population problem), Tōkyō, Nihon Hyōronsha, 1930, 268 pp.
    A general survey of Japan's population problem from early times through the Meiji period with emphasis on the Tokugawa period.

1267. Okazaki Ayanori 岡崎文規, *Nihon jinkō no jisshōteki kenkyū* 日本人口の実証的研究 (Factual studies of Japanese population), Tōkyō, Hokuryūkan, 1950, 602+50 pp.
    An analysis of Japan's post-Restoration population problem by the president of the Research Institute for Public Health and Population Problems. There is a list of suggested reading.

1268. Sekiyama Naotarō 関山直太郎, *Kinsei Nihon jinkō no kenkyū* 近世日本人口の研究 (Studies of population in Tokugawa Japan), Tōkyō, Ryūginsha, 1948, 282 pp.
    A collection of basic studies of Japan's pre-modern population problems. The final chapter on the transition from Tokugawa to Meiji population figures is particularly valuable.

1269. Takahashi Bonsen 高橋梵仙, *Datai mabiki no kenkyū* 堕胎間引の研究 (Abortion and infanticide), Tōkyō, Chūō Shakai Jigyō Kyōkai Shakai Jigyō Kenkyūsho, 1936, 286 pp.

1270. Takahashi Bonsen 高橋梵仙, *Nihon jinkōshi no kenkyū* 日本人口史の研究 (A study of the history of population in Japan), Tōkyō, San'yūsha, 1941, 853 pp.
    The most extensive study of pre-twentieth century population in Japan. The author begins with Japan's early history but focuses his attention upon the Tokugawa period and its regional population problems. Special studies are made of the problem of mabiki and the population policies of the shogunate and various daimyō. The work is extensively documented.

1271. Watanabe Shin'ichi 渡辺信一, *Nihon nōson jinkōron* 日本農村人口論 (An analysis of Japan's agricultural village population), Tōkyō, Nankōsha, 1938, 482 pp.
    A basic analysis of the role of the rural community as the source of Japan's modern industrial manpower.

f. Customs and Manners

    Works devoted to the history of Japanese life, customs, and manners are of several widely different varieties. First from point of time have been the studies of the antiquarian specialists such as Sekine Masanao, Sakurai Shigeru, and Wada Hisamatsu, the most substantial of which have been listed above in Part II, Chapter 2 c among the antiquarian dictionaries. Such works are concerned chiefly with the formal official life of the ruling classes in Japanese history, that is, the court and feudal nobility. Another group of scholars, represented by Ema Tsutomu, Nishioka Toranosuke, and Tamura Eitarō, have attempted to obtain more comprehensive insight into not only the public but the domestic life of the various classes in Japan. Ema's photographic reconstructions of historic settings and typical costumes (Entry 1272) are especially valuable for the foreign student of Japanese history. A third group of writers has consisted of folklorists and ethnologists working under the leadership of Yanagida Kunio. The chief emphasis of this group has been placed on the folk society of Japan. With headquarters in the Minzokugaku Kenkyūsho (Ethnological Institute) in Tokyo, the methodology and interests of the group are best described in the work by Yanagida and Seki entitled *Nihon minzokugaku nyūmon* (Introduction to the study of Japanese folklore) (Entry 1289). Finally, the following works included some which are concerned primarily with the recording of contemporary Japanese life. These are the gazetteers and photographic surveys produced in the main by geographers and ethnologists.
    In the following sections, the first on Folkways and Customs contains works of a general nature. The other sections are devoted to more specialized and diversified materials which cannot be profitably commented upon in detail. Among the general works, a number should be singled out for special mention. Among the survey histories Ema Tsutomu's *Nihon seikatsushi* (History of life in Japan) (Entry 1274) and Inokuma Kaneshige's work of the same title (Entry 1277) are both authoritative and conveniently arranged. Nishioka Toranosuke's *Minshū seikatsushi kenkyū* (Historical essays on the life of the people) (Entry 1284) is widely read for the stimulating ideas it contains. For more detailed historical coverage, the ten-volume *Nihon fūzokuga taisei* (A compendium of illustrations of Japanese manners and customs) (Entry 1292) and the twelve-volume *Nihon fūzokushi kōza* (Series on the history of Japanese customs and manners) (Entry 1293), though somewhat out-of-date, are still standard. Among the contemporary pictorial surveys, the recent work entitled *Shashin chishi Nihon* (Photo-monograph of Japan) (Entry 1287) is modern in conception and contains excellent photographs. Kumagai's *Ōchi mura* (Ōchi village) (Entry 1279) is unique for its ability to capture the life of a mountain village in photographs.

1) Folkways and Customs

1272. Ema Tsutomu 江馬務, *Rekidai fūzoku shashin taikan* 歴代風俗写真大観 (A photographic survey of customs and manners by historical periods), Tōkyō, Shinkōsha, 1931-32, 2 v.
    A pictorial survey of pre-twentieth century Japanese customs and manners. Photographs are of reconstructed scenes and activities in which contemporary figures dressed in authentic costumes are placed in historically authentic settings. Each illustration is explained and a brief survey of costumes and customs is appended.

1273. Ema Tsutomu 江馬務, Nihon fūzokushi 日本風俗史 (History of Japanese manners and customs), Tōkyō, Chijin Shokan, 1943, 442 pp.
    Published as part of the Taikan Nihon bunkashi sensho series (Entry 749). This work constitutes a summary of Ema Tsutomu's research into customs, costumes, manners, and festivals of the past. This volume includes a discussion of the Meiji period. Unfortunately, the paper is poor and the format is small so that the illustrations are far from satisfactory.

1274. Ema Tsutomu 江馬務, Nihon seikatsushi 日本生活史 (History of life in Japan), Tōkyō, Ogawa Shobō, 1947, 9+272 pp.
    The latest of Ema's surveys of Japanese customs. This work covers in general interpretive fashion by periods the salient features of the material life, the customs, and manners of the Japanese. The work concludes with a delightful chapter on the "Makkuāsā" period of postwar Japan.

1275. Fujioka Kenjirō 藤岡謙二郎 and others, Nihon no fūdo 日本の風土 (Japanese folkways), Kyōto, Ōyashima Shuppan K.K., 1948, 396 pp.
    A survey of Japanese folkways by region. The compilers are members of the Ritsumeikan Geographical Institute.

1276. Fujioka Sakutarō 藤岡作太郎 and Hiraide Kenjirō 平出鏗次郎, Nihon fūzokushi 日本風俗史 (History of Japanese manners and customs), Tōkyō, Tōyodō, 1895, 3 v.
    A pioneer study of Japanese manners and customs and still one of the most detailed and best illustrated. The treatment is by major historical periods from early times to 1868. For each period the authors describe the social class system, customary law, productive capacities, educational systems, religious practices, food and clothing, housing, family and social observances, pastimes and amusements.

1277. Inokuma Kaneshige 猪熊兼繁, Nihon seikatsushi 日本生活史 (History of living habits in in Japan), Kyōto, Sekai Shisōsha, 1952, 210 pp.
    An analytical survey of life in Japan, its historical developments, and its class differentiation. Chapters deal with agricultural life, court life, feudal life, and the life of the "common people." The last chapter is a penetrating analysis of the influence of the West and the "modernization process" on Japanese living habits.

1278. Katō Totsudō 加藤咄堂, Nihon fūzokushi 日本風俗志 (Notes on Japanese customs), Tōkyō, Daitō Shuppansha, rev. ed., 1941, 4 v.
    A description of folk customs and their regional peculiarities, first published in 1917-18. Volume 1 covers the Kantō area, 2 the Tōhoku and Chūbu, 3 the Hokuriku and Kinki, and 4 the Chūgoku and Kyūshu areas.

1279. Kumagai Gen'ichi 熊谷元一, Ōchi-mura 会地村 (Ochi village), Tōkyō, Ōsaka, Asahi Shimbunsha, 1938, 176 pp.
    An intimate photographic record of the life of a mountain village. The author, an art instructor and amateur photographer, depicts the passage of the seasons, the struggle for existence, family life, social pastimes, and religious activities of the village.

1280. Minzokugaku Kenkyūsho 民俗学研究所 (Ethnological Institute), Minzokugaku no hanashi 民俗学の話 (Lectures on folklore), Tōkyō, Kyōdō Shuppansha, 1949, 2+2+199 pp.
    Postwar introductory essays on Japanese folklore by members of the Yanagida school.

1281. Minzokugaku Kenkyūsho 民俗学研究所, Minzokugaku shinkō 民族学新講 (New lectures on folklore), Tōkyō, Meiseidō, 1947, 3+296 pp.
    Postwar introductory essays based on lectures delivered in 1946 at Tokyo University by Yanagida, Wakamori, Mrs. Segawa, and others of the Yanagida school. Pages 273-80 comprise a bibliography of works on Japanese folklore.

1282. Motoyama Keisen 本山桂川, Nihon minzoku zushi 日本民俗図誌 (Illustrated survey of Japanese folklore), Tōkyō, Tōkyōdō, 1942-44, 20 v.
    The most extensive illustrated survey of Japanese folkways.

1283. Nakama Teruhisa 仲摩照久, Nihon chiri fūzoku taikei 日本地理風俗大系 (Outline of Japanese geography and customs), Tōkyō, Shinkōsha, 1929-32, 19 v.
    A voluminous illustrated gazetteer of Japan, Korea, Formosa, and some of the islands formerly held by Japan in the Pacific. The work deals with the land, cities, the people, and their material civilization in contemporary times.

1284. Nishioka Toranosuke 西岡虎之助, Minshū seikatsushi kenkyū 民衆生活史研究 (Historical essays on the life of the people), Tōkyō, Fukumura Shoten, 1948, 692 pp.
    Collected essays on a broad variety of subjects related to the history of the Japanese people. Chapters deal with the concept of popular life as against aristocratic, the Japanese peasantry, the people as seen in Japan's early and medieval literature, peasant life in the Tokugawa period, social status and classes. The author is one of the senior historians living today and an expert on the Nara and Heian periods.

1285. Saito Ryūzō 斎藤隆三, Kinsei Nihon sesōshi 近世日本世想史 (History of modern Japanese life), Tōkyō, Hakubunkan, 1925, 1237 pp.
    An illustrated survey of the life and customs of Tokugawa, Meiji and Taisho Japan (1600-1925). The author describes social structure, clothes, food, amusements, arts and accomplishments, education, and religion.

1286. Tamura Eitarō 田村榮太郎, Nihon fūzokushi 日本風俗史 (History of Japanese customs), Tōkyō, Mikasa Shobō, 1936, 307 pp.
    Divided into three parts: 1) primitive Japan; 2) the period of court and military houses; 3) period of military houses.

1287. Tōkyō Daigaku Rigakubu Chirigaku Kyōshitsu Shashin Chishi Nihon Henshū Iinkai 東京大学理学部地理学敎室寫眞地誌日本編集委員会 (Committee for the Compilation of the Photo-monograph of Japan, Geographical Institute, Faculty of Science, Tokyo University), Shashin chishi Nihon 寫眞地誌日本 (Photo-monograph of Japan), Tōkyō, Dai Nihon Yūbenkai Kōdansha, 1952, 282 pp.
    Edited by such outstanding scholars as Tsujimura Tarō, Tanaka Kaoru, Kiuchi Shinzō, and Satō Hisashi, this work presents a vivid pictorial description of Japan today. Chapters deal with land forms, seasons, settlements and land utilization, folklore, and modernization. Illustrations are explained in detail in Japanese but captions carry English translations.

1288. Wakamori Tarō 和歌森太郎, Nihon minzokugaku gaisetsu 日本民俗学概説 (Introduction to Japanese ethnology), Tōkyō, Tōkai Shobō, 1947, 297 pp.
    Parts 1, 2 and 3 deal with ethnology as a science and the methodology of the Yanagida school. Part 4 is a general survey of Japanese customs, folklore, clothing, food, pastimes, religion, etc. Pages 279-297 comprise a useful bibliography of the field.

1289. Yanagida Kunio 柳田国男 and Seki Keigo 関敬吾, Nihon minzokugaku nyūmon 日本民俗学入門 (Introduction to the study of Japanese folklore), Tōkyō, Tōkyōdō, 1948, 2 v.
    A systematic discussion of the ethnological methodology of the Yanagida school, useful for the detailed classification of the field. Each segment of the field is analyzed and a reading list is suggested.

1290. Yanagida Kunio 柳田国男 and Miki Shigeru 三木茂, Yukiguni no minzoku 雪国の民俗 (People of the land of snow), Tōkyō, Nihon Shuppan Haikyū K.K., 1944, 367 plates + 64 pp.
    A photographic record of the daily life, clothing, housing, technology, festivals and beliefs of the peasants of Akita Prefecture, one of the more remote regions in Japan.

1291. Yanagida Kunio 柳田国男 and Ōtō Tokihiko 大藤時彦, Sesōshi 世相史 (History of material life), Tōkyō, Tōyō Keizai Shimpōsha Shuppambu, 1943, 10+386 pp. [= volume 18 of the Gendai Nihon bummeishi series (Entry 722)].
    This work provides a detailed description of the material life of the Japanese from 1868 to 1940. Chapters deal with clothing and houses, communications, the household and labor, production, social organization and contacts, education, speech, recreation, sickness and death, superstition and religion. Emphasis is upon the modernization process in Japanese life. There is a list of selected reference works.

1292. Yasuda Yukihiko 安田靫彦 and others, Nihon fūzokuga taisei 日本風俗畫大成 (A compendium of illustrations of Japanese manners and customs), Tōkyō, Chūō Bijutsusha, 1929, 10 v.
    One of the most useful illustrated histories of Japanese manners and customs. Volumes 1-8 cover Japanese society by period. Each volume contains numerous illustrations of the life and customs of the period taken from contemporary art. Illustrations are explained and each volume concludes with a brief survey of the period. Volumes 9-10 contain photographs of reconstructed scenes and of actual artifacts of the past. Coverage is from early times to the twentieth century.

1293. Yūzankaku 雄山閣, Nihon fūzokushi kōza 日本風俗史講座 (Series on the history of Japanese customs and manners), Tōkyō, Yūzankaku, 1927-29, 12 v.
    The collective work of 56 contributors, this series is a vast compendium of materials on Japanese historical manners and customs. Volumes 1-3 contain a chronological survey of the field from early times to 1911. Volumes 4-12 contain essays on specialized subjects such as court ceremonies, games, the tea ceremony, houses, gardens, music, drama, the bath, religion, Western influence, etc. The entire work is profusely illustrated.

2) Food, Clothing, and Ornaments

1294. Ema Tsutomu 江馬務, Zōtei Nihon fukushoku shiyō 増訂日本服飾史要 (The essentials of the history of Japanese dress, revised), Kyōto, Hoshino Shoten, 1944, 10+282+17 pp.
    First published in 1936, this work is an illustrated survey of pre-modern styles of dress in Japan.

1295. Gotō Moriichi 後藤守一, Fukushokushi gaisetsu 服飾史概説 (Outline history of costume and ornaments), Tōkyō, Shikai Shobō, 1943, 400 pp.

1296. Itazawa Takeo 板澤武雄, Ishokujū no rekishi 衣食住の歴史 (History of clothing, food, and housing), Tōkyō, Haneda Shoten, 1948, 219 pp.

1297. Kon Wajirō 今和次郎, Kurashi to jūkyo 暮しと住居 (Daily life and houses), Tōkyō, Mikuni Shobō, 1944, 235 pp.

1298. Miyamoto Seisuke 宮本勢助, Minkan fukushokushi, hakimono no bu 民間服飾史, 履物の部 (History of folk costume and ornaments—footwear), Tōkyō, Yūzankaku, 1933, 199 pp.

1299. Nagashima Nobuko 永島信子, Nihon ifukushi 日本衣服史 (History of Japanese dress), Kyōto, Geisōdō, 1933, 48+694 pp.
A history of Japanese styles in dress from early times to the present. Well illustrated.

1300. Sakurai Shigeru 櫻井秀, Nihon fukushokushi 日本服飾史 (A history of Japanese costume and ornaments), Tōkyō, Yūzankaku, 1929, 359 pp.
A sketchy survey of Japanese dress from ancient times to 1853. Emphasis is on the Heian period. Illustrations are few.

1301. Sakurai Shigeru 櫻井秀 and Adachi Isamu 足立勇, Nihon shokumotsushi 日本食物史 (History of Japanese food), Tōkyō, Yūzankaku, 1934, 479 pp.
A history of food and eating habits in Japan from prehistoric times to c. 1560. This work is continued by Sasagawa and Adachi (Entry 1302).

1302. Sasagawa Rimpū 笹川臨風 and Adachi Isamu 足立勇, Kinsei Nihon shokumotsushi 近世日本食物史 (History of Japanese food in early modern times), Tōkyō, Yūzankaku, 1935, 502 pp.
Continues the historical coverage begun by Sakurai and Adachi (Entry 1301) through the Azuchi, Momoyama, Tokugawa and Meiji periods.

1303. Segawa Kiyoko 瀬川清子, Kimono きもの (Kimono), Tōkyō, Rokuninsha, 1943, 283 pp.
An important folkloristic study of Japanese kimono, their patterns, uses, etc.

1304. Sekine Masanao 関根正直, Zōtei kyūden chōdo zukai 増訂宮殿調度図解 (Illustrations of palace furnishings—revised and enlarged), Tōkyō, Rikugōkan, 1928, 158 pp.
A brief survey, with illustrations, of the development of palaces in Japan, their furnishings, carriages used by the nobility, etc.
1304a. Sekine Masanao
1304a. Sekine Masanao 関根正直, Zōtei shōzoku zukai 増訂装束図解 (Illustrations of military attire—revised and enlarged), Tōkyō, Rikugōkan, 1928, 2 v.
Volume 1 covers military dress and armor; Volume 2 is devoted to weapons of pre-modern Japan.

1305. Sekine Masanao 関根正直, Fukusei no kenkyū 服制の研究 (A study of dress regulations), Tōkyō, Kokon Shoin, 1925, 275 pp.
A study of the history of regulations with respect to costume in Japan from ancient times to the Meiji period. These are regulations applying chiefly to classes, ranks, sex, etc.

1306. Suzuki Keizō 鈴木敬三, Fukusō to kojitsu: yūshoku kojitsu zukai 服装と故実 有職故実図解 (Dress and ceremonial practices: illustrations of Japanese court ceremony and practices), Kyōto, Kawahara Shoten, 1950, 246 pp.

1307. Takahashi Kenji 高橋健自, Nihon fukushoku shiron 日本服飾史論 (History of Japanese costume and ornaments), Tōkyō, Daitōkaku, 1927, 215 pp.
An historical survey by periods.

1308. Takahashi Kenji 高橋健自, Rekisei fukushoku zusetsu 歴世服飾図説 (An illustrated commentary on costumes and ornaments of the various periods), Tōkyō, Shūseidō, 1929, 2 v.
Covers the subject to c. 1850.

1309. Tani Shin'ichi 谷信一, Zusetsu Nihon fukusōshi 図説日本服飾史 (Illustrated history of Japanese costume), Tōkyō, Shirogane Shoin, 1927, 165 pp.

1310. Yanagida Kunio 柳田国男, Hi no mukashi 火の昔 (History of fire), Tōkyō, Jitsugyō no Nihonsha, 1944, 2+6+2+216 pp.
One of Yanagida's masterpieces, it deals with fire, its uses for light, heating, etc., and its social and religious significance.

3) Marriages, Funerals, and Festivals

1311. Ariga Kizaemon 有賀喜左衛門, Nihon kon'in shiron 日本婚姻史論 (Essays on the history of Japanese marriage practices), Tōkyō, Nikkō Shoin, 1948, 2+296 pp.
A technical study from the sociological point of view of Japanese marriage practices and the problems of age, blood relationship, social status, etc., in the peasant community. The author documents his work by both written records and field studies. There is an excellent bibliographical introduction.

1312. Ema Tsutomu 江馬務, Nihon saijishi (Kyōto no bu) 日本歳事史（京都の部）(History of Japanese festivals, Kyoto), Kyōto, Naigai Shuppan K.K., 1922, 35+599+20 pp.

1313. Hagiwara Masanori 萩原正徳, Kon'in, tanjō, sōrei 婚姻, 誕生, 葬礼 (Marriage, birth, and funeral rites), Tōkyō, Isseisha, 1933, 9+196+328 pp.
Collected essays by various experts.

1314. Hayakawa Kōtarō 早 川 孝 太 郎 , <u>Hanamatsuri</u> 花 祭 (Flower festival), Tōkyō, Oka Shoin, 1930, 2 v.

    A detailed field study of the <u>hanamatsuri</u> in rural Aichi Prefecture.

1315. Hayakawa Kōtarō 早 川 孝 太 郎 , <u>Nō to matsuri</u> 農 と 祭 (Agriculture and festivals), Tōkyō, Guroria Sosaete, 1942, 296 pp.

1316. Hozumi Nobushige 穂 積 陳 重 , <u>Inkyoron</u> 隠 居 論 (Essays on retirement), Tōkyō, Yūhikaku, rev. ed., 1914, 724+22+37 pp.

    An interesting study of the Japanese customs of retirement, its origin and development, and laws governing it.

1317. Miyamoto Tsuneichi 宮 本 常 一 , <u>Minkan koyomi</u> 民 間 暦 (Folk calendars), Tōkyō, Rokuninsha, 1942, 277 pp.

    A study of the cycle of seasons and festivals in Japan.

1318. Nakayama Tarō 中 山 太 郎 , <u>Nihon kon'inshi</u> 日 本 婚 姻 史 (History of Japanese marriage), Tōkyō, Shun'yōdō, 1928, 6+32+971 pp.

    A detailed description of Japanese marriage by a foremost expert on social customs. The approach is historical by periods.

1319. Satō Seiya 佐 藤 誠 也 , <u>Kōkoku nenchū gyōji seigi</u> 皇 国 年 中 行 事 精 義 (A commentary on the calendar of observances of Imperial Japan), Tōkyō, Hakkōsha, 1940, 8+262 pp.

1320. Takeda Hisayoshi 武 田 久 吉 , <u>Nōson no nenchu gyōji</u> 農 村 の 年 中 行 事 (Seasonal activities of agricultural villages), Tōkyō, Ryūseikaku, 1943, 590 pp.

    Studies of the cycle of seasons and the distribution of labor in Japanese agricultural communities.

1321. Yanagida Kunio 柳 田 国 男 , <u>Kon'in no hanashi</u> 婚 姻 の 話 (Explanations of marriage customs), Tōkyō, Iwanami Shoten, 1948, 4+2+312 pp.

1322. Yanagida Kunio 柳 田 国 男 , <u>Nihon no matsuri</u> 日 本 の 祭 (Japanese festivals), Tōkyō, Kōbundō, 1932, 4+1+280 pp.

4) Recreation and Sports

1323. Maruyama Sanzō 丸 山 三 造 , <u>Dai-Nihon jūdōshi</u> 大 日 本 柔 道 史 (History of Japanese <u>jūdo</u>), Tōkyō, Kōdōkan, 1170 pp.

    A voluminous work covering only briefly the pre-modern history of <u>jūdo</u> wrestling in Japan. The bulk of the work is devoted to a description of the development of <u>jūdo</u> in post-Restoration Japan, to the various schools of <u>jūdo</u> instruction, and to an analysis of the art of <u>jūdo</u> wrestling.

1324. Nishibori Ichizō 西 堀 一 三 , <u>Nihon sadōshi</u> 日 本 茶 道 史 (History of the tea ceremony in Japan), Tōkyō, Sōgensha, 1940, 255 pp.

    A standard history of the art of tea ceremony in Japan.

1325. Nishitsunoi Masayoshi 西 角 井 正 慶 , <u>Mura no asobi</u> 村 の 遊 び (Recreation in the village), Tōkyō, Jiipusha, 1950, 1+1+278 pp.

    Describes rural folk dances, plays, festivals, and songs with their antecedents such as <u>dengaku</u> and <u>kagura</u>.

1326. Sakai Kin 酒 井 欣 , <u>Nihon yūgishi</u> 日 本 遊 戯 史 (History of Japanese games), Tōkyō, Kensetsusha, 1933, 937 pp.

    A standard survey of Japanese games, pastimes, and various social arts describes by historic periods. The work is well documented and illustrated.

5) Folklore and Mythology

1327. Fujisawa Morihiko 藤 澤 衛 彦 , <u>Nihon densetsu sōsho</u> 日 本 傳 説 叢 書 (Series on Japanese mythology), Tōkyō, Rokubundo, 1917-20, 13 v.

    A detailed coverage of Japanese folklore grouped by region.

1328. Higo Kazuo 肥 後 和 男 , <u>Nihon no shinwa</u> 日 本 の 神 話 (Japanese mythology), Tōkyō, Kōbundō Shobō, 1942, 200 pp.

    A survey of Japanese mythology by a leading folklorist.

1329. Matsuoka Shizuo 松 岡 静 雄 , <u>Nihon koyū minzoku shinkō</u> 日 本 個 有 民 族 信 仰 (Folkloristic beliefs of the Japanese), Tōkyō, Tōkō Shoin, 1941, 380 pp.

    By a specialist in primitive religious practices and beliefs, this work deals with special aspects of Japanese folk religion. Chapters deal with the <u>kami</u>, shrines, rituals, incantations, taboos, superstitions, etc.

1330. Seki Keigo 関 敬 吾 , <u>Nihon mukashibanashi shūsei</u> 日 本 昔 話 集 成 (Series on Japanese mythology), Tōkyō, Kadokawa Shoten, 1950—.

    A series of collected folk tales and myths. Of the three volumes published to date, volume 1 contains stories of animals and birds, 2 trees, and 3 humorous stories. The author attempts to explain the myths and to relate the stories to the folklore of other peoples. Bibliographic citations are made.

1331. Takagi Toshio 高 木 敏 雄 , <u>Nihon shinwa densetsu no kenkyū</u> 日 本 神 話 傳 說 の 研 究 (Studies in Japanese mythology and folklore), Tōkyō, Ogiwara Seibunkan, 1943, 570+2 pp.

    Describes Japanese myths and folklore and compares them with those of the Pacific island peoples.

1332. Yanagida Kunio 柳 田 国 男 , <u>Densetsu</u> 傳 說 (Legend), Tōkyō, Iwanami Shoten, 1940, 2+4+180 pp.

8. EDUCATION

    Histories of Japanese education have been written in the main by educational experts, such as Ototake Iwazō, Ishikawa Ken, Yoshida Kumaji, and Kaigo Tokiomi. The works of these men are considered standard and give fairly complete coverage of modern and pre-modern educational systems and policies. Recently a number of professional historians have begun working in the field of education history. Among them Momo Hiroyuki and Ōkubo Toshiaki are listed below.

1333. Ishikawa Ken 石 川 謙 , <u>Nihon shomin kyōikushi</u> 日 本 庶 民 敎 育 史 (A history of the education of the Japanese common people), Tōkyō, Tōkō Shoin, 1929, 458 pp.

    A standard history of popular education in Japan by a specialist in the field of education.

1334. Kaigo Tokiomi 海 後 宗 臣 and others, <u>Nihon kyōikushi</u> 日 本 敎 育 史 (History of Japanese education), Tōkyō, Meguro Shoten, 1938, 6+336 pp.

    An analytical survey of education through the ages in Japan. Treatment is by periods. Within each period the work describes the educational system in its entirety, the spirit of education, the content of instruction, and the method of teaching.

1335. Matsushita Takeo 松 下 丈 夫 , <u>Kindai Nihon kyōikushi</u> 近 代 日 本 敎 育 史 (History of Japanese education in recent times), Tōkyō, Meiji Tosho Shuppansha, 1949, 379 pp.

    A detailed description of education in Japan from 1868 to 1948. Chapters deal with Meiji educational philosophy, early educational systems, the influence of the West, the Imperial Rescript on Education, education and the development of the Japanese state, education and the Pacific War, postwar developments. A selected reading list is appended.

1336. Momo Hiroyuki 桃 裕 行 , <u>Jōdai no gakusei no kenkyū</u> 上 代 の 学 制 の 研 究 (Studies of the educational system of ancient Japan), Tōkyō, Meguro Shoten, 1947.

1337. Ōkubo Toshiaki 大 久 保 利 謙 , <u>Nihon no daigaku</u> 日 本 の 大 学 (Japanese universities), Tōkyō, Sōgensha, 1938, 394 pp.

    A chronological survey of the development of centers of higher education in Japan from the eighth century to the present. Each chapter concludes with a list of references.

1338. Ototake Iwazō 乙 竹 岩 造 , <u>Nihon kokumin kyōikushi</u> 日 本 国 民 敎 育 史 (History of the education of the Japanese people), Tōkyō, Meguro Shoten, 1940, 8+412 pp.

    A standard survey of education in Japan from early times through 1925. Emphasis is placed on the development of popular education. The author, professor emeritus at Tokyo Bunrika University, is a pioneer in the field of educational history.

1339. Ototake Iwazō 乙 竹 岩 造 , <u>Nihon shomin kyoikushi</u> 日 本 庶 民 敎 育 史 (History of education of the Japanese common people), Tōkyō, Meguro Shoten, 1929, 3 v.

    A detailed analysis of the development of popular education from the twelfth century to 1868. The author has covered in special detail the growth of temple schools (<u>terakoya</u>) during the late Tokugawa period.

1340. Satō Seijitsu 佐 藤 誠 実 , <u>Shūtei Nihon kyōikushi</u> 修 訂 日 本 敎 育 史 (History of Japanese education, revised), Tōkyō, Dai Nihon Tosho K.K., 1903, 600 pp.

    First published in 1890 by the Ministry of Education. Though old fashioned, this work is still of use today. The author deals in great detail with educational institutions from early times to 1902. Of special value is his description of the transmission of craft and art traditions and modern education in technological fields.

1341. Takahashi Shunjo 高 橋 俊 乗 , <u>Nihon kyōiku bunkashi</u> 日 本 敎 育 文 化 史 (A cultural history of Japanese education), Tōkyō, Dōbun Shoin, 624 pp.

    A broad interpretive view of Japanese education from ancient times through the 1920s.

1342. Tsuji Kōzaburō 辻 幸 三 郎 , <u>Nihon kyōiku tsūshi</u> 日 本 敎 育 通 史 (A survey history of Japanese education), Tōkyō, Meguro Shoten, 5th ed., 1940, 553+6 pp.

    First published in 1933, this work surveys the development of educational institutions in Japan with emphasis on the period since 1868.

1343. Uno Tetsuto 宇 野 哲 人 and others, <u>Hangaku shidan</u> 藩 学 史 談 (Historical studies of <u>han</u> schools), Tōkyō, Bunshōdō Shoten, 1943, 509 pp.

> An uneven collection of essays contributed by a large number of writers on educational systems in the several domains (<u>han</u>) of the Tokugawa period (1600-1868).

1344. Yoshida Kumaji 吉 田 熊 次 , <u>Hompō kyōikushi gaisetsu</u> 本 邦 教 育 史 概 説 (An introduction to the history of Japanese education), Tōkyō, Meguro Shoten, 1925, 644 pp.

> This work covers the development of educational theory and practice in Japan from early times to the time of writing. The author, a specialist in comparative education, emphasizes the influence on Japan of the Chinese educational system and compares the development of modern education in Japan with that of the West.

9. HISTORY OF RELIGION, THOUGHT, AND PHILOSOPHY

The field of religious and intellectual history in Japan is one of the most difficult of access to the non-Japanese scholar. Those who wish for more detailed orientation in this field may find the chapters on Buddhism and Shinto in <u>A Guide to Japanese Studies</u> published by the Kokusai Bunka Shinkōkai (Tokyo, 1937) of value. The following sections represent the standard categories under which the Japanese have published in this field. These cover a variety of subjects ranging from religions such as Buddhism and Christianity to intellectual movements such as Dutch studies.

Trends in the study of thought and religion have followed at a somewhat slower pace those noted for general historiography. Early writers on philosophical and religious history were for the most part teachers of philosophy or instructors in seminaries. Their work was thus directed primarily towards the explanation of philosophical and religious systems or the narration of sectarian movements. During the 1930s a few writers in the field began to assume the broader approach of the cultural historian, while the post-World War II era saw the first appearance of studies from the social science or ethnological points of view.

Aside from the works listed below, students in this field will find that the prewar historical series compiled in the cultural history tradition such as the <u>Sōgō Nihonshi taikei</u> (Synthetic survey of Japanese history (Entry 748), the <u>Nihon bunkashi</u> (Cultural history of Japan) (Entry 730), and the <u>Nihon bunkashi taikei</u> (Survey of Japanese cultural history) (Entry 731) devote a great deal of space to religious and intellectual movements. It should be pointed out also that the series entitled <u>Iwanami kōza: Tōyō shichō</u> (Iwanami series on Oriental thought) (Entry 1412) contains a variety of material covering the entire field of thought and religion in Japan.

a. Survey Histories of Religion

In the following brief selection the work of Hiyane Yasusada is outstanding for its detailed and impartial coverage of Shinto, Buddhism, and Christianity both in pre-modern and contemporary Japan (Entries 1345 and 1346). A brief introduction, Saigusa and Torii's <u>Nihon shūkyō shisōshi</u> (History of Japanese religion and thought) (Entry 1349), is written from the point of view of the modern social historian.

1345. Hiyane Yasusada 比 屋 根 安 定 , <u>Nihon shūkyōshi</u> 日 本 宗 教 史 (A history of religion in Japan), Tōkyō, Sankyō Shuppansha, 1925, 1141 pp.

> A monumental factual history of the religious faith of the Japanese people from primitive times to the time of writing. The author divides his history into 18 periods and covers the development of Shinto, Buddhism, and Christianity. The author himself is Christian. A 1951 edition of this work brings coverage up to the postwar period.

1346. Hiyane Yasusada 比 屋 根 安 定 and Anezaki Masaharu 姉 崎 正 治 , <u>Shūkyōshi</u> 宗 教 史 (History of religion), Tōkyō, Tōyō Keizai Shimpōsha Shuppambu, 1941, 4+14+490+22 pp. [= v. 16 of the <u>Gendai Nihon bummeishi</u> (Entry 722)].

> Anezaki contributes a short essay on science and religion in modern Japan. The rest of the work by Hiyane is an authoritative history of religious movements from the late Tokugawa period to the time of writing. The author treats of Shinto, Buddhism, and Christianity impartially.

1347. Naganuma Kenkai 長 沼 賢 海 , <u>Nihon shūkyōshi no kenkyū</u> 日 本 宗 教 史 の 研 究 (Studies in the history of Japanese religion), Tōkyō, Kyōiku Kenkyūkai, 1928, 1019 pp.

> A collection of articles on a wide variety of subjects involving Japanese religious institutions and religious leaders. These include studies of Shinran, religious uprisings, the deity Ebisu, <u>wakō</u> and <u>bahan</u> ships, the Shimabara Christian uprising, Christians at Hirado, Christianity and Buddhism, etc. Most of the articles are of a technical nature. The author, a professor at Kyushu University, is a specialist on Kamakura Buddhism and on the local history of northern Kyushu.

1348. <u>Nihon shūkyō daikōza</u> 日 本 宗 教 大 講 座 (Series on Japanese religion), Tōkyō, Tōkō Shoin, 1929-30, 12 v.

> Collected essays on religious sects in Japan. Content is largely non-historical, with emphasis on matters of doctrine. Volumes 1-2 cover Shinto; 3-8, Buddhism; 9-11, Christianity; and 12, religious art.

1349. Saigusa Hiroto 三 枝 博 音 and Torii Hiroo 鳥 井 博 郎 , <u>Nihon shūkyō shisōshi</u> 日 本 宗 教 思 想 史 (History of Japanese religion and thought), Tōkyō, Sekai Shoin, 1948, 292 pp.

> A convenient survey of the history of religious sects and movements in Japan. The authors approach the subject from the point of view of social historians.

1350. Toyota Takeshi 豊 田 芀 , Nihon shūkyō seidoshi no kenkyū 日本宗教 制度史の 研究 (Historical study of Japanese religious systems), Tōkyō, Kōseikaku, 1938, 297 pp.
>An extremely useful study of the history of laws and regulations governing religious orders in Japan. The work covers the development of the Buddhist church down through the Tokugawa period, discusses the religious problems of the Meiji period, the revival of Japanese state Shinto, and touches upon the question of religious freedom during the 1930s.

1351. Tsuchiya Senkyō 土屋 詮教 , Nihon shūkyōshi 日本宗教史 (A history of religion in Japan), Tōkyō, Keibundō, rev. ed., 1933, 24+826+108 pp.
>The second revised edition of a work first published in 1907. Covering the entire history of religious movements in Japan from early times to 1930, the author traces the origin and growth of each religious sect, its doctrine, and its influence upon life and society of the times.

1) Shinto

The subject of Shinto history has several varied facets. The term Shinto embraces not only the popular folk beliefs of the Japanese but a sophisticated philosophical system borrowing heavily from Confucianism and Buddhism, a number of active popular sects, and a highly institutionalized national creed. Much of what the Japanese have published on Shinto was stimulated by the nationalistic revival of the 1930s. Consequently, emphasis has been placed on the ideal, philosophical side of Shinto to the neglect of its folk basis, recent sectarian developments, or the subversion of Shinto to nationalistic ends. Representative Shinto scholars of prewar Japan such as Kiyohara Sadao and Katō Genchi carried on chiefly in the tradition of the ethnocentric Kokugaku scholars of the eighteenth and nineteenth centuries. For a more objective and comprehensive treatment of the development of Shinto, therefore, the reader is referred to the two works by Hiyane Yasusada mentioned above (Entries 1345 and 1346). The intellectual historian Muraoka Maretsugu, whose works are listed in Section 9 b 1 below (Entry 1420), has also contributed a great deal to the critical study of Shinto thought. One of the few postwar critiques of Shinto to appear is Tsuda Sōkichi's Nihon no Shinto (Japanese Shinto) (Entry 1360).

Recent expansion of ethnological studies in Japan has given rise to a number of works on the folk foundation of Shinto. Yanagida Kunio's Shin-kokugaku-dan (New national studies series) (Entry 1362), though somewhat disjointed, represents the most authoritative work in this field. The reader should be reminded that most of the popular Shinto sects have published histories which describe their doctrine and institutional development. Such works have had to be eliminated from the following list because of their great variety.

1352. Harada Toshiaki 原田敏明 , Kodai Nihon no shinkō to shakai 古代日本の信仰と社会 (The religion and society of early Japan), Tōkyō, Shōkō Shoin, 1948, 210 pp.

1353. Kiyohara Sadao 清原貞雄 , Shintōshi 神道史 (A history of Shinto), Tōkyō, Kōseikaku, 1932, 18+652+21 pp.
>One of the most substantial historical surveys of Japanese Shinto. Chapters deal with native Shinto, the types and characteristics of kami, early ritual, the influence of Confucianism and Buddhism, influence of geomancy, Shinto in the middle ages, the Shinto revival of the Tokugawa period, and Shinto after the Meiji Restoration. There is an extensive index.

1354. Kobayashi Kenzō 小林健三 , Nihon Shintōshi no kenkyū 日本神道史の研究 (Studies in the history of Japanese Shinto), Tōkyō, Shibundō, 1934, 341 pp.
>Collected essays on Japanese Shinto. Those on the Kurozumi sect and on Shinto sects and Shinto theory are of some interest.

1355. Kōno Shōzō 河野省三 , Shintō bunkashi 神道文化史 (Cultural history of Shinto), Tōkyō, Chijin Shokan, 1940, 15+230 pp.
>Part of the Taikan Nihon bunkashi sensho series (Entry 749), this work is of use as an introduction to the historical study of Shinto. The author surveys the historical position of Shinto in Japanese culture, emphasizing the relationship of Shinto and the pre-modern state, the development of Shinto sects, and the development of Shinto theory during the Tokugawa period.

1356. Miyaji Naokazu 宮地直一 , Jingishi kōyō 神祇史綱要 (An outline of Shinto history), Tōkyō, Meiji Shoin, 1938, 10+212+33 pp.
>An orthodox outline survey of the development of Shinto thought and institutions in Japan. Taken from the author's lectures at Tokyo University.

1357. Miyaji Naokazu 宮地直一 , Jingishi taikei 神祇史大系 (Outline history of Shinto), Tōkyō, Meiji Shoin, 1943, 13+250+56 pp.
>An amplification of the author's previously published outline (see previous entry). This volume contains many useful maps indicating the location of shrines, tables of shrines and their feudal land holdings, etc. There is an index.

1358. Shintō Kōkyūkai 神道攷究会 (Society for the Study of Shinto), Shintō kōza 神道講座 (Lectures on Shinto), Tōkyō, Shintō Kōkyūkai, 1929-31, 12 v.
>Contains 56 essays on Shinto history, shrines, theory, literature, etc. Contributors include Miyaji, Kōno, Adachi, Katō Genchi, Kurita Motoji, Kiyohara Sadao, Tsuji Zennosuke, Uozumi Sōgorō, Hiraizumi Chō, Nakamura Naokatsu, and others. Several essays deal with methodology.

1359. Saeki Ariyoshi 佐伯有義, Dai Nihon jingishi 大日本神祇史 (A history of Japanese Shinto), Tōkyō, Kokkōkan, 1913, 1324 pp.
     A detailed description by historical periods of shrines, deities, ceremonies, and Shinto theory. The subject is covered up to 1868.

1360. Tsuda Sōkichi 津田左右吉, Nihon no Shintō 日本の神道 (Japanese Shinto), Tōkyō, Iwanami Shoten, 1949, 414 pp.
     Collected essays on Shinto and Japanese thought by a leading non-conformist thinker in Japan. Essays cover Shinto phrases and their meaning, the thought of the Nara and Heian periods, Ise Shinto, Shinto theory of the Edo period, the Kokugakusha, the concept of unity of church and state (sai-sei itchi), etc.

1361. Yanagida Kunio 柳田国男, Shintō to minzokugaku 神道と民俗学 (Shinto and folklore studies), Tōkyō, Meiseidō, 1943, 144 pp.

1362. Yanagida Kunio 柳田国男, Shin-kokugaku-dan 新国学談 (New national studies series), Tōkyō, Koyama Shoten, 1946–.
     A series of studies of the religious and folkloristic background of the Japanese people. Three volumes had appeared by 1948. Volume 1 (1946) deals with festivals; volume 2 (1947) with mountain and natural deities; and volume 3 (1947) with ujigami, worship and prayer, and Shinto ritual.

1363. Yoshii Yoshiaki 吉井良晁, Jinja seido no kenkyū 神社制度の研究 (Studies in the institutional history of Shinto shrines), Tōkyō, Yuzankaku, 1935, 502 pp.
     Deals with the historical development of Shinto rituals, shrines, shrine hierarchy, shrine lands, Shinto priesthood, etc.

2) Buddhism

     The history of Buddhism in Japan is fairly well covered in the standard cultural histories, especially in the works of such men as Nishida Naojirō (Entry 706), Kurita Motoji (Entry 694), and Tsuji Zennosuke (Entry 716) and in the survey series such as the Nihon bunkashi (Cultural history of Japan) (Entry 730) and Nihon bunkashi taikei (Survey of Japanese cultural history) (Entry 731). For a more detailed and objective survey of Buddhism in recent and historic times, Hiyane Yasusada's works listed earlier (Entries 1345 and 1346) are quite satisfactory.
     The more specialized works listed below are either the products of instructors in Buddhist seminaries or of the cultural historians. Of the first category, Tamamuro Taijō's Nihon Bukkyōshi gaisetsu (Introduction to the history of Japanese Buddhism) (Entry 1375) is recommended because of its systematic organization of material. Among the cultural historians, Tsuji Zennosuke (Entry 1379) is outstanding.

1364. Asano Kenshin 淺井研眞, Nihon Bukkyō shakai jigyōshi 日本佛教社会事業史 (History of Buddhist social work in Japan), Tōkyō, Bonjinsha, 1934, 260 pp.
     Part 1 is a general introduction to the theory of Buddhist participation in social welfare activities. Part 2 deals with the history of the social work of the Buddhist church in Japan by periods from the introduction of Buddhism to 1911. Part 3 takes up individual aspects of Buddhist social work: moral teaching, efforts to eliminate the death sentence, the anti-prostitution movement, the prohibition movement, efforts to protect children, etc.

1365. Fujiwara Yusetsu 藤原猶雲, Nihon Bukkyōshi kenkyū 日本佛教史研究 (Studies in the history of Japanese Buddhism), Tōkyō, Daitō Shuppansha, 1938, 716 pp.

1366. Hashikawa Tadashi 橋川正, Gaisetsu Nihon Bukkyōshi 概説日本佛教史 (An outline history of Japanese Buddhism), Kyōto, Bunken Shoin, 1929, 387 pp.
     A survey history of institutional Buddhism, temples, sects, and priests from the sixth century to the twentieth.

1367. Hashikawa Tadashi 橋川正, Sōgō Nihon Bukkyōshi 綜合日本佛教史 (A general history of Japanese Buddhism), Tōkyō, Meguro Shoten, 1932, 598 pp.
     Posthumously published under the editorship of Nishida Naojirō and Tokushige Senkichi, this work deals in detail with Buddhism's impact upon Japanese society, state, economy, and culture. The work concludes with three essays entitled: Buddhism and Shinto, Buddhism and Japanese spirit, Buddhism and art.

1368. Kaneko Taiei 金子大榮, Nihon Bukkyōshi-gan 日本佛教史眼 (Survey of the history of Japanese Buddhism), Tōkyō, Iwanami Shoten.
     The emphasis of this work is on the formative period of Buddhism in Japan, covering Buddhism under Shōtoku Taishi, Nara Buddhism, new Heian sects, and the Kamakura Buddhist revival. Useful for an understanding of the doctrines and special characteristics of Japanese sects.

1369. Murakami Senjō 村上専精, Nihon Bukkyōshi-kō 日本佛教史綱 (An outline history of Japanese Buddhism), Tōkyō, Kinkōdō, 1898, 2 v.; Sōgensha, 1939, 2 v.
     A pioneer survey of Buddhism in Japan. The writing is stilted, but the work is full of factual material. Emphasis is on sects, leaders, and the institutional aspects of Japanese Buddhism up through the early Meiji period. Reproduced in 1939 as one of the Nihon bunka meicho sen (Japanese cultural classics series).

1370. Murakami Senjō 村上 寧精 , Zōtei Shinshū zenshi 増訂真宗全史 (Complete history of Shinshū Buddhism—revised and enlarged), Tōkyō, Heigo Shuppansha, 1918, 822 pp.
  A detailed account of the origin and the development of the Shin sect in Japan up to 1911. There is a subject and name index.

1371. Nishimitsu Gijun 西光義運 , Nihon Bukkyōshi gaisetsu 日本佛敎史槪說 (Introduction to the history of Japanese Buddhism), Kyōto, Heirakuji Shoten, 1947.

1372. Saitō Yuishin 斉藤唯信 , Jōdokyōshi 浄土敎史 (History of Jōdo Buddhism), Tōkyō, Heigo Shuppansha, 1927, 627 pp.
  A standard survey of the origins of Pure Land teachings in India and their development in China and Japan. One-third of the book is devoted to a systematic coverage of the growth of the Jōdo sect in Japan up to the time of writing.

1373. Shimaji Daitō 島地大等, Nihon Bukkyō kyōgakushi 日本佛敎敎学史 (History of Buddhist doctrine in Japan), Tōkyō, Meiji Shoin, 1933, 505+32+76 pp.
  An analysis of Buddhist sects, leaders, and doctrine in Japan up to the middle of the fourteenth century. Treatment is by periods. The author prefaces each period with a general introduction on the religious atmosphere of the time and then proceeds to an analysis of the major doctrines. There is an index.

1374. Shimaji Daitō 島地大等, Tendai kyōgakushi 天台敎学史 (History of Tendai doctrine), Tōkyō, Meiji Shoin, 1929, 520 pp.
  A standard survey of the development of the Tendai doctrines in China and their spread to Japan.

1375. Tamamuro Taijō 圭室諦成 , Nihon Bukkyōshi gaisetsu 日本佛敎史槪說 (Introduction to the history of Japanese Buddhism), Tōkyō, Risōsha, 1940, 444 pp.
  An outline survey of the history of Buddhism in Japan up through the Meiji period. The author's organization of his material is especially useful for the introductory student. Each sect is treated separately and notes are provided on chief religious leaders and on bibliography. The author is particularly interested in pointing out the social and cultural backgrounds which accounted for the rise of each sect.

1376. Tamamuro Taijō 圭室諦成 , Nihon Bukkyōron 日本佛敎論 (An analysis of Japanese Buddhism), Tōkyō, Mikasa Shobō, 1939, 3+4+226 pp.
  Part of the Nihon rekishi zensho series (Entry 737). This work is similar in arrangement but less detailed than the previously mentioned work by the author.

1377. Tsuchiya Senkyō 土屋詮敎, Meiji Bukkyōshi 明治佛敎史 (History of Buddhism during the Meiji period), Tōkyō, Sanseidō, 1939, 226 pp.

1378. Tsuchiya Senkyō 土屋詮敎, Taishō Bukkyōshi 大正佛敎史 (History of Buddhism during the Taisho period), Tōkyō, Sanseidō, 1940, 236 pp.

1379. Tsuji Zennosuke 辻善之助, Nihon Bukkyōshi 日本佛敎史 (History of Japanese Buddhism), Tōkyō, Iwanami Shoten, 1944—.
  A voluminous and authoritative survey of Buddhism in Japan. By 1947 two volumes, which carried the coverage into the Kamakura period, had appeared. The work is fully annotated from primary sources and recent scholarship. Professor Tsuji's chief forte is the analysis of the cultural role played by Buddhism in Japan.

1380. Tsuji Zennosuke 辻善之助 , Nihon Bukkyōshi no kenkyū 日本佛敎史ノ研究 (Studies in the history of Japanese Buddhism), Tōkyō, Kinkōdō, 1919, 793 pp.; second series, 1931, 974 pp.
  Collected essays on Japanese Buddhism covering all major periods up through the early Meiji era.

1381. Washio Junkei 鷲尾順敬, Bukkyō to kokumin shisō 佛敎と国民思想 (Buddhism and Japanese thought), Tōkyō, Kokūshi Kōshūkai, 1922, 103 pp.
  A survey of the intellectual influence of Buddhism upon the Japanese people from the time of its introduction to the mid-nineteenth century.

3) Confucianism

  The Japanese do not consider Confucianism a religion. Furthermore, because of the decline of institutionalized Confucianism after the Meiji Restoration, they have comparatively neglected its study. While a number of specialized studies, particularly of individual schools or philosophers, have been written, satisfactory survey histories in the field are hard to come by. It is especially difficult to find works which cover equally well the early period of Confucian development (600-1600) and the Tokugawa Confucian revival period (1600-1868). Few writers have given any attention to the period after 1868.
  Early writers on Confucianism, such as Inoue Tetsujirō, concentrated their attention upon Confucianism as a philosophy. This philosophical approach has been carried on by Muraoka Maretsugu, whose Nihon shisoshi kenkyū (Studies in Japanese intellectual history) (Entry 1420) should be consulted in this field. Among those who have taken the broader view of the social and cultural historian, Bamba Masatomo's Nihon Jukyōron (Japanese Confucianism) (Entry 1382) and Takada Shinji's Nihon Jugakushi (History of Japanese Confucianism) (Entry 1393) are recommended. Critical evaluations of the role of Confucianism in pre-modern Japanese society may be obtained from Tsuda Sōkichi's Shina shisō to Nihon (Chinese thought and Japan) (Entry 1396) and Nagata Hiroshi's Nihon hōkensei ideorogii (Japanese feudal ideology) (Entry 1422).

1382. Bamba Masatomo 萬 羽 正 朋, Nihon Jukyōron 日 本 儒 教 論 (Japanese Confucianism), Tōkyō, Mikasa Shobō, 1939, 328 pp.
    Published as part of the Nihon rekishi zensho series (Entry 737), this work provides a convenient summary of the historical development of Confucian institutions in Japan. The author is particularly concerned with the relationship between Confucianism and Japanese social and intellectual currents. The greater portion of the book deals with the Tokugawa revival of Confucianism. The author offers suggested reading lists at the end of his chapters.

1383. Inoue Tetsujirō 井 上 哲 次 郎, Nihon Kogakuha no tetsugaku 日 本 古 学 派 の 哲 学 (The philosophy of the Kogaku school in Japan), Tōkyō, Fuzambō, 1915, 841+18 pp.
    A survey of the Tokugawa school of Confucianism which had its origins in the thought of Yamaga Sokō, Itō Jinsai, and Ogyū Sorai.

1384. Inoue Tetsujirō 井 上 哲 次 郎, Teisei zōho Nihon Shushigakuha no tetsugaku 訂 正 増 補 日 本 朱 子 学 派 の 哲 学 (The philosophy of the Shushi school in Japan, revised and enlarged), Tōkyō, Fuzambō, 1915, 838 pp.
    A history of the orthodox Chu Hsi school of Confucianism during the Tokugawa period.

1385. Inoue Tetsujirō 井 上 哲 次 郎, Nihon Yōmeigakuha no tetsugaku 日 本 陽 明 学 派 の 哲 学 (The philosophy of the Yōmei school in Japan), Tōkyō, Fuzambō, 1897, 678 pp.
    A survey of the Wang Yang-ming school of Confucianism made popular in Tokugawa Japan by Nakae Tōju.

1386. Itō Chimazō 伊 藤 于 眞 三, Nihon seishin kenkyū: Nihon Jukyō 日 本 精 神 研 究 日 本 儒 教 (Studies on Japanese spirit: Japanese Confucianism), Tōkyō, Tōyō Shoin, 1934, 318 pp.
    A series of essays covering a wide variety of topics in the field of Japanese Confucianism.

1387. Iwahashi Junsei 岩 橋 導 成, Dai Nihon rinri shisō hattatsushi 大 日 本 倫 理 思 想 発 達 史 (History of the development of ethical thought in Japan), Tōkyō, Meguro Shoten, 1915, 2 v.
    A detailed description of the influence of Confucianism on the ethical thought of the Japanese. The author places his chief emphasis on the Tokugawa period and analyzes the teachings of the main Confucian schools of that period.

1388. Makino Kenjirō 牧 野 謙 次 郎, Nihon Kangakushi 日 本 漢 学 史 (History of Chinese studies in Japan), Tōkyō, Sekaidō, 1938, 10+336 pp., 1943, 13+336 pp.
    A chronological survey of the study of Chinese texts, literature, and philosophy in Japan.

1389. Nakayama Kyūshirō 中 山 又 四 郎, Nihon bunka to Jukyō 日 本 文 化 と 儒 教 (Japanese culture and Confucianism), Tōkyō, Tōkō Shoin, 1935, 150 pp.
    A short survey of the development of Confucian studies in Japan up through the Meiji period.

1390. Nishimura Tokihiko (Tenshū) 西 村 時 彦 (天 囚), Nihon Sōgakushi 日 本 宗 学 史 (History of Neo-Confucianism in Japan), Ōsaka, Sugimoto Ryokodo, 1909, 431 pp. Also in Asahi bunko (Asahi library), Tōkyō, Asahi Shimbunsha, 1951, 9+8+279 pp.
    A survey of the transmission of Neo-Confucian philosophy and the development of the Sung school in Japan up through the Tokugawa period. The writing is old fashioned but the work is authoritative.

1391. Ōe Fumiki 大 江 文 城, Hompō Jugakushi ronkō 本 邦 儒 学 史 論 考 (History of Japanese Confucianism), Tōkyō, Nihon Shuppan Haikyū K.K., 1945, 572 pp.
    A documentary history of the development of Confucian studies in Japan from their early origins to the Tokugawa period. Recent and authoritative.

1392. Okada Masayuki 岡 田 正 之, Nihon Kambungakushi 日 本 漢 文 学 史 (History of Chinese literature in Japan), Tōkyō, Kyōritsusha, 1929, 680 pp.
    A history of the study of Chinese classics and Chinese literature in Japan together with the influence of Chinese thought on Japan. Coverage is limited to the period prior to the sixteenth century.

1393. Takada Shinji 高 田 眞 治, Nihon Jugakushi 日 本 儒 学 史 (History of Japanese Confucianism), Tōkyō, Chijin Shokan, 1941, 278 pp.
    Published as part of the Taikan Nihon bunkashi sensho series (Entry 749). This work affords a convenient outline of the development of Confucianism in Japan. It concludes with a brief list of suggested reading.

1394. Takeuchi Yoshio 武 内 義 雄, Jukyō no seishin 儒 教 の 精 神 (The spirit of Confucianism), Tōkyō, Iwanami Shoten, 1939, 2+2+214 pp.
    A useful outline of the basic doctrines of Confucianism. Beginning with Confucius and his teachings, the author covers the development of Confucian philosophy in China through the Han, Tang, and Sung periods and goes on to discuss in detail the doctrinal characteristics of the various Confucian schools as they developed in Japan up through the mid-nineteenth century.

1395. Tokugawa-Kō Keisō Shichijūnen Shukuga Kinenkai 徳 川 公 継 宗 七 十 年 祝 賀 記 念 会 (Society for the Celebration of the Seventieth Anniversary of the Succession of Tokugawa Ietatsu as Head of the Tokugawa House), Kinsei Nihon no Jugaku 近 世 日 本 の 儒 学 (Japanese Confucianism in the modern age), Tōkyō, Iwanami Shoten, 1939, 20+1150 pp.
    A voluminous collection of 47 essays brought together in honor of the head of the Shibunkai, the foremost Confucian society in Japan. Essays give a nearly exhaustive coverage to Confucianism and Confucianists

during the Tokugawa period. Of particular interest are the interpretive essays on the participation of the Tokugawa shogunate and the various shogun in Confucian studies, the development of the shogunate's Confucian college and libraries, the specialized studies of Confucianism in various regions in Japan, the study of Chinese language and literature, Confucianism and art, and Confucianism and book publishing. Authors are leading scholars in the field.

1396. Tsuda Sōkichi 津田左右吉, Shina shisō to Nihon 支那思想と日本 (Chinese thought and Japan), Tōkyō, Iwanami Shoten, 1938, 14+2+200 pp.
A stimulating discussion of the basic premises of Chinese thought and the influence of Chinese culture on Japan. The author is of the opinion that Confucianism, because of its origin in China, is fundamentally uncongenial to Japanese society. The effort of the Japanese to adopt Chinese culture and ideas has been a detriment to Japanese development.

1397. Uda Hisashi 宇田尚, Nihon bunka ni oyoboseru Jukyō no eikyō 日本文化に及ぼせる儒教の影響 (Influence of Confucian doctrine on Japanese culture), Tōkyō, Tōyō Shisō Kenkyūsho, 1935, 32+1120+14 pp.
A voluminous study of the effect of Confucian thought on Japanese culture. Chapters deal with Confucianism and the imperial household, the year names (nengō), Shinto, morals, education, laws, literature, and economic thought.

1398. Yasui Kotarō 安井小太郎, Nihon Jugakushi 日本儒学史 (History of Japanese Confucianism), Tōkyō, Fuzambō, 1939, 296+172+24 pp.
Divided into three parts. Part 1 consists of essays on Japanese Confucianists and Confucian schools; part 2 is a survey of the Japanese study of Chinese classics and literature up through the Kamakura period; and part 3 is a list of the author's library and his published works.

4) Christianity

So much has been written in Western languages about the activity of Christian missionaries in Japan that it is difficult to discover works in Japanese which can contribute further to our knowledge of the subject. The following works are selected from the rather limited literature which deals with the so-called "Christian century," roughly 1550 to 1650. They should be supplemented by several titles listed under the section on foreign relations (Chapter 5 f above). Okamoto Ryōchi's Jūrokuseiki Nichi-Ō kōtsūshi no kenkyū (Studies of Japanese intercourse with Europeans during the sixteenth century) (Entry 931) and Shimmura Izuru's Namban kōki (Studies of foreign relations) (Entry 935) and its successor volumes are especially recommended.
Of the following works Anezaki Masaharu's Kirishitan shūmon no hakugai to sempuku (Persecution of Christianity and its movement underground) (Entry 1401) covers a broad field and uses native sources not available to Western scholars. For the development of Christianity in Japan after the Restoration of 1868, the work of Hiyane and Anezaki, Shūkyōshi (History of religion) (Entry 1346) is valuable for its balanced treatment of Christianity in relationship to government policy and the other competing religions, Shinto and Buddhism.

1399. Anezaki Masaharu 姉崎正治, Kirishitan dendo no kōhai 切支丹伝道の興廃 (History of Christian missionary work), Tōkyō, Dōbunkan, 1930, 4+19+820 pp.
A detailed history of the "Christian century" in Japan.

1400. Anezaki Masaharu 姉崎正治, Kirishitan hakugaishi-chū no jimbutsu jisseki 切支丹迫害史中の人物事蹟 (Facts about the individuals who appear in the history of Japanese Christian persecution), Tōkyō, Dōbunkan, 1930, 5+10+584 pp.
Descriptions of the lives of early Japanese Christians.

1401. Anezaki Masaharu 姉崎正治, Kirishitan shūmon no hakugai to sempuku 切支丹宗門の迫害と潜伏 (Persecution of Christianity and its movement underground), Tōkyō, Dōbunkan, 1925, 6+5+390 pp.
A detailed study from Japanese sources of the official attempts to eradicate Christianity in Japan in the period after the great persecutions. Especially valuable are the author's descriptions of the methods of Christian surveillance (shūmon aratame).

1402. Ebizawa Arimichi 海老澤有道, Kirishitanshi no kenkyū 切支丹史の研究 (Studies of the history of Christianity in Japan), Tōkyō, Unebi Shobō, 1942, 6+6+372 pp.
Essays on Christians and Christianity of the early period in Japan.

1403. Shimmura Izuru 新村出, Nihon Kirishitan bunkashi 日本切支丹文化史 (The cultural history of Christianity in Japan), Tōkyō, Chijin Shokan, 1940.
The most convenient one-volume survey.

b. Thought, Ethics, and the "Japanese Spirit"

The titles listed below embrace a broad and rather ill-defined category into which the Japanese have grouped works on thought (shisō) and "Japanese spirit" (Nihon seishin). The best of these works would fit into our category of intellectual history. Such in fact are Muraoka Maretsugu's Nihon shisōshi kenkyū (Studies in Japanese intellectual history) (Entry 1420), Tsuda Sōkichi's Bungaku ni arawaretaru waga kokumin shisō no kenkyū (A study of our national thought as manifested in literature) (Entry 1431), and Watsuji Tetsurō's Nihon seishinshi kenkyū (Studies in the history of Japanese spirit) (Entry 1432).

Many of the following works have been written for more ulterior purposes, however, and attempt to demonstrate the uniqueness of the Japanese way of thought and life. Motivation for such works was especially acute during the 1930s and the war years when Japanese scholars joined the nationalistic trend to exalt Japanese values above those of other peoples. Writings in the category of Japanese spirit and national polity (see Chapter 5 b above) form the chief contribution of Japanese historians to the ultra-nationalist aims of their country. Among the authors listed below, Hiraizumi Kiyoshi, Kiyohara Sadao, Kōno Shozō, Minoda Muneki, and Ōkawa Shūmei wrote extensively in the nationalistic vein. The last of these was prosecuted as a war criminal.

Not all attempts to describe Japanese national characteristics have been so nationalistically oriented. Besides the intellectual historians such as Muraoka, Tsuda, and Watsuji listed above, literary critics like Hasegawa Nyozekan maintained an objectivity in their approach to Japanese intellectual traditions and value systems. Further works of this nature in the literary and aesthetic fields are listed in Chapters 10 and 11 below.

At the conclusion of this section, separate lists on Bushido, Kokugaku, and Yōgaku (Dutch Studies) have been added. Although these intellectual movements were largely limited to the Tokugawa period, it was felt that they were of enough importance to warrant special bibliographical attention.

1) General

1404. Hasegawa Nyozekan 長谷川如是閑, Nihonteki seikaku 日本的性格 (Japanese character), Tōkyō, Iwanami Shoten, 1938, 3+240 pp.
A stimulating discussion of Japanese national characteristics by a foremost Japanese critic and liberal essayist.

1405. Higo Kazuo 肥後和男, Nihon kokka shisō 日本国家思想 (Theories of the Japanese state), Tōkyō, Kōbundō, 1939, 171 pp.
Written by a foremost folklorist during his nationalistic phase. This work attempts to analyze the development of Japanese attitudes and theories concerning the nation. The subject is traced through the various stages of national development from early times through the Meiji period.

1406. Hiraizumi Kiyoshi 平泉澄, Dentō 傳統 (Tradition), Tōkyō, Shibundō, 1940, 649 pp.
A member of the ultra-nationalist Kemmu Gikai and the Shukōkai, this writer had great influence on the wartime officer class. A prolific writer in the field of Japanese thought, Shinto, and nationalism, he is here represented by one of his more general works on Japanese spirit.

1407. Ienaga Saburō 家永三郎, Nihon shisōshi no shomondai 日本思想史の諸問題 (Problems in the history of Japanese thought), Tōkyō, Saitō Shoten, 1948, 259 pp.
The author is a leading historian and editor of the new postwar history textbook for primary schools (Kuni no ayumi).

1408. Inoue Tetsujirō 井上哲次郎, Nihon seishin no hattatsushi 日本精神の発達史 (History of the development of the Japanese spirit), Tōkyō, Kōbundō Shoten, rev. ed., 1941, 510 pp.
One of the best prewar works in the field, this book consists of essays on the development of Japanese thought prior to modern times. Emphasis is placed on Shintoism and the special nature of Japanese thought due to Shinto influence. The final essay on methodology and bibliography is especially valuable.

1409. Ishida Bunshirō 石田文四郎, Shintei zōho Nihon kokumin shisōshi kōwa 新訂増補国民思想史講話 (Lectures on the history of the thought of the Japanese people—revised and enlarged), Tōkyō, Nishōdō, 1929, 441 pp.
A popular survey of the development of political, economic, and religious thought in Japan.

1410. Itō Chimazō 伊藤于真三, Nihon seishinshiron 日本精神史論 (Essays on the history of Japanese spirit), Tōkyō, Shinkyōsha, 1937, 320 pp.
Essays by a number of contributors on spiritual trends and leaders of religious, political and social movements in pre-modern Japan.

1411. Iwanami kōza: Rinrigaku 岩波講座倫理学 (Iwanami series on ethics), Tōkyō, Iwanami Shoten, 1930-31, 15 cases.
A comprehensive collection of essays on ethical systems of the West, Asia, and Japan. These are dispersed in random order throughout the 15 cases, but an index is contained in case number 15. Essays are arranged in 3 groups: 1) general surveys, 2) historical surveys, and 3) subject studies, dealing with customs, morals, and human relations. The historical surveys of Japanese ethics are written by Watsuji Tetsurō, Muraoka Maretsugu, Hani Gorō, and others.

1412. Iwanami kōza: Tōyō shichō 岩波講座東洋思潮 (Iwanami series on Oriental thought), Tōkyō, Iwanami Shoten, 1934-36, 14 v.
Edited by Tsuda Sōkichi, this collection of essays covers folklore, social systems, philology, culture, philosophy, and religion in Japan, China, and India.

1413. Kiyohara Sadao 清原貞雄, Kaitei Nihon kokumin shisōshi 改訂日本国民思想史 (A history of the thought of the Japanese people, revised), Tōkyō, Hōbunkan, 1937, 646+39 pp.
A revised edition of a work first published in 1925. This is perhaps the author's most substantial contribution to this field. In it he surveys the development of Japanese thought and religious beliefs from early times to 1868, with emphasis on the strength of native characteristics as against the influence of Confucianism and Buddhism.

1414. Kiyohara Sadao 清原貞雄, <u>Nihon dōtokushi</u> 日本道徳史 (A history of Japanese ethics), Tōkyō, Chūbunkan, 1932, 756 pp.
    An amplification of the sections on ethics in the author's <u>Nihon kokumin shisōshi</u> (see above). The treatment is brought down to 1925.

1415. Kiyohara Sadao 清原貞雄, <u>Nihon shisōshi</u> 日本思想史 (History of Japanese thought), Tōkyō, Chijin Shokan, 6th ed., 1944, 289 pp.
    Part of the <u>Taikan Nihon bunkashi sensho</u> series (Entry 749). This work is perhaps the most accessible of the author's works on Japanese thought. In it he surveys the history of Japanese thought and the development of the idea of <u>kokutai</u> (national polity) from early times to the time of writing. There is an appended list of selected references.

1416. Kōno Shōzō 河野省三, <u>Nihon seishin hattatsushi</u> 日本精神発達史 (History of the development of the Japanese spirit), Tōkyō, Ookayama Shoten, 1932, 354 pp.
    An extensively documented survey of the history of "Japanese spirit." Chapters deal with the special characteristics of Japanese spirit, the national structure and the special nature of the Japanese people, the origins of Bushido, the growth of national self-consciousness during the Tokugawa period, and national thought during the Meiji period. The author quotes extensively from literary sources and gives many bibliographic citations.

1417. Kōno Shōzō 河野省三, <u>Nihon seishin no kenkyū</u> 日本精神の研究 (Studies of the Japanese spirit), Tōkyō, Ōokayama Shoten, 1934, 404 pp.
    A collection of essays supplementing the author's previous work (see above).

1418. Minoda Muneki 蓑田胸喜, <u>Gakujutsu ishin</u> 学術維新 (The academic restoration), Tōkyō, Gengen Nihonsha, 1941, 828 pp.
    An intellectual supporter of the ultra-nationalist movement, the author defends the position of "Japanese spirit" in the intellectual climate of his day. Chapters discuss Marxism, Nishida philosophy, Tsuda Sōkichi, Japanese spirit and Naziism, etc.

1419. Mombushō 文部省, <u>Kokutai no hongi</u> 国体の本義 (The meaning of national entity), Tōkyō, Mombushō, 1937, 156 pp.
    The official prewar exposition of Japan's <u>kokutai</u> (see Entry 849).

1420. Muraoka Maretsugu 村岡典嗣, <u>Nihon shisōshi kenkyū</u> 日本思想史研究 (Studies in Japanese intellectual history), Tōkyō, Oka Shoin, 1930, 1939, 1948, 1949, 4 v.
    By the foremost intellectual historian in Japan, four volumes of this series have appeared to date. Volume 1 was revised in 1940. Volumes consist of collected essays and are not systematically arranged. These cover methodology, Shinto studies, "Japanese spirit," the <u>kokugaku</u> movement, individual thinkers, and various intellectual movements. The bibliographical article in volume 3 (pp. 3-34) and the long survey articles on Japanese thought, philosophy, and spiritual life in volume 4 are especially valuable.

1421. Nagata Hiroshi 永田廣志, <u>Nihon yuibutsuronshi</u> 日本唯物論史 (History of materialist theory in Japan), Tōkyō, Hakuyōsha, 1936, 340 pp.
    A discussion of the origins of materialism in Europe and its growth and spread in Meiji Japan.

1422. Nagata Hiroshi 永田廣志, <u>Nihon hōkensei ideorogii</u> 日本封建制イデオロギー (Japanese feudal ideology), Tōkyō, Hakuyōsha, 1938, 425 pp.
    A study of Japanese feudal thought in its broadest implications. The author compares Japanese feudal thought with that of Europe, analyzes the influence of Buddhism and Confucianism on the feudal mind, and discusses the <u>nōhei</u> (peasant-warrior) and <u>sonnō</u> (pro-emperor) controversies of the Tokugawa period.

1423. Nagata Hiroshi 永田廣志, <u>Nihon tetsugaku shisōshi</u> 日本哲学思想史 (History of Japanese philosophy and thought), Tōkyō, Mikami Shobō, 1938, 325 pp.
    An analysis of the intellectual history of the Tokugawa period. The author deals in detail with the influence of the absolute Tokugawa government, Tokugawa Confucian schools, beginnings of dissension (<u>kokugaku</u>, <u>shingaku</u>, and science), and anti-feudal thinking (Western studies and the Shinto revival).

1424. Nishimura Shinji 西村眞次, <u>Nihon minzoku risō</u> 日本民族理想 (The ideals of the Japanese people), Tōkyō, Tōkyōdō, rev. ed., 1939, 322 pp.
    Chapters deal with the foundations of Japanese culture, characteristics of the early Japanese people, basic communal practices, Japanese culture and native characteristics of the people, the ideal life of the people, etc. The author is an historian, anthropologist, and archeologist.

1425. Nishioka Toranosuke 西岡虎之助, <u>Nihon shisōshi no kenkyū</u> 日本思想史の研究 (Studies in Japanese intellectual history), Tōkyō, Shōkasha, 1936, 400 pp.
    Collected essays by several experts in the field of intellectual history. These include a survey of Japanese intellectual history (Nishioka), the spiritual life of the Fujiwara nobles (Fujita Hiromasa), the legal concepts of the Kamakura <u>bushi</u> (Watanabe Tamotsu), scholarship of the Muromachi courtiers (Nakamura Mitsuru), and popular education in the Tokugawa period (Ōkubo Toshiaki).

1426. Ōkawa Shūmei 大川周明, Nihon seishin kenkyu 日本精神研究 (Study of the Japanese spirit), Tōkyō, Meiji Shobō, 1939, 332 pp.
  The author was prosecuted as a class A war criminal for his part as a leader of the ultra-nationalist movement in Japan. In this work he describes the lives and thinking of a number of pre-modern national figures whose lives exemplified various facets of Japanese spirit.

1427. Saitō Shō 斉藤晌, Nihonteki sekaikan 日本的世界観 (The Japanese world view), Tōkyō, Asakura Shoten, 1943, 531+11 pp.
  A nationalistic treatment of the concept of Japan's historical uniqueness. Chapters deal with the imperial way and the uniqueness of Japanese Buddhism, Confucianism, etc.

1428. Sakurai Shōtarō 櫻井庄太郎, Nihon hōken shakai ishikiron 日本封建社会意識論 (A study of the Japanese feudal mentality), Tōkyō, Nikkō Shoin, 1949, 244 pp.
  An objective analysis of the feudal mind. The author deals with such problems as feudal contract, name, honor, face, feudal morals, etc. He documents his study by frequent reference to the literature of the Tokugawa period.

1429. Shihō Hogo Kyōkai 司法保護協会 (Society for the Protection of Justice), Nihon bunka no seikaku 日本文化の性格 (Characteristics of Japanese culture), Tōkyō, Bunrokusha, 1941, 348 pp.
  Contains contributions by a number of leading scholars on such subjects as Japanese legal institutions, religion, mythology, literature, art, customs, etc. Contributors include Hasegawa Nyozekan, Maki Kenji, Ema Tsutomu, Tamamuro Taijō, and others.

1430. Takeoka Katsuya 竹岡勝也, Nihon shisō no kenkyu 日本思想の研究 (Studies of Japanese thought), Tōkyō, Dōbun Shoin, 1940, 5+312 pp.
  A mediocre survey of Japanese thought from early times through the nineteenth century. Introductory chapters on Japanese characteristics are followed by studies of individual thinkers and philosophical works. These include the Gukanshō, Jinnō shōtōki, Arai Hakuseki, Nakae Tōju, the Kokugaku leaders.

1431. Tsuda Sōkichi 津田左右吉, Bungaku ni arawaretaru waga kokumin shisō no kenkyū 文学に現はれたる我国民思想の研究 (A study of our national thought as manifested in literature), Tōkyō, Rakuyōdo, 1916-21, 4 v.
  One of the most influential works in its field, this series has been reprinted several times. A postwar edition was begun in 1951. The author attempts to trace the social development and intellectual climate of the Japanese people by an analysis of their literature. Volume 1 covers the period of aristocratic literature up to the Kamakura period (1185). Volume 2 deals with the period of feudal warrior literature up to the early Tokugawa period (c. 1650). Volumes 3-4 treat the Tokugawa period with emphasis on the literature of the common people.

1432. Watsuji Tetsurō 和辻哲郎, Nihon seishinshi kenkyū 日本精神史研究 (Studies in the history of the Japanese spirit), Tōkyō, Iwanami Shoten, 1926, 1935, 2 v.
  A major work by a pioneer non-conformist scholar in the field of intellectual history. Volume 1 is largely limited to studies of early thought, aesthetics, and religion. Volume 2 contains interpretive articles on Japanese spirit, Buddhism, art, etc. The author approaches Japanese thought primarily through an analysis of Japanese art and literature.

2) Bushidō

1433. Hashimoto Minoru 橋本実, Bushidō no shiteki kenkyū 武士道の史的研究 (Historical studies of Bushido), Tōkyō, Yūzankaku, 1934, 350 pp.

1434. Hashimoto Minoru 橋本実, Nihon Bushidōshi 日本武士道史 (History of Japanese Bushido), Tōkyō, Chijin Shokan, 1940, 246 pp.
  One of the best survey histories of the development of the concepts of Bushido in Japan.

1435. Inobe Shigeo 井野辺茂雄 and others, Bushidō zensho 武士道全書 (Complete series on Bushido), Tōkyō, Jidaisha.

1436. Kiyohara Sadao 清原貞雄, Bushidōshi jikkō 武士道史十講 (Ten lectures on the history of Bushido), Tōkyō, Meguro Shoten, 1927, 257 pp.
  Based on lectures delivered at the Hiroshima Military Academy. Part 1 is a history of the military man and his code from ancient times to the present. Part 2 is an exposition of the code of Bushido in the light of contemporary ethical concepts.

1437. Nagayoshi Jirō 永吉二郎, Nihon Bushidōshi 日本武士道史 (History of Japanese Bushido), Tōkyō, Chūbunkan, 1932, 295+16 pp.
  A general history of Bushido from early times to the twentieth century.

1438. Nishida Naojirō 西田直二郎, "Nihon Bushido 日本武士道 (Japanese Bushido)," in Iwanami kōza: Tōyō shichō (Iwanami series on Oriental thought), Tōkyō, Iwanami Shoten, 1934-36, v. 14.
  One of the most scholarly historical appraisals of the development and influence of the concepts of Bushido in Japan.

1439. Shigeno Yasunobu 重野 安繹 and Kusaka Hiroshi 日下寛, <u>Nihon Bushido</u> 日本武士道 (Japanese Bushido), Tōkyō, Taishūdō, 1909, 425 pp.
    An early eulogistic analysis of the concepts of Bushido and their borrowed Confucian, Buddhist, and Shinto ingredients.

3) Kokugaku

1440. Asano Akira 浅野晃, <u>Kokugaku kōyō</u> 国学綱要 (Elements of Kokugaku), Tōkyō, Daidōin Shokan, 1942, 260 pp.
    The essential characteristics of Japan's national intellectual tradition by a non-academic student of Asiatic thought and Japan's classical literature.

1441. Fujita Tokutarō 藤田徳太郎, <u>Waga Kokugaku</u> わが国学 (Kokugaku), Tōkyō, Shin Kōasha, 1942, 292 pp.
    A nationalistic approach to the study of Kokugaku in Japan.

1442. Hani Gorō 羽仁五郎, <u>Nihon ni okeru kindai shisō no zentei</u> 日本に於ける近代思想の前提 (The antecedents of modern thought in Japan), Tōkyō, Iwanami Shoten, 1949, 208 pp.
    Contains two interpretive essays on the development of Kokugaku philosophy in the context of Tokugawa feudal society.

1443. Itō Tasaburō 伊東多三郎, <u>Kokugaku no shiteki kōsatsu</u> 国学の史的考察 (An historical study of the Kokugaku movement), Tōkyō, Ookayama Shoten, 1932, 3+3+425 pp.
    An authoritative analysis of the Kokugaku movement of the Tokugawa period. Beginning with a discussion of the ideological background of Kokugaku and its reliance on Confucian, Shinto, and feudal thought, the author attempts to analyze in modern terms the basic ingredients of the Kokugaku philosophy. He gives particular consideration to the social context of the movement. There is an index.

1444. Kiyohara Sadao 清原貞雄, <u>Kokugaku hattatsushi</u> 国学発達史 (History of the development of Kokugaku), Tōkyō, Unebi Shobō, 1942, 2nd ed., 410+12 pp.
    An historical survey of the early Japanese classics and Shinto scriptures in their relation to the Tokugawa Kokugaku movement. Each of the major Tokugawa Kokugaku scholars is given extensive treatment. There is an index.

1445. Nomura Hachirō 野村八良, <u>Kokugaku zenshi</u> 国学全史 (Complete history of the Kokugaku movement), Tōkyō, Seki Shoin, 1928-29, 2 v.
    Largely a collection of biographies and descriptive articles on the chief Kokugaku scholars of the Tokugawa period. Volume 2 concludes with chronological tables and an index.

1446. Yamada Yoshio 山田孝雄, <u>Kokugaku no hongi</u> 国学の本義 (The fundamentals of Kokugaku), Tōkyō, Unebi Shobō, 1942, 225 pp.
    A nationalistic presentation of the fundamentals of Japan's spiritual tradition as revealed through the study of the early classics.

1447. Yamamoto Masahide 山本正秀 and Watanabe Shū 渡辺秀, <u>Kokugakuron</u> 国学論 (A survey of Kokugaku), Tōkyō, Mikasa Shobō, 1939, 208 pp.
    One of the Nihon rekishi zensho series (Entry 737), this work presents a convenient interpretive outline of the development of the study of Japan's intellectual tradition as revealed in her literature. Chapters deal with the antecedents of the Kokugaku movement, Kamo Mabuchi, Motoori Norinaga, Hirata Atsutane, and the "New Kokugaku" scholars of post-Restoration Japan. There is a list of suggested reading.

4) Yōgaku

1448. Itazawa Takeo 板澤武雄, "Rangaku no hattatsu 蘭学の発達 (The development of Dutch studies)," in <u>Iwanami kōza: Nihon rekishi</u> (Iwanami series on Japanese history), Tōkyō, Iwanami Shoten, 1933, v. 18.
    A brief survey of Dutch studies in Japan.

1449. Numata Jirō 沼田次郎, <u>Bakumatsu Yōgakushi</u> 幕末洋学史 (History of Western studies in the late Tokugawa period), Tōkyō, Tōko Shoin, 1950, 283 pp.
    A survey of Dutch studies in Japan of the late Tokugawa period. The author minimizes the revolutionary influence which the students of Western science had upon Japanese society.

1450. Takahashi Shin'ichi 高橋碩一, <u>Yōgakuron</u> 洋学論 (Treatise on Western studies), Tōkyō, Mikasa Shobō, 1939, 224 pp.
    A general survey of Western studies in Tokugawa Japan. The author is inclined to credit Japanese scholars of the Yōgaku tradition with considerable influence in shaping the political and social currents of the late Tokugawa period.

10. LITERATURE

The field of Japanese literature is a broad one in which the literary historian has played a conspicuous role. The following list seeks only to provide a minimum working bibliography for the historian with non-specialized interests. The reader will find this field amply supplied with essay series (kōza) which provide excellent introductory material on almost any phase of literary history and interpretation. The postwar series published by Kawade Shobō (Entry 1461) contains valuable essays on bibliography and methodology. Of the general historical surveys, the thirteen-volume Nihon bungaku zenshi (Complete history of Japanese literature) (Entry 1463) is recommended as a standard factual reference work. Shorter interpretive histories are quite plentiful and difficult to choose from. The works of Fujioka Sakutarō and Haga Yaichi, though rather old by now, are still useful for their stimulating interpretations. Tsugita Jun's Kokubungakushi shinkō (New lectures on the history of Japanese literature) (Entry 1464) is of more recent origin and is quite authoritative. The most convenient one-volume survey to appear out of postwar Japan is undoubtedly Asō Isoji's Nihon bungakushi (History of Japanese literature) (Entry 1453).

a. General

1451. Ara Masahito 荒 正 人 and others, Gaisetsu gendai Nihon bungakushi 概 説 現 代 日 本 文 学 史 (Introduction to contemporary Japanese literature), Tōkyō, Hanawa Shobō, 1949, 340 pp.
> A series of survey articles on Japanese literature since 1868, divided as follows: Meiji literature, realistic literature, non-realistic literature, Taisho literature, early Showa and late Showa literature. Contributors are leading contemporary literary critics.

1452. Ara Masahito 荒 正 人, Shōwa bungaku jūnikō 昭 和 文 学 十 二 講 (Twelve essays on Showa literature), Tōkyō, Kaizōsha, 1950, 321 pp.
> Essays by leading contemporary critics on Japanese literature from 1926 to the postwar period.

1453. Asō Isoji 麻 生 磯 次, Nihon bungakushi 日 本 文 学 史 (History of Japanese literature), Kyōto, Shibundō, 1949, 4+332+18 pp.
> The most convenient one-volume survey of Japanese literature. Treatment is by periods and by genre within periods. Literary works are analyzed for their contents and meaning. Brief chronological tables and an index are appended.

1454. Fujimura Saku 藤 村 作, Kaitei kokubungakushi sōsetsu 改 訂 国 文 学 史 總 説 (Survey of the history of Japanese literature, revised), Tōkyō, Chukōkan, 1928, 360+16+8 pp.
> First published in 1926 as a text for higher school teachers, the revised edition is made more suitable for general use. This work is a general survey of the history of Japanese literature by periods from early times through the Meiji period. Representative writers and their works are discussed and characteristic excerpts quoted. The author includes useful bibliographical information on the existence of more detailed studies of the works he cites. There are chronological tables, an index, and numerous illustrations.

1455. Fujioka Sakutarō 藤 岡 作 太 郎, Kokubungakushi kōwa 国 文 学 史 講 話 (Lectures on the history of Japanese literature), Tōkyō, Kaiseikan, 1908, 442 pp.
> Perhaps the most famous interpretive history of Japanese literature, it is still valuable for its stimulating ideas and its brilliant style. The author describes Japanese literary development in broad strokes, using the point of view of the cultural historian. Coverage is up to the time of writing. Many editions of this work are available. The latest is a revised postwar edition, Iwanami Shoten, 1947, 360 pp.

1456. Haga Yaichi 芳 賀 矢 一, Kokubungakushi jikkō 国 文 学 史 十 講 (Ten lectures on the history of Japanese literature), Tōkyō, Fuzambō, rev. ed., 1903, 267+11 pp.
> Although these lectures were delivered in 1898, this work is of lasting worth for the clarity with which it sketches the main currents of Japanese literature and explains the characteristics of various literary works and styles. The revised edition contains notes on reference and research materials. Coverage is through the early Meiji period.

1457. Hisamatsu Sen'ichi 久 松 潜 一, Nihon bungaku hyōronshi 日 本 文 学 評 論 史 (History of literary theory and criticism in Japan), Tōkyō, Shibundō, 1936-38, 3 v.
> A detailed study of Japanese writings on literary theory and criticism from early times to the time of writing. The author analyzes the basic aesthetic concepts which the Japanese have applied to their prose and poetry. Volumes 2 and 3 contain bibliographical lists and indices.

1458. Homma Hisao 本 間 久 雄, Meiji bungakushi 明 治 文 学 史 (History of Meiji literature), Tōkyō, Tōkyōdō, 1935-43, 3 v.
> Volumes 1 and 2 of this series are included as part of the Nihon bungaku zenshi series (Entry 1463). Still incomplete, this work is none the less the standard treatment of Meiji literature.

1459. Iwanami kōza: Nihon bungaku 岩 波 講 座 日 本 文 学 (Iwanami series on Japanese literature), Tōkyō, Iwanami Shoten, 1931-33, 20 v.
> Edited by Fujimura Saku, Hashimoto Shinkichi, Yoshizawa Yoshinori, and Yamada Yoshio, this collection of some 187 essays on all phases of Japanese literature contains much material of historical importance. Essays include historical surveys by periods, surveys by genre, discussions of methodology, bibliography, etc.

1459a. Miura Keizō 三 浦 圭 三, Sōgō Nihon bungaku zenshi 綜 合 日 本 文 学 全 史 (Synthetic survey of the history of Japanese literature), Tōkyō, Bunkyō Shoin, 1924, 741 pp.
> A survey history of Japanese literature which seeks to synthesize the many approaches of previous scholars. The author combines interpretation with extensive bibliographical detail. Coverage is through Meiji.

1460. <u>Nihon bungaku kōza</u> 日本文学講座 (Series on Japanese literature), Tōkyō, Kaizōsha, 1933-35, 17 v.

A voluminous survey of Japanese literature by genre. Volumes cover: 1) general survey; 2) people's literature; 3-4) novels and short stories; 5) diaries and miscellanies; 6-7) <u>waka</u>; 8) <u>haiku</u>; 9) new poetry; 10) drama; 11) Meiji literature; 12) Meiji and Taisho; 13) Taisho; 14) popular literature; 15-17) special topics, grammar, tables, and bibliography.

1461. <u>Nihon bungaku kōza</u> 日本文学講座 (Series on Japanese literature), Tōkyō, Kawade Shobō, 1951—, 8 v.

An excellent series of essays covering the entire field of Japanese literature and literary aesthetics. Subject matter is divided as follows: volumes 1-2) ancient literature through the Heian period; 3) medieval literature; 4) Tokugawa literature; 5-6) post-Restoration; 7) Japanese literary theory and aesthetic principles; 8) methodology in bibliography, literary history, etc. Volumes 1-6 contain articles on literary movements, genres, individual works, and major authors. Volume 8 is of special use as a reference work and bibliography.

1462. <u>Nihon bungaku kōza</u> 日本文学講座 (Series on Japanese literature), Tōkyō, Shinchōsha, rev. ed., 1931, 15 v.

Contains some useful historical essays. Volume 2, covering Japanese literature and social life, is of special interest.

1463. Sasaki Nobutsuna 佐々木信綱 and others, <u>Nihon bungaku zenshi</u> 日本文学全史 (Complete history of Japanese literature), Tōkyō, Tōkyōdō, 1937, 13 v.

The outstanding multi-volume historical survey of Japanese literature. Volumes 1-2 cover the Nara period (Sasaki), 3-4 the Heian (Igarashi), 6-7 the Kamakura and Muromachi periods (Yoshizawa), 8-9 the Edo period (Takano), and 10-11 the Meiji period (Homma). Remaining volumes include general surveys and tables. Each volume is indexed and profusely illustrated. The approach is more descriptive and factual than interpretive.

1464. Tsugita Jun 次田潤, <u>Kokubungakushi shinkō</u> 国文学史新講 (New lectures on the history of Japanese literature), Tōkyō, Meiji Shoin, 1932-36, 2 v.

An outstanding interpretive survey of Japanese literature based on more up-to-date research than those of Haga or Fujioka (Entries 1456 and 1455). Coverage is limited to the pre-Meiji period. Each chapter contains a list of suggested references. There is an index.

b. **Special Studies**

1465. Ihara Toshirō 伊原敏郎, <u>Nihon engekishi</u> 日本演劇史 (History of Japanese drama), Tōkyō, Waseda Daigaku Shuppambu, 1904, 762 pp.

The author later published in this same series: <u>Kinsei Nihon engekishi</u> (History of Japanese drama of the Tokugawa period), 1913, and <u>Meiji engekishi</u> (History of Meiji drama), 1934. The author surveys briefly the origins of Japanese drama and provides detailed coverage to the Tokugawa (principally the <u>kabuki</u>) and Meiji periods.

1466. Nishishita Keiichi 西下経一, <u>Waka shiron</u> 和歌史論 (Historical interpretation of the <u>waka</u>), Tōkyō, Shibundō, 1944, 16+636 pp.

An interpretive survey of the history of the 31-syllable poem, the <u>waka</u>. The author traces the development of the principles of <u>waka</u> composition and the poetic spirit of <u>waka</u> writers from the origins to contemporary times.

1467. Sasaki Nobutsuna 佐々木信綱, <u>Nihon kagakushi</u> 日本歌学史 (History of Japanese poetry), Tōkyō, Hakubunkan, 1910, 559+75 pp.

A standard history of the development of <u>waka</u> poetry in Japan from the Heian through the Tokugawa periods. Several useful tables, indices, and bibliographic lists are appended.

1468. Sasaki Nobutsuna 佐々木信綱, <u>Zōtei wakashi no kenkyū</u> 増訂和歌史の研究 (Studies of the history of <u>waka</u> poetry, revised), Tōkyō, Kyōbunsha, 1927, 446 pp.

Significant interpretive essays which cover the history of Japanese <u>waka</u> poetry by period down to modern times.

1469. Takano Tatsuyuki 高野辰之, <u>Nihon engekishi</u> 日本演劇史 (History of Japanese drama), Tōkyō, Tōkyōdō, 1947—.

Scheduled to run to 3 volumes, this work is a collection of lectures and essays on the origins and development of the dramatic medium in Japan. Volume 1 covers the years up to the beginning of the Tokugawa period.

1470. Takano Tatsuyuki 高野辰之, <u>Nihon kayōshi</u> 日本歌謡史 (A history of Japanese songs), Tōkyō, Shunjūsha, 1926, 1090+27 pp.

A definitive study of the development of songs in Japan from ancient times to 1868. The work covers folk songs, religious songs, the chants in <u>nō</u> drama, <u>jōruri</u> singing, etc.

1471. Yamada Yoshio 山田孝雄, <u>Renga gaisetsu</u> 連歌概説 (Introduction to <u>renga</u>), Tōkyō, Iwanami Shoten, 1937, 295 pp.

1472. Yoshihara Toshio 吉原 敏雄, Gaikan tankashi 概 觀 短 歌 史(Introduction to the history of tanka), Tōkyō, Kadan Shimpōsha, rev. ed., 1948, 208 pp.
    Completed in 1938 and first published in 1942, this work affords a useful survey of tanka writing in Japan up to modern times.

11. ARTS AND CRAFTS

    The Japanese are noted for their many illustrated works on fine arts and crafts. The extensiveness of this field has precluded the possibility of providing more than a cursory survey of Japanese publications of this type. The general historian will no doubt find illustrated art histories of most service for introductory purposes. Of these, the one by Miyamoto Toyomune (Entry 1483) has obtained considerable fame by virtue of its translation into English. Others of this variety are Fujikake Shizuya's Nihon bijutsu zusetsu (A pictorial survey of Japanese art) (Entry 1475) and Ōoka and Tazawa's Zusetsu Nihon bijutsushi (An illustrated history of Japanese art) (Entry 1489). For short interpretive surveys the Teishitsu Hakubutsukan's Nihon bijutsu ryakushi (An abridged history of Japanese art) (Entry 1490) is recommended among prewar works. In post-World War II Japan the work edited by Kuno Kenji of the Institute of Art Research entitled Nihon bijutsushi (History of Japanese art) (Entry 1480) attempts a new approach to art history by relating art to social and political movements. The reader is reminded that a number of the standard cultural histories, notably Nishida Naojirō's Nihon bunkashi josetsu (An introduction to the history of Japanese culture) (Entry 706) and the Nihon bunkashi taikei (Survey of Japanese cultural history) (Entry 731), provide stimulating discussions of art in the cultural context of their times.

a. Fine Arts in General: Painting and Sculpture

1473. Fujikake Shizuya 藤 懸 静 也, "Bijutsushigaku no hatten 美 術 史 学 の 発 展(The development of the study of art history)," Nihon shogaku, v. 1, n. 1, 1942, 153+173 pp.
    A survey of the development of professional art history from the Tokugawa period to contemporary times. Describes the various schools of art history and their approaches.

1474. Fujikake Shizuya 藤 懸 静 也, ed., Nihon bijutsu taikei 日 本 美 術 大 系 (Outline of Japanese art), Tōkyō, Seibundō Shinkōsha, 1942, 555 pp.

1475. Fujikake Shizuya 藤 懸 静 也, Nihon bijutsu zusetsu 日 本 美 術 図 説(A pictorial survey of Japanese art), Tōkyō, Asahi Shimbunsha, 1950, 349 pp. + 80 pp. illus.
    A general survey of Japan's pre-modern art based on a broad selection of illustrative materials. The work covers all fields of art, crafts, and architecture. Individual specialists have written introductory passages for each field and supply explanations for the illustrations.

1476. Fujikake Shizuya 藤 懸 静 也, Ukiyoe no kenkyū 浮 世 絵 の 研 究 (A study of ukiyoe), Tōkyō, Yūzankaku, 1943, 3 v.
    The standard scholarly survey of ukiyoe, illustrated but not in color.

1477. Fujioka Sakutarō 藤 岡 作 太 郎, Kinsei kaigashi 近 世 絵 画 史(History of modern Japanese painting), Tōkyō, Kinkōdō, 1903, 399+13+32+26 pp.
    An analytical survey of Japanese painting of the Tokugawa and Meiji periods. The author, a specialist in literary history, relates the development of painting to social and intellectual movements. There was a revised edition in 1906 and a 1926 reprint.

1478. Hamada Kōsaku 濱 田 耕 作, Nihon bijutsushi kenkyū 日 本 美 術 史 研 究 (Studies in the history of Japanese art), Tōkyō, Zayūhō Kankōkai, 1941, 20+424 pp.
    Essays by a leading archeologist and specialist in early Japanese art. The essays cover Japanese fine art from earliest times to the end of the sixteenth century. Emphasis is upon sculpture.

1479. Kobayashi Takeshi 小 林 剛, Nihon chōkokushi kenkyū 日 本 彫 刻 史 研 究 (Studies in the history of Japanese sculpture), Nara, Yōtokusha, 1947, 399 pp.
    Essays covering the history of Japanese sculpture from the Nara through Kamakura periods by a foremost expert on the subject.

1480. Kuno Kenji 久 野 健 氏, ed., Nihon bijutsushi 日 本 美 術 史 (History of Japanese art), Tōkyō, Zayūhō Kankōkai, 1949-50, 2 v.
    A collaborative work by nine art historians, chiefly of the Bijutsu Kenkyūjo (Institute of Art Research). Essays cover Japanese art history by periods, attempting to relate developments in the field of fine arts to the social and political movements of the times.

1481. Kuroda Hōshin 黒 田 鵬 心, Dai Nihon bijutsushi 大 日 本 美 術 史 (History of Japanese art), Tōkyō, Seibundō, 1922, 27+1002+22 pp.
    Based on lectures delivered in 1891 by one of the early pioneers in the field of art history.

1482. Kuroda Hōshin 黒 田 鵬 心, Nihon bijutsushi gaisetsu 日 本 美 術 史 概 説(Outline history of Japanese art), Tōkyō, Seibundō, 1933, 897+21 pp.
    A comprehensive survey of Japanese art from earliest times to 1925. The author divides Japanese art history into 12 periods. Within each period he takes up the main fields of artistic creation including architecture and crafts.

1483. Minamoto Toyomune 源 豊 宗 , Nihon bijutsushi zuroku 日 本 美 術 史 図 錄 (Illustrated history of Japanese art), Kyōto, Hoshino Shoten, 1932, 50+219+100 pp.
> A standard survey of Japanese art as seen through important examples. The work emphasizes painting and sculpture and covers the years up to the Meiji Restoration. There is an English translation: Harold G. Henderson, An Illustrated History of Japanese Art, Kyōto, Hoshino, 1935.

1484. Naitō Tōichirō 内 藤 藤 一 郎 , Nihon Bukkyō zuzōshi 日 本 佛 敎 図 像 史 (A history of Buddhist iconography), Tōkyō, Toho Shoin, 1932, 3+7+33 pp.
> Studies in detail of the iconography of Yakushi and Amida Nyorai.

1485. Ōguchi Masao 大 口 理 夫 , Nihon chōkokushi kenkyū 日 本 彫 刻 史 研 究 (Studies in the history of Japanese sculpture), Kanagawa, Sōgeisha, 1948, 210 pp.

1486. Okuyama Kindō 奥 山 錦 洞 , Nihon shodōshi 日 本 書 道 史 (A history of Japanese calligraphy), Tōkyō, Seikyōsha, 1943, 46+496 pp.
> Largely concerned with the lives of great calligraphers, this work covers by period the entire history of calligraphic art in Japan. There is an appended chronological table and bibliographical list of sources.

1487. Ōmura Seigai 大 村 西 崖 , Kō Nihon kaigashi 廣 日 本 繪 畫 史 (A complete history of Japanese painting), Tōkyō, Hōunsha, 1948, 3 v.
> A detailed history of Japanese painting by an authority. Volume 1 covers early Japanese painting and Buddhist pictorial art through the first half of the Ashikaga period. Volume 2 extends through the early Tokugawa period, and volume 3 completes the Tokugawa period.

1488. Ono Gemmyō 小 野 玄 妙 , Bukkyō bijutsu gairon 佛 敎 美 術 概 論 (Introduction to Buddhist art), Tōkyō, Heigo Shuppansha, 1917, 263 pp.
> An authoritative survey of Buddhist art and iconography by a foremost expert.

1489. Ōoka Minoru 大 岡 実 and Tazawa Yutaka 田 澤 坦 , Zusetsu Nihon bijutsushi 図 説 日 本 美 術 史 (An illustrated history of Japanese art), Tōkyō, Iwanami Shoten, 1933, 297 pp.
> An extremely useful outline history of Japanese art and architecture as seen through illustrations.

1490. Sakai Seisui 酒 井 犀 水 , Nihon mokuchōshi 日 本 木 彫 史 (History of Japanese wood carving), Tōkyō, Taimusu Shuppansha, 1929, 23+562+32 pp.
> A somewhat popular survey of wood carving and sculpture in Japan from the seventh century to the Meiji period.

1491. Sawamura Sentarō 澤 村 專 太 郎 , Nihon kaigashi no kenkyū 日 本 繪 畫 史 の 研 究 (Studies in the history of Japanese painting), Tōkyō, Hoshino Shoten, 1931, 552+13 pp.
> Contains 27 essays arranged chronologically and covering the history of Japanese painting from early times through the Tokugawa period.

1492. Seki Mamoru 関 衛 , Dai Nihon kaigashi 大 日 本 繪 畫 史 (History of Japanese painting), Tōkyō, Kōseikaku, 1934, 669+62 pp.
> A standard survey of Japanese painting from pre-historic cave drawings and the figures on dōtaku to the Western influenced art of the 1920s.

1493. Shigemori Sanrei 重 森 三 玲 , ed., Kyōto bijutsu taikan 京 都 美 術 大 觀 (Survey of the fine arts of Kyōto), Tōkyō, Kozandō Shoten, 1936, 12 v.
> Since Kyōto was for many hundreds of years the art center of Japan, this comprehensive pictorial survey of Kyōto and her environs affords one of the most complete and intimate views of Japanese art in all its aspects. Volumes deal with: 1) architecture, 2) gardens, 3) tea houses, 4-5) painting, 6-7) sculpture, 8) portraiture, 9) stonework, 10) ceramics, lacquer, metal work, etc., 11-12) calligraphy and inscriptions. Each volume is profusely illustrated and contains both a general historical survey and explanatory notes to the pictures. The series is the joint effort of an impressive array of leading art historians of the Kyoto area.

1494. Tajima Shiichi 田 嶋 志 一 and Ōmura Seigai 大 村 西 崖 , Tōyō bijutsu taikan 東 洋 美 術 大 觀 (Survey of Oriental art), Tōkyō, Shimbi Shoin, 1908-18, 15 v.
> Somewhat outdated in its approach, this series still is useful for the detailed factual information it presents. Eight volumes are devoted to Japanese art: 1) Asuka-Nara, 2) Heian-Kamakura, 3-4) Ashikaga Toyotomi, 5-7) Tokugawa, 15) Japanese sculpture. Each volume contains an introductory analysis of the art of the particular period. Illustrations follow and are given full explanation.

1495. Tani Shin'ichi 谷 信 一 , Nihon bijutsushi gaisetsu 日 本 美 術 史 概 說 (An introduction to the history of Japanese art), Tōkyō, Tōkyōdō, 1948, 13+431 pp.
> One of the best of the postwar works on Japanese art history, this is a survey of painting and sculpture by periods to 1868. The author, a specialist in Buddhist art, is especially able in his handling of medieval art and in explaining the technical problems and spiritual motivations of the artists of the past.

1496. Teishitsu Hakubutsukan 帝 室 博 物 館 , Nihon bijutsu ryakushi 日 本 美 術 略 史 (An abridged history of Japanese art), Kyōto, Benrido, 1940, 14+252 pp., 130 plates.
> A standard survey of Japanese art and architecture published by the Imperial Museum (now the National Museum) and based largely on the collection of that museum.

1497. Tōyō bijutsu bunko 東洋美術文庫 (Oriental art library), Tōkyō, Atoriesha, 1938-40, 24 v.
A series of excellent short studies of the leading artists of Japan. Included are Kazan, Sōtatsu, Kiyonaga, Kōetsu, Sesshū, Kōrin, Enshū, Tessai, Harunobu, Ōkyo, and others. Each volume includes representative illustrations (approximately 50) plus a short biographical essay on the artist and an analysis of his art by a specialist.

1498. Yashiro Yukio 矢代幸雄, Nihon bijutsu no tokushitsu 日本美術の特質 (Characteristics of Japanese art), Tōkyō, Iwanami Shoten, 1943, 7+5+465+15+15 pp., 64 illus.
An original and somewhat nationalistic analysis of the spirit of Japanese art. Influenced by the thinking of Bruno Taut. The author, now director of the Institute of Art Research, is a foremost specialist.

b. Architecture and Gardens

1499. Adachi Kō 足立康, Nihon kenchikushi 日本建築史 (History of Japanese architecture), Tōkyō, Chijin Shokan, 1940, 11+192 pp.
One of the Taikan Nihon bunkashi sensho series (Entry 749). This work affords one of the best general introductions to the history of public architecture in Japan. There is a glossary of terms and the whole work is well illustrated.

1500. Amanuma Toshiichi 天沼俊一, Nihon kenchikushi yō 日本建築史要 (Principles of the history of Japanese architecture), Nara, Asukaen, rev. ed., 1928, 2 v.
A comprehensive survey of Japanese public architecture from early times through the Tokugawa period. Treatment is by historic period and in terms of representative architectural monuments within each period. The author covers temples, shrines, palaces, and castles. Volume 2 consists of illustrations.

1501. Fujita Motoharu 藤田元春, Nihon minkashi 日本民家史 (History of Japanese domestic dwellings), Tōkyō, Tōkō Shoin, rev. ed., 1937, 784 pp.
A detailed and well-illustrated study of the history, characteristics, and varieties of Japanese domestic dwellings. Emphasis is on rural house types.

1502. Furukawa Shigeharu 古川重春, Nihon jōkakukō 日本城郭考 (A study of Japanese castles), Ōsaka, Kojinsha Shoten, 1936, 96+13+4+607 pp.
A detailed study of the origins and development of castle architecture in Japan, the location of castles, and their varieties. One half of the work is devoted to an analysis of the castles which remained in preservation in Japan at the time of writing. Profusely illustrated with photographs, maps, and drawings.

1503. Harasawa Tōgo 原澤東吾, Nihon kenchiku keizaishi 日本建築経済史 (An economic history of Japanese architecture), Tōkyō, Fuzambō, 1944, 464 pp.
A socio-economic approach to the history of Japanese architecture. The author attempts to explain architectural types and usages in terms of the economic and social background of the builders. Chapters are divided as follows: clan culture; court aristocracy, their life and architecture; feudal lords, their life and architecture; the development of people's architecture.

1504. Hattori Shōkichi 服部勝吉, Kenchikushi 建築史 (History of architecture), Tōkyō, Juken Kōza Kankōkai, 1930, 366 pp.
One of the Kokushi kōza (Series on Japanese history). A standard academic survey of public architecture.

1505. Kitao Shundō 北尾春道, ed., Sukiya shūsei 数寄屋集成 (Collected illustrations of tea houses), Tōkyō, Kōyosha, 1935, 20 v.
Large illustrations with explanatory notes on Japanese tea house architecture.

1506. Kon Wajirō 今和次郎, Nihon no minka 日本の民家 (Japanese domestic architecture), Tōkyō, Oka Shoin, rev. ed., 1927, 8+8+334 pp.
A work first published in 1922. The author is influenced by the folkloristic school of Yanagida Kunio. Part 1 deals with general principles. Part 2 is a regional survey of Japanese domestic architecture, primarily rural, consisting of illustrations and explanatory notes. Part 3 is devoted to a study of mountain village architecture.

1507. Negishi Eiryū 根岸榮隆, Torii no kenkyū 鳥居の研究 (A study of torii), Tōkyō, Kōseikaku, 1943, 445 pp.

1508. Ōrui Noboru 大類伸 and Toba Masao 鳥羽正雄, Nihon jōkakushi 日本城郭史 (History of Japanese castles), Tōkyō, Yūzankaku, 1936, 732 pp.
A scholarly historical survey of the development of castles and the part they played in Japanese history. Beginning with the fortified strongpoints of the sixth and seventh centuries, the authors trace the location, military significance, and architectural form of major castles. Profusely illustrated and carefully documented.

1509. Sekino Masaru 関 野 克 , Nihon jūtaku shōshi 日 本 住 宅 小 史 (Short history of Japanese dwellings), Tōkyō, Sagami Shobō, 1942, 161 pp. + 134 illus.

    A short but excellent survey of Japanese domestic architecture from pit dwellings to "ranch-style" modern. The introductory chapter deals with the influence of natural environment, life, and art on domestic architecture. The concluding chapter attempts to analyze the influences upon Japanese house types through a series of diagrams. Illustrations are poorly printed but the work is well annotated.

1510. Sekino Tadashi 関 野 貞 , Nihon no kenchiku to geijutsu 日 本 の 建 築 と 藝 術 (Japanese architecture and art), Tōkyō, Iwanami Shoten, 1940, 2 v.

    A collection of articles by a foremost authority on architecture, art, and archeology. Essays range from an analysis of primitive architecture and its relationship to the arts of the time to studies of the influence of continental styles on Japanese architecture, a survey history of Japanese architecture, Buddhist architecture, notes on architectural monuments still extant, a history of Japanese craft arts, an analysis of ancient tiles, etc.

1511. Shigemori Sanrei 重 森 三 玲, Nihon teien rekiran 日 本 庭 園 歴 覧 (Chronological tables of Japanese gardens), Tōkyō, Kobunsha, 1935, 376 pp.

    A useful list of gardens arranged regionally and chronologically according to date of construction within each area. Short explanatory notes accompany each citation.

1512. Shigemori Sanrei 重 森 三 玲 , Nihon teien shōshi 日 本 庭 園 小 史 (Short history of Japanese gardens).

    A short survey by the leading authority on the history of Japanese gardens.

c. Music and Dance

1513. Iba Takashi 伊 庭 孝 , Nihon ongakushi 日 本 音 樂 史 (History of music in Japan), Tōkyō, Ongaku no Tomosha, 1950, 224 pp.

1514. Kodera Yūkichi 小 寺 融 吉 , Buyō no ayumi 舞 踊 の 歩 み (Steps of the dance), Tōkyō, Jiipusha, 1950, 3+2+224 pp.

1515. Suzuki Koson 鈴 木 鼓 村 , Nihon ongakushi 日 本 音 樂 史 (A history of Japanese music), Tōkyō, Hajime Shobō, 1944, 9+292 pp.

    Part 1 is a history of the development of music in Japan from early times to the twentieth century. Part 2 is a study of musical traditions as currently extant in Japan. The author analyzes the music and the instruments, attempting to reduce melodies to modern notation for the piano.

1516. Tanabe Hisao 田 辺 尚 雄 , Nihon ongakushi 日 本 音 樂 史 (A history of Japanese music), Tōkyō, Yūzankaku, 1932, 320 pp.

    A history of music and musical instruments in Japan from earliest times to 1868. The author emphasizes the transmission of musical traditions and instruments from the Asiatic continent. There is little analysis of the music itself.

d. Industrial Arts and Crafts

1517. Aida Tomiyasu 会 田 富 康 , Nihon koin shinkō 日 本 古 印 新 攷 (New studies of old Japanese seals), Tōkyō, Hōunsha, 1947, 4+197+21 pp.

    The art of seal making, learned largely from China, is highly prized by Japanese artists and calligraphers. This work is a well-illustrated survey of seals and the history of seal engraving by a specialist in the actual manufacture of seals. There is an index.

1518. Akashi Kunisuke 明 石 国 助 , Nihon senshokushi 日 本 染 色 史 (A history of Japanese dyeing), Tōkyō, Yūzankaku, 1928, 526+16 pp.

    A survey of the art of dyeing in Japan. Emphasis is upon the early period prior to the 9th century. The later development of dyeing is treated in general outline fashion.

1519. Arisaka Yotarō 有 阪 與 太 郎 , Nihon gangushi 日 本 玩 具 史 (A history of Japanese toys), Tōkyō, Kensetsusha, 1931-32, 2 v.

    A detailed study of Japanese toys of the Edo period (1600-1868). The author has drawn extensively from literary, graphic, and documentary sources.

1520. Gōroku Teiji 郷 六 貞 治 , Nihontō bunrui mokuroku 日 本 刀 分 類 目 録 (A classified catalogue of Japanese swords), Tōkyō, Nihon Shuppan Haikyū K.K., 1944, 138+18+8 pp.

    A classified list of famous Japanese swords. Each entry provides the following information: name of sword, swordsmith, type, and present owner.

1521. Harada Michihiro 原 田 道 寛 , Dai Nihon tōkenshi 大 日 本 刀 劍 史 (A history of Japanese swords), Tōkyō, Shunjūsha, 1940-41, 3 v.

    A voluminous history of swordmaking in Japan.

1522. Homma Hisao 本 間 久 雄 , Nihontō 日 本 刀 (Japanese swords), Tōkyō, Iwanami Shoten, 1939, 225 pp.

1523. Katori Hozuma 香 取 秀 眞 , Nihon kinkōshi 日 本 金 工 史 (History of metalcraft in Japan), Tōkyō, Yūzankaku, 1932, 2+4+390 pp.
　　A study of metal working in Japan from the early bronze age through the Heian period. The author devotes an introduction to an explanation of technology and materials, then takes up the history of the production of metal implements and articles and religious figures by period. Emphasis is on the analysis of aesthetic and technological aspects of the subject.

1524. Koyama Fujio 小 山 富 士 夫 , Satsumayaki no kenkyū 薩 摩 燒 の 研 究 (A study of Satsuma ceramics), Tōkyō, Tōyō Tōki Kenkyūsho, 1940, 309 pp.

1525. Okuda Seiichi 奥 田 誠 一 , Nihon kōgeishi 日 本 工 藝 史 (History of Japanese industrial arts), Tōkyō, Yūzankaku, 1936, 135 pp.
　　A brief survey by a leading authority. Part 1 discusses special characteristics of Japanese industrial and craft arts. Part 2 is a history of industrial art in Japan.

1526. Sawaguchi Goichi 澤 口 悟 一 , Nihon shikkō no kenkyū 日 本 漆 工 の 研 究 (A study of Japanese lacquer), Tōkyō, Maruzen, 1933, 717+19 pp.
　　Part 1 is a survey history of the lacquer craft in Japan. Part 2 is an analysis of the lacquer production and the export of lacquer ware from Japan.

1527. Tamura Eitarō 田 村 策 太 郎 , Nihon kōgyō bunkashi 日 本 工 業 文 化 史 (A cultural history of Japanese industry), Tōkyō, Kagakushugi Kōgyōsha, 1943, 784 pp.
　　An encyclopedic reference work on crafts and industry in pre-modern Japan. The following major fields are covered: vehicles and palanquins, clothing, civil engineering, lighting, weapons, machinery, weaving, and mining. Information is provided on origins and development of craft and industrial technology, and on the uses to which pre-modern equipment was put. Well illustrated and documented.

1528. Tōki kōza 陶 器 講 座 (Series on ceramics), Tōkyō, Yūzankaku, 1935-38, 25 v.
　　An extensive series of articles covering the field of ceramics in Japan, Korea, and China. Emphasis is on Japan. Many essays are of historical interest. The chronologies and bibliographical lists are of particular value.

1529. Yamagami Hachirō 山 上 八 郎 , Nihon katchū no shin-kenkyū 日 本 甲 冑 の 新 研 究 (A new study of Japanese armor), privately published, 1928, 2 v.
　　A detailed description of Japanese armor by a noted authority. There is an index.

12. APPLIED SCIENCE

1530. Arakawa Hidetoshi 荒 川 秀 俊 , Nihon kishōgakushi 日 本 氣 象 学 史 (History of meteorology), Tōkyō, Kawade Shobō, 1941, 2+8+191 pp.
　　A brief survey of the history of meteorological observations in Japan from approximately 1835 to 1937. Chapters include a general history, the establishment of observatories and meteorological institutions, leading figures in the meteorological world, and characteristics of Japanese weather. The work contains an index and a useful bibliographical list.

1531. Araki Toshima 荒 木 俊 馬 , Nihon rekigakushi gaisetsu 日 本 曆 学 史 概 説 (Introduction to the history of calendrical science in Japan), Tōkyō, Yamaguchi Shoten, 1943, 236+29 pp.
　　A survey of calendrical systems in Japan from early times to 1873. Chapters deal with the archaic calendar, the period of reliance on the Chinese system (554-1550), the beginnings of a native system, the Yoshimune period (1716-1750), and subsequent changes.

1532. Chūō Kishōdai 中 央 氣 象 台 (Central Observatory), Nihon kishō shiryō sōran 日 本 氣 象 史 料 綜 覧 (Survey of historical materials on weather conditions in Japan), Tōkyō, Chijin Shokan, 1943, 248 pp.
　　A chronological listing of historically recorded unusual weather phenomena from earliest times to 1887. Each entry includes date, place of recording, condition (storm, wind, flood, earthquake, etc.), and source of information.

1533. Endo Toshisada 遠 藤 利 貞 , Dai Nihon sūgakushi 大 日 本 數 学 史 (A history of Japanese mathematics), Tōkyō, Iwanami Shoten, rev. ed., 1918, 702+40+45 pp.
　　A pioneer study of pre-modern mathematics in Japan. The work covers the entire field from early times to 1877.

1534. Fujikawa Yū 富 士 川 游 , Nihon igakushi 日 本 医 学 史 (A history of Japanese medical science), Tōkyō, Shōkabō, 1904, 1036 pp.
　　A scholarly study of medicine and medical scientists in Japan from early times to the time of writing. Especially useful for its explanations of old medical terms, lists of pre-modern medical literature, and its extensive bibliography.

1535. Fujikawa Yū 富 士 川 游 , Nihon shippeishi 日 本 疾 病 史 (A history of Japanese diseases), Tōkyō, Tohōdō, 1904, 302 pp.
　　A basic history of diseases, epidemics, and their cures in pre-modern Japan. A useful bibliographical list is included.

1536. Fujita Motoharu 藤 田 元 春 , Nihon chirigakushi 日本 地 理 学 史 (History of Japanese geographical science), Tōkyō, Tōkō Shoin, rev. ed., 1943, 16+8+7+667 pp.

     An inquiry into the origins and development of geographical science and cartography in Japan. There are numerous reproductions of old Japanese maps. One unique feature of the work is the analysis of maps of Japan found in Korea.

1537. Hosoi Sō 細井綜 , Wasan shisō no tokushitsu 和 算 思 想 の 特 質 (Characteristics of Japanese mathematical theory), Tōkyō, Kyōritsusha, 1941, 343 pp.

     An authoritative analysis of the characteristic features of Japan's pre-modern mathematical tradition.

1538. Ishihara Jun 石 原 純 , Kagakushi 科 学 史 (History of natural science), Tōkyō, Tōyō Keizai Shimpōsha, 1942, 489 pp.

     One of the Gendai Nihon bummeishi (Entry 722) series. This work provides a brief sketch of scientific development in pre-Restoration Japan. It is chiefly devoted to an analysis of the development of the main branches of natural science from 1868 to 1925.

1539. Itō Shirō 伊 藤 至 郎 , Nihon kagakushi 日本 科 学 史 (History of science in Japan), Itō Shoten, 1941, 310 pp.

     A survey of the development of pre-modern scientific technology in Japan.

1540. Mizuki Kozue 水 木 梢 , Nihon sūgakushi 日 本 数 学 史 (A history of mathematics in Japan), Tōkyō, Kyōiku Kenkyūkai, 1928, 535 pp.

     A survey of Japanese mathematics and mathematicians from ancient times to approximately 1877. Emphasis is on the Edo period (1600-1868).

1541. Mori Senzō 森 銑 三 , Kinsei Nihon no kagakushatachi 近 世 日 本 の 科 学 者 達 (Scientists of Tokugawa Japan), Tōkyō, Seiun Shoin, 1948, 2+12+302+16+6 pp.

     Intended for a popular audience, this work describes the lives and activities of some 50 scholars, scientists, and technologists of the Tokugawa period (1600-1868). The work terminates with a useful bibliographical list of works related to each of the figures mentioned in the text.

1542. Nihon kagakushi 日 本 科 学 史 (History of science in Japan), Tōkyō, Yūzankaku, 1942, 289 pp. [= v. 19 of the Shinkō Dai Nihonshi series (Entry 744)].

     Contains the following chapters: general survey (Nakaseko Rokubei), mathematics (Mikami Yoshio), the calendar (Takeda Ryūji), Tokugawa geography (Abe Makoto), medicine (Oshima Ranzaburō), and natural science (Mukōzaka Michiharu).

1543. Ogura Kinnosuke 小 倉 金 之 助 , Sūgaku kyōikushi 数 学 教 育 史 (History of education in mathematics), Tōkyō, Iwanami Shoten, 1932, 256 pp.

1544. Shimizu Fujitarō 清 水 藤 太 郎 , Nihon yakugakushi 日 本 薬 学 史 (History of Japanese pharmacology), Tōkyō, Nanzandō, 1949, 531 pp.

     An extremely detailed and fully documented history of Japanese pharmacology from early times to 1949. There is an introductory bibliographical note and a chronological list (pp. 473-488) of works on pharmacology. An index is appended.

1545. Terajima Masashi 寺 島 柾 史 , Nihon kagaku hattatsushi 日 本 科 学 発 達 史 (History of the development of Japanese science), Tōkyō, Keibunsha, 1937, 326 pp.

     A general survey of the history of technological and scientific development in Japan from ancient times to the present.

1546. Tominari Kimahei 富 成 喜 馬 平 , Nihon kagakushiyō 日 本 科 学 史 要 (Outline history of Japanese science), Tōkyō, Kōbundō, 1939, 4+1+169 pp.

     A survey of Japanese activity in the scientific and technological field from the arrival of Westerners in the sixteenth century to the end of the Tokugawa period. There is an appended bibliographic list.

1547. Tominari Kimahei 富 成 喜 馬 平 , Gendai Nihon kagakushi 現 代 日 本 科 学 史 (History of contemporary Japanese science), Tōkyō, Mikasa Shobō, 1941, 267 pp.

     A brief survey in popular style of the development of science and technology in post-Restoration Japan. There is an appended bibliographical list.

1548. Ueda Sampei 上 田 三 平 , Nihon yakuenshi no kenkyū 日 本 薬 学 史 の 研 究 (A study of the history of Japanese medicinal herb gardens), Tōkyō, Maruzen, 1930, 224 pp.

     A study of Japanese gardens for the cultivation of medicinal herbs. The work traces the history of such gardens from their origins in Japan to the end of the Tokugawa period. The types and varieties of plants cultivated are analyzed. There is an index to botanical names.

1549. Ueno Masuzō 上 野 益 三 , Nihon seibutsugaku no rekishi 日 本 生 物 学 の 歴 史 (History of biology in Japan), Tōkyō, Kōbundō, 1939, 188 pp.

1550. Watanabe Toshio 渡 辺 敏 夫 , Koyomi 暦 (Calendars), Tōkyō, Kōseisha, 1940, 298 pp.

     A comprehensive study of calendrical systems in China and Japan.

1551. Yamamoto Narinosuke 山 本 成 之 助 , Nihon kagakushi 日 本 科 学 史 (History of science in Japan), Tōkyō, Nihon Shuppan K.K., 1947, 194 pp.

     A study of Chinese and Western scientific traditions, their influence upon Japan, and their Japanization.

List of Publishers*

A

Achikku Myuzeamu　アチック　ミューゼアム (Attic Museum)　Tōkyō
Akita Sōsho Kankōkai　秋田叢書刊行会　Akita
Ankusha　安苦社　Tōkyō
Aoki Shoten　青木書店　Tōkyō
Asada Bummeidō　麻田文明堂　Kyōto
Asahi Shimbunsha　朝日新聞社　Tōkyō and Ōsaka
Asahi Shobō　朝日書房　Tōkyō
Asakura Shoten　朝倉書店　Tōkyō
Asukaen　飛鳥園　Nara
Asano Shoten　淺野書店　Tōkyō

B

Baifukan　培風館　Tōkyō
Benkyōdō　勉強堂　Tōkyō
Benridō　便利堂　Kyōto
Bijutsu Kenkyūsho　美術研究所 (Institute of Art Research)　Tōkyō
Bijutsushi Gakkai　美術史学会 (History of Art Society)　Tōkyō
Bonjinsha　凡人社　Tōkyō
Bōsō Sōsho Kankōkai　房總叢書刊行会　Chiba
Bukeseido Kenkyūkai　武家制度研究会 (Research Society for Feudal Institutions)　Tōkyō
Bukkyō Bijutsusha　佛教美術社　Nara
Bukkyō Daijiten Hakkōsho　佛教大辞典発行所　Tōkyō
Bukkyō Taikei Kanseikai　佛教大系完成会　Tōkyō
Bun'eidō　文永堂　Tōkyō
Bungei Shunjūsha　文藝春秋社　Tōkyō
Bunka Gakkai　文化学会 (Cultural Association)　Tōkyō
Bunkashi Gakkai　文化史学会 (Cultural History Association)　Kyōto
Bunken Shoin　文献書院　Kyōto
Bunkyōdō　文教堂　Tōkyō
Bunkyō Shoin　文教書院　Kobe
Bunrokusha　文録社　Tōkyō
Bunshinsha　文信社　Tōkyō
Bunshōdō Shoten　文祥堂書店　Tōkyō
Bunshōkaku　文章閣　Tōkyō
Buntokusha　佛德社　Ōsaka
Bunyūdō Shoten　文友堂書店　Tōkyō
Busō Kōkokai　武相考古会 (Busō Archeological Society)
Busō Sōsho Kankōkai　武相叢書刊行会　Chiba
Bussho Kankōkai　佛書刊行会　Tōkyō

C

Chihōshi Kenkyū Kyōgikai　地方史研究協議会 (Committee for the Study of Local History)　Tōkyō
Chijin Shokan　地人書館　Tōkyō
Chikuma Shobō　筑摩書房　Tōkyō
Chikura Shobō　千倉書房　Tōkyō
Chiri Chōsasho　地理調査所 (Geodetic Office)　Tōkyō
Chiri Kyōiku Kenkyūkai　地理教育研究会 (Geographical Instruction Society)　Tōkyō

Chōryūsha　潮流社　Tōkyō
Chōyōkai　朝陽会　Tōkyō
Chūbunkan Shoten　中文館書店　Tōkyō
Chūgai Shōgyō Shimpōsha　中外商業新報社　Tōkyō
Chūkōkan　中興館　Tōkyō
Chūō Bijutsusha　中央美術社　Tōkyō
Chūō Kōronsha　中央公論社　Tōkyō
Chūō Sangyō Chōsakai　中央産業調査会 (Central Production Survey Society)　Tōkyō
Chūō Shakai Jigyō Kyōkai Shakai Jigyō Kenkyūsho　中央社会事業協会社会事業研究所 (Central Social Work Association, Research Institute of Social Work)　Tōkyō

D

Daidōin Shokan　大同印書館　Tōkyō
Daidō Shoin　大同書院　Tōkyō
Daigaku Shimbun Remmei Shuppambu　大学新聞連盟出版部 (University Newspapers Union Press)　Tōkyō
Dai Nihon Bukkyō Zensho Hakkōsho　大日本佛教全書発行所　Tōkyō
Dai Nihon Bummei Kyōkai　大日本文明協会 (Japan Cultural Association)　Tōkyō
Dai Nihon Chishi Taikei Kankōkai　大日本地誌大系刊行会　Tōkyō
Dai Nihon Fukyō Sōsho Kankōkai　大日本風教叢書刊行会　Tōkyō
Dai Nihon Meishozue Kankōkai　大日本名所図会刊行会　Tōkyō
Dai Nihon Rengō Seinenkai　大日本聯合青年会 (Japan Combined Youth Association)　Tōkyō
Dai Nihon Sanshikai　大日本蚕系会 (Japan Filature Association)　Tōkyō
Dai Nihon Seiji Shisōshi Kankōkai　大日本政治思想史刊行会　Tōkyō
Dai Nihon Shisō Zenshū Kankōkai　大日本思想全集刊行会　Tōkyō
Dai Nihon Shoga Meika Taikan Kankōkai　大日本書畫名家大鑑刊行会　Tōkyō
Dai Nihon Shuppan Kabushiki Kaisha　大日本出版株式会社　Tōkyō
Dai Nihon Tosho Kabushiki Kaisha　大日本図書株式会社　Tōkyō
Dai Nihon Yūbenkai Kōdansha　大日本雄辯会講談社　Tōkyō
Daishinsha　大浸社　Tōkyō
Daitōkaku　大鐙閣　Tōkyō
Daitō Shimbunsha　大東新聞社　Tōkyō
Daitō Shokan　大東書館　Tōkyō
Daitō Shuppansha　大東出版社　Tōkyō
Daiyamondosha　ダイヤモンド社　Tōkyō
Daizōkyō Sakuin Kankōkai　大藏經索引刊行会　Tōkyō
Daizō Shuppan Kabushiki Kaisha　大藏出版株式会社　Tōkyō
Denki Gakkai　傳記学会 (Biographical Society)　Tōkyō
Doboku Gakkai　土木学会 (Civil Engineering Society)　Tōkyō

---

*In the following list definitions have been provided for the names of non-commercial publishers such as universities, research institutes and government offices. No definitions have been affixed to organizations brought together for the purpose of publishing a single work or series. Most such groups are identified by the term kankōkai (publication society) contained in their titles.

Dōbunkan 同文館 Tōkyō
Dōbun Shoin 同文書院 Tōkyō
Dōjinsha Shoten 同人社書店 Tōkyō
Dokusho Kenkyūkai 讀書研究会 Tōkyō

E

Edo Sōsho Kankōkai 江戸叢書刊行会 Tōkyō
Eishinsha 榮進舎 Tōkyō

F

Fukuda Shobō 福田書房 Tōkyō
Fukumura Shoten 福村書店 Tōkyō
Fukushima-ken Shigakkai 福島縣史学会 (Fukushima Prefecture Historical Society) Tōkyō
Fuzambō 富山房 Tōkyō
Fūzoku Kenkyūkai 風俗研究会 (Institute for the Study of Customs) Tōkyō

G

Gaimushō 外務省 (Ministry of Foreign Affairs) Tōkyō
Gaimushō Bunshoka Toshogakari 外務省文書課図書係 (Ministry of Foreign Affairs, Archives, Chief Archivist) Tōkyō
Gaimushō Jōyakukyoku 外務省條約局 (Ministry of Foreign Affairs, Treaty Division) Tōkyō
Gakusei Shobō 学生書房 Tōkyō
Ganshōdō Shoten 巖松堂書店 Tōkyō
Geisōdō 藝草堂 Kyōto
Gengen Nihonsha 原現日本社 Tōkyō
Genrin Shobō 玄林書房 Kyōto
Getsuyō Shobō 月曜書房 Tōkyō
Gunjishi Kenkyūkai 軍事史研究会 (Society for the Study of Military History) Tōkyō
Guroria Sosaete グロリアソサエテ (Gloria Society) Tōkyō
Gyōmeisha 曉明社 Tōkyō

H

Hajime Shobō 肇書房 Tōkyō
Hakkōsha 八光社 Tōkyō
Hakubundō 博文堂 Tōkyō
Hakubunkan 博文館 Tōkyō
Hakujitsu Shoin 白日書院 Tōkyō
Hakutōsha 白東社 Tōkyō
Hakuyōsha 白揚社 Tōkyō
Hanawa Shobō 塙書房 Tōkyō
Hanazono Daigaku Zengaku Kenkyūkai 花園大学禪学研究会 Kyōto
Haneda Shoten 羽田書店 Tōkyō
Hattensha 発展社 Tōkyō
Hattensha Shuppanbu 発展社出版部 Tōkyō
Heibonsha 平凡社 Tōkyō
Heigo Shuppansha 丙午出版社 Tōkyō
Heirakuji Shoten 平楽寺書店 Kyōto
Herarudosha ヘラルド社 Tōkyō
Hibiya Toshokan 日比谷図書館 (Hibiya Library) Tōkyō
Hibonkaku 非凡閣 Tōkyō
Higashifushimi no Miya-ke 東伏見の宮家 (Prince Higashi Fushimi) Tōkyō
Hinode Shimbunsha 日の出新聞社 Kyōto
Hiroshima Bunrika Daigaku Shigaku Kenkyūkai 廣島文理科大学史学研究会 (Hiroshima University, Historical Society)
Hōbunkan 宝文館 Tōkyō, Ōsaka and Kōbe
Hōbunsha 峰文社 Tōkyō
Hōgaku Shoin 法学書院 Tōkyō

Hōkei Shobō 芳惠書房 Tōkyō
Hokkaidō-chō 北海道庁 (Hokkaido Territorial Office) Sapporo
Hokuryūkan 北隆館 Tōkyō
Hōritsu Jisho Kankōkai 法律辞書刊行会 Tōkyō
Hoshino Shoten 星野書店 Tōkyō and Kyōto
Hōunsha 宝雲社 Tōkyō
Hyōgensha 表現社 Tōkyō

I

Ibundō Shoten 彙文堂書店 Kyōto
Iga Shobō 伊賀書房 Tōkyō
Ikeda Shoten 池田書店 Tōkyō
Ikuhōsha 育芳社 Tōkyō
Ikuseikai 育成会 Tōkyō
Ikuseisha 育生社 Tōkyō
Imin Mondai Kenkyūkai 移民問題研究会 (Society for the Study of the Immigration Problem) Tōkyō
Ishiguro Bunkichi 石黒文吉 Tōkyō
Ishikawa-ken 石川縣 (Ishikawa Prefecture) Kanazawa
Ishin Shiryō Hensan Jimukyoku 維新史料編纂事務局 (Office for the Compilation of Historical Materials Concerning the Restoration) Tōkyō
Isseidō Shoten 一誠堂書店 Tōkyō
Isseisha 一誠社 Tōkyō
Itō Shoten 伊藤書店 Tōkyō
Iwanami Shoten 岩波書店 Tōkyō
Iwasaki Shoten 岩崎書店 Tōkyō
Iwate Shigakkai 岩手史学会 (Iwate Historical Society Morioka

J

Jichōsha 時潮社 Tōkyō
Jidaisha 時代社 Tōkyō
Jiipusha ジープ社 Tōkyō
Jiji Tsūshinsha 時事通信社 Tōkyō
Jikkyō Shuppan Kabushiki Kaisha 実教出版株式会社 Tōkyō
Jimbun Chiri Gakkai 人文地理学会 (Institute of Human Geography) Kyōto
Jimbun Gakkai 人文学会 (Society of Humanistic Science) Kyōto
Jimbun Kagaku Iinkai 人文科学委員会 (Committee on Humanistic Science) Tōkyō
Jimbun Shoin 人文書院 Kyōto
Jingū Kyōin 神宮敬院 (Institute of Shinto Studies) Tōkyō
Jingū Shichō 神宮司庁 (Office of Shrine Affairs) Kyōto
Jinji Kōshinsho 人事興信所 Tōkyō
Jitsugyō no Nihonsha 実業の日本社 Tōkyō
Juichi Kumi Shuppanbu 十一組出版部
Juken Kōza Kankōkai 受験講座刊行会 Tōkyō

K

Kadan Shimpōsha 歌壇新報社 Tōkyō
Kadokawa Shoten 角川書店 Tōkyō
Kagakushugi Kōgyōsha 科学主義工業社 Tōkyō
Kagawa-ken 香川縣 (Kagawa Prefecture) Takamatsu
Kagoshima-ken 鹿兒島縣 (Kagoshima Prefecture) Kagoshima
Kaibō Shiryō Kankōkai 海防史料刊行会 Tōkyō

Kaigun Yushukai 海軍有終会 (Navy
  Perfection Society   Tōkyō
Kaikōsha 偕行社   Tōkyō
Kaiseikan 開成館   Ōsaka
Kai Shiryō Kankōkai 甲斐志料刊行会   Kōfu
        (Yamanashi)
Kaizōsha 改造社   Tōkyō
Kaji Sekai Shisha 加持世界支社   Tōkyō
Kamakura Bunko 鎌倉文庫   Tōkyō
Kamigata Kyōdo Kenkyūkai 上方郷土研究会
    (Society for the Study of the Kamigata
    Area)   Ōsaka
Kaname Shobō 要書房   Tōkyō
Kangensha 乾元社   Tōkyō
Kantōsha 甜燈社   Tōkyō
Kasumigaseki Shobō 霞関書房   Tōkyō
Katsuragi Shoten 葛城書店   Tōkyō
Kawade Shobō 河出書房   Tōkyō
Kawahara Shoten 河原書店   Kyōto
Keibundō 敬文堂   Tōkyō
Keibunsha 啓文社   Tōkyō
Keimeisha 啓明社   Tōkyō
Keiō Gijuku Daigaku Mita Shigakkai 慶應義
    塾大学三田史学会 (Keiō
    University, Mita Historical Society) Tōkyō
Keiō Gijuku Daigaku Rizai Gakkai 慶應義塾
    大学理財学会 (Keiō University,
    Finance Society)   Tōkyō
Keiō Gijuku Keizaishi Gakkai 慶應義塾
    經済史学会 (Keiō University, Economic
    History Society)   Tōkyō
Keiō Shobō 慶應書房   Tōkyō
Keiō Shuppansha 慶應出版社   Tōkyō
Keiseisha 啓成社   Tōkyō
Keisetsu Shoin 螢雪書院   Tōkyō
Keizai Zasshisha 經済雑誌社   Tōkyō
Kembunkan 賢文館   Tōkyō
Kembunsha 健文社   Tōkyō
Kensetsusha 建設社   Tōkyō
Kenshinsha 研進社   Tōkyō
Kibi Gunsho Shūsei Kankōkai 吉備群書
    集成刊行会   Okayama
Kibōkaku 希望閣   Tōkyō
Kichō Tosho Eihon Kankōkai 貴重図書影本
    刊行会   Kyōto
Kingensha Shoten 紀元社書店   Tōkyō
Kindai Shisōsha 近代思想社   Tōkyō
Kinkōdō 金港堂   Tōkyō
Kinseidō 金星堂   Tōkyō
Kinsei Jikata Keizai Shiryō Kankōkai 近世地
    方經済史料刊行会   Tōkyō
Kinseisha 錦正社   Tōkyō
Kinseki Hōryūdō 金剌芳流堂   Tōkyō
Kōbundō 弘文堂   Tōkyō
Kōbundō Shobō 弘文堂書房   Tōkyō
        and Kyōto
Kōbunko Kankōkai 廣文庫刊行会   Tōkyō
Kōbunsha 光文社   Tōkyō
Kōbunsō 弘文荘   Tōkyō
Kōchō Hikyū Kankōkai 皇朝秘笈刊行会 Tōkyō
Kōdansha 講談社 (See Dai Nihon Yūbenkai
    Kōdansha)   Tōkyō
Kōdōkan 講道館   Tōkyō
Kōdōsha 公道社   Tōkyō
Kōgakkai 工学会 (Engineering Association) Tōkyō
Kōjinsha Shoten 巧人社書店   Ōsaka
Koji Ruien Kankōkai 古事類苑刊行会 Tōkyō
Kōjunsha 交詢社   Tōkyō
Kokka Gakkai 国家学会 (Political Science
    Society)   Tōkyō
Kokkasha 国華社   Tōkyō
Kokkōkan 国光館   Tōkyō
Kokon Shoin 古今書院   Tōkyō

Kokubun Tōhō Bukkyō Sōsho Kankōkai 国文東
    方佛教叢書刊行会   Tōkyō
Kokudosha 国土社   Tōkyō
Kokugakuin Daigaku 国学院大学
    (Kokugakuin University)   Tōkyō
Kokugakuin Daigaku Kokushi Gakkai 国学院
    大学国史学会 (Kokugakuin University,
    Japanese History Society)   Tōkyō
Kokugakuin Daigaku Shintō Shūkyō Kenkyūshitsu
    国学院大学神道宗教研究室
    (Kokugakuin University, Institute of Shinto
    Studies)   Tōkyō
Kokugakuin Daigaku Shuppambu 国学院大
    学出版部 (Kokugakuin University
    Press)   Tōkyō
Kokuhon Shuppansha 国本出版社   Tōkyō
Kokumin Bunko Kankōkai 国民文庫刊行会
        Tōkyō
Kokumin no Rekishi Kenkyūkai 国民の歴史
    研究会 (People's History Society) Tōkyō
Kokumin Tosho Kabushiki Kaisha 国民図書
    株式会社   Tōkyō
Kokuritsu Kokkai Toshokan 国立国会図
    書館 (National Diet Library)   Tōkyō
Kokuritsu Shoin 国立書院   Tōkyō
Kokuryūkai 黒龍会 (Amur River [Black
    Dragon] Society)   Tōkyō
Kokusai Bunka Jōhōsha 国際文化情報社
Kokusai Bunka Shinkōkai 国際文化振興
    会 (Society for International Cultural
    Relations)   Tōkyō
Kokusai Kōtsū Bunka Kyōkai 国際交通
    文化協会 (Society for International
    Communications)   Tōkyō
Kokusai Shichōsha 国際思潮社   Tōkyō
Kokushi Kenkyūkai 国史研究会
    (Japanese History Research Society) Tōkyō
Kokushi Kōshūkai 国史講習会 (Japanese
    History Lecture Association)   Tōkyō
Kokusho Kankōkai 国書刊行会 (Society
    for the Publication of Japanese Texts) Tōkyō
Kokusho Shuppan Kyōkai 国書出版協会 Tōkyō
Kōkyō Shoin 弘敎書院   Tōkyō
Kondō Kappansho 近藤活版社   Tōkyō
Kondō Shobō 近藤書房   Tōkyō
Kondō Shuppanbu 近藤出版部   Tōkyō
Koronasha コロナ社   Tōkyō
Kōronsha 公論社   Tōkyō
Kōseikaku 厚生閣   Tōkyō
        and Kyōto
Kōseisha 恒星社   Tōkyō
Kōshaku Hosokawa-ke Hensansho 侯爵細川
    家編纂所 (House of Marquis Hosokawa,
    Compilation Office)
Kosho Hozonkai 古書保存会 (Society
    for the Preservation of Historical Works) Tōkyō
Koten Hozonkai 古典保存会 (Society
    for the Preservation of Classics)   Tōkyō
Kōten Kōkyūsho Jingū Hōsaikai 皇典講究所
    神宮奉斎会 (Institute for the Study
    of Imperial Classics, Shinto Scripture Society) Tōkyō
Kōtō Shoin 高桐書院   Kyōto
Koyama Shoten 小山書店   Tōkyō
Kōyasan Daigaku Mikkyō Kenkyūkai 高野山大
    学密敎研究会 (Kōyasan University,
    Esoteric Buddhism Society)   Kōyasan
        (Wakayama)
Kōyōsha 洪洋社   Tōkyō
Kōyūkan 光融館   Tōkyō
Kōzandō Shoten 向山堂書店   Tōkyō
Kōzan Konwakai 鑛山懇話会 (Mining
    Association)   Tōkyō

Kunaishō 宮内省 (Imperial Household Ministry)   Tōkyō
Kyōbunsha 京文社   Tōkyō
Kyōchōkai 協調会 (Conciliation Society)   Tōkyō
Kyōdō Shuppansha 協同出版社   Tōkyō
Kyōiku Chiri Rekishi Remmei 教育地理歴史聯盟 (Union of Teachers of Geography and History)   Tōkyō
Kyōiku Kenkyūkai 教育研究会 (Education Research Society)   Tōkyō
Kyōiku Tosho Kabushiki Kaisha 教育図書株式会社   Tōkyō
Kyōritsusha 共立社   Tōkyō
Kyōseikaku 共生閣   Tōkyō
Kyōto Daigaku Jimbun Kagaku Kenkyūsho (Kyoto University, Institute of Humanistic and Social Sciences)   Kyōto
Kyōto Daigaku Keizai Gakkai 京都大学経済学会 (Kyoto University, Economic Society)   Kyōto
Kyōto Shigaku Chirigaku Dōkōkai 京都史学地理学同攻会 Kyoto Joint Society of History and Geography)   Kyōto
Kyōto Shiyakusho 京都市役所 (Kyoto City Office)   Kyōto
Kyōto Sōsho Kankōkai 京都叢書刊行会 Kyōto
Kyōto Teikoku Daigaku Bungakubu Chirigaku Kyōshitsu 京都帝国大学文学部地理学教室(Kyoto Imperial University, Faculty of Letters, Geographical Institute)   Kyōto
Kyōto Teikoku Daigaku Fuzoku Toshokan 京都帝国大学附属図書館 (Kyoto Imperial University Library)   Kyōto
Kyōto Teikoku Daigaku Keizai Gakkai 京都帝国大学経済学会(Kyoto Imperial University, Economics Association)   Kyōto
Kyōto Teikoku Daigaku Shigaku Kenkyūkai 京都帝国大学史学研究会 (Kyoto Imperial University, Historical Association)   Kyōto
Kyōto Yakugyō Jironsha 京都薬業時論社   Kyōto
Kyūdai Shigakkai 九大史学会 (Kyūshū University, Historical Society)   Fukuoka

M

Mainichi Shimbunsha 毎日新聞社   Tōkyō
Mamiya Shoten 間宮書店   Tōkyō and Ōsaka
Manchōhōsha 満朝報社   Tōkyō
Maruyamasha 丸山舎   Tōkyō
Maruzen Kabushiki Kaisha 丸善株式会社 Tōkyō
Masu Shobō 鱒書房   Tōkyō
Meguro Shoten 目黒書店   Tōkyō
Meibundō 明文堂   Tōkyō
Meicho Kankōkai 名著刊行会   Tōkyō
Meiji Shobō 明治書房   Tōkyō
Meiji Shoin 明治書院   Tōkyō
Meiji Shuppansha 明治出版社   Tōkyō
Meiji Tosho Shuppansha 明治図書出版社   Tōkyō
Meiseidō 明正堂   Tōkyō
Meitokudō 明德堂   Tōkyō
Mikami Shobō 三上書房   Tōkyō
Mikasa Shobō 三笠書房   Tōkyō
Mikkyō Jiten Hensankai 密教辞典編纂会   Kyōto
Mikuni Shobō 三国書房   Tōkyō
Minami Ajia Bunka Kenkyūsho 南亜細亜文化研究所 (Research Institute for South Asian Culture)   Tōkyō
Minkan Denshō no Kai 民間傳承の会 (Society of Folklore Tradition)   Tōkyō
Minshu Hyōronsha 民主評論社   Tōkyō

Minshushugi Kagakusha Kyōkai 民主主義科学者協会 (Association of Democratic Scientists)   Tōkyō
Misuzu Shobō みすず書房   Tōkyō
Miwa Shoten 三輪書店   Tōkyō
Mochizuki Hakase Kanreki Kinenkai 望月博士還暦記念会   Tōkyō
Mombushō 文部省 (Ministry of Education) Tōkyō
Moriyama Shoten 森山書店   Tōkyō
Musashino Shoin 武蔵野書院   Tōkyō

N

Nagasaki Kenritsu Toshokan 長崎縣立図書館 (Nagasaki Prefectural Library)   Nagasaki
Nagasaki Shiyakusho 長崎市役所 (Nagasaki City Office)   Nagasaki
Naigai Shoseki Kabushiki Kaisha 内外書籍株式会社   Tōkyō
Naigai Shuppan Kabushiki Kaisha 内外出版株式会社   Kyōto
Naikaku Insatsukyoku 内閣印刷局 (Cabinet Printing Office)   Tōkyō
Naikaku Kirokukyoku 内閣記録局 (Cabinet Archives Office)   Tōkyō
Naikaku Shokikanshitsu Kirokuka 内閣書記官室記録課 (Cabinet, Secretariat, Archives Section)   Tōkyō
Naimushō 内務省 (Ministry of Home Affairs)   Tōkyō
Naimushō Chihōkyoku 内務省地方局 (Ministry of Home Affairs, Local Affairs Office)   Tōkyō
Naimushō Keihokyoku 内務省警保局 (Ministry of Home Affairs, Police Department)   Tōkyō
Naimushō Toshokyoku 内務省図書局 (Ministry of Home Affairs, Bureau of Books) Tōkyō
Nambokusha 南北社   Tōkyō
Nambu Sōsho Kankōkai 南部叢書刊行会 Aomori
Naniwa Sōsho Kankōkai 浪速叢書刊行会 Ōsaka
Nanki Tokugawashi Kankōkai 南紀德川史刊行会   Wakayama
Nankōsha 南郊社   Tōkyō
Nanzandō 南山堂   Tōkyō
Nara-ken Kyōikukai 奈良縣教育会 (Nara Prefecture Educational Society)   Nara
Naukasha ナウカ社   Tōkyō
Nichiyō Shobō 日用書房   Tōkyō
Nihon Chiri Gakkai 日本地理学会 (Association of Japanese Geographers)   Tōkyō
Nihon Chosakuken Kyōgikai 日本著作權協議会(Japan Copyright Council)   Tōkyō
Nihon Daizōkyō Hensankai 日本大藏經編纂会   Tōkyō
Nihon Dempō Tsūshinsha 日本電報通信社   Tōkyō
Nihon Dokusho Kumiai 日本讀書組合 Tōkyō
Nihon Dokusho Shimbunsha 日本讀書新聞社   Tōkyō
Nihon Gakujutsu Fukyūkai 日本学術普及会   Tōkyō
Nihon Haisho Taikei Kankōkai 日本俳書大系刊行会   Tōkyō
Nihon Hōri Kenkyūkai 日本法理研究会 (Japan Jurisprudence Society)   Tōkyō
Nihon Hōshakai Gakkai 日本法社会学会 (Japan Society of Sociology of Law) Tōkyō
Nihon Hyōronsha 日本評論社   Tōkyō
Nihon Hyōron Shinsha 日本評論新社   Tōkyō
Nihon Insatsu Gakkai 日本印刷学会 (Japan Printing Society)   Tōkyō

Nihon Jinrui Gakkai 日本人類学会
(Japan Anthropological Society) Tokyo
Nihon Kagakushi Gakkai 日本科学史学会
(Japan History of Science Society) Tokyo
Nihon Keizaishi Hensankai 日本經育史編
纂会 Tokyo
Nihon Keizaishi Kenkyūsho 日本經済史
研究所 (Japan Institute of Economic
History) Kyōto
Nihon Keizai Sōsho Kankōkai 日本經済叢
書刊行会 Tokyo
Nihon Kokuhō Zenshū Kankōkai 日本国宝全
集刊行会 Tokyo
Nihon Kokusai Kyōkai 日本国際協会
(Japan Foreign Affairs Society) Tokyo
Nihon Kokusui Zensho Kankōkai 日本国粋全
書刊行会 Tokyo
Nihon Kōsho Tsūshinsha 日本古書通信社 Tokyo
Nihon Koten Zenshū Kankōkai 日本古典全
集刊行会 Tokyo
Nihon Mingei Kyōkai 日本民藝協会
(Japan Folk Art Association) Tokyo
Nihon Minzoku Gakkai 日本民俗学会
(Japanese Society of Ethnology) Tokyo
Nihon Rekishi Chiri Gakkai 日本歴史地
理学会 (Japan Historical Geography
Society) Tokyo
Nihon Rōdō Kumiai Undōshi Kankōkai 日本勞
働組合運動史刊行会 Tokyo
Nihon Sanrinshi Kankōkai 日本山林史刊
行会 Tokyo
Nihon Shakai Gakkai 日本社会学会
(Japan Sociological Association) Tokyo
Nihonshi Kenkyūkai 日本史研究会
(Society for the Study of Japanese History) Kyōto Tokyo
Nihon Shimbun Kyōkai 日本新聞協会
Nihon Shiseki Hozonkai 日本史籍保存会
(Society for the Preservation of Japanese
Historical Materials) Tokyo
Nihon Shiseki Kyōkai 日本史籍協会
(Association for Japanese Historical Texts) Tokyo
Nihon Shobō 日本書房 Tokyo
Nihon Shoshi Gakkai 日本書誌学会
(Japan Bibliographical Society) Tokyo
Nihon Shuppan Haikyū Kabushiki Kaisha 日本出
版配給株式会社 Tokyo
Nihon Shuppan Kyōdō Kabushiki Kaisha 日本出
版協同株式会社 Tokyo
Nihon Shuppan Kyōkai 日本出版協会 Tokyo
Nihon Shūshikyoku Shiryō Hensangakari 日本修
史局史料編纂係 Tokyo
Nihon Tosho Kabushiki Kaisha 日本図書株
式会社 Tokyo
Nihon Toshokan Kyōkai 日本図書館協会
(Japan Library Association) Tokyo
Nikkō Shoin 日光書院 Tokyo
Nishi Nihon Shigakkai 西日本史学会 (Western
Japan Historical Society) Fukuoka
Nishōdō 二松堂 Tokyo
Nisshin Shoten 日新書店 Tokyo
Nōgyō Keizai Gakkai 農業經済学会
(Association for the Study of Agrarian Economy) Tokyo
Nōgyō Sōgō Kenkyū Kankōkai 農業綜合研
究刊行会 Tokyo
Nōgyō Sōgō Kenkyūsho 農業綜合研究所
(National Research Institute of Agriculture) Tokyo
Nōgyō to Kikaisha 農業と機械社 Tokyo
Nōgyō to Suisansha 農業と水産社 Tokyo

O

Ocha no Mizu Shobō 御茶の水書房 Tokyo
Ogawa Shobō 小川書房 Tokyo
Ogiwara Seibunkan 荻原屋文院 Tokyo
Ōhata Shoten 大畑書店 Tokyo

Oka Shoin 岡書院 Tokyo
Okayama Shiyakusho 岡山市役所
(Okayama City Office) Okayama
Ōkura Seishin Bunka Kenkyūsho 大倉精神
文化研究所 (Ōkura Institute of
Spiritual Research) Yokohama
Ōkura Kōbundō 大倉廣文堂 Tokyo
Ōkurashō 大藏省 (Ministry of Finance) Tokyo
Ōkura Shoten 大倉書店 Tokyo
Ongaku no Tomosha 音樂の友社 Tokyo
Ōokayama Shoten 大岡山書店 Tokyo
Ōsaka Furitsu Toshokan 大阪府立図
書館 (Osaka City Library) Ōsaka
Ōsaka Kyōiku Tosho Kabushiki Kaisha 大阪
教育図書株式会社 Ōsaka
Ōsaka Rekishi Gakkai 大阪歴史学会
(Osaka Historical Society) Ōsaka
Ōsaka Ryōgaesho Kumiai 大阪両替商
組合 (Osaka Exchange House Union) Ōsaka
Ōsaka Shiritsu Daigaku Bungakkai 大阪市立
大学文学会 (Osaka City University,
Literary Society) Ōsaka
Ōsaka Shiritsu Jōto Toshokan 大阪市立城
東図書館 (Osaka City Jōto Library) Ōsaka
Ōsakashi Sanjikai 大阪市参事会
(Osaka Municipal Council) Ōsaka
Ōsaka Shōka Daigaku Keizai Kenkyūsho 大阪
商科大学經済研究所 (Osaka
Commercial University, Economic Research
Institute) Ōsaka
Ōsakayagō Shoten 大阪屋号書店 Tokyo
Ōtsuka Kōgeisha 大塚巧藝社 Tokyo
Ōyashima Shuppan Kabushiki Kaisha 大八洲
出版株式会社 Tokyo
and Kyōto

R

Rakuyōdō 洛陽堂 Tokyo
Ranshobō 蘭書房 Tokyo and Kyōto
Rekishibunka Kenkyūkai 歴史文化研
究会 (Society for the Study of the History
of Japanese Culture) Tokyo
Rekishichiri Gakkai 歴史地理学会
(Historical Geography Association) Tokyo
Rekishigaku Kenkyūkai 歴史学研究会
(Historical Science Society) Tokyo
Rekishi Kyōiku Kenkyūkai 歴史教育研
究会 (Historical Instruction Society) Tokyo
Ressei Zenshū Hensankai 列聖全集編纂会 Tokyo
Rikkyō Daigaku Shigaku Kenkyūkai 立教大学
史学研究会 (Rikkyō University, Historical Society) Tokyo
Rikugōkan 六合館 Tokyo
Rikugun Bunko 陸軍文庫 (Army Archives) Tokyo
Rikugunshō 陸軍省 (Army Ministry) Tokyo
Rimpei Shoten 林平書店 Tokyo
Risōsha 理想社 Tokyo
Rōdō Bunkasha 勞働文化社 Tokyo
Rokubundō 六文堂 Tokyo
Rokuninsha 六人社 Tokyo
Rōnōsha 勞農社 Tokyo
Ruisan Kankōkai 類纂刊行会 Tokyo
Ryūbunkan 隆文館 Tokyo
Ryūbunsha 隆文舍 Tokyo
Ryūginsha 龍吟社 Tokyo
Ryūkoku Daigaku 龍谷大学 (Ryūkoku
University) Kyōto
Ryūkoku Daigaku Shigakkai 龍谷大学史
学会 (Ryukoku University, Historical
Society) Kyōto
Ryūkoku Daigaku Shuppanbu 龍谷大学出
版部 (Ryukoku University Press) Kyōto
Ryūkoku Gakkai 龍谷学会 (Ryukoku
Association) Kyōto

Ryūseikaku 龍星閣   Tōkyō

S

Sagami Shobō 相模書房   Tōkyō
Saitō Shoten 斎藤書店   Tōkyō
Sakai Shiyakusho 堺市役所 (Sakai City Office)   Sakai (Ōsaka)
Sambō Hombu 参謀本部 (General Staff)   Tōkyō
Sangensha 三元社   Tōkyō
Sangyō Kumiai Chūōkai 産業組合中央会   Tōkyō
San'ichi Shobō 三一書房   Kyōto
Sankyō Shoin 三教書院   Tōkyō
Sankyō Shuppansha 三共出版社   Tōkyō
Sanseidō 三誠堂   Tōkyō
Sanseisha Shoten 三星社書店   Tōkyō
Sanryūsha 三立社   Tōkyō
Seibundō 誠文堂   Tōkyō
Seibundō Shinkōsha 誠文堂新光社   Tōkyō
Seikadō Bunko 静嘉堂文庫 (Seikadō Library)   Tōkyō
Seikatsusha 生活社   Tōkyō
Seikisha 正旗社   Tōkyō
Seikyōsha 政教社   Tōkyō
Seishi Kakei Daijiten Kankōkai 姓氏家系大辞典刊行会   Tōkyō
Seitō Shobō 西東書房   Tōkyō
Seiun Shoin 青雲書院   Tōkyō
Seizōdō 成象堂   Tōkyō and Ōsaka
Sekaidō 世界堂
Sekai Shisōsha 世界思想社   Kyōto
Sekai Shoin 世界書院   Tōkyō
Seki Hironao 瀬木博尚   Tōkyō
Seki Shoin 関書院   Tōkyō
Sendai Shiyakusho 仙台市役所 (Sendai City Office)   Sendai
Sendai Sōsho Kankōkai 仙台叢書刊行会   Sendai
Senkusha 先駆社   Tōkyō
Senshinsha 先進社   Tōkyō
Setonaikai Sōgō Kenkyūkai 瀬戸内海総合研究会 (Joint Association for the Study of the Inland Sea)   Okayama
Shakai Keizai Shigakkai 社会経済史学会 (Tokyo Social and Economic History Society)   Tōkyō
Shakai Shisō Kenkyūsho 社会思想研究所 (Institute for the Study of Social Thought)   Tōkyō
Shakai Shisō Kenkyūsho Shuppanbu 社会思想研究会出版部 (Institute for the Study of Social Thought, Publications Department)   Tōkyō
Shibundō 至文堂   Tōkyō and Kyōto
Shibunkai 斯文会 (Shibun Association)   Tōkyō
Shibun Shoin 斯文書院   Tōkyō
Shihōshō 司法省 (Ministry of Justice)   Tōkyō
Shikai Shobō 四海書房   Tōkyō
Shimbi Shoin 審美書院   Tōkyō
Shimbun Kenkyūsho 新聞研究所 (Newspaper Research Association)   Tōkyō
Shimizu Shoin 清水書院   Tōkyō
Shinano Kyōdo Kenkyūkai 信濃郷土研究会 (Shinano Local Studies Society)   Matsumoto (Nagano)
Shinano Kyōikukai Shimoina Bukai 信濃教育会下伊那部会 (Shinano Educational Society, Shimoina Branch)   Nagano
Shinano Shiryō Sōsho Hensankai 信濃史料叢書編纂会   Nagano
Shinchi Shobō 新地書房   Tōkyō
Shinchōsha 新潮社   Tōkyō
Shin Kōasha 新興亜社   Tōkyō
Shinkōsha 新光社   Tōkyō
Shinkō Shuppansha 新興出版社   Tōkyō

Shinkyōsha 新興社   Tōkyō
Shinkyō Shuppansha 新教出版社   Tōkyō
Shin Nihonsha 真日本社   Ōsaka
Shintō Kōkyūkai 神道攷究会 (Society for the Study of Shinto)   Tōkyō
Shirogane Shoin 銀書院   Tōkyō
Shiryō Hensangakari 史料編纂係 (Department of Historiography)   Tōkyō
Shiryō Hensansho 史料編纂所 (Historiographical Institute)   Tōkyō
Shiryō Tsūshin Kyōkai 史料通信協会 (Society for the Collection of Historical Sources by Correspondence)   Tōkyō
Shiseki Bijutsu Dōkōkai 史迹美術同攷会 (Joint Society of Historic Remains and Art)   Kyōto
Shishiō Bunko 獅子王文庫   Tōkyō
Shishi Shuppansha 史誌出版社   Tōkyō
Shizen Gakkai 史前学会 (Prehistory Society)   Tōkyō
Shizuoka-ken 静岡県 (Shizuoka Prefecture)   Shizuoka
Shizuoka Kyōdo Kenkyūkai 静岡郷土研究会 (Shizuoka Local Studies Society)   Shizuoka
Shōkasha 章華社   Tōkyō
Shōkōkan Bunko 彰考館文庫 (Shōkōkan Library)   Tōkyō
Shōkō Shoin 彰考書院   Tōkyō
Shomotsu Tembōsha 書物展望社   Tōkyō
Shōwa Shobō 昭和書房   Tōkyō
Shūhōkaku 聚芳閣   Tōkyō
Shunjūsha 春秋社   Tōkyō
Shun'yōdō 春陽堂   Tōkyō
Shuppan Nyūsusha 出版ニュース社   Tōkyō
Shūrakusha 聚楽社   Tōkyō
Shūseidō 聚精堂   Tōkyō
Sōbisha 草美社   Tōkyō
Sōbunkaku 叢文閣   Tōkyō
Sōgabō 草臥房   Takamatsu (Kagawa)
Sōgensha 創元社   Tōkyō and Osaka
Sōmeisha 蒼明社   Tōkyō
Sugimoto Ryōkōdō 杉本梁江堂   Ōsaka
Sunnansha 駿南社   Tōkyō
Suwa Shiryō Sōsho Kankōkai 諏訪史料叢書刊行会   Nagano

T

Taigadō 大雅堂   Tōkyō and Kyōto
Taihōkaku 大鳳堂   Tōkyō
Taikōdō 泰光堂   Kyōto
Taikōsha 大洽社   Tōkyō
Taimusu Shuppansha タイムス出版社   Tōkyō
Taiseikan 大成館   Tōkyō
Taishō Daigaku Shigakkai 大正大学史学会 (Taishō University Historical Society)   Tōkyō
Taishō Issaikyō Kankōkai 大正一切経刊行会   Tōkyō
Taishūdō 大修堂   Tōkyō
Taiyōdō 太陽堂   Tōkyō
Takagi Toshita 高木利太   Ōsaka
Takubundō 拓文堂   Tōkyō
Tamba Shorin 丹波書林   Tōkyō
Teikoku Daigaku Shimbunsha Shuppanbu 帝国大学新聞社出版部 (Imperial University Newspaper Press)   Tōkyō
Teikoku Himitsu Tanteisha 帝国秘密探偵社   Tōkyō
Teikoku Toshokan 帝国図書館 (Imperial Library)   Tōkyō
Teishinshō 逓信省 (Communications Ministry)   Tōkyō
Teishitsu Rinyakyoku 帝室林野局 (Imperial Household, Forrestry Division)   Tōkyō
Teito Shuppansha 帝都出版社   Tōkyō
Tenri Toshokan 天理図書館 (Tenri Library)   Tambaichi (Nara)

Tetsudōshō 鉄道省 (Railroad Ministry)　　　Tokyo
Tetsugaku Shoin 哲学書院
Tōdai Kyōdō Kumiai Shuppanbu 東大協同組
　　合出版部　　　　　　　　　　　　　Tokyo
Tōgakusha 東学社　　　　　　　　　　　Tokyo
Tōhō Bunka Gakuin 東方文化学院
　　(Academy of Oriental Culture)　　　Tokyo
Tōhō Bunka Kenkyūsho 東方文化研究所
　　(Institute of Oriental Culture)　　　Kyoto
Tohōdō 吐鳳堂　　　　　　　　　　　　Tokyo
Tōhō Shoin 東方書院　　　　　　　　　Tokyo
Tōhoku Shigakkai 東北史学会 (Tohoku
　　Historical Association)　　　Sendai (Yamagata)
Tōkai Shobō 東海書房　　　　　　　　　Tokyo
Tōkō Shoin 刀江書院　　　　　　　　　Tokyo
Tōkyō Asahi Shimbunsha (see Asahi Shimbunsha) Tokyo
Tōkyō Bunrika Daigaku Ōtsuka Shigakkai 東京
　　文理科大学大塚史学会 (Tokyo
　　University of Literature, Ōtsuka Historical
　　Society)　　　　　　　　　　　　　Tokyo
Tōkyō Daigaku Kyōdō Kumiai Shuppanbu 東京
　　大学協同組合出版部 (Tokyo
　　University Cooperative Press)　　　Tokyo
Tōkyō Daigaku Shiryō Hensansho 東京大学
　　史料編纂所(Tokyo University His-
　　toriographical Institute)　　　　　Tokyo
Tōkyō Daigaku Shūkyōgaku Kenkyūkai 東京大学
　　宗教学研究会 (Tokyo Uni-
　　versity Institute of Religious Studies)　Tokyo
Tōkyō Daigaku Shuppanbu 東京大学出版部
　　(Tokyo University Press)　　　　　Tokyo
Tōkyōdō 東京堂　　　　　　　　　　　Tokyo
Tōkyō Koshosekishō Kumiai 東京古書籍
　　商組合　　　　　　　　　　　　　Tokyo
Tōkyō Kyōiku Kenkyūkai 東京教育研究会
　　(Tokyo Educational Research Society)　Tokyo
Tōkyō Shakai Kagaku Kenkyūsho 東京社会
　　科学研究所(Tokyo Institute of Social
　　Science)　　　　　　　　　　　　Tokyo
Tōkyō Shisei Chōsakai 東京市政調査会
　　(Tokyo Municipal Research Society)　Tokyo
Tōkyō Shosekishō Kumiai Jimusho 東京書籍
　　商組合事務所　　　　　　　　　　Tokyo
Tōkyō Shuppan Kyōkai 東京出版協会　　Tokyo
Tōkyō Taimususha 東京タイムス社　　　Tokyo
Tōkyō Teikoku Daigaku 東京帝国大学
　　(Tokyo Imperial University)　　　　Tokyo
Tōkyō Teikoku Daigaku Fuzoku Toshokan 東京
　　帝国大学附属図書館 (Tokyo
　　Imperial University Library)　　　　Tokyo
Tōkyō [Teikoku] Daigaku Keizai Gakkai 東京帝
　　国大学経済学会 (Tokyo [Imperial]
　　University Economic Society)　　　Tokyo
Tōkyō [Teikoku] Daigaku Shigakkai 東京帝国
　　大学史学会 (Tokyo [Imperial] Uni-
　　versity Institute of Historical Science)　Tokyo
Tōkyō Toshokan 東京図書館(Tokyo
　　Library)　　　　　　　　　　　　Tokyo
Tonan Shobō 図南書房　　　　　　　　Tokyo
Tōrin Shobō 東林書房　　　　　　　　Kyoto
Toshokan Jigyō Kenkyūkai 図書館事業研
　　究会 (Society for Study of Libraries) Tokyo
Toshokan Shiryōsha 図書館資料社　　　Urawa
Tosho Kenkyūkai 図書研究会 (Book
　　Research Society)　　　　　　　　Tokyo
Tosho Shimbunsha 図書新聞社　　　　　Tokyo
Toshokan Shiryōsha 図書館資料社　　　Urawa
Toyama-ken 富山県 (Toyama Prefecture)
　　　　　　　　　　　　　　　Urawa (Saitama)
Tōyō Bunka Kyōkai 東洋文化協会
　　(Oriental Culture Association)　　　Tokyo
Tōyō Bunko 東洋文庫 (Oriental Library)　Tokyo
Tōyōdō 東陽堂　　　　　　　　　　　Tokyo
Tōyō Gakkai 東洋学会 (Oriental Society)　Tokyo

Tōyō Gakujutsu Kyōkai 東洋学術協会
　　(Research Department, Oriental Library)
　　　　　　　　　　　　　　　　　Tokyo
Tōyō Keizai Shimpōsha 東洋経済新報社
　　　　　　　　　　　　　　　　　Tokyo
Tōyō Shimpōsha 東洋新報社　　　　　Tokyo
Tōyō Shisō Kenkyūsho 東洋思想研究所
　　(Research Institute of Oriental Thought)
　　　　　　　　　　　　　　　　　Tokyo
Tōyō Shoin 東洋書院　　　　　　　　Tokyo
Tōyō Shokan 東洋書館　　　　　　　Tokyo
Tōyō Tōki Kenkyūsho 東洋陶器研究所
　　(Oriental Ceramics Institute)　　　Tokyo
Tōyō Tosho Kabushiki Kaisha 東洋図書株
　　式会社　　　　　　　　　　　　Tokyo
Tōyō Tosho Kankōkai 東洋図書刊行会　Osaka
Tōzai Shuppansha 東西出版社　　　　Tokyo
Tsukuba Kenkyūbu 筑波研究部 (Tsukuba
　　Research Institute)　　　　　　　Tokyo

U

Ueno Shoten 上野書店　　　　　　　Tokyo
Umiguchi Shoten 海口書店　　　　　Tokyo
Unebi Shobō 畝傍書房　　　　　　　Tokyo
Ushio Shobō 潮書房　　　　　　　　Tokyo
Usui Shobō 碓氷書房　　　　　　　Tokyo

W

Wakaihito Sha 若い人社　　　　　　Tokyo
Waseda Daigaku Shigakkai 早稲田大学
　　史学会 (Waseda University Historical
　　Society)　　　　　　　　　　　Tokyo
Waseda Daigaku Shuppanbu 早稲田大学出
　　版部 (Waseda University Press)　Tokyo
Waseda Hōgakkai 早稲田法学会
　　(Waseda Society of Law)　　　　Tokyo

Y

Yabuki Masae 屋葺政衛　　　　　　Tokyo
Yamaguchi Shoten 山口書店　　　　Tokyo
Yamakawa Shuppansha 山川出版社　Tokyo
Yamanaka Shoka 山中書家　　　　　Tokyo
Yokohama Shiyakusho 横浜市役所
　　(Yokohama City Office)　　Yokohama (Kanagawa)
Yokohama Bōeki Shimposha 横浜貿易新
　　報社　　　　　　　Yokohama (Kanagawa)
Yoneyamadō 米山堂　　　　　　　Tokyo
Yoshikawa Hanshichi 吉川半七　　　Tokyo
Yoshikawa Kōbunkan 吉川弘文館　　Tokyo
Yōtokusha 養徳社　　　　　　　Tambaichi (Nara)
Yoyogikai 代々木会 (Yoyogi Society)　Tokyo
Yūhikaku 有斐閣　　　　　　　　　Tokyo
Yūhōdō 有朋堂
Yuibutsuron Kenkyūsho 唯物論研究所
　　(Institute for Materialistic Studies)　Tokyo
Yuibutsuron Kenkyūkai 唯物論研究会
　　(Society for Materialistic Studies)　Tokyo
Yūkan Seikadō 又間精華堂　　　　Tokyo
Yūkōsha 有光社　　　　　　　　　Tokyo
Yūrindō 有隣堂　　　　　　　　　Tokyo
Yūseidō 有精堂　　　　　　　　　Tokyo
Yūzankaku 雄山閣　　　　　　　　Tokyo
Yūtoku Zaidan 有徳財団

Z

Zaisei Keizai Gakkai 財政経済学会
　　(Society for the Study of Finance and Econom-
　　ics)　　　　　　　　　　　　　Tokyo
Zayūhō Kankōkai 座右宝刊行会　　Tokyo
Zenkoku Shobō 全国書房　　　　　Kyoto
Zoku Gunsho Ruijū Kanseikai 続群書類従
　　完成会　　　　　　　　　　　Tokyo
Zōkyō Shoin 蔵経書院　　　　　　Kyoto
Zuihitsu Taisei Kankōkai 随筆大成刊行会
　　　　　　　　　　　　　　　　Tokyo